MICA POLLOCK is the director of the Center for Research on Educational Equity, Assessment, and Teaching Excellence (CREATE) at the University of California, San Diego. The editor of *Everyday Antiracism* (The New Press), she lives in southern California.

School

alk

Rethinking
What We Say About —
and to — Students
Every Day

MICA POLLOCK

THE NEW PRESS
25 YEARS

NEW YORK
LONDON

Requests for permission to reproduce selections from this book should be mailed to: Permissions Department, The New Press, 120 Wall Street, 31st floor, New York, NY 10005.

Published in the United States by The New Press, New York, 2017

Distributed by Two Rivers Distribution

ISBN 978-1-62097-103-1 (pb)
ISBN 978-1-62097-104-8 (e-book)
CIP data is available

The New Press publishes books that promote and enrich public discussion and understanding of the issues vital to our democracy and to a more equitable world. These books are made possible by the enthusiasm of our readers; the support of a committed group of donors, large and small; the collaboration of our many partners in the independent media and the not-for-profit sector; booksellers, who often hand-sell New Press books; librarians; and above all by our authors.

www.thenewpress.com

Book design and composition by Lovedog Studio

This book was set in Adobe Garamond

Printed in the United States of America

20 19 18 17 16 15 14 13 12 11

To my family, past and present,
who have always acted like I had something to say.

Contents

How to Read This Book

A note on the chapters and activities to come.

This book is designed to support everyday exploration and inquiry by many people. You can read it alone or with others. I wanted the book to be accessible to people with a wide variety of backgrounds, and applicable to a wide variety of work and life situations. I write informally throughout this book, in short paragraphs to aid "digestion."

I designed this book's sections to be read in order. The Introduction gives you an overview of the whole book and foundational ideas to which we return repeatedly. "A (Brief) Guide to Talking Effectively with Colleagues" (which appears in full in the Appendix) sets you up to talk with others as you read. Then, seven chapters walk through key aspects of schooltalking for equity. A Conclusion sets you up for ongoing equity effort. I cite resources along the way that I hope you'll pursue. They appear as endnotes so they don't distract you while you read.

To promote ongoing reflection and application, you'll see **THINK/DISCUSS** questions peppered throughout each chapter. I've placed **THINK/DISCUSS** questions that are best tackled after reading at the back of every chapter ("More schooltalk scenarios"). Even if you don't engage in all of those discussions, I hope you'll read all the **THINK/DISCUSS** questions and select the ones that resonate most for your work.

Right as each chapter ends, **Action Assignments** invite you to engage and share key schooltalk issues with others and to share examples of schooltalking for equity. This book quotes many researchers and educators, plus students and parents; Action Assignments will ask you to tap more youth and adult voices. I hope to continue the dialogue online using the hashtag #schooltalking. Together, let's redesign schooltalk with equity in mind.

Introduction

Schooltalk seeks to support you to redesign the most basic thing people do in education: talk about young people and with them.

With all the work we need to do in education, why focus a whole book on designing new schooltalk?

Because everybody talks;

And because **communication is action: talk about (and with) young people shapes their lives.**

Schools are where we shape the next generation and through them, the world.

And the most basic thing we do all day in schools is talk.

Equity work—active effort to develop the full human talents of every young person, and all groups of young people—starts with our words.

We talk about a million things in schools as we educate young people. We talk about math and science and literature and social studies; we discuss the nation and the world.

In this book, we're redesigning the most foundational form of schooltalk: talk about young people themselves. That's because such schooltalk causes some of our most fundamental problems for young people.

All school pathways *for* students are shaped by basic communications *about* students.

Sometimes, single communications change our paths.

THINK / DISCUSS

Did anyone ever say anything about you in school that particularly supported your school success, or slowed you down? Try to remember one story.

I always loved to write. I remember one librarian telling me that a little book I wrote in kindergarten was so good she was going to put a copy in the library. (Then she actually did it.) She was the first person to call me an "author." And I remember my dad telling me that one day maybe I'd become a "writer." His expressed confidence in me shaped my identity—as did the opportunities teachers then gave me to develop my writing skills.

I also remember that once in grad school, a professor told me that I "probably shouldn't become a writer." I still hear his voice in my head along with the others', making me doubt my abilities.

I know countless people who remember comments in school classrooms or offices that either fostered or threatened their own potential. For example, a high school counselor told my colleague Daniela* that as a Latina, she just shouldn't try to make it to a top university. Daniela remembered that uninformed comment for the rest of her life. The same type of comment from counselors deflated many of her Latino peers—who didn't hear much from counselors about how to get to college, either.

Daniela actually defied that counselor's prediction and went to Berkeley, then Stanford, to become a professor of education who studies how to support Latino students through college. After Daniela got her PhD, she went back to that counselor to make sure he never talked down the potential of another young person.

Whenever I tell that story, listeners have something similar to share.

THINK / DISCUSS

Have you ever explicitly challenged a common comment about young people as harmful to young people? What was the comment, and how did you challenge it? Did your strategy work?

Can you think of a common comment that you did not challenge, even though it bothered you? Why didn't you?

Millions of common things we say about and then to young people can shape students' fates in schools. Consider each of these examples:

＊   A teacher or peer calls a student's community "ghetto." How might this shape young people's sense of themselves, their classmates, and their school?

---

*Names of individual students or educators in this book are pseudonyms for real people; they represent common schooltalk experiences. Names of researchers are real so that readers can find published resources.

✳   A counselor calls the student body "not college material" in a faculty meeting about whether to offer more AP sections. How might the comment affect the group's thinking?

✳   A teacher's aide or specialist describes students in the car ride to school with words like "Special Ed kids" or "losers," or, conversely, describes a few students as unusually "gifted" or "smart." How might he or she treat each of these students in class?

✳   Administrators explain a chart of achievement outcomes, broken down by race, language group, gender, or disability, in a faculty meeting as they make decisions about hiring additional support staff. What happens to the analysis of student needs when someone says summarily that one group of kids "just doesn't want to learn"?

✳   In a college or graduate school classroom, future teachers try to discuss why some students drop out of school and end up in prison. What happens to planning for student support when someone says that it must be because these students' parents "don't care about education" enough?

Each communication is an action with serious equity implications. As we'll see throughout this book, the things people say about students in schools shape how adults think about and treat students, how students feel about themselves and their peers, and who offers students which opportunities and assistance. Words lead to treatment and to self-concepts, to expectations internalized by adults and students, and to the distribution of material resources by adults. Who gets which dollars, teachers, daily supports, and opportunities to learn—schooltalk is involved in all of this. Schooltalk about history, current events, and policy similarly shapes how opportunities get to young people, by shaping who we think "deserves" opportunities and who we hold responsible for providing which opportunities to whom. Even schooltalk far away from schools matters. Think of the consequences if a politician talking about schools in "the inner city" frames young people as totally uninterested in reading, then floats a school funding bill.

Schooltalking isn't the only action we can shape for equity in education. It's just a foundation of equity work—where it begins. And it's a realm of equity action available all day, every day. Redesigning schooltalk just requires reshaping what we already do.

As an educator friend of mine put it after reading this introduction,

"How I talk about students and the messages I convey to them or to others will influence the decisions we make about how we instruct and support students."

What folks say about young people has consequences for them. But school-talk has another common problem: what we fail to say.

In and around schools, we routinely fail to share necessary and accurate information about who young people are, what they can do, what they need, and how they are doing. These failures to communicate have consequences for students too; they regularly keep adults from understanding young people and offering them sufficient supports.

As a new teacher I had a tenth-grade student, Jake, who had trouble reading aloud and acted silly a lot. I learned late in the year that he got special supports in another class for a learning need nobody had ever talked to me about. I knew from a teaching partner that Jake's mom worked late and that he stayed up anxiously waiting for her, but Jake and I never talked about this and I never met his mom. Jake made me laugh and drove me crazy. I never really got to know him, and I didn't support him successfully as a reader, either.

And one day two years later, Jake almost didn't graduate because school staff had told him inaccurate information about the credits he needed for graduation. I found him sitting dejected on the school steps on graduation morning. He had just heard he wasn't graduating after all. We went to the office and had an accurate discussion of his credits with school administrators, clarifying that he had completed every credit adults had told him he needed. The counselors adjusted his transcript. Jake graduated.

Those eleventh-hour communications changed Jake's life. I'm glad I was there that day.

But I could have helped Jake far more if I and others had talked earlier about specific things he was experiencing and specific ways of supporting him in school.

THINK / DISCUSS

Have you ever seen a young person harmed because people failed to share some piece of necessary information about him or her?

Have you ever insisted that others add a crucial piece of information to a discussion about a young person or group of young people you know? Have you ever hesitated to do so? Why, and what happened?

Just like the things we say about young people in schools, the schooltalk we *don't* hear is predictable and patterned too. In schools across the country, many educators know too little about students' experiences, skills, and needs. Every year, many students vanish from the graduation stage without adults really knowing why.

In fact, school communities are full of structural cracks in communications—gaps in necessary schooltalk that keep many students from being better known and better served.

Consider a student, Paula, who's experiencing these common gaps:

✳ Paula's teachers and administrators rarely hear straight from students or families about issues in the local neighborhood and instead proceed based on assumptions, because they didn't grow up there.

✳ People in Paula's school and community never consider ways to improve school disciplinary policies that are particularly harsh for boys and girls of color, because people don't ever review who is being disciplined and why.

✳ Paula doesn't hear from her counselor about signing up for the SAT, because Paula's counselor has six hundred other students to attend to whose parents haven't been to college either.

✳ Paula doesn't tell the teacher about a family issue that affects her attendance, because teachers in her school rarely take time to build personalized relationships with their students.

✳ Teachers and other school staff rarely ask Paula what she enjoys learning or is good at, either.

✳ Paula's teachers rarely discuss how they could support Paula and her peers in rigorous math, because adults rarely take sufficient time to discuss student progress with students or each other.

✳ The people running youth programs in Paula's community have no idea how Paula or her peers are doing in school—and school adults have no idea what Paula and her peers do in community programs or at home.

✳ An administrator emails home a handout in English about a workshop on college financial aid, but Paula's parent/guardian primarily speaks Spanish and doesn't have consistent Internet.

✳ In a local discussion on graduation rates at Paula's school, nobody talks about which opportunities to learn Paula's school actually offers and doesn't.

Each of these common gaps in necessary schooltalk has consequences. Across the country, educators don't know important facts about young people's neighborhoods or communities, know why specific students are absent, or discuss why they are suspended; adults don't review key details about students' progress or can't find such information when they need it. Too few adults ask students what they experience inside or outside of school or what they can do; people fail to discuss crucial opportunity information with each other or with parents or students themselves. And so, we don't figure out together how to get young people essential opportunities and supports.

You get the point—we can derail young people significantly when our schooltalk harms them, or when we fail to say things that can help them.

But when we take charge of schooltalk as a foundational action for equity, we can change the game.

This book seeks to support you to *design new ways to talk about and with young people* in schools, so that everything we say helps to develop the full human potential of all young people rather than limiting what young people can do.

Position yourself from here forward as an *equity designer*—as someone who asks, daily, which actions and situations need to be improved so all young people get the opportunities and supports they need and deserve. For this book's purposes, we're focused on redesigning how people talk about students and with them. As equity designers, we'll return throughout the book to the following three elements.

1. The Equity Line of *Schooltalk*

Equity efforts in education provide supports to give *every* young person and *all groups* of young people a full chance to develop their vast human talents.

Equity efforts treat all young people as equally and infinitely valuable. And so, they seek to remedy any situation where opportunities for some are insufficient or expectations low, particularly when young people have long been underserved by schools.

With this book, I hope to get you in the habit of asking this foundational question about every example of schooltalk you encounter:

Does this communication help support **equity** (the full human talent development of *every* student, and *all groups* of students)? Or not?

The Equity Line helps us evaluate which actions and situations offer students sufficient opportunities and supports, and which don't. I've used the line to prompt discussion of the pros and cons for young people of countless everyday actions and situations.[1] The Equity Line appears throughout this book as a reminder to evaluate the consequences for young people of everything folks *say* about and to young people—in schools and in society at large.

2. The Foundational Principles of Schooltalking for Equity

Each chapter of this book will begin with a specific principle and chapter goal for designing schooltalk to pursue equity. But I'll often refer back to the following Foundational Principles of Schooltalking for Equity.

Equity-oriented schooltalk about young people urgently does the following:

* Conveys belief in all young people's equal human value and potential, and care and respect for their development and well-being;
* Describes young people more accurately as individuals and members of communities, including their experiences with others in opportunity contexts;
* Pinpoints and collectively addresses students' needs precisely, not vaguely, and regularly and rapidly, not rarely;
* Shares opportunities to learn (and to meet needs) widely, not just with some.

Sound obvious? You may be surprised at how much schooltalk fails to do this.

Finally, let's consider who this book is about and for.

3. The Foundational Image of Schooltalk: A sample of the people who help shape a young person's fate in school every day

Our Foundational Image (see next page) represents some of the key people who shape any young person's fate each day through their everyday actions—one of which is schooltalk. In addition to school district people, an outer ring of people (not shown) whose acts shape young people's lives would include politicians, journalists, and other media makers, community leaders, industry and university people, and everyone observing schools. If you're one of those people, read on. Your schooltalk matters tremendously, too, because it shapes public conversations, policies, and resource decisions.

In this book, I ask you to *think like an educator*—like one of the people in our Foundational Image—in order to really get concrete about communications' everyday implications for young people. Throughout this book, we'll consider the consequences of what the powerful people in our Foundational Image say and do not say, even as we treat their schooltalk as shaped by a shared society.

Indeed, this book is for anyone interested in improving young people's lives. You may be a veteran educator or a beginner; you may not work in a school at all. If you're a student or a parent yourself, or if you serve on the school board, make media, or just discuss education at the dinner table, your talk also shapes how young people are seen, treated, and offered opportunities. If you work in higher education or a child- or youth-serving program, everything here can be translated to your setting as well. This book seeks to support you to support young people in whatever work you do each day. We'll do so by asking you to think like an educator about everyday schooltalk and its implications.

A friend described the potential *Schooltalk* reader to me:

"Teachers haven't had this level of introspection on how critical their talk is. But this allows the superintendent, parents, the secretary, everyone to join the work. It brings a level of ownership to equity work that nobody can disavow. We all talk."

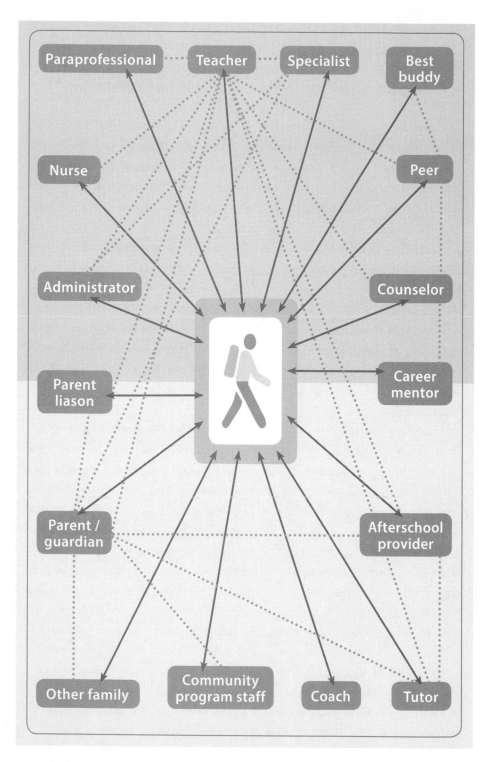

The Foundational Image

Let's just imagine that the young person at the center of that image is a young person you care about a lot. You dream of his or her contributions to our society.

What do you want these people saying about and to him or her? What do you *not* want them saying?

You'll see that this isn't about being "politically correct" or trying to just be nice to kids. And it's not about adding some extra work to our already overcrowded lives. This is about rethinking—and then redesigning—the most foundational ways our daily words support young people or don't.

Designing schooltalk for equity

Generations of thinkers you'll encounter in *Schooltalk* have shaped this book's lofty definition of equity effort. Equity efforts in education refuse insufficient opportunity or low expectations for any young person or group of young people. Instead, equity efforts actively arrange and provide supports to give *every young person* and *all groups* of young people a full chance to develop their vast human talents.

A few key quotes start to explain what I mean.

In 1897 John Dewey called for developing the full human "power" of each young person through education:

> *To prepare [a student] for the future life means to give him command of himself; it means so to train him that he will have the full and ready use of all his capacities.*[2]
> —*John Dewey*

And in 1865, just after the Civil War, black community members in Charleston, South Carolina, came together in an overflowing convention to call for basic human rights, equity, and justice. In defiance of Black Codes again restricting their human freedoms, they called for schools and fair trials; they claimed the right to assemble peacefully to discuss politics, to pursue "all avenues of trade, commerce, agriculture," and to "amass wealth by thrift and industry." And as historian Vincent Harding notes, "To all this they added a summary human right not normally found in the public documents of the nation":

> *The right to develop our whole being, by all the appliances that belong to civilized society.*[3]
>
> —*Vincent Harding*

Those two definitions of education's purpose combine in our definition of "equity." I hear them as demanding active effort by individuals and institutions to arrange necessary supports and opportunities so *each person* and *all communities of people* get a true chance to develop their full human "capacities" and potential contributions.

That makes the people in our Foundational Image tremendously important, because they have the chance to help support young people's full human talent development every day. Children don't develop their capacity alone; it takes a network to raise a child!

The concept of "full human talent development" in our definition of "equity" effort is clunky, but it's there for several reasons. First, as we'll see, people in the United States have too often suggested falsely that some "types of" young people innately have more value, potential, "intelligence," "capacity," or "talent" than others, or are worth more investment. Equity work counteracts that programming by insisting that *all* humans have vast potential and are equally valuable. Equity effort thus insists that necessary opportunities and resources reach all.

Our definition of equity effort also invites a wide variety of efforts to pursue and secure necessary opportunities for young people. Many efforts to develop the human talents of young people via schools primarily seek to ensure that all young people have access to "intellectually challenging learning."[4] Some focus first on ensuring all children have access to a well-trained teacher or rigorous coursework. Some insist first that all young people get foundational opportunities to learn to write, read, and calculate, in preparation for college and fulfilling careers. Some equity efforts insist first that more young people get the chance to analyze and then improve their communities, the nation, or the world. Still others insist first that more young people get the chance to express their views, feel valued and skilled, and be treated with dignity, on developing more young people artistically, or empowering them with history. Bud Mehan, who devoted much of his career to the idea of college for all, told me that "We have equity in society when every young person has the same opportunity to influence the course of democracy."[5] Put together, equity efforts seek to help develop each young person and all young people, in every community, to contribute their full human power to the world.

Finally, equity effort seeks to secure needed supports, opportunities, and resources for individuals and groups of students who typically haven't received what they need from schools. Blankstein and Noguera call equity effort "a commitment to ensure that every student receives what he or she needs to succeed."[6] As Paul Gorski put it, "Equity is a fair distribution of opportunity and access leading to the possibility for all students to reach their full potential." My colleague Makeba Jones calls equity effort "the flexible use of resources to tailor supports to kids." Equity effort seeks to get individuals from all "groups" necessary opportunities and resources, whether race/ethnic groups or income groups, boys or girls, students with or without labeled disabilities, English speakers or English learners, U.S.-born or immigrant students, religious groups, and more. In this book, because of my own history of work, we'll tend to focus on remedying situations that limit opportunities along race or income-based lines, and extend to other group experiences as intersecting examples.

The notion that every child in every community is worth such investment undergirds the lofty definition of "equity" we use in this book. Young people are the ultimate collective resource; educators are particularly powerful resource developers; society suffers if only some young people are sufficiently supported in schools. Because schools are where we shape the society we live in, equity effort to help develop all young people's human talents via schools isn't charity "for" kids, which is often the connotation of the word "equity" in education. Equity is the collective development of kids—of the people who will be in the driver's seat when we all get old.

Our bar for equity effort is high because children deserve it to be high—and because the world needs it to be high. Karolyn Tyson applies a parent's urgency to equity effort in education:

> If that child were yours, what would you want her school experience to be?[7]

Of course, parents often anxiously hoard school opportunities for their children alone, fearing that more opportunities for more children mean fewer opportunities for their own. But increasing opportunity for young people doesn't have to be a zero-sum game. Research shows that efforts to support and challenge more students in schools can make schools more interesting and rigorous for everyone.[8] Parents also experience how the success of more young people in a community can buoy the success of other young people. If other kids stay healthier, my child stays healthier. If the other children in my child's class love reading, he might end up inspired to read with them. As a parent in a diverse city or region, I want my child to be surrounded by skilled, employed, and healthy people from all corners of that city and region, doing interesting, challenging things that my child can learn from. As a parent who wants a functioning planet for my child to live on as an adult, I actually want lots of kids to help cure diseases and figure out how to halt global warming. I want my own kids doing great things, *and* I want my kids to benefit from other people equipped to fix collective problems. Martin Luther King Jr. articulated such collective interest beautifully in his famous "Letter from a Birmingham Jail": "We are caught in an inescapable network of mutuality, tied in a single garment of destiny."[9]

Thinking of equity in this common-interest way focuses equity efforts on making more opportunities for more young people whenever we can, not just fighting over the limited opportunities seemingly available.[10] Equity effort actually refuses to accept opportunity as limited to some.

A college student in one of my courses put it this way:

"I had not previously thought of education in that way . . . that we are not trying to help students learn and develop out of an abstract sense that we 'should,' but rather because it will benefit society as a whole to have students reach their full potential."

Another described the goal of equity effort as "unlocking the human potential of an individual to then share him with the world."

Students at Gompers Preparatory Academy in San Diego state this idea of collective interest out loud each fall as they head toward the goal of 100 percent graduation and college enrollment to benefit the entire community. "We are a family," they repeat. "No one will be left behind."

Apply that phrase to all of education and you have "equity" effort in a nutshell.

Unfortunately, though, schools typically leave a lot of kids behind. Schools typically don't sufficiently develop the full human talents of each young person and all groups of young people—or even seek to do so.

Indeed, every day, even without meaning to, we accept insufficient opportunities for millions of young people and reproduce low expectations for them in schools, as we simply talk about students and with them!

This is where you come in as an equity designer.

Look back at our Foundational Image and think about just one child you know. What do you want these people saying about and to the young person in the middle? What do you not want them saying?

You might be thinking that to help develop young people's full human talents, you most want the folks in our Foundational Image talking effectively inside classrooms about math or science, social studies or literacy. Supporting more students of all ages to talk deeply about rigorous content is critical to many contemporary school reforms.[11] Shaping such talk about content in a multilingual nation is another huge subject requiring its own book-length focus.[12] That's crucial schooltalk—and perhaps the subject of my next book.

Schooltalk necessarily lays the equity foundation first.

In this book, I suggest that it matters fundamentally how people talk about *students themselves*—about who students are, what their lives are like, what they can do, what opportunities and supports they need, and who might support them in specific ways.

I'm committed to supporting you to design such schooltalk for equity because I've spent two decades learning how with every word adults utter (or fail to utter) about students in schools, we either help support young people or we don't.

Where I'm coming from: The experiences and commitments behind *Schooltalk*

I started thinking about schooltalk's foundational role in equity effort in my early twenties, as I saw colleagues struggle to use and not use words like "black," "white," "Latino," "Filipino," "Samoan," or "Chinese" when discussing curriculum, discipline, student-teacher relationships, attendance, and achievement in the California high school where I taught tenth and eleventh graders. I saw people fail to provide students necessary supports when they failed to *talk* about supporting students better. And I started to understand that every word we say, or *don't* say, about young people in schools has consequences for how young people are treated.[13]

After graduate school I worked in the Office for Civil Rights of the U.S. Department of Education, investigating complaints filed by parents and educators arguing that students had been denied opportunity in schools along lines of race, gender, national origin, or disability. I saw teachers, administrators, parents, community members, and lawyers get stalled in unproductive, dead-end arguments as they tried to debate students' experiences and needs. And again, I wondered how people might discuss student supports more productively.[14]

In my first decade as a professor of education, I noticed how educators in my classes struggled to talk about supporting young people from various "groups." I saw how common schooltalk—even in academia—often exacerbates misinformation about young people. And in producing and teaching the book *Everyday Antiracism* with colleagues,[15] I also began to frame educators as powerful *equity designers* who can redesign each everyday action—including schooltalk—for student success.

In a large community project in Somerville, Massachusetts, called the OneVille Project (wiki.oneville.org), I then collaborated with teachers, students, administrators, and community partners to redesign the infrastructure shaping everyday communications in schools.[16] I worked with teachers to test whether texting might help teachers support students on the brink of quitting school. I watched teachers and students design online portfolios that let students describe a broad range of their own skills and talents. I worked with administrators, teachers, and staff to shape data displays to support more informed conversations about students' progress. I worked with parents and staff to design new mechanisms for translation and interpretation so parents could discuss opportunities across barriers of language. And overall, I started thinking about the *channels* through which communications travel—about the blend of technology-based, paper-based, and face-to-face talk that might support folks to communicate in support of young people in schools.

Back in California again, supporting teachers and students with my committed colleagues at UC San Diego's Center for Research on Educational Equity, Assessment, and Teaching Excellence (CREATE), I started working with educators and university staff to design new forms of schooltalk for equity. I learned from teachers who'd created advisory classes to communicate about college with every student every week. I met administrators innovating with Google Docs for communicating about students' missing assignments, and college outreach workers trying new ways of getting information to parents. I supported educators to test whether simple video tools could help English learners communicate their ideas to teachers, and to explore the face-to-face dialogue needed to support young people taking online courses.[17] My colleagues started designing a database enabling regional conversations about students' pathways to and through college. We launched a campus-wide conversation about leveraging university resources to create new learning opportunities for local young people. And I started to learn from colleagues about the schooltalk needed for rigorous instruction in math, science, literacy, and writing (http://create.ucsd.edu).

So at this point, I've worked on understanding and improving schooltalk as a teacher (*Colormute*, 2004), as a civil rights worker (*Because of Race*, 2008), as a professor inside two universities (e.g., teaching *Everyday Antiracism*, 2008), as an action researcher partnering with educators, community groups, students, and families (wiki.oneville.org), as a university center director (create.ucsd.edu), and as a parent in the two diverse communities where I've sent my kids to school. I've thought about communications that happen face-to-face, on paper, and via technology. And everyone I met in this work taught me something important. This book draws from literally thousands of people's ideas on improving everyday schooltalk with equity in mind.[18]

Thinking through these twenty years of work to understand and improve schooltalk in diverse schools, districts, cities, community organizations, universities, and the government, I've synthesized the Foundational Schooltalking Principles shared on page 8. I want to end by emphasizing the second Principle—this book's call for more *accurate and informed* talk about young people as foundational to equity effort. That's because I think it's potentially key to the others.

Caring about and believing in young people is obviously fundamental to student success. Increasing opportunity to learn is core to equity effort in education. So is precise and regular attention to students' needs.

But I've seen people move on each dimension when they were *more informed*—when they better understood not only fundamental facts about young people everywhere but also more about who *specific* young people really were, what they could do, and what they were really dealing with in specific opportunity contexts. When we understand young people better, we not only support them more effectively. We also value them more, perhaps the key to equity effort.

Young people today are demanding to be discussed more accurately and to be more fully known. That's because young people sense that what people know and say about youth matters to how youth are treated, inside and outside of schools.

In summer 2014, hundreds of young people contributed to a Tumblr site to call for more informed descriptions of young people, black youth in particular (http://iftheygunnedmedown.tumblr.com). After a policeman had shot unarmed Michael Brown in Ferguson, Missouri, media and others had circulated photos of Brown that portrayed him as a thug implicitly deserving his fate. By posting two photos each of themselves on Tumblr, young people demanded more informed, accurate, and compassionate portrayals of youth. One photo in each pair was a photo or exaggerated selfie of the young person acting tough or partying. These were the photos the submitters thought the media would likely choose to memorialize them negatively if police "gunned me down." But these young people argued that more informed portraits of them would include the other photos they posted, in which they beamed from graduation gowns, hugged relatives, or just looked happily at the camera. In this self-portrait exercise, students called for *more accurate* description, here communicated with images as well as words. They called for a more fully informed conversation about who they actually were.

> ## THINK / DISCUSS
>
> Can you imagine candid or staged photos you've taken of yourself that, if shared publicly as "you," would distort who you actually are? What other pictures would you want added to your portrait to describe you more accurately?
>
> Have you ever felt misdescribed by words used by someone who didn't really know you? Think of an example and your reaction to it.

Here's another image made by a student of mine at UC San Diego, demonstrating just a few pieces of information she'd want added to any typical conversation about her as a Latina student. In reaction to a quote from an earlier draft of *Schooltalk*, she decided that the single message "Get to Know Me" was her top schooltalking strategy. She sensed that more accurate information communicated by her, and then about her, could get people to understand her better, believe in her more, and respond to her actual needs:

Hang on to her call to "Get to Know Me." Throughout this book, we'll seek to describe young people and their experiences in opportunity contexts more accurately, as a foundation of equity work in education. If we can't see young people clearly—or the contexts around them that shape their lives—why would we fully believe in them, or offer them opportunities that develop their human talents and meet their needs? As Solórzano and Yosso note, a quote from Ralph Ellison's *Invisible Man* applies to far too many young people in our schools: "I am invisible, understand, simply because people refuse to see me."[19]

The organization of this book

We'll begin with "A (Brief) Guide to Talking Effectively with Colleagues," designed to support you in dialogue as you read this book (the full guide appears in the Appendix). In the first half of the book ("Flipping Scripts"), we'll then design ways to counteract classic underinformed claims about young people with more-informed claims, leveraging foundational information every U.S. resident and certainly every educator should know. Often, we'll see, "flipping scripts" just requires talking more accurately about the people, interactions, and factors that shape young people's lives and our own.

In the book's second half ("Designing Schooltalk Infrastructure"), we'll design ways that the folks in our Foundational Image can learn and share more accurate information about supporting the specific young people they serve. Often, we'll learn to listen to young people themselves.

Part 1: Flipping scripts: Countering fundamental misinformation about young people

In our schooltalk, all of us sometimes repeat common, habitual comments about young people or their communities that are fundamentally inaccurate and underinformed. Such "scripts" are the simplifying, familiar claims we reach for when we talk about young people and about education. Much of the time, these "scripts" have a shallow grasp on facts about young people's lives and instead adhere to premade ideas about young people. Dangerously, scripts misrepresenting young people in general can keep adults from fully supporting actual young people—and keep young people believing false-hoods about themselves and their peers.

So we have to correct education's most basic misinformation about young people.

In the first four chapters of *Schooltalk*, we'll pursue this overall goal for redesigning schooltalk:

> Part 1 goal: Flip the scripts. Counter fundamental misinformation about young people with more fact-based talk.

We'll learn essential information needed to correct some fundamental mis-understandings about young people that plague U.S. schooltalk and block opportunities from getting to students. We'll get in the habit of questioning the classic labels we use for students (Chapter 1: Group Talk), the ways we sum up their opportunities and outcomes (Chapter 2: Inequality Talk), how we frame their abilities (Chapter 3: Smarts Talk), and the claims we make about their communities (Chapter 4: Culture Talk). These four chapters will mark four key domains of schooltalk needing our close attention.

And in each chapter, we'll gain tools for strengthening schooltalk's fact foundation—for replacing classically underinformed claims about young people anywhere with more informed, accurate statements about young people and the contexts that shape them.

By the end of Part 1, we'll have flipped so many underinformed scripts about young people in general that we'll have one overall aim in mind: to learn more about supporting specific young people in specific places.

In Part 2, we'll design ways for education communities to do that.

Part 2: Designing schooltalk infrastructure: Enabling routinely informed schooltalk that supports young people

Look at our Foundational Image again (page 10) and think of a young person in an education community you know.

To help support equity—the full human talent development of every student and all groups of students—in that education community,

> Who in this school/classroom/community needs to communicate what information to whom? (How often? When?)

> What are the barriers to needed communication, and how could those barriers be overcome?

> What channel (face-to-face conversation, paper, technology) might allow necessary communications to occur?

Imagine turning one of the dotted lines between speakers in the Foundational Image into a stable pipe that allows people to *regularly* discuss some issue of student support that needs to be discussed. That's what we mean by designing *schooltalk infrastructure*: the schooltalk that's necessary for supporting young people now occurs more easily. Habits for parent-teacher or teacher-student conferencing designed to *regularly* spark more informed conversations about supporting student development, a student website or quarterly face-to-face presentation designed to *routinely* invite students to communicate their own accomplishments to teachers, a focus group *repeatedly* asking students for input on improving their school experiences, or a bulletin board or community calendar designed to allow parents from all groups to *consistently* share opportunity information and ideas are all examples of schooltalk infrastructure we can design for equity in schools. Schooltalk infrastructure can steer people to communicate in new ways face-to-face (a regularly scheduled student-teacher meeting), on paper (a weekly backpack handout), and using technology. Like adding new pipes to a building to carry water to new places, schooltalk infrastructure helps necessary information flow as needed between potential partners, improving student support.

> Part 2 goal: Design schooltalk infrastructure for equity. Help people routinely get informed about young people's experiences and the supports specific young people need to keep developing their full human talents. Then insist that young people get those supports.

We'll design ways schooltalk can better monitor students' progress and development (Chapter 5: Data Talk), respond to students' personal situations (Chapter 6: Life Talk) and share opportunities for young people (Chapter 7: Opportunity Talk). As we design infrastructure that reshapes school Data Talk, Life Talk, and Opportunity Talk, we'll learn from lots of other designers who have attempted to do the same.

Ready to design schooltalk for equity?

Let's get going, with *you* as our key equity designer.

> *Look closely at the present you are constructing: it should look like the future you are dreaming.*
> —*Alice Walker*

First, let's consider how we talk with other potential supporters of young people—the folks you might talk to as you read this book. If we want to talk so that every young person is supported, that requires setting up productive conversations with each other.

1. Ask a colleague, friend or family member to look at our Foundational Image (page 10) and consider: can he or she recall one comment or routine communication *about himself or herself* that was helpful or harmful to his or her success in school? (In answering this question, people have recalled motivating or crushing comments by counselors, teachers, or coaches—or typical, repeated ways their needs, skills, or experiences were or were not discussed by various people at school.) Ask the person if his or her peers experienced similar schooltalk.

   Use our Equity Line to consider his/her example.

   Did this communication help support **equity** (the full human talent development of *every* student, and *all groups* of students)? Or not?

   NOT supporting each/all
   students' talent development   SUPPORTING each/all students'
                                                  talent development

   In a journal or verbally to someone else (without naming the person you talked to), briefly describe your interaction and pinpoint one thing you learned from the person about schooltalking for equity. Was his or her example of schooltalk similar to or different from something you experienced in K–12?

2. Ask someone else to read this chapter. Then, discuss.

   > Choose one idea about "equity" from this chapter that particularly resonates with you (or doesn't). Discuss your reaction with your partner.

   > This book frames schools as critical for changing the world and frames *schooltalk* as a foundational equity action. What do you think so far of this argument?

A (Brief) Guide to Talking Effectively with Colleagues

This is a shortened reference guide; a full version appears in the Appendix. Especially if you know you'll be discussing this book with others, I suggest you read the Appendix version before starting the rest of the book. Here, I'll just list core suggestions to help you talk with colleagues as you read.

> **STRATEGY** Use the Equity Line to matter-of-factly invite inquiry into the consequences for young people of specific actions and situations.

For this book's purposes, keep asking:

Does **this communication** help support **equity** (the full human talent development of *every* student, and *all groups* of students)? Or not?

| NOT supporting each/all students' talent development | SUPPORTING each/all students' talent development |

> **STRATEGY** Focus discussion on evaluating specific things that people can do to support young people better (not on debating people's presumed intentions or character).

If someone says something you consider harmful,

> **STRATEGY** Position someone's comment as a common thing said by many people.

> **STRATEGY** Attack the script, not the speaker. (Go after the thing said, not the person who said it.)

`STRATEGY`   Act like a learner.

`STRATEGY`   Plan to stay engaged even if there is some conflict.

`STRATEGY`   Don't ignore your feelings; try to notice them and dialogue through them with young people in mind.

And as you talk,

`STRATEGY`   Ask people to consider (or offer) additional evidence related to their claims.

`STRATEGY`   Seek three forms of clarifying takeaways for equity effort while you talk:

1. Name **Great Quotes** that clarify equity efforts.

2. Name **Principles, Strategies,** and **Try Tomorrows** for equity effort.

    A **Principle** is a lofty statement in your own words about what should be done to support young people.

    A **Strategy** offers a concrete plan for action that someone could take in many places to pursue equity.

    A **Try Tomorrow** is a really specific action to take with particular people in a specific setting.

3. Name **Core Tensions** of equity effort.

    A **Core Tension** articulates an unsolvable dilemma of equity effort—a way people are "trapped between a rock and a hard place" when they try to take action for equity.

This discussion model can help you discuss or write about the **THINK/ DISCUSS** questions in this book and about real situations in settings you know. (See Appendix for more explanation of each element.)

Discussion model

A. **Discuss** a real-world issue affecting young people.

B. **Evaluate** existing situation or possible actions using the Equity Line, considering the pros and cons for young people. Ask for perspectives:

Does **this action/situation** (for this book's purposes, **this communication)** help support **equity** (the full human talent development of *every* student, and *all groups* of students)? Or not?

NOT supporting each/all students' talent development   SUPPORTING each/all students' talent development

C. As you go and definitely before ending the conversation, **restate some clarifying takeaways** regarding equity effort.

✳ Do any **Great Quotes** from colleagues or other sources help you think about equity effort?

✳ Can you name a **Principle, Strategy,** or **Try Tomorrow** for equity effort that came up in this discussion?

✳ Can you name one or more **Core Tensions** (unresolvable dilemmas) of equity effort that came up in this discussion?

Discuss
Evaluate
Pinpoint

- **Great Quote**
- **Principle / Strategy / Try Tomorrow**
- **Core Tension**

Finally, if you are dialoguing with others as you read this book, I recommend you pinpoint group norms you'd like to follow with colleagues. Someone should keep a list.

Supporting ongoing dialogue for equity if you're using this book in professional development or in a course.

✳ I've typically asked people to remain in a small discussion group for the duration of a learning experience. Building relationships helps people to discuss tough issues and to develop their thinking over time.

✳ I've also typically asked people to collect a clarifying takeaway from every chapter or assigned reading in a private journal. (I ask people to use each chapter's endnotes to find, then share, additional resources of interest.) We use these journals to write responses to **THINK/DISCUSS** questions and to document the Action Assignments that end each chapter.

✳ I often ask people to post some or all of their journal responses online so that small-group members and I can respond in writing to each person's thoughts. My favorite tool for online dialogue about equity is a wiki (a website enabling collaborative writing). A wiki allows me to comment in a new color right in the middle of people's ideas. For example, Anna might write the following, and I might respond (typing in green after my initials):

> *I think I'll redesign the labels we use on the report card at school. (MP: sounds promising, Anna! At the Try Tomorrow level, which label would you tweak first on the report card, and why?)*

So let's get started in redesigning schooltalk. Our first goal in Part 1 is to *flip scripts*—to respond with more fact-based information to habitual comments about young people that can get in the way of young people's success.

Part One
Flipping Scripts →

Part One Goal:
Flip the scripts. Counter fundamental misinformation about young people with more fact-based talk.

Ready to lay a new foundation for equity in education?

Let's reconsider the most fundamental information and misinformation about young people that we learn in the United States and carry into schooltalk.

Our scripts!

We're going to tackle four foundational ways we talk about young people in education and in schools: how we think and talk about their *groups*, their *opportunities and outcomes*, their *intelligence*, and their *cultural communities*.

Our goal is to counteract classic underinformed claims about young people with more informed claims. We'll get prepared for conversations with adults and with young people themselves.

Go back to page 8 and look at our Foundational Principles of equity-oriented schooltalk.

Start thinking about the pros and cons *for* young people of what folks so commonly say *about* young people. To *flip scripts*, we first seek particularly to get more accurate in what we say.

Chapter 1

Group Talk

Wield words only to support young people.

Chapter Goal:
Question our descriptions of young people. As a starter, consider when labels for "types of kids" enable student support and when they get in the way.

Let's start with a fundamental form of schooltalk that has major consequences for young people.

In our conversations in schools, how do we handle labels for "types of kids"?

Labels are everywhere in schools. They're schooltalking "scripts" because they are common, pre-existing ways of talking about young people—in this case, as members of groups.

Some group labels for "types of kids," like race, ethnicity, or gender labels, are made outside of schools and reinforced within them. Others are primarily made inside schools, like some ability or disability labels ("gifted"; "special needs"), program participation labels, or the other labels in the cartoon on the next page. As in the cartoon, most labels exist before we arrive and then they're applied to us.

So when do labels help young people, and when do they harm them?

Take a minute to remember our Foundational Principles of schooltalking for equity (page 8).

Now look again at the cartoon.

A denigrating label like "failure" or "slow" is probably obviously harmful.

It certainly doesn't convey belief in young people or a sense of care for them. But we often apply such labels in schools without thinking much about it.

We tend to worry a lot more about using labels not on the cartoon—words that to some, sound purely descriptive. Should I call Jim "the autistic student," or is that offensive? Should a school let students start a Black Student Union? How about a student "white club"? Which groups should be represented or named on a syllabus? Should we explicitly label someone's race, national origin, gender, or income group when determining admission to a program? When educators organize school assemblies, which groups will be named or celebrated, and why?

It's dizzying. Does schooltalk about types of kids help us pursue equity or not?

It depends on whether we're using labels to support young people. So as equity designers, our first task is to get in the habit of asking that very question.

Use our Equity Line to evaluate the consequences of every label use you encounter.

Does this label use seem to support **equity** (the full human talent development of *every* student, and *all groups* of students), or not?

NOT supporting each/all   SUPPORTING each/all students'
students' talent development   talent development

Evaluating Group Talk: Grappling with the pros and cons (for young people) of labels

Let's start with examples that most obviously violate our Foundational
Principles. It's clear that a slur—an insulting word that explicitly denigrates
people—is harmful. A colleague once told me about visiting a school where
she heard teachers calling their kids "hookers" and "trash." She thought: if
teachers would use labels like these in the presence of a stranger who could
even be someone's parent, how might they treat students in the classroom?
But even she found it hard to speak up against their use in the moment.

More often, we use seemingly gentler but inherently critical labels in
schools, like the words "problem" or "impaired" or "underachiever" in the
cartoon above. Should we not respond when others use them, by saying
these words are harmful to children?

Sometimes young people use denigrating words to describe themselves and
each other. For example, schools are plagued with debate over whether to
outlaw students' use of "the n word." Educators often agree that the ——er
version is a historical slur and should be prohibited. The ——a version has
long been part of youth culture, and some educators deem it allowable. As

a teacher I opted for disallowing even the ——a version, arguing that it de-valued youth. Many argue that the most powerful solution is for educators to discuss the label's consequences for young people *with* young people and colleagues, to devise a response all understand.[1] Similarly, we can talk with students about the consequences of "hate speech" in schools—like what it's like to hear a label that you claim shouted hatefully *as* a slur.[2] (As one ex-ample, researchers urge school allies to actively reject pejorative uses of the word "gay" [e.g., "that's so gay"], which most LGBT youth hear regularly at school and find deeply distressing.)[3]

Note that our Foundational Principles call for conveying belief in (and support and respect for) those being described. For a label to help rather than harm, the person using it has to frame the person described as a per-son with potential, strengths, and value. For example, clubs like "Women in Science and Engineering" use labels to empower morale and self-confi-dence in fields employing too few women. At one university in California, staff who were planning a summer session for the Philosophy department invited women to come experience a department that historically had few women. The program reached out proactively to women in its public com-munications and did not exclude men. The program got hundreds of female applicants, far more applicants than the program had ever had from pro-spective students of either sex. The staff found that it can be useful to reach out to a group that has not yet accessed an opportunity, to say explicitly that they have potential and are welcome. In contrast, calling out a woman as if women are unlikely to succeed in a field ("Ha! So you're the *girl* engineer!") does not empower.

So we have to think about whether we're *using* labels to support young people, too.

For example, can you think of a school label designed to help that's ac-tually often used with a negative connotation? Formal "disability" labels are designed to catalyze support services in schools, but they often come with stigma for kids. Labels like "at risk" are designed to flag students who need additional support, but they sum up an entire child as likely to fail.

As equity designers, we have to continuously evaluate the consequences for young people of every label we use to describe them. Do labels express belief in young people and care for them? Do they describe youth accurately rather than falsely? Pinpoint a need, strength, or real experience? Enable opportunity? If not, the label use is probably a problem.

Wield words only to support young people.

Sometimes, adults just want to delete labels altogether from descriptions of young people and ourselves, so we can stop thinking about all this and avoid any risk of harm. People do this with race labels in particular. Have you heard this script (or one similar to it) before?

"I don't use labels. I just see people as people." ("I don't care whether they're black, white, polka-dotted, or purple.")

In my research, I've called the common habit of deleting race labels specifically *colormuteness*.[4] That's because when we refuse to use race labels when talking, we're still thinking with them. And we aren't getting rid of their effects on people's lives.

It's a Core Tension: even as we may want to *stop* labeling people, sometimes, we need labels to accurately describe people's experiences in a world that has treated us *as* members of such "groups" for a long time.

For example, I talked to one school's administrators who had conducted a school climate survey. Black students particularly had reported that they felt misunderstood and disrespected by peers. Administrators were so worried about inappropriate Group Talk that they feared even inviting black students to dialogue in a group as "black students." But they realized they couldn't discuss or address the experiences students noted on the survey without using the label "black"—and that by anxiously deleting the very *word* "black" as if it were problematic, they were disrespecting the students further. In the end, administrators decided to respect black students by addressing their experiences. They decided to personally invite all of the school's students who identified as black (either in the school database or in person) to come to a meeting to discuss the survey if they so desired. They also planned to teach more African American history at the school so that all students had more information about their unique and shared histories; to encourage students to visit each others' neighborhoods; and to spark more dialogue in all classrooms about honoring the many groups various students identified with and didn't—their various "we's" as well as "I's."

By taking these steps, they were questioning label use *with* young people, while using those labels to enable discussion of current and historic experiences.

Labels help when they prompt inquiry into real experiences requiring attention. Labels harm when people *refuse* to question them—more precisely, when we fail to look beyond labels so that students are more fully known.

"Well, it's because they're Asians."

"Oh, he's a Special Ed kid."

"Yeah, that LTEL [Long Term English Learner]."

All labels are shorthand scripts that *could* prompt us to look no further into students' full, actual lives.

Consider a teacher who never asks students what they like reading or what's going on in their neighborhoods, and proceeds instead on his assumptions about "Latinos." Consider a specialist who knows just a fraction of her students' skills or talents, but still describes "the Special Ed kids" or "the LTELs" to colleagues as if the very labels suggest they lack skills of all kinds. The equity solution in each case is to look beyond labels to see and respect complex people—even as we stay open to learning about experiences that may require a description and response.

CORE TENSION   Schooltalk for equity describes all people as individuals too complex for labels. Schooltalk for equity *also* labels shared experiences and needs in order to address them.

The first step toward schooltalking for equity is not just to delete labels from schooltalk. It's to empower ourselves to grapple with all words' pros and cons for young people. We can start with the labels we use to describe them.

STRATEGY   Treat labels critically, as words that people *make* and thus can question with student support in mind.

When you think about it, all the categories we use to describe "types of children" in and out of schools were created by people. Thinking about labels as things people make gives us more power in deciding what to do with them in schools. We put ourselves more in charge of labels, rather than only at their mercy.

Later in this chapter, we'll dive deep into the particular history of how race categories were made by people, as taking charge of race labels is particularly key to schooltalking for equity. In this most extreme example of creating "types of people," as we'll discuss in depth later, Europeans and European Americans imagined human "races" as fundamentally different subtypes to the human species and organized centuries of resource distribution around that myth, fundamentally shaping contemporary inequality (including in schools) and creating a slew of harmful myths still requiring our attention as equity designers. Today, supporting young people requires both explicitly challenging these false and devaluing myths about types of people, and recognizing our real and powerful experiences *in* a racialized world.

But really, any group label has been made by people.

While labeling "types of things" is considered a human solution for cognitive overload,[5] anthropologists have shown that humans naming "types of people" routinely define Group A vs. Group B, presume traits held by each, and oversimplify who people actually are. The bigger problem is that those with more power and resources often use labels to benefit themselves, naming and ranking "types of people"—nations, ethnic groups, castes, sexuality "types"[6]—to organize access to resources and to opportunities, rights and privileges of various kinds. Labels harm when they *stratify or rank* "types of people," distribute opportunities accordingly, and then normalize hierarchies as if they're natural. In schools, as the cartoon jokes, we have named and created many additional "types of students" to organize learning experiences, resources, supports, and the school day.[7]

Over time, speakers (especially those getting the privileges) then sometimes stop questioning the categories they've made, as if those "types of people" just exist naturally. We also forge powerful identities around labels as we *experience* a world of "groups." As Henze and colleagues put it, human "classifications, while cultural inventions, are deeply internalized, feel real and natural, and shape how we experience the world."[8]

It's tempting to delete all labels for types of children when so many labels at their origin restrict opportunity only to some.

But because we categorize people, often distribute opportunities accordingly, and forge powerful identities along the way, ignoring categories can translate into ignoring aspects of our lived experience.

I'm always the complex, individual Mica Pollock, but you'd misunderstand aspects of my life if you failed to consider some experiences I've had as a woman in a gendered world. As I'll describe more in Chapter 2, my family was labeled "white" over several generations in the United States, shaping my life fundamentally even while the label "white" is only sometimes at the forefront of my mind. Typically I'm not thinking about myself much as a secular "Jewish" person who does a couple of holidays a year, but I am driven deeply by my grandparents' experiences as Jews in the Holocaust, which distributed the opportunity *to live* around a group label. (My mother's first language as a new immigrant was Yiddish, and she was teased in school for it; born here, I unfortunately learned only English and was praised in school for it.) I never was given a disability label in school, but a few classes tried to label me "gifted" or an "honors" student. That experience, while brief, shaped my opportunities and sense of self. Few people label my economic experience on an everyday basis, but "upper middle class" or "the 10 percent" would accurately describe my total household income, even though I rarely think about myself using either label. And the world would call me "straight"; I'm happily married to a man, and I've enjoyed the legal benefits that provides, too.

THINK / DISCUSS

Think of one category of group membership that describes you, without which you could not fully be understood. Now consider how it also does *not* easily fit your life. Is there any other label people try to put on you that you feel really doesn't fit you at all, or fits you particularly well? Has any such label "organized" your experience of opportunity?

The problem with just relying on any one of my labels to support me would be if you decided to look no further—if you presumed my experience without asking more, if you assumed false things about my "group," or if you forgot to analyze how all of these experiences intersect in my individual life and just described me with one of these many labels. You'd need to keep learning about me, right?

But if you refused to recognize my experiences in these categories, you'd ignore my actual experiences—and supporting me would be more difficult.

As we wield labels only to support young people in schools, then, this Strategy can help:

STRATEGY   Only use labels to help recognize a need or experience and support young people accordingly.

I learned this Strategy while working at the Office for Civil Rights (OCR) of the U.S. Department of Education.[9]

In a nutshell, civil rights laws designed to protect students (specifically, students with "disabilities" and students learning English in an English-dominant school system) say that sometimes you have to label a need or experience to be able to address it and support a child.

The laws also suggest that labels should accurately describe needs and experiences students actually have—and offer supports people actually want.

When I worked at OCR, for example, I saw some parents fight to get schools to apply disability labels to their children, for one simple reason: securing opportunities to learn. By law, a professional has to deem a particular learning need or physical need a disability if a student is to get funded supplemental services to accommodate that need in school. Parents have the civil right to request and receive an evaluation of a child's potential "disability" in the quest to secure supports for a given need in school. Parents struggling to get more support for their children often argued very explicitly that a formal disability label accurately described their child's needs and experiences. He was a student with a visual processing disorder, or she was "ADD."

Note that parents didn't want disability labels, per se. The label was simply a vehicle to get supports for the child. Parents who could afford it spent substantial money and time to get these formal labels and, then, to get schools to provide the services these labels demanded.

THINK / DISCUSS

Should students be given such supports without the labeling process? Could they?

But in some OCR complaints, parents or advocates argued that children were *inaccurately* being given a disability label, violating the accuracy principle of equity-oriented schooltalk.

STRATEGY   Refuse inaccurate labels for young people.

The field calls it "overrepresentation" or "disproportionality" when students of a racial-ethnic group or language group are given disability labels out of proportion to their slice of the population, as this raises suspicions about the basic accuracy of the labeling processes. In the high school where I taught in California, for example, a small proportion of the school's youth were black, but most of the students in what we called "Special Ed" classes were black. We investigated demographics like this often in OCR complaints. Research shows that in schools across the country, Special Education demographics are indeed suspiciously skewed, often due to diagnostic conversations that place disability labels on students inappropriately. Research shows that many students of color, particularly black students, are overdisciplined for minor behavior infractions for which white students often receive lesser or no consequences, then evaluated for vague disabilities, labeled officially, and finally placed in some form of Special Education—often in a separate room, not with personalized accommodations in regular classrooms as the law dictates. (Under the law, students with disabilities should only be educated in separate spaces if this is absolutely necessary to their learning.) Research also shows that many students learning English get inappropriately evaluated for disabilities when what they actually need are better school supports as they learn English.[10] In each case, educators schooltalking *for equity* would question labels' accuracy and explore how to use labels only to pinpoint and serve needs young people actually have.

Equity-oriented schooltalk leverages a label *only* to accurately recognize a student's actual need or experience and to support him or her accordingly. Why else should we label a child, after all?

At OCR, I saw another example of people trying to wield labels to secure supports—in this case, to address English learners' actual needs. Civil rights law requires schools to formally recognize students learning English as English learners so that the adults around them are accountable to support their language development and ensure they understand classroom instruction. A famous 1974 Supreme Court case, *Lau v. Nichols*, declared it illegal to let English learners "sink or swim" in English-only classrooms without targeted supports for their English language development. The *Lau* court found, for example, that a Chinese speaker in an all-English classroom with no accommodations for his or her language needs was not experiencing "equal" opportunity to learn in comparison to a native English speaker in the room. Over time, *Lau* has been interpreted to require educators to regularly assess and label which English learners in the classroom need what level of English instructional support.[11] Again, the logic is not that labels themselves are the goal, but that accurate descriptions of student need and experience can secure desired assistance. Further, *needs not named might never be met.*

I remember two examples from teaching high school when needs not mentioned became needs not met. Lutita, a student in my room who had just arrived from rural Samoa, wasn't notated in any record I saw as needing special assistance of any kind. She sat there silent in my fast-paced English 10 class. I'm not sure I ever supported her to write and read in academic English. Kyle was a student who had an IEP that no one ever showed me. (An IEP is a written Individualized Education Plan, part of the legal process outlining required supports for students with labeled disabilities.) I had no idea Kyle was considered to have a specialized learning need until someone told me at the end of the year that he was also in Special Ed classes. To this day I don't know what his learning need was.

In some ways, the absence of simple labels in my schooltalk about Lutita and Kyle let me just treat them as complex individuals. If I had known better how to pinpoint and then address students' academic needs and strengths myself, I might have figured out their learning situations without any formal descriptions by others. However, each student also had real learning needs that I was supposed to be serving but didn't know about. Could I have helped them more if someone had formally labeled those needs for me and held me accountable for meeting them?

When we fail to describe a student's situation, we can fail to respond to it.

Many English learners are offered little or no targeted support for their English language development in school.[12] OCR colleagues spent a lot of time insisting that English learners in English-only classes be assessed and labeled and then offered strategic instruction to build skills next. But labeling doesn't help students if they are *just* labeled and not actually attended to appropriately: equity-oriented schooltalk uses labels as portals to actual assistance. Ted Hamann writes about students who were kept in low-level ESL (English as a second language) classrooms long after they'd mastered sufficient English because they could help teachers translate for the other kids. In this case, the label "ESL" wasn't being wielded to help the young people any more. Now misapplied, it actually masked their skills and kept students from opportunities they also needed.[13] (In another example of label misapplication, a college student of mine told me about his friend, a fluent English speaker who was put inappropriately into ESL classes as a child just because she was the child of Spanish-speaking parents. She took unnecessary English language development classes through high school and so missed out on many other course opportunities that could have prepared her for college.)

Also, a vague label for a student's situation often doesn't assist like a precise description does. For example, the more recently created label LTEL (long-term English learner) describes secondary students not yet achieving English fluency as hoped. Some educators I know feel the label starts to name a critical student situation but then is too vague to shape precise assistance. Others argue that "limited English proficient" similarly frames young people as not meeting expectations, rather than clarifying needed supports (or validating students' abilities in other languages!). As Laurie Olsen puts it, "English learners" become "long term English learners" through years of inconsistent and inadequate English support; by high school, students need continued targeted assistance on specific aspects of their English language development. Instead, she writes, "most districts lack any definition or means of identifying or monitoring the progress and achievement of this population."[14] As one district administrator put it, vague labels like "LTEL" can become "just an excuse for why a student may not succeed," violating our Foundational Principle of pinpointing and addressing students' precise situations and needs.

Inaccurate labels that come with stigma are of course not at all supportive, but they still get applied to many young people in schools. Teresa McCarty and Tiffany Lee note that because many Native American students raised as English speakers "speak varieties of English influenced by their Native languages," many are "subjected to school labeling practices that stigmatize them as 'limited English proficient,'" rather than engaged via (or valued for) their actual language skills.[15]

Accurate and precise descriptions of young people, linked to actual provision of support when needed, are key to schooltalking for equity.

Giving a child a disability label when he actually has been having bad relationships with teachers or a "limited English proficient" label when she's actually fluently multilingual overlooks a child's actual situation. Calling a child "Chinese" when she is actually Korean American or "Mexican" when he is actually from El Salvador misrepresents a child. (School mascots that label, distort, and disrespect entire groups harm; many children still hear such labels screamed in game after game.[16]) And of course, using a label that at its core denigrates a child violates every Foundational Principle we've laid out.

Still, this happens all the time in schools.

Let's walk through more label usage worth questioning.

Our Foundational Principles (page 8) call for precise description. Labels that come to *stand for the entire person* (especially when used by person X to describe person Y) can distort our sense of young people. As we've seen, efforts to specify and support children's English development needs are critical, but overarching labels used to describe entire types of people—like even the seemingly purely descriptive "English learner"—can risk overlooking the rest of students' skills and experiences. (Indeed, a friend's colleague once described "English learners" matter-of-factly as "having *no* language," even as research shows how much multilingual skill young people learning English must employ to navigate English-dominant settings.[17])

When we routinely use overarching labels like "Special Ed kid," we also imply a "type of person" and say nothing about the real goal—supporting specific aspects of students' learning. For example, I heard one student speak passionately about what it meant to him to stop riding a bus labeled generally as for "Special Ed kids" in middle school. At his new school, which "mainstreamed" students marked as "Special Ed" into classes with everyone else, people stopped publicly using the overarching generic label "Special Ed kid" to describe him but continued to precisely (and in this case, privately) label, discuss, and support his specialized learning needs and strengths, wielding funding secured through the labeling process. He graduated and enrolled in college.

Thinking about how we use labels in sentences can also keep them from being equated to "the kid." The organization Kids Included Together (www.kitonline.org/) calls for "socially responsible language" that considers how children labeled with disabilities might prefer to be described. One solution is using "person-first" language, like "student with [*specific special need*]" rather than "Special Needs kid," or "child with autism" instead of "autistic kid." As one of their leaders put it, "Person-first language reminds educators that children are more alike than they are different":

> "We find that viewing a child by their label first ('Downs kid,' 'autistic kid') can lead to stereotyping by the adult. When a teacher or child-care provider hears 'you are getting an autistic child in your class,' they can jump to a lot of assumptions about that child's needs. If they, instead, hear 'you are getting a boy named Tommy in your class, he loves dinosaurs and he has autism,' the picture in the teacher's head is completely different."

THINK / DISCUSS

Can you think of a label you want used only to describe one aspect of your experiences or needs, rather than used as if it equals you? Give an example of such label use that you would welcome.

We can also try to question lump-sum labels used *constantly*, rather than contextually and in combination, to describe any individual child. That's because any given label *sometimes* captures an important experience and sometimes fails to describe our experiences and needs precisely. Let's say a student whose family immigrated from Korea when she was in fifth grade describes herself sometimes by middle school as "Asian," due to expectations from forms, peers, and media and because she feels positively connected to the term. At the same time, perhaps she still needs some specific school supports for translating from Korean to English; perhaps she might connect most with other "immigrant students" with extended families still in the country of origin. Depending on her family's legal status, as she ages she might most need information on applying to college as the child of "undocumented" parents. Right now, maybe she most needs to talk to other girls struggling with body image or early-adult sexuality. Perhaps the primary thing affecting her life is a family struggle with money for unmet medical needs, meaning a referral to a local program offering health care services to "low-income" families could actually be most helpful. Or maybe she'd most like to connect to people who share her love of hip-hop, or her skills in gaming. *Just* calling her "Asian" wouldn't capture her full complexity; "Asian" is one of the terms she claims.

How would you know which labels accurately describe aspects of her experience, and when? Perhaps you'd respectfully ask her or her family about the supports she wants most right now. One school I visited wrestled with the related question of how to group students in support discussions with others who might share various life experiences. In the end, they decided to ask students who they wanted to get support from. Other schools and community organizations decide to support young people through inviting group conversations (e.g., about community history or tradition) that adults think might support and fuel them, even if the students didn't yet ask for the support.

Patricia Gándara notes that it can be helpful to students to get "cocooned" at times in support groups with students who may share some group experiences. For example, she argues that even while educators must emphasize individuality and diversity within "Latino" populations, students can sometimes benefit from voluntary time to discuss their range of experiences as "Latinos" in a school or community.[18] The goal is not to ghettoize or homogenize Latinos but to invite discussion of experience that may (or may not) be shared—and let students decline if they wish. As a superintendent put it to me once, educators can seek a "smorgasbord" of activities that invite young people to discuss a variety of community and individual experiences—like offering various "cocoons" at different times to care for students. Research suggests that college students, for example, benefit *both* from invitations to join people in their same racial or ethnic identity "groups" in discussion *and* from talking across such group lines as members of other groups—say, as "freshmen" or "bio majors" or "calculus students."[19] (Such discussions help if students are approached as capable of success, not as likely to fail.) Then, students can debrief on experiences shared along various dimensions and realize that everyone is stressing about school, not just members of their "group."

THINK / DISCUSS

Consider a group "cocoon" *you* would have welcomed in K–12 school or afterwards. What would you have wanted to discuss? How would others have reacted to that cocooning?

No single "cocoon" can likely meet all of our needs. Poet Walt Whitman put it accurately: we all "contain multitudes." Others have called multiculturalism "the normal human experience": we belong simultaneously to multiple communities that shape our lives.[20] Scholars have termed complex experiences of power dynamics in race, gender, class, and sexuality communities simultaneously *intersectionality*.[21] As a colleague who studies race, gender, and religious identities said succinctly in an email, "people are members of multiple communities and have multiple, often intersecting identities, some of which are context-dependent."

Shaun Harper and his colleagues demonstrate such "intersectionality" through a personal profile of Tyson, a "biracial gay male undergraduate student with salient academic and spiritual identities who straddles two disparate socioeconomic statuses." They point out that few college programs are set up to support complex individual Tyson. "In most places, he would have to go to the Black culture center for matters pertaining to his Blackness, to a discussion series for men to explore his masculine identity, to the LGBT Center to connect with other non-heterosexual students, and so on." So, Tyson is often forced to "rank order the multiple dimensions of his identity," and asked to "prioritize and value some identities over the others" in various social environments. A solution, Harper and colleagues argue, is for educators to pay "increased attention to students as individuals" who are negotiating many group experiences simultaneously.[22] Educators can offer each individual Group Talk options of multiple kinds.

Inflexibly and imprecisely labeling students with single labels often misses more specific life experiences (positive and negative), making educators less able to fully support and understand young people. At the same time, to ignore group experience ignores our Foundational Principle of accurate description. Ignoring unique experiences of being gay, born in Korea, or a student learning English does not assist students; it just refuses to fully understand or engage their lives.

So rather than just ignore or delete labels, we can instead work with youth and their supporters to understand, describe, and address students' complex experiences and meet their actual needs.

Young people often question labels' utility for such tasks. At the high school where I taught, students were always debating which labels fit them and which didn't. A student might describe himself at one moment as "part Salvadoran and part Filipino and part black" and ask at another moment to be represented as "Latino" in the school assembly or on a classroom syllabus. I called this strategic use of labels "race bending." Students proudly used many labels to describe their complex identities *and* used single, "lump-sum" labels to identify themselves in consequential struggles over representation and resource. Sometimes they made up some new labels (like "japapino"); mostly they worked with the ones society handed them.[23] In race bending, they asked to value and learn about particular group experiences that mattered to them *even as* they lived complex multicultural lives. Young people constantly have to choose which preexisting ideas about groups to use and which to contest, particularly as others position them as single group members and offer opportunities accordingly.[24]

Research shows that young people around the world debate and challenge categories and labels of race, nation, gender, class, sexuality, religion, neighborhood, and peer group even as they use them to navigate their societies and communities. Students both defy and adopt simple race categories in their popular culture use.[25] Immigrant students struggle to challenge U.S. race categories even as they start to use them.[26] For *Tough Fronts*, Lory J. Dance talked with youth struggling to earn the label "hard" (tough) to ward off real aggression from peers, even as they knew the label oversimplified who they actually wanted to be.[27] Other label use empowers youth tremendously: many Native youth use tribal names that connect them pow-erfully to relationships, historic knowledge, and heritage languages in their communities, *even as* they also navigate complex contemporary communi-ties that are multilingual and multicultural. Many programs exploring group histories and identities *with* youth fuel them for life.[28]

As equity designers, then, we can consider all descriptions of "types of people" *with young people*—proactively, and in response to their questions. The simplest Group Talk strategy of all? Be ready for inquiry into labels' accuracy, pros, and cons for youth when youth raise the subject.[29]

THINK / DISCUSS

Here's a question to ask a young person or yourself: do you ever use a long list of labels when taking the freedom to describe some aspect of your own complex identity? Do you ever use single "lump-sum" labels to identify yourself when trying to secure a resource, resist some experience of unequal opportunity, or connect to a community that empowers you? How does that feel, and what are the pros and cons for you of using the labels in question?

Are you starting to sense that we have to resist labels *and* use them when needed to describe an actual experience or need and to support and respect a child?

Let's finish our Group Talk chapter by actively questioning the toughest labels of all: race labels. These are words both flawed at their core *and* now necessary to describe various realities in American life.

I've spent a lot of time helping people in schools take charge of race labels for antiracist purposes. Race labels involve some of our deepest misconceptions about "types of people"—scripts that require active chal-lenge if we want to support young people. We'll explore many such scripts throughout this book, but let's start with a particularly fundamental one. Many people don't know one critical fact essential to equity effort: that genetically speaking, there are no valid racial subgroups to the human species. We just have long treated each other *as if* there are, creating deep inequalities and real human experiences we now need to describe and ad-dress in schools.

This might be a deeper dive into race labels than you were expecting. But after working with thousands of educators on this material, I'm convinced that a head-on discussion of *race labels themselves* equips us for equity effort of all kinds. It helps us get in the habit of questioning various *inaccurate and devaluing* notions about "types of people," while recognizing how real experiences *with* grouping shape our lives and require attention in schools.

So, collect any gold nugget ideas that you might use later with others, and draw parallels to other labels we use in schools whenever you can. The **THINK/DISCUSS** questions along the way and at the end of the chapter should help you out.

Race labels and schooltalk

Are you used to thinking about the U.S. population as a handful of fundamentally different "kinds of people"? Here's one chart for California:

Population Today:
California vs. the United States:

	CA	US
White persons, percent, 2011	74.0%	78.1%
Black persons, percent, 2011	6.6%	13.1%
American Indian and Alaska Native persons, percent, 2011	1.7%	1.2%
Asian persons, percent, 2011	13.6%	5.0%
Native Hawaiian and Other Pacific Islander persons, percent, 2011	0.5%	0.2%
Persons reporting two or more races, percent, 2011	3.6%	2.3%
Persons of Hispanic or Latino Origin, percent, 2011	38.1%	16.7%
White persons not Hispanic, percent, 2011	39.7%	63.4%

Source: http://quickfacts.census.gov/qfd/states/06000.html.

These categories aren't genetically valid subgroups of humans. But the census collects real social data—it collects data on groups long *labeled* as being "races." At this point, race labels are a social reality built on a biological fiction.

Race labels embody what Ashley Montagu called "man's most dangerous myth."[30] It's the myth that our variations in appearance indicate that we are fundamentally different types of people on the inside.

Over the past five or six hundred years, this myth has undergirded several linked falsehoods about humans that have shaped U.S. life fundamentally and still affect us deeply in schools:

MYTH 1: There are subgroups to the human species called "races" that are different biologically.

MYTH 2: Your inner worth, abilities, skills, traits, and talents are linked to your outer appearance.

MYTH 3: Some such subgroups are more worthy of rights, opportunities, and privileges.

These myths still shape how we see and treat students every day in schools. So, let's gallop through six hundred years of history to share some critical facts we need for our schooltalk. We'll explore how:

✳   Racial categories were created by human beings, even though they are genetically inaccurate.

✳   Laws made racial categories central to who got which opportunities, creating race-class inequalities still with us today.

✳   Science supported false ideas about racial "types of people" to justify such distributions of opportunity, bolstering harmful and false ideas about "races" that remain with us—including in schools.

You'll see that this gallop leaves us at the brink of a Core Tension for Group Talk today. To support young people, we have to *both* reject these false labels for types of people, *and* wield such labels to describe and address a world long organized around them.

So to lay the foundation for equity effort, let's flip some scripts about human difference that have done folks some serious harm.

A gallop through six hundred years
of history—for educators

In the mid-1400s in Spain, the early Spanish word "raza," or "race," first
appeared in "purity of blood" laws that forced people to try to prove their
family ancestry was Christian, not Jewish or Muslim, in order to get status
positions and other privileges.[31] Yes, this matters to schooltalk today.

Europeans colonizing the New World circa 1500 and beyond enslaved
Africans, and in some locations indigenous Americans, to work land.
Simultaneously, they developed deep and lasting ideologies to explain those
being dominated economically and socially as inferior types of people deserving such treatment. Audrey Smedley calls this justificatory ideology a
"racial worldview" that persists today.[32] In essence, this worldview was the
idea that racial subtypes of humans existed and that some deserved opportunity more than others.

As anthropologist Roger Sanjek notes, people have long divided up resources
along various made-up lines of rank or caste.[33] Some have tried to dominate
or even own other people and accordingly called them inferior types of people, sometimes along lines of appearance and sometimes not. Smedley notes
that for centuries (starting in the 1100s), for example, the English called the
Irish "savages" and "heathens" who deserved or even needed colonial domi-
nation; James Sweet details the Portuguese denigration of Africans long before Columbus.[34] Europeans carried this same ideology to the New World,

treating diverse Native Americans across the Americas as an inferior type of person who could be displaced from land or forced into labor.[35] Post-1400s colonialism and slavery extended and solidified such ideology in a particular way to limit access to wealth, power, and social privilege. For the first time, Europeans built a systemic hierarchy focused on physical appearance, through both laws and pseudoscience. As Carol Mukhopadhyay puts it, "racial labels and categories, like all terms and concepts, are human-made classifying devices that we learn, internalize, and then use to interpret the everyday world in which we live. But conventional American racial categories are rooted in colonialism, slavery, and an elaborate ideology developed to justify a system of racial inequality."[36]

THINK / DISCUSS

As we continue to gallop, consider: how are laws, and appeals to science, involved in producing and reinforcing the other categories we use in schools?

The role of laws in making categories

The word "white" formally entered the American vocabulary in our slave laws, to gradually name Europeans as a type of "free" person who could be paid for their labor in contrast to African slaves.[37] As historian Winthrop Jordan put it, "After about 1680, taking the colonies as a whole, a new term appeared—*white*."[38] Laws and public documents increasingly declared that "Negroes," or "black" people, could be permanently unpaid and "owned."

The label "white" was all about restricting opportunity to some. European Americans gaining legal privileges as "whites"—to earn wages, vote, own land, and more—then wrote more laws to keep those privileges, threatening with physical violence anyone disobeying the laws.[39] Resistance continued from those enslaved and displaced; laws got even harsher. Laws gradually named "Negroes" as a type of person whose descendants would be enslaved and who wasn't even allowed to learn to read or write, in case such learning would incite more rebellion. (African Americans pursued literacy nonetheless.)

U.S. laws also gradually named many other European immigrants, migrating largely at first from Western and Northern Europe, as "whites"—a type of person who could become a citizen, own property, and vote (if male, that is). The Naturalization Act of 1790 explicitly reserved U.S. citizenship and its benefits to "free white persons."[40] (This racial restriction of the ability to become a citizen was not fully rescinded until 1952; as Ian Haney López sums up, "From the earliest years of this country until just a generation ago, being a 'white person' was a condition for acquiring citizenship."[41]) In 1882, the literally named "Chinese Exclusion Act," intended to restrict U.S. jobs to "whites," labeled "Chinese" immigrants as a type of person not allowed to migrate to the U.S. at all. (This law was not repealed until 1943, and stringent quotas still restricted the immigration of Asians for decades after.)[42]

After the U.S. incorporated much of Mexico in 1848 as California and the Southwestern states, laws (e.g., in California) extended U.S. citizenship rights primarily to "White male citizen[s] of Mexico."[43] Tomás Almaguer describes how labeling again restricted opportunity to some. Wealthier, land-owning Mexicans seen as descended more directly from Spaniards were more likely to be seen as deserving "white" citizenship and rights in the United States, while the lower class Mexican majority, often darker skinned and seen as more indigenous, were typically not deemed "white" by custom nor offered "white" privileges in practice, "despite being eligible for citizenship rights." Instead, they were treated more like the "Indians" laboring at the bottom of California's racial hierarchy.[44] As Gilbert González describes, U.S. families still tagged as "Mexican" were framed as "natural" laborers who had to be led by "whites," and were gradually segregated into poorly resourced schools separate from "whites" in the Southwest and California— just as black people were. By the 1930s, several hundred thousand U.S. citizens of Mexican descent busy contributing to U.S. life were even erroneously deported to Mexico.[45]

U.S. lawmakers continued to restrict the classification "white" and its attendant privileges to people of European descent. For example, Ian Haney López's book *White by Law* shows U.S. residents from East Asia, South Asia, and the Middle East suing, typically unsuccessfully, to be labeled "white" throughout the late nineteenth and early twentieth centuries, in order to access the benefits of citizenship as they lived U.S. lives.[46] Over the nineteenth and twentieth centuries, various European immigrants initially discriminated against as "not quite white" (or as inferior subtypes of "whites") in employment, housing, and immigration policy (like Irish Catholics in some cases, and Southern and Eastern Europeans in others) got socially included over time in the homogenized category "white" and its economic benefits, while migration from Asia and citizenship chances for Asians in the United States were long restricted.[47] By law and by custom, the segregation of neighborhoods, schools, social spaces, and jobs was shaped along the made-up white/non-white binary, limiting access to U.S. opportunity even as "non-white" people contributed mightily to U.S. life.[48]

In Chapter 2 (Inequality Talk), we'll discuss in a bit more detail a specific aspect of this story: how centuries of "white"-made laws and customs ensuring that "whites" could get paid for their labor, secure better jobs and property, go to publicly funded schools and universities, and vote meant that "whites" overall accumulated more wealth than non-"whites," forming the basis of the race-class inequality that still shapes our neighborhoods and schools. But for now, let's start considering another issue foundational to schooltalk overall: how myths about "the races" got made. For centuries, "white" scientists led an effort to prove right a race-based system of opportunity, pumping myths into American life that still saturate our Group Talk today and disrupt efforts to accurately *see* every child.

The role of science in making categories

Remember, all ideas about "types of people" are made by people. Let's gallop back for a second to 1735, when the slave trade was still going strong. A naturalist and botanist named Carl Linnaeus began classifying humans into four varieties: Europaeus, Americanus (by which he meant Native Americans), Asiaticus, and Africanus. He would publish this schema in a 1758 edition of his *Systema Naturae*. Rather than just describing such simplified types physically, Linnaeus presumed inner traits linked to "groups'" physical appearance. For example, he described Europaeus as not just "white . . . eyes—blue" but also as "gentle, acute [smart], inventive . . . governed by laws."[49]

For several hundred years after this, scientists published presumptions that racial types existed and that these types were internally different— differentially moral, hard-working, attractive, peaceful or threatening, and smart. Through the 1800s and 1900s, European and U.S. researchers (including from emerging disciplines like anthropology and psychology) produced studies they argued "proved" the presumed inferiority of non-"whites"; the studies served to justify an economic and social hierarchy that already benefited "whites."[50] As the evolutionary biologist Stephen Jay Gould documented, these scientists, deeming themselves "white," mismeasured skulls, assessed noses, and presumed character, repeatedly putting "white" on top and "black" at the bottom, with all other groups ranked in between.[51] Advertisements and media then broadcast pseudo-science about "white" people as beautiful and morally pure; circulated "science"-fed anxieties about "Negro" people as threatening, aggressive, and hypersexual; and denigrated "Asians" and "Mexicans" respectively as inscrutable or lazy, to name just a few myths. As Gilbert González documents, for example, researchers studying what they called "the Mexican problem" cited each other's unfounded claims well into the twentieth century, to argue that Mexican parents (working hard in U.S. companies on both sides of the border) "dislike[d] work," "undervalued education, lacked leadership abilities, and were intellectually inferior," as were supposedly their children.[52]

Hand in hand with "science," media distorting a diverse nation trained U.S. eyes and brains to see and *judge* people as members of separate races, hierarchically arranged. Such assumptions about presumed inner traits linked to outer appearance became a key aspect of what Smedley calls the U.S. racial worldview, a set of myths rooted in several centuries of "scientific" classification effort.

Consider which such worldviews affect other categories we use in schools today:

1. Idea of race categories as rigid and simple and permanent;
2. Outer appearances presumed to be indicators of inner traits and worth;
3. Simplicity of race categories, ignoring the true diversity of humanity;
4. Classifications hierarchically structured;
5. Classifications made by "scientists" made these race categories seem natural and legitimate.[53]

Each of these scripted falsehoods about racial "types of people" still requires active challenge in our schooltalk today as we seek to accurately see and value every child. Research finds that U.S. viewers still associate positive traits more quickly with faces that look "white," for example, or have physiologically negative reactions to images or scenarios involving "black" people (brow furrowing; sweating).[54] Scholars call this *implicit bias*, a bias we have but may not even consciously recognize.[55] Such unconscious reactions aren't born in babies. They develop out of lived immersion in centuries-old scripts about differentially valued "groups" that still circulate in the media, public life, and everyday conversations. We'll address many of them in the chapters to come.

So how do we even start counteracting such long-standing, ingrained bias about "types of people"? One key step is to recognize our programming to assume false things about "groups."

Even now, we still need to challenge six hundred years of programming to imagine fundamentally different subtypes of humans. If left unchallenged, deep notions about racial groups as fundamentally different (and differentially valuable) "types of people" derail equity efforts of all kinds. To create schools where we truly support every child, we can start by actively busting the myth that races are genetically real human subgroups.

THINK / DISCUSS

In addition to racial assumptions, what other assumptions about inner abilities, personalities, or values do we make in schools, based on outer characteristics? Name one example. Do those assumptions also need to be "busted" with equity in mind?

Here are additional points I often share in my own schooltalk with educators, university students, or youth, to start the process of flipping foundational scripts about race groups as genetic subgroups of human beings. I've truly needed every point to convince others as part of caring for young people. As an equity designer, which of the following facts might you share with an adult or young person, to pursue more accurate schooltalk about "types of people"?

Race facts to strengthen and inform your schooltalk

* We are one human species sharing a gene pool without boundaries, not sub-races to the human race with fundamentally different genes.[56]

✳   Our various visual differences as humans—like skin color, hair type, nose shape, eye shape—are too insignificant (and arbitrary) a portion of our genetics to use to categorize human beings into a set of genetically distinct subgroups.[57]

✳   As anthropologist Nina Jablonski (author of *Skin*) wrote me in an email, for example, "Skin pigmentation genes account for a tiny proportion of our genetic makeup. . . . Taken together, all genes accounting for portions of the visible human phenotype [your appearance] constitute only a tiny fraction of our genome. The physical traits that have been used to classify people into 'races' are directly controlled by genes that constitute far less than 1% of our genome."[58]

✳   The traits we use to mark "race" are also arbitrary. The authors of *How Real Is Race?* invite students to notice the many examples of human physical variability—like hairiness, height, hand shape, the ability to curl your tongue—and to ask, "why do U.S. racial categories emphasize some traits and ignore all the rest?"[59]

✳   Humans are 99.9 percent "the same," genetically speaking. As a genome researcher put it bluntly in response to questions on www.genome.gov, "racial groups are not distinct biological groups."[60]

✳   Why does skin look different? Our human ancestors originated in Africa, close to the equator. Natural selection favored darker skin (more melanin) to protect against folate deficiency (a threat to reproduction) caused by high UV radiation from intense sunlight. As humans migrated to areas with less sunlight, natural selection favored lighter skin to allow for sufficient absorption of Vitamin D.[61] So, darker or lighter skin tells us mainly "about a human's amount of ancestry relative to the equator."[62]

✳   Our ancestors moved around the globe and had children with each other. As the *Race: The Power of an Illusion* website puts it, "No human group has been isolated long enough to evolve into a genetically distinct race."[63]

✳ If you zoom in and look at a human's genetic code, there are no clear markers on it saying what "race" you are. You can only see the regions of the world through which some of your genetic ancestors migrated.[64]

✳ "We are all more related than we have been taught to think."[65] The National Geographic film *Human Family Tree* showed a diverse community in Queens exploring their ancestors' migration histories—and realizing they were far more related as humans than they expected!

✳ If you got all humans in one room, you'd see physical traits (nose shapes, skin colors) scattered and shared all over the world.[66] We'd then walk across the room to join new groups if you asked us to categorize ourselves by hair type, vs. nose shape, vs. tooth type! If we arbitrarily used height to create new "races" of people, Mukhopadhyay and colleagues point out in *How Real Is Race*, "African Tutsis and European Swedes would be in the same race. African Mbuti, Filipinos, Vietnamese, and some Eastern Europeans and Russians would end up in the same race."[67]

✳ And even if you lined us all up by skin tone, there would be no clear line where one "race" ends and another begins. As Alan Goodman puts it, "Skin color, the physical characteristic that Americans most often use to falsely distinguish racial groups, itself cannot be classified into clear-cut 'types' of 'colors.'"[68]

✳ Genetically, humans are more diverse *inside* any population we've called a "race group" than genetically different from people from other "race groups." Most genetic variability actually exists between individuals. And Africa, with more than a billion individuals, contains the most genetic diversity in the world.[69]

People often bring up disease patterns (like susceptibility to sickle cell anemia) or sports (the many Africans or African Americans who have won high-profile track competitions) at this point in an effort to argue that races "really exist" biologically. Here are responses I've collected for this purpose. Again, I've needed every one in my schooltalk:

✳ The "Race: Are We So Different?" exhibition by the American Anthropological Association clarifies that "certain diseases are more common among people with a particular ancestry than among the general population. But racial categories are just too big and imprecise to indicate anything medically meaningful about a person's ancestry. In order to be truly pertinent, the data gathered in medical studies must track ancestry at the level of specific country or region." For example, sickle cell anemia (an environmental adaptation to the threat of malaria) is more prevalent in western Africa than southern Africa and in southern Europe than northern Europe. Those of northern European ancestry are more at risk for cystic fibrosis than those of southern European ancestry, even while both are considered "white" on the U.S. Census.[70]

✳ Acquired diseases that are more prevalent in certain populations, such as a disproportionate experience of heart disease among African Americans, are a function of lived experiences, such as poverty, stress, discrimination, diet, or pollution.[71]

✳ While different countries often do well at different sports in the Olympics, this doesn't show that biologically we are different "races," but rather that we pursue different sports. Some of our ancestors may have passed us body parts shaped well for a particular sport, but that doesn't mean we are different subgroups of the human species.[72]

✳ Finally, the very perception of the "race group" we are in shifts depending on context. If a person considered "white" in Brazil comes to the U.S. and is relabeled "black" or "Latino," the fabricated nature of these groupings becomes apparent.[73] The groups we call "races" are social categories that people made and perpetuate—categories that even shift depending on context. As the authors of *How Real Is Race* conclude, "there are no reliable procedures for dividing humans into races!"[74]

I often say flippantly to teachers that Americans could have organized power and privilege along the lines of foot size; or that organizing opportunity around blood type would have made more sense in genetic terms.

Instead, those in power organized much of our opportunity around skin color, noses, eye shape, and hair—genetically insignificant characteristics that could simply be seen. Every time we look at people with different appearances and think they are fundamentally different on the inside, we are activating six hundred years of programming to think so.

Do you feel like you knew all that? Many people don't. Sharing and discussing these facts is foundational to schooltalk for equity, because it reminds us that we are all *equally human*—and equally valuable.

THINK / DISCUSS

Do educators need to learn and talk to each other (or to students) about the history of race categories in order to teach successfully in America? Why or why not?

STRATEGY Share our six-hundred-year "gallop" and other information in this chapter to communicate to colleagues and students that race categories are not genetic realities—humans made them socially real through six hundred years of unequal treatment.

Schooltalk for equity has to bust a lot of myths about "types of people." As we'll discuss in later chapters, the scripted and programmed biases and snap judgments of prior centuries stay in our brains automatically despite our best intentions. We also still have the opportunity systems "race" built—and we've come up with all sorts of mythic explanations for those too.

I often walk around my campus noting how my brain automatically categorizes people racially, even as I know this history. Historian Robin Kelley succinctly notes that race "is not about how you look, it is about how people assign meaning to how you look."[75] If I stay aware, I can literally feel my brain assign meaning. That is, I note how in addition to categorizing people, my brain automatically attaches judgments to categorizations. Without intending to, I make snap presumptions about who might be a hard worker, or about who might steal something from my car if I don't lock it. In "Bike Thief," a videoed experiment testing such stereotypes, two boys and a girl (who respectively looked "white," African American, and "white") each pretended in sequence to be sawing a bike lock off a bike in a mostly white suburban neighborhood. People walked past the white boy without much reaction. They angrily asked the black boy why he was trying to steal the bike. Many asked the white girl if she needed help.[76]

Whenever I find myself snapping to judgment without really knowing people, I remind myself that I'm programmed to think with such "scripts." Acknowledging my programming helps me start to actively reject it. Researchers have shown that we can begin to counteract this automated "assignment of meaning" if we become conscious of it and try to refuse it with "counter-stereotypic thoughts" and accurate facts about real people.[77]

As Jordan, an African American high school student, told researcher Na'ila Nasir,

> "I think [stereotypes about African American students] just has been instilled in the American mindframe . . . even though I don't want to categorize someone, but there are certain stereotypes that pop in your head and you have to catch yourself and say, no, that's not true. But it's gonna take a lot."

As Nasir notes, Jordan understood "that the stereotypes about black males (a demographic group to which he belongs) are so strong that he had to actively work to remind himself that they lacked truth."[78] He had to flip the script about himself.

We'll explore various schooltalk scripts about "types of people" in the chapters to come. For now, note that researchers suggest that if we notice how we snap to old ideas about some "types of people" as more or less threatening, moral, hardworking, beautiful, trustworthy, smart, and deserving of opportunity, we can begin to resist such thoughts and replace them with a refusal to stereotype—and with a commitment to seeking accurate facts about actual people. And so, to counteract my own programming, I notice it and work to reject it. I sometimes think silently to a stranger on campus, "I actually know nothing about you. But my brain is programmed to categorize you. And the world still categorizes us both."

All of us get put in categories by others every time we walk outside.

And here's perhaps the toughest part to handle in our schooltalk—even as we resist stereotype, we often need to wield categories and labels to describe and handle the system already made.[79]

As we put it in *Everyday Antiracism*,

In a world that has been organized for six centuries around bogus biological categories invented in order to justify the unequal distribution of life's necessities, some antiracist activity refuses to categorize people racially. Other antiracist activity recognizes people living as racial group members in order to analyze and transform a racially unequal world.[80]

We'll consider a "world" (and schools) organized around such categories in next chapters, and the schooltalk needed to address student experiences in such a world. Even though we don't belong to biologically distinct or differentially valuable "types of people," we do need labels to describe real experiences with the inequalities and myths race labels have brought us— *and* to help describe the identities, strengths, and contributions people have forged along the way. So, while we work to counteract additional inaccurate scripted myths about "race groups," we'll work to *accurately* describe experience in a world that has treated us as members of "race groups" for a very long time. In short, we'll use race labels only to support young people!

For now, note that sometimes the same category that harmfully oversimplifies people when imposed by others can be seized on purpose by people in the group for self-description and self-empowerment. Researchers have called this (re: race categorization) "strategic racialization."[81] As Ta-Nehisi Coates muses in his opus on African American experiences, "They made us into a race. We made ourselves into a people."[82]

Such aggregated self-labeling negotiates a world of categories and helps to *describe and address actual shared experience* (negative and positive) in such a world, despite the vast human diversity inside any "group." At various moments in U.S. history, African Americans have strategically seized and positively reframed categories others used to harm, proudly reclaiming labels like "black" to analyze shared experience, claim social contributions, counteract damaging myths about African Americans, pursue economic empowerment, and connect to the larger African diaspora. Americans from many Latin American origins have aggregated as "Latinos" for political power, social recognition, representation in voting and labor, and community action.[83] Analysts note that both the more self-chosen category "Latino" (building in recent decades) and the more bureaucratic label "Hispanic" (used by the census starting in the 1970s) lump together a very diverse U.S. population with widely varying experiences, even as Latinos in the aggregate have various shared experiences in the U.S., including, as we'll see, patterns of access to opportunity.[84] Native Americans can describe shared experiences, including with non-Native institutions, *while* describing the vast diversity and knowledges across more than five hundred Native American tribal communities; activists wielding constitutional law have asserted critical language, cultural, and economic rights *as* Native American and Indigenous peoples.[85] As Yen Le Espiritu puts it, in "Asian American" movements in the 1960s, "the pan-Asian concept, originally imposed by non-Asians, became a symbol of pride and a rallying point for mass mobilization by later generations," with many lumping "panethnically" as "Asian American" "to be politically and economically effective" and to address common problems with exclusion and discrimination.[86] Today, many researchers and communities prioritize teaching such group histories to young people, so students can powerfully define themselves and position themselves (and others) accurately as part of long histories of rich contribution, struggle, and striving in a world of categories even while analyzing their own complex contemporary lives.[87] We'll just scratch the surface of such necessary stories in the chapters to come, in our ongoing quest for accurate description and schooltalk that values every child.

THINK / DISCUSS

Can you think of any school category that is both imposed on people, and wielded for strength by the people in it? When is the category helpful or harmful for those described? (Gilberto Arriaza writes that as a Guatemalan forced to migrate to the United States by the civil wars of the 1980s, "upon arrival, I was immediately labeled . . . as Latino, brown, second-language speaker. The options for me, then, were to be colonized by the labels or adopt the labels as sources of power. I took the latter option."[88])

People "lumping" themselves together for specific purposes (including to address real experiences in a world of "groups") doesn't indicate a lack of internal diversity. The U.S. census "mark one or more races" (check all that apply) policy in 2000 allowed for fifty-seven different possible self-reported category combinations; youth increasingly insist on multiple "boxes."[89] Indeed, people labeling themselves on the 2010 census wrote in more than twenty categories just under the umbrella of "Asian."[90] And every individual human counted on that census had a complicated individual life.

Let's end by again expanding these Group Talk issues beyond race. To communicate toward equity with any Group Talk, educators may have to accept a Core Tension:

CORE TENSION   Schooltalk for equity describes all people as individuals too complex for labels. Schooltalk for equity *also* labels shared experiences and needs in order to address them.

That's why the foundation of schooltalking for equity is to consider the pros and cons (for young people) of every word we use and encounter in schools.

The chapters to come are full of examples of how to do this.

ACTION ASSIGNMENTS

1. Talk to a young person or adult you know about a key categorization or label that has affected him or her personally in an educational context. You might have him or her read part of this chapter. Ask the following:

   > How has that category or label been helpful and/or harmful to your educational experience?

   > Was any group experience not labeled in school that should have been?

   Use our Equity Line with him/her to assess the pros and cons of the label use experienced. Ask:

   Did this communication (**about "types of people"**) help support **equity** (the full human talent development of *every* student, and *all groups* of students)? Or not?

NOT supporting each/all students' talent development	SUPPORTING each/all students' talent development

   > In a journal or to a colleague, briefly report on the interaction. What did you learn about Group Talk in this interaction? What about the category or label seemed helpful to the person described by it, and what about it seemed harmful? Why? Do you see any related ideas in this chapter?

   > What went well and not so well in the conversation? What would you do differently next time in this conversation?

   > If you now could change one thing about the discussion of this category or use of this label in an educational setting you know well, what would it be and why? Name a Principle or Core Tension behind your suggestion.

2. Practice talking with a conversation partner of any age about the fact that race categories aren't genetically valid subgroups to the human species but have shaped very powerful and real experiences. (You might find yourself even more equipped for this conversation by the end of Part 1.) To start, try sharing one or more of the ideas or resources in this chapter with your partner. Then, briefly report on the interaction in a journal or to a colleague. Answer these questions:

> What did you learn in this interaction? What went well and not so well? What would you do differently next time in this conversation?

> If you could change one thing about how race categories are discussed in an educational setting you know well, what would it be and why? Name a Principle or Core Tension behind your suggestion.

> Compare race categorizations to some other form of categorization used in schools. What are the similarities and differences?

3. Turn one idea or fact from this chapter into a #schooltalking tool that lots of other people could learn from. For example, create a poster or PowerPoint slide, short video, or other multimedia image to share the idea or fact publicly.

Consider and choose one audience: children (ages 6 to 10), youth (ages 10 to 18), young adults (ages 18 to 30), parents, or teachers. Imagine that your message could reach people anywhere online, or in a specific school community you know well. Public messages really matter! Geneva Gay calls school walls "valuable 'advertising' space," as "students learn important lessons from what is displayed there."[91] And as the OpEd Project notes, clear, succinct messaging can go "viral" online.[92]

Here's one example from Renate Ward, a school psychologist I know, who describes herself as a "multiracial woman working with both Deaf and hearing special needs students." She envisioned a poster asking youth to consider this question:

Source: Mark Gabrenya via iStock. By Getty Images.

Why are racial categories like trying to fit a square peg into a round hole?

To accompany your main message, create a brief user's guide of five related information points or ideas from this chapter that can help users be more fully informed about the issue at hand and have a productive conversation sparked by your tool. (This guide should be no more than a few paragraphs long. It could be a few paragraphs on the back of a poster image, a slide or two following a main PowerPoint slide, or a voiceover for a video.) Finally, in this short guide to your message, be sure to address one Core Tension you expect to be present in the conversation that ensues from your tool, so that users are prepared.

List works referenced so that you share resources with others.

4. In person or via the Internet, find an educator or young person who you feel is already schooltalking for equity in their Group Talk. Document (with their permission) and share (#schooltalking) some example of their work—a photo, a video, an image, a quote from them, or something they have produced.

More schooltalk scenarios

To talk or write about these questions, you might use the Discussion Model offered in the Brief Guide, page 26. You might also prioritize analysis of real education settings you could influence.

THINK / DISCUSS

Think back to the story about my students Lutita and Kyle (pages 40–41). Should I have used their official "English learner" or "Special Education" labels as a portal to assisting them? How? Consider a Principle and Core Tension behind your answers. For example, I might offer these:

PRINCIPLE   Consider already-applied labels critically when you design student supports. (Don't just ignore a label altogether if someone else thought it could help the child.)

CORE TENSION   Labels can distort our thinking about young people, so sometimes it's best not to know the labels others gave them in school. But when labels could be levers for serving a student's needs, we do need to know the labels others have applied.

THINK / DISCUSS

Educators in a K–8 school wondered whether to hold lunchtime dialogues after a student used a racial slur on the playground. A parent suggested they invite students into race-based lunchtime conversations about their experiences at the school. Others wondered whether that was segregating students rather than integrating them. Others asked: should adults create these groups for students, or should students create them for themselves?

They discussed the question using the Equity Line and came up with the following ideas for their school:

(continued)

PRINCIPLE   If students need a chance to discuss possible common experiences, they should be given the option.

STRATEGY   Explore any affinity groups that students would find useful.

TRY TOMORROW   Offer a fall survey asking students about whether they'd appreciate affinity groups for support and, if so, in which groupings.

What's your take on the solutions the school came up with? Come up with your own Principle, Strategy, and Try Tomorrow for the situation. Name a Core Tension of it. (Note: A student I know who considers herself "biracial, black and Latina" was frustrated when her school used its record-keeping system, which allowed only one label per student, to invite students to a dialogue for "black" students. Nobody invited her to the dialogue, as she was listed in the system as "Latino/a.")

To conclude, consider: would your Strategy differ if the slur had been a homophobic slur, or hate speech against a religious group? Why or why not?

THINK / DISCUSS

Do you think it makes a difference to use "people-first" phrases like "student with [*specific special need*]" versus "Special Needs student," as does the Kids Included Together organization I mentioned early in the chapter? Why or why not?

At the Try Tomorrow level, try describing a young person labeled with a disability in a way that you think might be most useful to the child. If possible, ask a colleague, parent, or student for their take on the situation. Then, name a Principle or Core Tension behind your proposed description.

THINK / DISCUSS

Can you think of a category or label used inaccurately, in a school you know, to represent the entire child in a way that masks or distorts the rest of the child? Consider a Strategy for handling the label, and a Principle or Core Tension behind your idea.

THINK / DISCUSS

The census used to have a "multiracial" category and then decided in 1997 to let respondents check as many categories as they felt applied. As noted earlier, that allowed for fifty-seven different possible category combinations.

You are a principal. A white woman (who also considers herself Irish American) and a Jamaican man (who also calls himself "black"), parents of one of your new sixth-grade students, have come to complain that the forms their child filled out for your school only had boxes for "black," "Latino," "white," "Asian," and "other non-white." They felt that their child was pressured to choose between her parents when filling out the form. In past districts they lived in, she got to check "multiracial." They want you to rethink your forms. What will you say?

Practice a response at the Try Tomorrow level. At the level of Strategy, consider what you as principal will do regarding the checkboxes on your form. Name a Principle or Core Tension behind your ideas.

Finally, consider: would your response differ at all if the parents were a Filipina American and Indian American who felt they didn't relate to the category "Asian"? Why or why not?

THINK / DISCUSS

At my university, students often are invited into clubs as they walk down a common pedestrian pathway. Other students give them flyers or just verbally invite them to come to a group. Some clubs are designed around race or ethnic or national origin identity, others around gender or politics. Some students really enjoy the active invitations to join communities. Other students say they avoid this area of campus altogether, either because they don't want to be approached as a group member or because they don't want to feel excluded when no one hands them a flier (e.g., if an engineering club doesn't hand a flier to a woman).

Imagine you are an advisor to one of the clubs. A student in the club has just asked you: should we continue to approach peers with fliers based on their perceived "group"? What will you advise club leaders to do or to say when they approach someone to join the club? Name a Principle or Core Tension behind your ideas.

THINK / DISCUSS

Imagine that you have just received an invitation to discuss a group experience someone thinks you share. What words written on the invitation would make you feel comfortable going to this dialogue group? Consider a phrase at the Try Tomorrow level, and a Principle or Core Tension behind it.

THINK / DISCUSS

In an education community you know, do any written policies explicitly state which "type of student" gets which opportunities to learn? Are there any informal habits of offering some "types of students" more opportunities than others? Do any such ideas about "types of young people" in your school get justified by "science," and do you consider any of these ideas "mismeasurements"? Consider how you might react the next time this issue comes up in a conversation. Then consider a Principle and Core Tension behind your idea.

THINK / DISCUSS

In her chapter in *Everyday Antiracism*, Carol Mukhopadhyay notes that most people labeled "Caucasian" have no ancestral link to the Caucasus region. Since the word insinuates some false biological bond among "Caucasians," she urges that we replace the word "Caucasian" with the more precise ancestry word "European American." (I often choose the term "white," to engage historic experiences with this category in the United States.)

Consider: What might you say the next time a student or colleague refers to someone as "Caucasian"? Role-play possible responses. Then, name a general Strategy for handling the word and a Principle or Core Tension behind your idea.

THINK / DISCUSS

A high school in California wrestled with the question of starting a "Caucasian" club (www.sfgate.com/news/article/Club-for-Caucasians-stirs-up-Oakley-High-school-2587527.php).

You are a high school teacher. For some time, the school has had a Latino club, an Asian American club, a Samoan club, and an African American club. Several white students have proposed a "White club," saying they also want to learn about their backgrounds. The vice principal thinks it should be allowed in order to be "fair." Several club leaders at the school say they don't really feel comfortable with a "White club," as they think it sounds racist. Others suggest a new "Multiracial Alliance" club. Consider your position on this situation. What might you say at the next gathering of representatives of all the clubs?

(As food for thought: Ali Michael and Eleonora Bartoli argue that "white students should never meet in an exclusively designated white space except for explicitly antiracist purposes." Beverly Daniel Tatum suggests that schools should create spaces for "antiracist white identity." Activities for an antiracist "white club" might include critical analysis of media messages (or biological myths) about "races," consideration of how to intervene in racist incidents,

(continued)

shared analysis of anxiety about race talk, and learning stories of white antiracism throughout history "so that white students can envision possible ways to be white and antiracist."[93])

What's your take on these suggestions? You might also consider Patricia Gándara's ideas about "cocooning" (pages 44–45): are "cocoons" good for any group, or particularly for more marginalized groups?

THINK / DISCUSS

In 2012 and after, national debates erupted over policing and school discipline—specifically, over how adults often approach black youth with a very old racial stereotype in mind, of black people as inherently "threatening."[94]

Do young people in any school community you know get approached through this false group lens, as likely troublemakers? What are the consequences for those young people? What's one question you could ask adults about their reactions to students, to get people to rethink this old group programming? (See the endnote for related resources.) Consider a Principle and Core Tension behind your answer.

THINK / DISCUSS:

(Can also do after reading Chapter 2): In 2003, a California ballot measure (Proposition 54) was proposed to prohibit state and local governments "from classifying any person by race, ethnicity, color, or national origin." Called the Racial Privacy Initiative (RPI), the initiative would have prohibited state agencies from "using race, ethnicity, or national origin to classify current or prospective students" in public education data.

Proponents of the initiative claimed that gathering race-based data perpetuated racism by imposing racial categories on California's extremely diverse citizens, particularly its children. Its main backer also spoke up in the name of the state's "multiracial" student population, arguing that "This initiative is for the growing population of kids who don't know what box to check—and shouldn't have to decide. Please give them freedom from race and let them just be Americans." Critics said the Racial Privacy Initiative would wreck anti-discrimination efforts in education, as well as in law enforcement and public health, by making it impossible to track racial patterns.

It is September 2003. You are the superintendent of a large district in California. You have been asked to take a stand on the Racial Privacy Initiative at the next school board meeting. What's your position? Why?

Utilizing any evidence from this chapter, evaluate the pros and cons of different positions you could take on the initiative. You might role-play different ways of stating your position at a school board meeting. To conclude, pinpoint a Principle that accompanies your decision on the RPI, and a Core Tension of the situation.

Now discuss the pros and cons of deleting another label that a school you know uses for record-keeping.[95]

Chapter 2

Inequality Talk

To motivate and inform student support efforts, keep trying to make more informed claims about the supports and opportunities young people have and need.

Chapter Goal:
Clean your lenses. Speak more precisely and thoroughly about student outcomes as a product of interactions in opportunity contexts over time.

In Chapter 1 we started evaluating the basic labels we use to describe young people.

Now let's consider the words we use to explain young people's lives.

Let's start by evaluating our typical claims about the opportunities young people have and how those relate to outcomes—key to what researchers call "inequality."

One of the main things we do when schooltalking is sum up how students fare in schools and in life.

And in those summations, we often grab scripted explanations readily available in the air—shorthand explanations that don't necessarily thoroughly explain students' experiences at all.

Have you heard shorthand claims like these?

"Poor kids drop out because they don't really try."

"The kids typically in college are just the kids who worked harder. (*She got in just because of her race.*)"

I have, often.

I last encountered the first scripted claim in a meeting of community leaders, as a local philanthropist argued that low-income young people generally didn't get past community college because they weren't that motivated.

A student in my class recounted how a Latina friend of hers heard the second scripted claim at a campus party. Several students—strangers—decided her university admission had nothing to do with her past twelve years of school achievement. She was hearing the claim questioning her place at the university often enough that she was starting to worry, thinking, "maybe they're right."

* Underinformed explanations have serious consequences for how students are treated—and how they feel about schools and themselves.

In a conversation about education, have you heard any speaker grab and share a quick explanation of why students end up in college or in jail, or about who is in advanced classes and who is hanging out on the street? How many of these claims seem to miss something?

To many ears, shorthand explanations of young people's life outcomes are familiar and comfortable. But often, they are deeply underinformed. Politics aside, they just lack critical information.

Schooltalk for equity requires more fully informed explanations. Because adults won't offer young people additional opportunities via schools if they sense kids don't need or deserve them.

Should this school get another college counselor? Does George deserve a shot in advanced algebra? Who should get financial aid? Every decision about offering more opportunity to young people contains an analysis of who has which opportunities already and how opportunity links to outcomes. If people sum up that George doesn't try (rather than analyzing available math supports), or that kids from the neighborhood don't shoot for college or strive to graduate (rather than analyzing existing counseling supports or financial need), why would anyone provide more math supports, counselors, or financial aid resources in schools?

What people claim about opportunities and outcomes shapes who offers which opportunities to whom.

In this chapter, we'll work on talking through even the most baseline opportunities necessary for success in schools—opportunities to have a trained teacher, take rigorous math, see a counselor, or graduate from high school ready for college, for example. Linda Darling-Hammond notes that "we often behave, as a nation, as though we are unaware of the . . . substantial inequalities in access to educational opportunity" that affect students from birth through college. "Indeed," she adds, "most ordinary Americans *are* unaware of these disparities."[1]

<u>We're "unaware" of lots of information about opportunity and outcome in education in part because so much typical Inequality Talk masks it.</u>

As we'll consider in this chapter, when we speak in scripted shorthand about young people's outcomes we often particularly fail to see how a young person's fate is shaped in an *opportunity context* over time.

That is, we rarely describe how any young person's outcome is produced as people provide or don't provide some basic opportunities to students and students and others react.

It's like looking at the image below—a 3-D version of our Foundational Image—with dirty glasses.

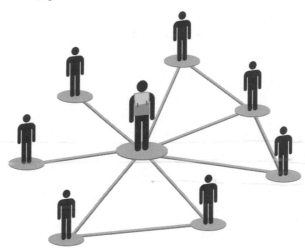

Imagine that you're struggling to explain why the child in the middle didn't graduate. But at first, you can only see the child in the middle because your glasses are so dirty!

Now let's say you only clean your lenses partially. You now might just see a few people who provide opportunity to the student, like a parent or a single teacher. Or you might just see a few opportunity factors in the student's context (like whether she had lots of books at home as a child), and fail to see the rest (like whether his school had sufficiently trained teachers in it).

Many shorthand scripted explanations just blame single actors, or consider just one opportunity factor in students' lives.

When we talk about student outcomes, we often assign blame and responsibility for processes that are far more complicated than we make them sound.

Why do some students read by third grade while others do not? Why are some students in AP Calculus whereas others never get past Algebra I? Why are some groups more represented in college than others?

Because in contexts where adults provide kids a given set of resources and opportunities to learn, young people's interactions with the many people around them pile up over time to produce students' school achievement.

It's a common script to skip all that and just say something simpler! But talking toward equity in schools requires more precise talk informed by facts.

As equity designers, let's get in the habit of cleaning our lenses and others'—that is, asking whether claims about opportunity and outcome are *informed enough* to get students the opportunities they need.

THINK / DISCUSS

Is there a claim about students' opportunities and outcomes that you have heard in an education community you know, that you suspect oversimplifies processes that are actually more complicated?

What's one aspect of young people's lives in opportunity contexts that you suspect folks need to investigate to support more thorough explanations?

Inequality Talk in action

Talk about inequality in education involves some of the most emotional questions of American life. *Which children deserve more opportunities, and why? Do I or my children deserve more, and why?*

But even when these conversations are fraught, we can stay in the realm of facts, by pushing beyond claims that can backfire by keeping causal thinking blurry.

Here's one example. How do people you know explain a very disturbing U.S. outcome—lots of young black men in jail instead of college?

"If current trends continue," according to the Sentencing Project, "one of every three black American males born today can expect to go to prison in his lifetime, as can one of every six Latino males—compared to one of every seventeen white males."[2] Any society might shudder at this much incarceration—this much stalled human contribution.

But many people react to such stats by just blaming the men incarcerated, because they don't analyze the opportunity-related *process behind* disparate incarceration. Indeed, as David Knight writes, listeners who are focused solely on the outcome of incarceration, rather than the factors and experiences leading to incarceration, might demand more incarceration rather than less.

In a recent study, psychologists Rebecca Hetey and Jennifer Eberhardt found that people shown evidence of extreme racial disparities in incarceration became *more* likely to support the punitive policies creating such disparities. As Hetey and Eberhardt noted,

an opinion

Many legal advocates and social activists assume that bombarding the public with images and statistics documenting the plight of minorities will motivate people to fight inequality. Our results call this assumption into question.... Perhaps motivating the public to work toward an equal society requires something more than the evidence of inequality itself.

Knight notes that the key is to move beyond naming unequal outcomes to discussing the lives and processes behind them. "The question before us is not simply about how we use statistics," he writes, "but a deeper concern with how our discourse about young black males needs to change. We can start by presenting larger, more complex stories about the lives they lead."[3]

THINK / DISCUSS

What is one image or statistic related to young people that you wish were presented along with a "larger, more complex story" so people could understand young people's situation better?

The call to tell larger, more complex stories is a call to clean our lenses about how young people end up where they do. Sociologist Mike Males's data website, YouthFacts.org, tries to counteract pervasive negative misinformation about youth by demanding more accurate use of statistics—for instance, by pointing out that in the past few decades, crime by California's increasingly diverse teenagers has fallen while crime by (majority-white) middle-aged people has increased.

THINK / DISCUSS

If you were in charge of YouthFacts' next post, which pervasive idea about which young people might you immediately hope to dislodge, with which initial information or "larger, more complex story"?

To help further clean our lenses on one piece of the story behind who's in prison, a group of researchers (including me), advocates, and youth supporters spent a couple of years working to explain a host of factors related to school discipline and opportunity that contribute to the disproportionate incarceration rate of black young men.[4]

Here's one "larger, more complex story" we found in the research. Black students today are suspended disproportionately, as early as preschool, for behaviors often overlooked in white students. Security guards, administrators, school police officers, and teachers often overreact to black boys and girls in American schools as "threatening": as with police officers, research links such overreactions in part to centuries-old, media-fed, even unconscious anxieties researchers call "implicit bias."[5] This happens even in middle-class, desegregated schools, where black students are asked routinely for hall passes or assumed to be troublemaking.[6] Particularly in schools serving low-income students of color predominantly, teachers serving students of color are also disproportionately inexperienced (and disproportionately white, from white communities), and their schools are frequently under-resourced and understaffed while concentrating students with many poverty-related needs. These opportunity conditions further strain efforts to build relationships.[7] When teachers disproportionately send black students to the office, administrators then disproportionately suspend them from school for long periods even for small infractions. In many cases, they are ejecting them into the streets of high poverty neighborhoods without sufficient youth supports. Educators, and school police (who are sometimes hired instead of counselors), also disproportionately refer youth of color into the justice system itself.[8] Police officers on streets also often overreact to black young people with excessive force and arrest, including when applying drug laws that they don't apply similarly to drug-using white youth (as Michelle Alexander points out, black students' parents are also disproportionately incarcerated, often for small drug offenses for which white parents are not jailed).[9] And these experiences often have cumulative consequences for young people's incarceration. Recent studies show that for U.S. youth, a single suspension in the ninth grade is correlated with a doubled chance of dropping out and a tripled chance of ending up in the criminal justice system itself.[10]

So, research makes clear that incarceration often results in part from interactions in schools. But because people see young people through dirty lenses, even just saying passionately that *black kids are imprisoned too much* doesn't clarify any of the process behind imprisonment—or what to do about it. Indeed, just saying *black kids are suspended too often* without investigating the larger story behind those suspensions analyzes an earlier outcome with dirty lenses, and leaves many folks just blaming the kids suspended.

Discussion of young people's outcomes doesn't automatically lead to analysis of processes behind the outcomes, leaving us underequipped to figure out how to support young people better. On the contrary, as a renowned psychologist wrote me via email, psychological research shows that people tend instead to "treat those who are the recipients of misfortune as somehow having deserved it." In a habit called "system justification," she noted, "everybody including the disadvantaged justify systems" of unequal outcomes as valid and deserved. (If you find yourself bristling at the very word "misfortune" to describe a young person ending up in prison, you see how routine it is to just blame the young person imprisoned.)[11] And in education, as Richard Valencia demonstrates, explanations of student "failure" routinely ignore students' experiences in opportunity contexts and just blame students for having presumed "deficits."[12]

Information on how young people end up where they do will not ensure student support, but thorough information on the processes producing outcomes has a better chance than facts about outcomes alone.

So let's start to gather some schooltalk Strategies and information that can make Inequality Talk more thorough.

Let me introduce my own tool for thinking and talking more accurately about how outcomes get produced every day in opportunity contexts over time: The Snowball.

Like a tiny ice chunk that rolls down a hill and accumulates in a giant ball, millions of acts in an opportunity context pile up to shape a child's fate. Any student gets to the graduation stage or a college campus through years of such interactions. In our schooltalk, situating everyday acts' contribution to each child's fate (e.g., all the interactions behind a suspension or incarceration) is key if we want to motivate ongoing support by each person involved.

But there's a big opportunity context around these daily interactions that we need to understand first. We are each born into opportunity contexts that we do not control, and any student's everyday opportunities are affected by historical opportunity provision that happened over generations *before* his or her life began.

So here's a more detailed frame I've used to discuss how opportunity contexts shape U.S. student outcomes over time.[13] I've adapted the specific frame from an article by Rebecca Blank, an economist,[14] but it links to ideas from many others.[15] It's the idea of *cumulative advantage and disadvantage*. The idea is that

✳ Inequality of opportunity and outcome take shape *across generations*;

✳ Inequality of opportunity and outcome take shape *across domains* like health, housing, employment, and schooling;

✳ Inequality of opportunity and outcome take shape *over the everyday life of a child*.

I'm going to talk through the frame using national facts that I think every educator and young person should know for thorough Inequality Talk, plus some facts specific to the state I live in now. Remember that each of these facts is an *average fact* from research: you may feel it doesn't quite describe your specific opportunity story or your family's. Just think about how the frame can help you talk more thoroughly about how opportunity contexts affected you and affect the young people you know now. Keep thinking:

> **THINK / DISCUSS**
>
> What other facts do you need to collect to see opportunity contexts where you live with cleaner lenses, so you can have a more effective discussion of opportunity and outcome in the schools you know?

> **THINK / DISCUSS**
>
> How does this presentation of information make you *feel*? Can you take any hints from those feelings, to learn how to talk to people about responding to the types of facts presented?

1. Inequality of opportunity accumulates across generations

You might hear national facts like these stated in discussions of schools: circa 2010, according to the Children's Defense Fund, more than one-fifth of all U.S. children under eighteen lived in poverty. (Sixty-five percent of poor families with children under eighteen had at least one member who was employed, indicating the critical role of living wage jobs.[16]) In 2010, 14.6 percent of white (not Hispanic) children under the age of five lived in poverty, as did 45.5 percent of African American children under the age of five, 37.6 percent of Latino children and 15.6 percent of Asian American children.[17] That's a lot of poverty. In fact, recent studies have noted that *51 percent* of public school children in the United States are now eligible for free and reduced lunch, a school-based measure of family poverty.[18]

As we'll discuss, "living in poverty," just like living in a wealthy household, is part of an *opportunity context* a child is handed when he or she is born. For now, let's ask a bigger question about that statistic that many of us struggle to discuss. How is it that white children are *less likely* to be born into poverty than children of color are?

As usual, thorough schooltalk requires some history.

For me, learning history makes opportunity facts bigger than any individual; they become personal but somehow not so personal. No baby asks for the context they're handed; I can't control what earlier generations did. But understanding how our opportunity contexts were shaped by prior people's opportunities over time is a key aspect of seeing others and ourselves through cleaner lenses—or of considering how to support each of us in our current situation.

As researchers have shown, being labeled "white" in early North America—as an immigrant or, later, a "native-born" person—enabled you to get paid for your labor, potentially accumulate wealth, and pursue your interests through the political system. Early indentured servants included both Africans and Europeans. As a race-based system of slavery grew, indentured servants labeled "whites" through law could get paid for their work, while workers labeled "black" could be enslaved and forced to work without pay.[19] Similarly, people who were classified as "free white" people, allowed or encouraged to immigrate, and offered the full benefits of citizenship (e.g., under the Naturalization Act of 1790 and later laws and policies), could more easily accumulate various forms of property and wealth while voting for people who would protect their economic interests.[20] Laws and customs originally restricted the right to vote to "white" propertied males, while long providing only "whites" access to higher-paying jobs and more lucrative property.[21]

These generations of wages and property accumulation caused cumulative economic advantage for many "free white people," as parents gained wealth to pass to the next generation. Many white children are still born poor today and some children of color are born extremely wealthy, but on average today, economists show, even Americans of color who take home salaries equivalent to white Americans do not on average have similarly accumulated intergenerational wealth—accumulated property and savings that shape what we can invest in, where we can live, and how we can weather economic troubles, like losing a job. Researchers suggest that it is this variation in the ability to weather economic troubles that in fact divides "the classes."[22]

The expansion of public schooling also shaped cumulative aggregated wealth in the nation's families today; it's another set of facts we need for fully informed Inequality Talk. In the decades before the Civil War, for example, reformers started expanding free publicly funded education in the United States; it long reached "white" children predominantly. Public school budgets in communities across the nation denied resources to many black students, Native American students, and the children of Asian immigrants. Strict anti-literacy laws denied enslaved African-descended children in the South the right to learn openly to read. Laws like the 1830 Indian Removal Act forcibly removed many Native Americans from economically sustainable ancestral lands, and for generations into the twentieth century, many were pressured and forced to attend white-run schools designed to erase cultural practices that had once undergirded Native livelihoods. Nationwide, free black children were still denied entrance to many publicly funded schools through the 1800s, and families often had to find money for their own schools (as did Chinese people living in California before and then despite the Chinese Exclusion Act). When offered slices of public school budgets, Mexican American, African American, and many Asian American children were typically segregated into separate and under-resourced classrooms or schools.[23] All of this sounds long ago, but by 1900, James Anderson notes, black people were still arguing for the extension of public school in the South (after a very brief, post–Civil War window of political power and school expansion), and by 1910 only one in every twelve black youth of high school age in the South was enrolled in school at all.[24] Historians Rubén Donato and Gilbert González help clean our lenses on another fact: in 1930, 85 percent of Mexican American children in the Southwest went to school in purposefully segregated, overcrowded, inferior-resourced environments, were tracked into vocational education, and were encouraged to drop out after elementary school in order to work in manual jobs and fields.[25]

Thinking cumulatively about such experiences in opportunity contexts over time, we can see how, over generations, education opportunity restrictions would contribute to lower wages for many families, while getting free and better-resourced public education (and then, better-paying employment opportunities) would contribute to more years of education, better jobs, and more money that could be handed down to children. (As Oliver and Shapiro put it of "white" wealth accumulation before and after the Civil War, for example, "White families who were able to secure title to land in the nineteenth century were much more likely to finance education for their children, provide resources for their own or their children's self-employment, or secure their political rights through political lobbies and the electoral process."[26]) We can also see how racial restrictions on wages, schools, property, and jobs restricted access to money. While U.S. folks often debate whether U.S. inequality is "about race" or "about class," historian Manning Marable called this a "false debate"—because inventing race hinged on distributing economic opportunity.[27]

All this wasn't that long ago. As Ta-Nehisi Coates notes, even the "period between now and slavery" is just "two old ladies back to back."[28] And in each of these generations, some kids were made more successful economically than others as tiny babies, before *they* did any work. It's not the "fault" of the baby; it's just a set of opportunity facts shaping each kid's life.

Here's a personal example of "cumulative advantage" over several more recent generations in my own family, making it so I and my own kids were *not* born into poverty. Christine Sleeter would call this kind of information "critical family history," gained through interviews with family or review of secondary sources.[29] Mara Tieken suggests that educators and students also can investigate the opportunity history of their school's local community, to clean their lenses on past generations in the place they live and work.[30]

I tell this story about my own family to my students, to illustrate how race and class got intertwined in my own opportunity context in ways aligned with average patterns.

My grandfather was born in Liverpool en route from Lithuania to the United States around 1910, then moved to a low-income Cleveland neighborhood where many Jews from Eastern Europe had gathered. Grandpa quit school in the ninth grade to support the family during the Depression. He delivered ice for a living, then helped the family junk business. Then, after serving in World War II, he went into distributing those goods. By the time I knew Grandpa and Grandma, they lived in a nice house in the suburbs of Cleveland.

Some unexpected advantages accumulated over those years from the war until I knew them.

Once vilified in American society (and restricted from entrance to various universities and neighborhoods), Jews increasingly were treated as "white" in U.S. life after World War II.[31] Our family remembers that Grandpa, who had no family wealth to buy a home and little high school education, benefited from the GI Bill. At the time, the GI Bill extended affordable home

loans, employment training and benefits, and educational subsidies disproportionately to white veterans, particularly because white-run banks and
loan programs disproportionately made it "very difficult, often impossible,
for blacks to qualify for mortgages"[32] and local officials blocked access to
other benefits (as did employers and segregated colleges).[33] Many Latino
and Filipino veterans experienced similar barriers.[34] Broader loan practices restricted non-white families from buying more lucrative property in segregated
white neighborhoods. As a result, white people could disproportionately invest in houses and accrue wealth. Because of how the GI Bill and related
policies played out in segregated America, scholars have called such policies
a massive "affirmative action" program for white people.[35] Beyond veterans,
analysts note, policies blocking loans to non-white Americans in the post–
World War II housing boom locked many people "out of the greatest mass-
based opportunity for wealth accumulation in American history."[36]

Grandpa and Grandma used his VA credit to buy their first house in an
all-white Cleveland neighborhood and soon sold it at a profit, moving to a
bigger house in Shaker Heights, Ohio—in a neighborhood that before the
war had typically excluded Jews like them.

That housing purchase also contributed to a tax base that supported well-
equipped public schools in their Shaker Heights neighborhood. U.S. public
schools are supported primarily by local property taxes and by the state,
and finally by the federal government. Communities with more money often have the ability to tax themselves to spend far more per pupil for their
schools, and to fundraise above that—and, as researcher Gary Orfield noted
to me, to keep property tax revenues high by refusing affordable housing.[37]

My father went to these schools, along with mostly white kids and a few
black kids (African American families would not become more substan-
tively integrated into Shaker neighborhoods until the 1970s and 1980s).[38]
That solid K–12 education helped my father get into college in the late
1960s, and then into grad school. And when my father got his first university job in the mid-1970s, Grandma and Grandpa helped him put the down
payment on a house, using some of the wealth they'd accumulated through
their own housing investments.

Growing up in a neighborhood of owned homes in a university town
(Iowa City, Iowa), I too attended sufficiently resourced public schools with
a similarly adequate tax base. I never imagined not attending college. I went
to college on a scholarship paid by my father's next university. My Cleveland
grandmother, Elsie, helped pay for my university housing and fees, using

extra cash stemming from two generations of accumulated housing and employment wealth. So I graduated from college without debt—and when I was ready to buy a house at the age of thirty, I had my down payment ready. It included not just my own personal savings from nearly fifteen years of working (including federally subsidized college work study and grad school financial aid) and my husband's personal savings, but also money saved from additional gifts from the grandparent generation. My job, the result of my education, then supported my mortgage payments on that house, subsidized the health care I bought for my children, and enabled me to pay for a childcare center that helped prepare my kids for kindergarten.

Many "whites" today remain poor or are experiencing downward economic mobility as jobs evaporate; wages and benefits are now insufficient for many U.S. families across race lines.[39] In fact, because white people are still the majority overall in the United States, "at least one-third of the 13 million children living in poverty are white,"[40] and by sheer numbers, "whites comprise the largest share of all low-income children."[41] But in the *aggregate*, economic benefits undergirding things like housing and schooling (and employment) accumulated to mean more houses, more college, and more money for "whites" over generations. Thorough Inequality Talk seeks to understand this cumulative history and its opportunity consequences for young people. Zoom out from my story to an aggregated statistic: owing in part to policies creating racial disparities in home ownership, "the wealth of white households was 13 times the median wealth of black households in 2013," and "more than 10 times the wealth of Hispanic households."[42] As Oliver and Shapiro sum up of black families specifically on average, "blocked from low-interest government-backed loans, redlined out by financial institutions, or barred from home ownership by banks, black families have been denied the benefits of housing inflation and the subsequent vast increase in home equity assets."[43]

These facts about the growth of dollars in my own family shape how I think about my own wealth today. As Peggy McIntosh's famous essay notes, the "white privilege" that started accruing centuries ago takes lots of other deeply consequential forms today, including in schools.[44] As we'll explore, people are less likely to question the intelligence or competence of white youth or adults; people often consider behaviors associated with "whites" the appropriate norm. But privilege is also about intergenerational dollars that shape young people's lives from birth. Many social scientists want us thinking about those.

Some claims about average opportunity and outcome can feel like misrepresentations when applied personally. To know me better, for example, you would need to know about the other side of my family—that my mother was born in a displaced persons camp in Germany after the Holocaust destroyed my extended family, and that she arrived in the United States with her penniless (though partially college-educated) parents in 1950 as a refugee from Eastern Europe. I'd want you to know that those grandparents, Eliot and Sabina Milman, also contributed to my parents' first mortgage payments; they used money made working long days running three nursing homes they owned, after managing to buy a house themselves in a mostly white neighborhood and then send my mother to college too. I also would want you to know that my Cleveland grandfather, Al Pollock, worked long hours every day, literally until the day he died; that my grandmother, Elsie Pollock, enabled his work by raising the kids; and that my dad still works more than he sleeps, in a job he got to choose because of the education opportunity he got to receive. To protect them all and maybe even myself, I might get snippy if you suggested that I had my job and house and daycare for my kids *only* because my family experienced a handout of privilege.

But I *also* got those things because of the schools I went to, because of the house we lived in, because of my dad's (and mom's) sufficiently funded schooling, because of my grandparents' housing investments, in part because of some help from the GI Bill and broader racialized housing policies. Families *not* treated as "white" worked as hard over those same generations; but our whole family, and many others, really did benefit cumulatively from some opportunities doled out disproportionately along racial lines. It's just the facts.

THINK / DISCUSS

How are you feeling?

This is an important moment to do a self check—to pause and think about the politics and emotions of Inequality Talk. For example, researchers have shown that how we frame "advantage" and "disadvantage" in our narratives either gets people fired up or turns them off. Sometimes our group experience relates to how we hear history.

For example, Brian Lowery and Daryl Wout found in experiments that white university students stopped fully engaging when a reading passage explained inequality in terms of unearned advantages for white people. But white students stayed engaged when the inequality story was framed as unfair disadvantage to people of color. Listeners of color had exactly the opposite reaction, turning off more to stories that emphasized their disadvantages and engaging more when stories emphasized white advantage.[45]

So as we describe any set of facts, we might note how it's natural to bristle when we feel oversimplified or misunderstood, or critiqued, pitied, or judged—or when we don't feel we fit the average pattern being described. We can also notice that we tend to bristle more when people claim average patterns about us than when those claims are about other people. We can even invite people to consider their reactions to facts as understandable and common—and then return together to thorough consideration of those facts, to consider necessary supports for today's children.

THINK / DISCUSS

Have you had any of these reactions already, in hearing these initial facts or frames about "cumulative advantage and disadvantage over generations"? Do you feel turned off? Fired up? Which facts triggered your reaction?

What do you make of your reaction? Does your own reaction start to clue you in to ways to support other people to talk through facts like these?

And did you feel your family story still wasn't mentioned here at all? It's crucial to note when our Inequality Talk names some patterns but not others.

Global patterns of who came to the United States when—or came as a refugee or migrant worker versus as an invited professional, or with no prior education versus some college education—also play a role in our intergenerational snowballs. Europeans who came first without limit (even those who came without education) obviously had longer to accumulate wealth than did those whose U.S. immigration was restricted or curtailed. Some people who accrue wealth in their home countries bring it here; other highly educated immigrants are forced to take lower-wage jobs. Some people come having experienced schooling opportunity, others don't. Today, nearly one in four schoolchildren is an immigrant or an immigrant's child, and when immigrants arrive, only some experience the opportunity to go to well-resourced schools. Immigrants plug in to neighborhoods and schools with existing patterns of economic advantage or disadvantage, with effects for their kids.[46] Kevin Kumashiro and John Lee ask students to investigate their own family experiences of immigration to consider factors *pushing* migrants out of home countries and *pulling* them into the United States, and then factors providing advantage or disadvantage once in the U.S. context.[47] Again, the goal is to clean our lenses on how we got where we are—to understand ourselves as well as others as people shaped by opportunity context.

Are you thinking now about the opportunity situations your family members experienced, and the consequences for your generation or others? Let's discuss a second form of "cumulative advantage and disadvantage"— that which accumulates *across opportunity domains*, like housing, health care, and schooling.

Take note of your reactions to this next part of the frame and the facts I present, so you can consider how to discuss such facts with others when analyzing how to improve on young people's opportunities and outcomes.

2.   Inequality of opportunity and outcome accumulates across domains

Let's go back to that starting fact. Today, as we noted, African American and Hispanic students are more likely than white students to be born into poverty. In 2010, "almost one in two young Black children and more than one in three young Hispanic children [were] living in poverty," compared to 14.6 percent of white children.[48] (Remember, circa 2010, according to the Children's Defense Fund, 65 percent of the U.S. families with children in poverty had at least one member who was employed at a job that could not support the family.)

And then they *also* tend to have less access to adequate health care and to affordable housing in economically stable neighborhoods, and they are more likely to attend schools that concentrate poor students—with inadequate physical facilities, fewer highly qualified and trained teachers, and fewer overall opportunities to learn.[49] As Linda Darling-Hammond sums up, "on every tangible measure—from qualified teachers and class sizes to textbooks, computers, facilities, and curriculum offerings—schools serving large numbers of students of color have significantly fewer resources than schools serving more affluent, White students."[50] In fact, white students often don't attend schools with lots of students of color at all, because in the United States we tend to allow school enrollment that concentrates students with peers who share their race as well as their income situation. Then we allow schools serving poor kids to offer *fewer* quality opportunities to learn than schools serving wealthier kids, rather than more to compensate for higher need. That is, our schools fail to counteract the wealth disparities kids come in with. Schools actually exacerbate them instead.

As the Civil Rights Project and NAACP report, for example, "The typical White public school student" attends a school that is nearly 75% white, while black and Latino students on average attend schools where just a quarter of students are white.[51] And since race correlates on average with family wealth in the United States, U.S. kids tend to go to school with kids who share their financial situation, too. As the Civil Rights Project puts it, racial segregation creates "a racial chasm in students' exposure to poverty." Southern California—where I live now—is one egregious example of national trends:

* "Keeping in mind that 56% of Southern Californian schoolchildren qualified for free or reduced priced lunches [FRL], the average white student in the region attended a school where FRL students made up just a third of the population. Contrast that figure to the school of the average black or Latino student, where more than half—63% and 69%, respectively—were FRL eligible students."[52]

* "Though poverty has dramatically increased in the region ["the West"] since 1991, students of different racial backgrounds are not exposed equally to existing poverty. The typical Latino student, followed by black student, goes to a school with much higher concentrations of poor students than the typical white or Asian student."[53]

* "Across nearly all of the highest-enrolling metropolitan areas in the region, Latino students experience the highest levels of exposure to poverty. In the Los Angeles metropolitan area, the average Latino student attends a school where nearly 75% of students are poor, while the average white student attends a school where only about a fourth are poor."[54] Black students in California tend to attend Latino-concentrated, high-poverty schools.[55] (Nationally, according

to the Civil Rights Project, in 2013 the average black student and Latino student attended a school where almost 70 percent of their peers were low income, while the average white student and Asian student attended a school where roughly 40 percent of their peers were low income.[56] Further, while "about half of all Black and Latino students attend schools in which three-quarters or more students are poor," "only 5% of white students attend such schools. In schools of extreme poverty [where poor students constitute 90–100% of the population], 80% of the students are Black and Latino."[57])

✳   In 2008, "just 5% of Southern California's Asian students attended intensely segregated minority schools, and 2% of the region's white students did the same." (Instead, Asian and white students were more often in higher-income schools together.[58])

An article exploring the Bay Area's version of such race-class segregation concluded bluntly that "overwhelmingly, low-income students are concentrated in schools with black and Latino students."[59] Gary Orfield and colleagues call this "double segregation."[60]

The economic situation in students' homes affects who eats what before school, who ends up moving schools because they can't afford stable housing, who has parents with insurance to afford glasses or asthma medicine, and who can access extracurricular opportunities that cost money, like music or science camp. Low-income children often get low-quality preschool or no preschool, while wealthier children's parents can pay for high-quality preschool (like I did) that immerses children in stimulating activities preparing them for kindergarten. A school filled with lower-income students thus aggregates many additional human needs, including kids experiencing untreated health issues, overcrowded housing, isolation as English learners, and parents with unreliable or exploitative employment.

This is the point researchers make about advantage and disadvantage accumulating across domains. As Richard Rothstein points out in his book *Class and Schools*,[61] schooling is affected by other "domains" of opportunity: if a child has no health care, and thus no glasses, she can't see the board and might fail the test. If she hasn't eaten a substantial breakfast because her parents can't routinely provide one (or because local supermarkets make less nutritious food available), she may have trouble concentrating on the work. If she is constantly moving between neighborhoods due to a lack of affordable housing, she may struggle to keep supportive relationships with her teachers or peers. If she lives near an environmental hazard (most often placed in poor neighborhoods), she may develop increased asthma or other health problems that keep her home from school. If she is staying up late caring for a sibling while a parent travels a long distance to an inflexible night shift he can't afford to lose, she likely has more trouble staying awake in class.[62] Conversely, more well-off families also can pay, overall, for stuff outside of school that affects school—glasses and health care, cars and gas, breakfast, stable housing, day care and preschool, tutors, extracurriculars, private counselors, and other socio-emotional counseling as needed. Schools that cluster middle- or high-income kids cluster kids with these advantages and also cluster connections to employment and college-educated professionals. And even as they have fewer crisis-level health, socio-emotional, and academic needs to take care of with their dollars, researchers note, wealthy districts can and do spend far more dollars on enriched supports to kids.[63] While schools serving poor students spend down their dollars on basics, parent fundraising in wealthier schools increases school resource disparities. In California circa 2012, "more affluent high schools were able to raise $20 for every $1 raised in high-poverty high schools."[64]

And to further exacerbate disparity, a concentration of poverty in a school has typically meant exposure to far *fewer* core academic opportunities via that school, rather than more.

In Southern California, for example:

* "Across Southern California counties, intensely segregated and segregated schools of color experienced a greater shortage of A-G courses [classes deemed college-prep by the University of California] and college preparatory teachers than majority white and Asian schools."

* "In 2008, students in intensely segregated schools were close to three times as likely to have a teacher lacking full qualifications than students attending majority white and Asian schools."

* "Over twice as many intensely segregated secondary schools were identified by the state as critically overcrowded compared to predominately white and Asian schools (those enrolling 0–10% underrepresented minority students)."

✳   "The higher the underrepresented [black and Latino] concentration of students in a Southern California high school, the less likely a rigorous mathematical curriculum was offered to its students."[65]

✳   In 2000, a state-level legal case, *Eliezer Williams, et al. v. State of California, et al.* argued that low-income students across the state lacked basic resources like safe facilities, books, qualified teachers, and even sufficient days of school.[66] The case led to a settlement, more funding, and ongoing requirements to report school resource conditions,[67] but as the stats above start to indicate, substantive inadequacies and disparities still persist today, and new funding formulae are just starting to address them.

Schools serving higher-income families also tend to have more district clout, meaning districts respond more quickly to school needs or listen to parents who insist on hiring highly successful staff. Such schools also typically offer more college prep or enrichment classes, specialists, libraries and tech resources, and more and better physical infrastructure. (Only such wealthier communities have been able to counteract, through self-taxation or fundraising, the years of budget cuts that have given California the worst student-staff ratios in the country.[68]) And on average in the United States, the most credentialed, degreed, trained, and experienced teachers—the holy grail of education opportunity—also teach disproportionately at higher-income students' schools, recruited by higher salaries and more-resourced working conditions. (To be clear, many new, energetic teachers in high-poverty schools are well-trained and fantastic student supporters—and not all teachers with long "experience" are. But research does show that students benefit more overall when teachers are highly trained and experienced, and that more such teachers teach in more-affluent schools.[69]) In 2016, the Office for Civil Rights found that nationally, black, Latino, and Native American students disproportionately attended schools "where more than 20 percent of teachers hadn't met state licensure requirements" and where "more than 20 percent of teachers are in their first year of teaching"—and where schools spent dollars on school police rather than counselors. On average, high-poverty schools also have few teachers trained to support the many students learning English, and more overall teacher turnover—often even leaving students in the hands even of untrained substitutes.[70]

I tend not to use the word "disadvantaged" to describe a child, but instead to describe an opportunity context as advantaging or disadvantaging. Kids who lack certain opportunities are just kids who lack certain opportunities, and kids with particular resources are just kids with particular resources. It's also not helpful to sum up any context as completely devoid of opportunity or saturated by privilege along every dimension: there are some very depressed wealthy kids and some poor kids with emotional resources money can't buy. Parents' own provision of opportunity is also a complex phenomenon: a poor parent might insist that her child access every free opportunity in the city, while a wealthy parent might destroy a family environment through alcoholism. Parents of any income level can offer young people valuable opportunities to learn of infinite kinds. Luis Moll has suggested the ironic label "LTEP," or "limited to English proficiency," to describe children who have *not* had the opportunity to become multilingual like many low-income children of color have.[71]

But how could basic disparities in health care, housing, employment stability, and school opportunity contexts not shape students' lives?

The role of my own school opportunity context struck me at my high school reunion, when I stood again on the stage in my sufficiently funded public high school in the stable-employment university town of Iowa City, Iowa. This auditorium enabled me to perform music and theater, fundamentally shaping my life experiences and my college application. The school system paid for lessons on free instruments. We had a hundred-piece orchestra, choirs, and a newspaper. These free opportunities were brought alive by trained teachers who chose to teach me and my friends. I was named a valedictorian on this stage.

The auditorium in the California public high school where I taught in the mid-1990s was dripping and crumbling; we had no orchestra, no choir, and no newspaper I recall. We served low-income students of color almost exclusively. When my aunt picked me up at the front door on a visit from

Massachusetts and saw the kids streaming out after school, her comment was, "So much for *Brown v. Board*."

Linda Darling-Hammond argues that we got closer to equalizing public education opportunities in the late 1960s and early 1970s, through public investments in desegregation, employment, school resources, and programs reducing family poverty. Low-income students and students of color then experienced large gains in academic performance by the early 1980s, she argues. Rollback of such programs during the 1980s then led to a spike in child poverty, homelessness, and inadequate access to health care, and to grossly under-resourced schools (again) for poor children and children of color. Indeed, she argues, "since the 1980s, national investments have tipped heavily toward incarceration rather [than] education," with "states that would not spend $10,000 a year to ensure adequate education for young children of color spend[ing] over $30,000 a year to keep them in jail."[72]

Analysts say the most important steps to take to counteract disparities and inadequacies in baseline opportunity across domains would be to invest simultaneously in living-wage jobs for parents (many call this action the key),[73] preschool and other health supports for children,[74] and high-quality professional supports for more teachers, while ensuring that schools concentrating low-income students get more resources and highly trained staff to handle the need. Others argue that breaking up concentrations of students by race and wealth through school enrollment policies and even housing desegregation is the real key to counteracting opportunity disparities in today's schools. But as it stands, we do surprisingly little to remedy opportunity gaps between schools. For decades, courts have gradually restricted active efforts to address segregation of districts by race, and active efforts to integrate by income are the exception rather than the rule. Instead, our housing patterns exacerbate and reinforce the segregation of schools. Affordable housing units have long been built more often in high-poverty areas, not in high-income areas, again concentrating poverty with poverty; lenders continue to favor white applicants for solid and reasonable-rate mortgages.[75] Research shows that realtors also still routinely show white people more homes and units in whiter areas, and that property owners often don't offer units to poor people or people of color; such actions exacerbate simultaneous dynamics of "choice," where people who can afford it often choose to live near more people who look like them and to send kids to more-resourced schools. Nationally, low-income white people still live closer to wealthier white people than low-income or even middle-income people of color do, and so they are more likely to experience higher-income schools and local amenities. (Research shows that middle-income black and Latino families tend to live in lower-wealth neighborhoods than do low-income white families, due in part to disparities in intergenerational wealth accumulation.[76]) Sometimes schools try to attract diverse populations across geographic regions, through "magnet" schools or charter schools with enticing foci. But often, families have to afford transportation to get to these schools. And state funding lawsuits have only partially addressed vast resource inadequacies. Today, where you go to school—and what basic opportunities you enjoy there—is predominantly a question of where you live and how much money your family has, plus how much investment officials decide to make in you and your teachers.[77]

Let's talk with nuance: not all poor students are black and Latino (many white and Asian students are poor), not all black and Latino students are poor, not all poor students go to school with other poor students, and not all white students attend more-resourced schools. (And this chapter hasn't even explored private versus public school resourcing.) Today, many Americans are struggling financially, across race lines—increasing the share of poor students in many schools[78] and leading many to argue that the real culprit is a business sector that underpays workers.[79] Many researchers argue crucially that the entire United States underinvests in child development, family well-being, and teacher development in comparison to other similarly wealthy nations, leaving many families of all groups trying to support children without a sufficient safety net.[80] Seeing specific schools and the opportunities they actually provide is also a critical part of cleaning our lenses: realtors and friends who steer white homebuyers away from even decently resourced and successful schools predominantly serving black and brown children inaccurately convey that all schools clustering these students of color are "lacking." Circularly, this reinforces segregation and all the resource disparities mentioned earlier.

But across the United States, internal disparities remain and require our attention in thorough Inequality Talk and public policy effort, as we seek to understand and address the opportunities students have and need. Low-income students are regularly concentrated in schools together, black and Latino students disproportionately attend such schools (while white students disproportionately don't), and these schools typically provide fewer baseline opportunities to learn than schools serving higher-income students.[81] Every such school I've ever known is full of amazing young people with talents of all kinds, but those young people rarely get to enjoy the same full set of baseline opportunities to learn that higher-income students do.

Note too that the aggregated facts above also mention "Asians" as disproportionately attending more-resourced schools alongside white students, specifically in California. As we'll discuss more thoroughly in Chapter 4, Asian immigrant families, often excluded from the United States before the 1960s, have migrated in greater numbers since the 1960s due to immigration policies that also favored professional skill sets. Simultaneously, various Asian national-origin groups have migrated disproportionately poor, often as war refugees, and have higher-than-average rates of poverty: in 2008, for example, the poverty rate among Hmong Americans was roughly 38 percent, among Cambodian Americans 29 percent, among Laotian Americans nearly 19 percent, and among Vietnamese Americans nearly 17 percent, and in 2006, the high school drop-out rates for Hmong, Cambodian, and Laotian American populations were respectively 40, 35, and 38 percent.[82] Many poor Asian immigrants attend under-resourced schools in low-income neighborhoods, and many struggle academically in them too. Research just suggests that Asian students *in the aggregate* are less segregated in high-poverty areas and more integrated in schools with white students than black or Latino students are—and that many Asian immigrants (who come disproportionately professionally skilled on average, and with more schooling) leverage their community information networks to attend more-resourced schools.[83] We'll "peel the onion" on that story in Chapter 4, as flipping distorting scripts about "Asian" achievement is critically needed schooltalk in the United States. It's still about how basic opportunity contexts shape children's achievement.

Do you feel like your family story wasn't mentioned here? Discussions of exceptions to average patterns are essential in Inequality Talk. For example, some students I've taught at the university level have pointed out crucially that as the child of poor Asian immigrants or middle-class Latinos in Southern California, their personal stories defy some of the average facts above on opportunity contexts. Yet many then note that their families found their way to the more-resourced, more-white contexts mentioned—or that *inside* their schools, the average dynamics of race-class segregation persisted. Some were the few low-income or non-white students in a high-opportunity school. Some accessed rare or restricted opportunities like the few AP, IB, or honors classes inside a mostly under-resourced, low-opportunity school.

So, the quest to describe opportunity and outcome patterns *precisely*—inside schools as well as between them—must be ongoing in any localized context if we're to help students receive necessary supports.

Let's work briefly on that key skill set for describing opportunity patterns *inside* a school opportunity context. At times, I've called this the struggle to figure out who is disadvantaged along which dimensions in comparison to whom—or more precisely, who needs which opportunities to support their school success.

An Inequality Talk skill set: Getting more precise about who needs which opportunities in specific places

Here's a key issue you may have encountered in Inequality Talk: educators trying to handle complex opportunity contexts by talking about how "all students" need help and support.

This is true, of course. All students need to be supported in schools.

But if any subgroup of young people experience particular aspects of an opportunity context, we need to discuss those experiences precisely in order to support them. As we'll see, inside many schools, some students are offered rigorous learning opportunities more than others; some are suspended more egregiously than others. Inside a school, some families might live in a neighborhood with particularly bad bus service that keeps failing to get kids to school on time. Some students might have to work after school to support their families; some might experience inconsistent housing rather than life in stably rented houses. Girls or boys, or LGBT students, may have particular experiences needing attention in a school community. When I taught high school, talk of "all students" masked subgroup experiences inside the school—like black students who were disproportionately suspended and placed in Special Education; Latino, Samoan, and African American students who disproportionately vanished from the graduation stage; and Filipino, Chinese, and Latino students' wide variety of needs as students learning English.

Some claims about subgroups' needs will need to be broken down even more. As Martha Gimenez notes, for example, Puerto Ricans or third-generation Mexican Americans may have very different experiences than "recent immigrants from Cuba, Central America, and South America," even as all may at times be called "Latinos."[84] Talk of "Asian immigrants" might fail to note low-income Chinese students' struggles to sleep in overcrowded multi-family housing, for example, in comparison to middle-class Chinese Americans living in single family homes across town. Researchers wading through a host of claims about "Asians" in education research noted that the "common mantra" of many studies seeking more locally nuanced claims was "disaggregate." "Once data is separated along ethnicity, gender, and a host of other variables" like family income, country of origin, or documentation status, researchers noted, "a more complex picture is revealed."[85]

So, disaggregation is often key to accurate Inequality Talk; but sometimes necessary Inequality Talk also recognizes shared needs that others may overlook. Even while speaking many languages and navigating varied opportunity contexts, for example, English learners in schools often share opportunity situations (including linguistic isolation from English-fluent peers) and often need targeted attention *as* a school's students learning English, even while each student's specific needs will be different.[86]

So, our Inequality Talk comparisons may shift depending on the local and school-specific situation, as we seek to pinpoint and secure necessary supports for students. Sometimes we need to compare the needs of kids from wealthy families to those of kids from poor families, sometimes to compare the needs of English learners to those of fluent English speakers, white students to students of color, kids labeled "disabled" to kids not so labeled, kids with immigration status X vs. Y, rural needs to urban, or specific subgroups vs. other subgroups.[87] Sometimes we need to compare an entire school's or community's resources to those in another school or community. And perhaps the holy grail of equity analysis is to compare an individual child's current opportunities to the opportunities necessary for *him or her* to thrive. Blankstein and Noguera argue that "the most important question that educators ask of themselves is this: 'Have we created learning environments that make it possible to serve the needs of every student?'"[88]

It's all a quest to figure out who needs which supports in specific contexts.

Naming a need for some along one dimension doesn't have to imply neglect of other students' other needs. This issue of Inequality Talk plagued the debate over the phrase "Black Lives Matter" circa 2015, during national debates over race and policing. The phrase insisted that black people's disproportionate experience of excessive force at the hands of police needed more specific discussion and address. To those using it, the phrase "Black Lives Matter" included the truism that all lives matter. As my professor friend

Kevin Foster put it to me, "Saying black lives matter doesn't mean other lives don't. Just like saying 'save the rainforests' doesn't mean 'hey, screw all other types of forests.' It's just naming a need requiring particular attention."

Thorough Inequality Talk also can name an average pattern in baseline opportunity *while* acknowledging outliers and deeper complexity. It's like zooming in on a state's border on a map and acknowledging it as rugged rather than straight.

In any claim we make, equity effort requires that we try to discuss with sufficient precision who needs which supports within specific opportunity contexts, rather than mask those details in vague talk.[89]

STRATEGY   Rather than talk simplistically about anyone's needs, educators can inquire:

Which needs are shared by subgroups, larger groups, or all our students? Which are specific to individuals?

Perhaps the bigger problem is that people discussing student outcomes too rarely talk through students' experiences in opportunity contexts in any detail, leaving people unequipped to make change. Only rarely are youth themselves encouraged to compare the school resources they have to the resources experienced by students in other schools, for example. It's also not typical for educators to talk with parents to truly understand the opportunities available in students' homes and neighborhoods, or for parents to fully analyze a district's provision of opportunity to students.

And often, we all treat both unequal and inadequate opportunities and disparate outcomes as just the way of the world—certainly nothing *we* can do anything about.[90] In fact, Linda Darling-Hammond calls our "continuing comfort with profound inequality" the "Achilles heel of American education," because too many of us normalize inadequate opportunity for so many—while too few of our young people get fully equipped to handle a global economy necessitating high-level skill.[91]

So there's a final aspect to Inequality Talk for equity: talking through what everyday people can do to *counteract* inequality and provide necessary opportunity to young people.

All of us can leverage informed Inequality Talk to insist on policy actions to provide more baseline opportunities to students. We can insist that governments fund more well-trained staff for schools, for example; we can demand a living wage for parents or universal, high-quality preschool, or press for fair housing and school integration.[92] We can work with university and industry partners to help pump new opportunities into school systems;[93] we can insist that districts spread crucial opportunities to all. We'll begin foundational work to expand opportunity systems with parents in Chapter 7!

But for the educators in our Foundational Image, the most immediate arena of effort is everyday interactions with kids. So more than many professionals, educators need to analyze how outcomes in education also take shape each day inside schools, through interactions that activate opportunity over the course of young people's lives.

I have a tool for this way of thinking and talking: The Snowball.

3.   Inequality of opportunity and outcome accumulate over young people's lives

As I said earlier, every child's outcome accumulates like a snowball does. Like a tiny ice chunk that rolls down a hill and accumulates in a giant ball, millions of interactions in an opportunity context pile up to shape a child's fate. To motivate everyday acts to support students, we can try this Strategy:

> **STRATEGY**   Talk about how each action in an opportunity context contributes to students' outcomes over time.

Like snowflakes in a snowball, single opportunity-related acts toward children—a single suspension, a placement in a specific math course—lead to *next people's reactions* (including the child's) and have a serious effect on children's overall experience of opportunity over time. While some people describe dropping out as just a student's personal choice, for example, each child's dropout happens over time, in an opportunity context that provides or doesn't provide specific opportunities and supports, through everyday interactions with actual people. When asked, young people often can remember specific interactions with teachers or counselors that finally prompted their dropout; each interaction was another layer of a snowball of interactions with lots of other people.[94]

Some experiences accumulate positively, others negatively: for example, research shows that kids who get accelerated learning opportunities early tend to get increasingly accelerated opportunities over time. Conversely, students who are given lower-level learning opportunities early keep getting lower-level opportunities; curriculum slows and gets more and more boring. Nationally, white students and middle-class students are disproportionately likely to be put early in accelerated groups and to have honors and AP classes made available later, compounding advantage over each child's life. We call this cumulative opportunity provision "tracking" in education.[95] We'll discuss this process in more detail in the chapters that follow. For now, take note of a critical issue for Inequality Talk to address: any school outcome —like a spot in an advanced course or a seat on a graduation stage—is the outcome of a long sequence of opportunity-related interactions with many people in an opportunity context. Students' academic fates are built through real-time *interactions*, as educators react to students, students to educators, and both to families, other students, and experiences outside of schools. Through these interactions, children become youth who are attached to schools and successful in schools, or youth who are not.

The parents I met while I worked at the U.S. Department of Education's Office for Civil Rights argued similarly that even single opportunity-related acts by educators led to *next* steps in a student's school experience, with cumulative consequences for students' experiences of opportunity in schools. A referral to Special Education, "gifted" education, AP, afterschool enrichment, or the local police; an overly harsh suspension; a day of unaddressed racial slurs by a peer; or a decision about language services for children learning English each led to students' reactions and adults'.

It was in trying to *improve on* any of these accumulating experiences in opportunity contexts that Inequality Talk often broke down. As I saw working at OCR, arguments often stalled when educators anxiously contested that parents or students insisting on the importance of single actions were making a mountain out of a molehill. Arguments also stalled when people deflected analysis completely onto others—like when educators claimed that only students or parents (not educators too) were responsible for students' outcomes.

The problem was discussing The Snowball.

So let's try to practice some classic Inequality Talk challenges related to everything we've discussed.

I'm going to offer three classic issues of opportunity and outcome in schools that folks find particularly hard to discuss. In considering each "Inequality Talk Challenge," think how you might use the frames and facts we've discussed to get someone else to think about student outcomes as snowballing over time, or to consider and address students' opportunity experiences in more precise detail.

Inequality Talk Challenge 1: Talking about the educators' role in student outcomes

Working at OCR and reading student files, I could *see* students' interactions with educators snowballing into student outcomes over time. For example, I saw educators give kids detention for minor infractions like chewing gum in class, then get embroiled in escalating conflicts with the students, then suspend them for long periods; students' relationships to educators and schools then corroded over time, with consequences for students' attendance and academic achievement. Partnering again to support any young person always required educators to discuss how their actions contributed to shaping a young person's outcomes, even while educators weren't solely responsible. But such discussions were hard. Many teachers could only see a "misbehaving" or truant student, not all the interactions—including with educators themselves—behind the current situation.

If we could slow down school life to watch interactions and their consequences, it would really help drive home how actions snowball into outcomes. Anthropologist George Spindler used to observe student-teacher interactions (like who teachers called on in class) and then get teachers to see how they offered opportunity to some young people more than others without knowing it.[96] Some researchers now sit with teachers to watch classroom interactions captured on videotape, to see how each partner's reactions shaped the others'.[97] In "restorative justice" circles, students and adults get the chance to explain the backstory behind school interactions that snowballed into conflicts.[98] And I've talked over the years to literally thousands of students who could remember everyday acts by single teachers that shaped their lives for the better.

Positioning educators as key contributors to students' fates (as does much research) doesn't mean educators alone are responsible for those fates. Educators can't be asked to overcome under-resourced systems alone, for example, or fix the insufficient wages of parents; that's seeing *educators* through dirty lenses.[99] Paul Gorski also reminds us critically that "teachers who teach at high-poverty schools, as well as an increasing number of their colleagues at all public schools, too often are themselves denied access to adequate resources," including professional opportunities to learn.[100] And as Pedro Noguera reasoned once to a Texas administrator worried about critics, "Why don't you tell them that we'll get a zero percent drop out rate in the schools when they start sending us zero percent of the children who are hungry, uninsured, un-immunized and un-housed?" Noguera's writing is full of important points that clean our lenses about the opportunity factors beyond educators' actions alone:

∗ "America doesn't just have an achievement gap, we have an allocation gap in school funding, a preparation gap due to limited access to quality pre-school, and a power gap, because poor parents are not able to exert as much influence over the schools that serve their children."

∗ "The reason why America continues to be characterized by pervasive disparities in student achievement that correspond closely to the race and class backgrounds of children, is not because our educators aren't working hard enough, or because parents don't care about their children (a commonly heard accusation), but simply because as a nation we have done very little to address racial inequality."

∗ "Our politicians want schools that will enable the United States to maintain its economic and technological dominance in the world, even though we continue to pay teachers salaries that make it unlikely that our top college students will enter the profession. They complain when our students do considerably less well on international tests than children in other wealthy nations, but they are not willing to do the things the nations we like to compare ourselves to do for their children—universal access to healthcare and pre-school, and generous parental leave policies."[101]

Jacqueline Jordan Irvine similarly writes pointedly of the core opportunity "gaps" needing address in education, beyond teachers alone:

The teacher quality gap; the teacher training gap; the challenging curriculum gap; the school funding gap; the digital divide gap; the wealth and income gap; the employment opportunity gap; the affordable housing gap; the health care gap; the nutrition gap; the school integration gap; and the quality childcare gap.[102]

All such issues require public policy attention. As Nelson Mandela put it, "poverty is not an accident. Like slavery and apartheid, it is man-made and can be removed by the actions of human beings." (Analysts call employing parents at a living wage the biggest fix for education too.[103]) Yet I've also seen that if we don't frame teaching's everyday interactions as a critical contribution to students' outcomes and life opportunities, teachers may reject their power to shape students' lives at all. Especially in opportunity contexts that lack many essential resources, educators start to lament, "What *can* I do?"[104]

In fact, research shows both that high-quality teachers are schools' most critical opportunity resouce, and that educators who analyze their own everyday acts' contributions to student success and well-being (rather than feeling overwhelmed by "systems" out of their control) actually do better by students.[105] It's teachers and other educators who have hours each day to *respond* to young people in opportunity contexts: educators are linchpin opportunity-to-learn providers. Indeed, Rich Milner notes that school people may particularly influence children living in poverty, because such students rely on schools for opportunity "in ways that other students from more affluent communities may not have to."[106] Research on highly successful leaders often shows them emphasizing this crucial everyday influence, by asking colleagues, "OK, but what can *we* do about this?"[107] by pinpointing aspects of systems that they can most impactfully change,[108] and by focusing dialogue on actions immediately within their control.[109] One principal I know starts many meetings by asking colleagues explicitly to speak of "our kids" rather than "those kids." He says that when they speak of "those kids," they have just thrown away their responsibility for students' success.[110] Jeff Duncan-Andrade calls on educators to combine critical analysis of inequality with "audacious hope" that they can contribute to changing it.[111]

So it's a Core Tension of Inequality Talk for teachers and other educators: they can't singlehandedly shape students' fates, but they still shape students' fates every day. In social science, we call this the combination of "structure" and "agency": we are handed opportunity situations, regardless of our preferences (structure), and then we react to them (agency). It's this combination of structure and agency that shapes every educator's career and every young person's life.

So imagine saying this in your own words, to an educator you care about: your everyday actions are not solely responsible for students' academic outcomes, but you contribute fundamentally to them over time. A teacher in one of my classes brought in this related quote from the Jewish legal text, the Talmud: "You are not obligated to complete the work, but neither are you free to abandon it." I've translated this for educators as, "You are not solely responsible for student achievement, but you are also fundamentally responsible for it, in interaction with many other people and factors."

THINK / DISCUSS

Think of a teacher whose everyday actions really affected you in your "snowball," positively or negatively. If you saw that teacher again, how might you convince him or her of those acts' role in your life?

The goal isn't blame—it's accurate analysis! To improve opportunity and outcome in education, people need to be ready to analyze how educators', students', and parents' actions intertwine to shape students' educational experiences, in opportunity contexts created by lots of other people. As I suggested in *Colormute*, people need to be ready to discuss the following about any student outcome using an "urgent language of communal responsibility":

*   The players involved in the phenomenon. Are all necessary players included in our analysis?

*   The precision of our analysis. Have we precisely described the problem in all its complexity?

*   The placement of responsibility and blame. Is our talk placing blame or responsibility accurately and fairly? Have we displaced responsibility from any key players?

So accurately discussing educators' role in students' fates is key. In upcoming chapters, we'll talk more about that and about the role of parents. For now, let's talk through the role of students themselves.

Inequality Talk Challenge 2: Talking about the students' role in their own outcomes

Are students responsible for their own school outcomes, or are other people? Well, both.

Talking through young people's role in their own fates has plagued social scientists for generations. Can people shape their own fates (agency)? Or are their fates largely shaped by the opportunity context they are handed (structure)?

As infants, people are handed opportunity situations, regardless of their preferences (structure); then they react to them (agency). Because opportunity contexts (structures) exist before students arrive, many social scientists hold them most responsible for student outcomes. As we've seen, some students show up in schools that lack books; some students show up in schools with extensive technology. Some students show up having attended private preschool, others with no preschool at all.[112] Some students are assigned teachers with extensive training, while others get teachers with none.

But quite often in our schooltalk, we forget how the opportunity context (the "structure") shapes the student's experiences, and we instead just talk about his outcome as only the consequence of his personal effort (his own "agency"). As John Dewey put it long ago, we often seem to ignore the context shaping everyone's education experience:

> In a word, we live from birth to death in a world of persons and things which is in large measure what it is because of what has been done and transmitted from previous human activities. When this fact is ignored, experience is treated as if it were something which goes on exclusively inside an individual's body and mind. It ought not to be necessary to say that experience does not occur in a vacuum. There are sources outside an individual which give rise to experience.[113]

Recent years' discussions of student "grit" or "resilience" (persistence past obstacles) embody this debate over how much to blame the student's reactions *to* the opportunity context rather than his or her experiences *in* opportunity context. Some researchers suggest that those with stamina to make it past obstacles make it, but others argue that this focus on student stamina actually downplays the obstacles.[114] As Alfie Kohn said of the "grit" debate,

"The more we focus on levels of grit (or self-discipline more generally), the less likely we'll be to question larger policies and institutions." Kohn argued of one journalist's take on "grit and resilience,"

> Consider Paul Tough's declaration that "there is no antipoverty tool we can provide for disadvantaged young people that will be more valuable than the character strengths . . . [such as] conscientiousness, grit, resilience, perseverance, and optimism." Really? No antipoverty tool—presumably including Medicaid and public housing—is more valuable than an effort to train poor kids to persist at whatever they're told to do? Whose interests are served by such a position?[115]

Yet we also distort structure and agency if we tell youth "the system" completely controls their fate. One mentor I know who gets a lot of very low-income young people into college with scholarships refers to the "tightrope of adolescence" and the danger of continually emphasizing obstacles: "If we tell youth there is danger below and not to look down," he said once, "youth look down" and lose confidence in their ability to handle challenges. Since educators can't just crumble the opportunity "structure" like Katniss Everdeen's arrow in *Catching Fire*, they have to help youth respond *to* opportunity systems each and every day.

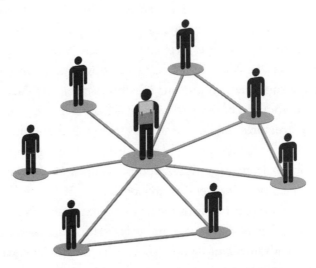

Here's a deep Core Tension of Inequality Talk that plagues adults and students alike:

CORE TENSION   If we only talk about student outcomes as being
students' fault, we miss the other actors, factors, and opportunity context around the student. But if we only talk about students as victims of
circumstance, we also fail to acknowledge their own agency in their own
lives.

The solution may still be accurate Inequality Talk! For example, research
shows that K–12 students benefit tremendously from analyzing opportunity
systems thoroughly in order to address them.[116] For example, having seen a
number of young people in his Arizona community respond to limiting opportunity contexts in either self-sabotaging or self-empowering ways (e.g.,
by cutting class or insisting on diplomas), anthropologist Julio Cammarota
noted that youths' reactions to their contexts seemed to depend on how
they came to "assess the role" school success would play in their fates. He
taught students research skills and had them read social science so they
could analyze their own personal experiences of poverty, health care, and
schooling as experiences in broader opportunity contexts and then consider
what to do for themselves and others via schools. Cammarota described one
student who had previously been depressed, "up at night thinking about
the injustices" of her family's inability to afford a doctor or sufficient food.
"After a year spent in social research and analysis, Kati came to believe that
she did not need 'fixing'—rather, it was time to address the socioeconomic
conditions" under her family's experience, and reading and writing about
those conditions were skills key to her agency to make a difference.[117]

Relatedly, students need not feel alone in their "agency": educators can
ask youth to consider collective challenges to opportunity systems, not just
individual personal ones. Proponents of youth participatory action research
have engaged youth in both low- and high-resource contexts in analysis of
opportunity structures and how to address them together through demanding specific policy changes, like changes to school funding or policing.[118]
New York youth from urban and suburban high schools joined together
with CUNY faculty and students to collaboratively study youth perspectives
on race, class, and opportunity in the region, culminating in a collaborative
performance and public reports arguing for critical education opportunities for all.[119] Ladson-Billings writes of teachers and students who together
informed the community about their outdated textbooks by writing letters
to the editor.[120] Villegas and Lucas call for designing school projects around
investigating specific issues in students' shared opportunity contexts, like

the quality of local water.[121] Gorski and Swalwell ask teachers to develop their own "equity literacy" along with students' by engaging young people in analyzing unequal resource distribution in schools and communities.[122] All such work can be buoyed by study of historic struggles for opportunity, within communities and across them.[123] And as high school teachers, researchers Jeff Duncan-Andrade and Ernest Morrell supported students to interview local agents of change—youth program leaders, dance instructors, former student activists, and other "everyday people" improving local lives—and then question "the prevailing logic about their community, including their own notions." After talking to local change agents, many students "discovered that they too had come to believe the dominant discourse about their own community and had lost sight of the countless indicators of hope and strength that are present on their blocks every day."[124]

Educators also can engage youth productively in considering immediate individual responses to opportunity contexts. Sonia Nieto suggests that educators best offer young people "critical care" by together analyzing how to handle specific obstacles without lowering expectations.[125] Similarly, when I asked him for an example of "ideal" Inequality Talk, Rich Milner shared what he considered a helpful vs. harmful discussion of a scenario involving a young person's need for money. To Milner, the first (harmful) "deficit"-focused lament just positions a student as someone who's experiencing problems. The helpful, "asset"-focused framing seeks to support a student to respond more powerfully to her opportunity context:

A high school student, Carla, works six to eight hours a day after school at a fast-food restaurant to help support her family financially. She passes all her classes and shows up at school every day, but her schoolwork is not exceptional.

A teacher's deficit perspective: "Poor Carla. She works too many hours. Although she passes my class, she could do so much better if she spent more time studying and less time working. Her work could be better."

A teacher's asset perspective: "Carla demonstrates the capacity to balance her schoolwork and her part-time job. I should talk with her about how I can assist her to make sure she is maximizing the class while she is working so hard in her part-time job. She is demonstrating the ability to balance school and work. This balancing act is commendable."[126]

Every college preparation program I've seen work successfully with low-income students empowers youth to leverage their agency to insist on AP and honors classes, tap scholarships, and doggedly complete college applications, *while* critically analyzing how opportunity contexts don't provide sufficient opportunities already and should. When I talk to students in such programs, I try to analyze their opportunity contexts with them just as I have done in this chapter, considering how students could fuel themselves to seize every opportunity made available *and* promising to do my own part at the university level to get more resources to schools' opportunity systems. When I talk to students in well-resourced systems, I try to clarify that their hard work leverages the opportunity contexts they are lucky enough to experience and to say it's in our collective interest if more students experience the same.

So let's tackle a final classic challenge of Inequality Talk that includes everything we've discussed so far: debating who "deserves" more opportunities.

Try discussing college admissions.

Inequality Talk Challenge 3: Talking about who "deserves" which additional opportunities

Remember the campus party I mentioned at the beginning of this chapter? A student described a freshman-year party where a group of (non-Latino) young men kept insisting that Latino/a students like her friend only got into the university because of "racial quotas" reserving slots for students because of their race.

Since then, the friend had heard multiple suggestions that she was "less qualified," or that she was at the university to fill a "racial quota." The experience had made her friend feel like she didn't belong at the university. She had actually considered dropping out. After the incident was discussed in my class, a second Latina student approached my teaching assistant to share that she experienced similar insinuations from peers. She told her TA that even while she "knew there were no racial quotas in UC admissions," the ongoing insinuations from peers "made her feel that she must not really be qualified."

For many students, the first year of college is full of make-or-break communications where students either start to feel they belong on the campus or don't. Lots of times, these communications are scripted, underinformed claims about who "deserves" a college slot after K–12 efforts. In a Tumblr, black students at Harvard reported similar comments questioning their place at the university.[127] Researchers call these comments (sometimes phrased as jokes) "microaggressions" that cause ongoing stress, consume major mental attention, and accumulate to an experience of exclusion from the campus environment.[128]

In 2015, an underinformed claim that several black students at UT Austin had been admitted over a white student "just because of race" went all the way to the Supreme Court. In reality, observers noted, the white student denied admission had lower scores and grades than most admitted UT students; 92 percent of UT students of all "races" were admitted just because they had finished in the top 10 percent of their class. A highly competitive process distributed the remaining slots by reviewing students' accumulated grades, test scores, essays, activities, and various personal factors that might contribute to a well-rounded campus, of which race was just "a factor of a factor of a factor."[129] Even so, a Supreme Court justice considering the case (and the future of college admissions policies generally) blurred analysis of admits' K–12 efforts by questioning whether black students generally belonged at "slower" schools than UT. As Richard Reddick, a professor at UT Austin, pointed out to me after Justice Scalia's comments went viral, "the challenges for underrepresented students still exist when they arrive on the campus, manifested in chilly campus climate. Justice Scalia's words certainly caused many Black students to question their worth and belonging at UT."[130]

Misunderstandings about students' efforts in opportunity contexts enter our schooltalk all of the time, with serious consequences for young people. So we need to clean young people's lenses as well.

I distilled this chapter into a few sentences for Upward Bound students visiting my campus. Many were the children of Latino immigrants and worried about their own potential place in college. I told them:

> "The people in college before you don't belong there more—they just are people who had the opportunity to get to college before you did. People who were here earlier in the U.S., or folks who got certain advantages through laws or policies, just had the opportunity to get to college before you did. People congregated in more-resourced schools just had the opportunity to get to college before you did. While *we*

work on improving the opportunity context for more students, what *you* do to react to the opportunity context you are handed also matters tremendously. But don't ever think you don't deserve to be in college just because people other than your families got to college before you did."

To talk in more depth with my own University of California students about the thorny question of who "deserves" a spot in the UC system, I've also had to gather more facts about how young people get slots in college admissions processes themselves.

✳   For cleaner lenses, my students have needed to hear first that nobody is handed a college slot because of a quota. Quota-based admission is illegal in U.S. universities: you can't reserve a number of slots for one group or admit students "just because of their race." The Supreme Court has said that universities can attempt to produce a more diverse incoming class by considering students' race, ethnicity, and national origin "narrowly" as just one of many factors in a student's application, with the logic that it benefits all students to learn on a campus that resembles the diversity of our society. Today, researchers note, admissions officers who do consider race at all consider it as a tiny slice of a factor after determining academic competence, alongside the many other aspects of an individual's accumulated experience that could contribute to a fully diverse campus.[131] (Elite institutions tend to award slots on a host of factors other than scores and grades—like whether relatives went to the institution.[132]) But because of a 1996 statewide California proposition, at the University of California race is not considered in undergraduate admissions at all. And in reading huge stacks of applications "holistically" to understand every student's potential contributions to campus, admissions officers most weigh the "academic core" as measured by students' course completion, grades, and test scores.[133]

Cleaning our lenses further on those admissions decisions requires discussing how applicants' applications are themselves produced in often very *different* opportunity contexts. My students and I talk through how, even as budget woes have eroded resources across many California public schools[134]—and even as the UCs have tried to address state budget cuts by admitting an additional layer of out-of-state and international students who pay more tuition—students in higher-resourced schools and families in California still tend disproportionately to get the opportunities that get rewarded in in-state college admission. I share facts like these about California students and schools, to start to think more clearly about UC admissions and necessary improvements to K–12 opportunity contexts in California:

✳ In California, baseline eligibility for a coveted spot on a UC or CSU campus relies on students accessing and passing the "A-G," a sequence of courses that UC has deemed sufficiently college-preparatory through syllabus review. A-G courses are offered in a higher quantity and variety at higher-income students' schools.[135]

✳ The UC system offers you a spot at one of its campuses if your academic achievement positions you in the top 9 percent of the state (measured by your grade point average [GPA], A-G course completion, and test scores) or in the top 9 percent of your high school class (measured by your GPA and A-G completion). But if you want to be *competitively* eligible for a UC slot at one of the most competitive campuses, you really need a particularly high grade point average. (The *average* incoming GPA at UC San Diego was recently a 4.13.)[136] You can get a higher GPA if you take AP and honors courses, which offer a "weight" bumping up a GPA even over the traditional "4.0." At UC San Diego in 2010–11, 76 percent of entering freshmen had taken one or more weighted honors courses during tenth and eleventh grade; 23 percent of admitted students had taken more than four.[137] (52 percent of freshmen admitted in 2015 had taken 15 or more honors or AP courses between seventh and twelfth grade.[138]) AP and honors courses too are available far more often (and in a wider variety) at higher-income students' schools.[139] Black and Latino students in California (and nationally) disproportionately attend schools that do not offer as many such courses.[140] And inside schools, only some students typically get to take them.

✳ A next important ticket to competitive UC admission is SAT score. The average SAT score at UCSD was recently "651, 699 and 668, respectively, for Critical Reading, Math, and Writing," out of a possible score of 800 on each.[141] High SAT scores today are the product not only of solid K–12 preparation by well-trained and experienced teachers, who work more often at higher-income students' schools, but also often of SAT test prep, which costs money from parents or schools. In fact, studies often show that your SAT score correlates with your income level.[142]

✳ While the "academic core" of A-G course completion, grades, and test scores is central to UC admission, UC admissions officers also review and reward sustained participation in extracurricular activities as "value added" evidence of potential contributions to campus. Through California's budget crunch, activities like music and the arts—key to my own college application—have persisted more often in higher-income schools in California in part because parents demand and fundraise extra money to provide these subjects. Many sustained out-of-school activities you might also put on your college application—lessons, clubs—require parent payment. (John Rogers and colleagues note that "on average, families of 15–17-year-olds with earnings above $98,000 spent more than seven times as much on education-related expenses as families earning less than $57,000."[143]) In my region, higher-income parents with science degrees and engineering jobs are coaching their kids' science clubs and robotics teams after school, leading to championships recorded on applications. Low-income students in many other parts of the region have no such clubs or teams at all.

✳ Overall, a UC application is comprised of many components, including a personal statement. Higher-income families are increasingly hiring private college advisors to help put those components together. (John Rogers and colleagues note that "one recent national survey of students who performed well on the SAT or ACT found that more than one quarter hired a private educational consultant to help them with the college admissions process."[144]) Or, as one of my UCSD students put it, "My (college-educated) mom was the one that helped me fill out all my applications."[145] California has "less than one counselor for every 1000 students enrolled in K12 public schools,"[146] and particularly in high schools serving low-income youth, students have no person to see regularly about transcripts, required courses, financial aid, or college application processes even while they have no one at home or nearby who has been through the process either. Research shows that nationally, many high-achieving low-income students don't even apply to selective colleges they're qualified for and could succeed in, because they aren't sufficiently informed that they can.[147]

＊ In sum, research suggests that on average, California students of all demographics who are able to attend predominantly white, higher-income, more-resourced schools end up more often at the most competitive UCs.[148]

＊ Meanwhile, as a UC admissions official put it to me, when reviewing all applicants holistically as individuals (prioritizing the "academic core" of A-G completion, grades, and test scores, reading personal statements, and considering extracurriculars as "value added"), admissions readers at the most competitive campuses do try to recognize students who took "*full advantage of* the educational opportunities available" in their local context. So, in their holistic review, reviewers will prioritize "the applicant who took full advantage of all that the school has to offer," including in a less-resourced or overall "underperforming" school that offered fewer baseline opportunities in comparison to other schools in the state (e.g., an applicant who took all of the few available AP or honors courses), over a "student attending a high performing or well-resourced school who did not take full advantage of the educational opportunities available."

In allotting the few remaining slots on competitive campuses, admissions officials use various factors as "tiebreakers" to make tough decisions. As the admissions official put it, "we do use low income or first generation as a tie breaker" in deciding in favor of a student who has also excelled academically and taken advantage of all local opportunities, while prioritizing "students in the top 9% of their local graduating class." In considering low-income or first-generation status, admissions officers are acknowledging a college applicant who has excelled despite common barriers—and so, might contribute to a learning environment in a way that benefits others as well. Every student has to have sufficient grades, A-G completion, and test scores.[149]

THINK / DISCUSS

Consider a low-income student who seized every opportunity in her school, excelled, and finally benefited from such a "tiebreaker." Ask your gut: is her admission fair?

In sum, no UC student, including the young woman at the party, is admitted "because of her race." Students are admitted because they tapped the opportunities they could access. Of course, including race as one of many real "factors" in a student's cumulative life experience might help reviewers understand even better what students have overcome and accomplished, and what they might contribute to campus life. But UC reviewers are restricted from reviewing that "factor."

And of course, it's also quite possible that the young woman at the party was not a low-income student or the first in her family to attend college at all. Perhaps she went to a fancy private school and was the third generation in her family to go to college. Maybe she was last year's world champion Scrabble player or the top recruit for the school softball team. You actually have no idea, right? All we know is that she tapped the opportunities she could access.

Yet the very fact that her peers assumed her inadequacy *even in a race-blind admissions process* indicates that a key aspect of experience in any opportunity context actually is navigating the beliefs about "merit" circulating in it. As Richard Reddick noted to me, white students securing slots on university campuses after review of their various "factors" more rarely experience questions about their "merit"; a student who has excelled over time despite widespread, scripted myths about his or her potential might well contribute particular strength to a college. Indeed, research suggests that nationwide, both students and faculty of color often prefer to go to schools that recognize this explicitly—that can explicitly value racial and ethnic diversity, too, when weighing outstanding applicants' potential contributions to campus life.[150]

But we'll tackle these myths about student "potential" more in Chapter 3, not now.

In sum, at the moment of college admission, thoughtful reviewers essentially review prior experiences in opportunity contexts. In doing so, they must grapple with a classic Inequality Talk issue: whether giving young peo-

ple context-blind treatment is fair (e.g., reviewing a GPA without considering how many weighted AP or honors courses were available), or whether
analyzing and addressing prior opportunity differences is fair (e.g., considering available courses when reviewing a GPA; appreciating a student who
has excelled despite a less-resourced context). Many colleagues considering
K–12 settings have shared this image online to convey the concept of "equitable," context-responsive treatment (on the right) versus "the same," context-blind treatment (on the left):

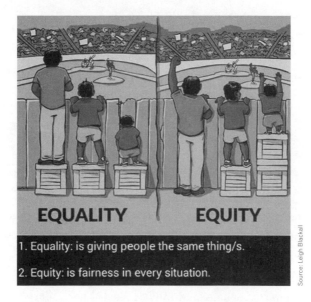

If I were to redo this graphic, I would call the picture on the left "same"
treatment (which some call "equal" treatment) and have another picture
on the far right called "equality"—the desired outcome where everyone has
been offered needed supports to access opportunity (equity) and is standing triumphantly on the other side of the fence. To many, the outcome of
"equality" is still where we're going; "equity" is how to get there, by providing supports that equalize the opportunity to succeed.

A teacher friend uses the image of throwing your shoes in a pile to describe "equal" (the same) vs. "equitable" treatment of students in K–12 opportunity contexts. To walk at all, everyone at least needs an *equal* two shoes
back from the pile. But they really only help you walk if they actually fit
your feet. Supports that "fit" are to him, "equity." Similarly, throughout a
student's life, if we just review every student "equally" without considering
the opportunities available in the student's prior life, we can't tailor next
supports to "fit." A more thorough, equity-oriented analysis checks to see

what opportunities have been provided and assesses necessary opportunities accordingly.

The ultimate equity-oriented Inequality Talk asks, *which students need which supports to have an equal shot at getting over the fence?*—and then offers the opportunities needed *along the way.* Think how improved the college journey would be for so many—and the country for us all—if adults reviewed young students' needs carefully on a regular basis, and actually gave each young person the opportunities he or she needed to succeed!

That's why we keep asking if our lenses are sufficiently clean—if we can clearly see how young people are accessing needed opportunities, and what supports they actually need.

Keep trying to make more informed claims about the supports and opportunities young people have and need. As usual, the ongoing work of schooltalking for equity requires interrogating the accuracy of what we say.

ACTION ASSIGNMENTS

1. Try talking to a friend, family member, colleague, or young person you know about some issue of opportunity and outcome in education that you personally find difficult to discuss. Using any tool or fact from this chapter, try to discuss with them: how are student outcomes produced as people interact in an opportunity context? Then report:

   > Describe the interaction you had. Did any typical challenges or "scripts" of discussing inequality referenced in this chapter show up in your conversation? Which ones? How could your conversation have addressed them better?

   > What in the conversation would you "redo" with equity in mind, and why?

   > What do you think you and other people need to learn more about in order to have a more informed and useful conversation about addressing this issue of opportunity and outcome? How would you go find and share this information?

   > If you could change one thing about the *typical* conversation about this aspect of opportunity and outcome in an education setting you know, what would you change? How might you go about this? What would be some Core Tensions of your effort?

2. Do #1 again, talking to someone in a school community you know now (and could actually improve) about some issue of opportunity and outcome there that requires attention.

3. Try to turn one gold nugget idea or fact from this chapter into a #schooltalking tool that lots of other people could learn from. For example, create a poster or PowerPoint slide, short video, or other multimedia image publicly sharing that gold nugget quote or idea. To accompany your main message, create a brief user's guide of five related information points or ideas from this chapter that can help users be more fully informed about the issue at hand and have a productive conversation sparked by your tool. See Chapter 1, pages 65–66 for more instructions.

    Here's one I might make:

    ### No individual is an independent being. We rely on opportunities from each other to succeed.

    And I'd love to make a poster for teachers out of this fortune cookie message I got once. To me, it offers a way to challenge "structures" through collective "agency":

    ### Pulled together, spider webs can trap a lion.

4. In person or via the Internet, find an educator or young person who you feel is schooltalking for equity in their Inequality Talk. Document (with permission) and share (#schooltalking) some example of their work—a photo, a video, an image, a quote from them, or something they have produced.

More schooltalk scenarios

THINK / DISCUSS

Does your experience feel different than the average opportunity patterns mentioned in this chapter? Does it in some way fit these patterns?

Name some information we'd need to know about your family or prior life in order to fully "clean our lenses" when looking at your own achievement up until now. You might address the following:

(continued)

✳ What were the race-class demographics of the school system where you grew up, in comparison to the typical dynamics of segregation discussed in this chapter? (Were those demographics ever discussed? Were they framed as normal?)

✳ Did you go to a school with lots of AP and honors classes or not? How did that opportunity context affect your grade point average? If you had been in a different high school with different course offerings, how might your college chances have been affected?

✳ Think of the framework of "cumulative advantage and disadvantage," and its application to your own opportunity context. Did any family experiences across generations help you to get where you are right now, or almost derail you? (If you don't know, how could you investigate some family history to learn more?) How about experiences across the opportunity "domains" of schooling, health care, and housing?

✳ Self-check: how did this chapter make you feel about your own school achievement? How would you present any information in it to someone who had a similar opportunity context as you did? Why?

THINK / DISCUSS

Look back at the popular image defining "equity" effort (page 119). If you were the artist, would you edit the image at all to make any point about opportunity and outcome? Consider a Principle or Core Tension behind your response.

THINK / DISCUSS

You are a principal appearing on a radio program to discuss a new state funding formula that is going to give more money to schools serving large concentrations of low-income students and English learners, including yours. An educator from a district that serves higher-income students and few English learners calls in to argue that the funding formula is "inequitable" to his own district. How would you respond? Consider a Try Tomorrow response (what you would actually say), a more general Strategy for such responses, and a Principle or Core Tension behind your response.

THINK / DISCUSS

Try using this Strategy to discuss a school community you know:

STRATEGY   Rather than talk simplistically about anyone's needs, educators can inquire:

Which needs are shared by subgroups, larger groups, or all our students? Which are specific to individuals?[151]

| individual students | sub-groups | larger groups | all students |

Then consider: can you think of one example when schooltalk for equity requires discussion of subpopulations with specific needs in the school you know, and one example when it's been necessary to speak "in aggregated terms about goals for 'all'"? What else do people need to learn in order to have a more precise conversation that pinpoints necessary student supports? Consider a Principle and Core Tension behind your suggestions.

THINK / DISCUSS

At OCR, I investigated a low-income school serving mostly Latinos, in which students with diagnosed learning disabilities spent much of the day in a basement room without any credentialed or consistent teachers to provide specific assistance they needed. One teacher complaining to OCR said this was unequal opportunity. Another teacher rebutted that the whole segregated school had revolving teachers, was understaffed, and had too few resources. She said everyone at the school had unequal opportunities in comparison to other schools in town.

Evaluate the pros and cons of different ways you could call for more opportunity for the students in the basement. If you were going to call for "equal" or "equitable" opportunity for them, to whose opportunities would you compare? Would you instead call for "more" opportunity? For "necessary" opportunities? For whom? End with a Principle behind your comment or a Core Tension of such Inequality Talk.

THINK / DISCUSS

Look at our Foundational Image with the student at the center, surrounded by potential supporters (page 10). Who (representing what contextual factors) do you feel is missing from this diagram, but affects young people's outcomes nonetheless? (You might consider far-away parents buying homes, realtors making suggestions, district administrators assigning teachers, organizations offering enrichment, banks giving loans, judges writing school assignment decisions, and more.) How would you adjust the diagram to clarify this? (What other image or information might you use to convince one such actor of his/her role in student outcomes?)

THINK / DISCUSS

Lots of people argue that the phrase "achievement gap" places blame for a "gap" on the children who fail to "achieve." Others have used the phrases "opportunity gap"[152] or "education debt" to describe opportunity provision to young people over time and, as Gloria Ladson-Billings puts it, to use "a discourse that 'holds us all accountable.'"[153]

Which phrase about "gaps" do you find most effective for Inequality Talk? Why? Does it matter who you are talking to? Name a Principle and Core Tension behind your response.

The Preuss School at UC San Diego, a grade 6–12 school, enrolls solely low-income students who will be the first in their family to attend college. Applicants are selected for admission randomly from a lottery. Preuss requires AP curriculum for all students and offers a range of supports to prepare students for college. These supports include a longer school day, twenty-three extra school days a year, and an advisory where students are supported by a teacher for seven years. Parents raise small amounts of money in PTA fundraisers, but Preuss raises most of its extra money from local donors. University professors and students regularly contribute time and expertise to the school, as do local mentors. In advisory class and on weekends, students get information about college application processes and support to draft personal statements and complete financial aid forms. More than 90 percent get accepted to four-year universities.[154]

If someone said to you that all this "extra" support to prepare Preuss students for college "isn't fair," what would you say? Consider a Try Tomorrow (what you'd actually say), a Principle behind your comments, and a Core Tension of talking about offering such substantial college prep supports to students who otherwise would not have them.

Chapter 3

Smarts Talk

⊙ **PRINCIPLE**

Communicating toward equity means actively counteracting the myth— all day, every day—that some young people or some groups are just "smarter" than others.

Chapter Goal:
Stomp the myths. Gather and *actively share* accurate information to counter ill-defined and dangerous notions about intelligence.

Smarts Talk scripts are everywhere in schools.

When I taught at a high school serving low-income students of color, I was sitting outside on a bench with a senior, an African American young woman I'd taught as a tenth grader. She was struggling with finishing her credits for graduation. She glumly explained her struggle with a phrase that has haunted me since: "This school is where the dumb kids go."

Two years before, I'd been carpooling to school with some other teachers, just munching my bagel in the back seat. A teacher in front sipped her coffee while taking about the upcoming city Academic Decathalon. "We never win," she said, adding that at the school across town, "They get all the smart kids and we get all the losers." I winced, but I'm not sure I said a thing.

In the city we lived in, people said all the time that other schools, not ours, got all the "smart kids." The script seeped into our everyday ways of talking about students and students' ways of talking about themselves. One time, my students and I were discussing how our school needed more resources from the district in order to do things like fix the broken wall outside our classroom door. One of my students said sarcastically, "you really think if we had carpets and stuff it would make us smarter?"

And as a professor, I met a graduate student who had just asked a teacher in Los Angeles why there were no "gifted" classes at her all-Latino school. The teacher had answered matter-of-factly, "Well, because there are no gifted kids here!"

In Smarts Talk scripts, we routinely, easily, and *falsely* assign "smarts" to individuals or groups of kids. I'll leave the very word "smart" in quotes to keep us questioning it!

There may be no more influential schooltalk. What we say about students' abilities and potential shapes how students feel about themselves and how adults offer students opportunities to learn.

Smarts Talk often violates all of the Foundational Principles of equity-minded schooltalk (page 8).

So, how will you respond the next time you hear scripts like these?

> "This school is where the dumb kids go."
>
> "They get all the smart kids and we get all the losers."
>
> "There are no gifted kids here."

In this chapter, we'll equip you as a myth-buster. That's because Smarts Talk scripts contain some of our most dangerous myths in education. These myths come from a very long history of thinking and talking inaccurately about intelligence and ability. Here are two main ones:

Intelligence is not an objectively or simply measured quantity of stuff "in your head." But we keep talking as if it is!

No child or group is "smarter" than any other, but we routinely talk as if some are.

Given how pervasive these myths about intelligence are, if you don't respond when you hear inaccurate claims about people's "smartness" or "dumbness" or "giftedness," you'll let deeply inaccurate thinking about young people's abilities and intelligence go on unabated. That teacher in the carpool stayed on for years before retiring. Thousands of students went through a school some labeled as for "the dumb kids."

Keep using our Equity Line to evaluate the consequences of everything people say about intelligence and ability in schools, asking:

> Does this communication (**about intelligence and ability**) help support **equity** (the full human talent development of *every* student, and *all groups* of students)? Or not?

NOT supporting each/all students' talent development ←————————→ SUPPORTING each/all students' talent development

Smarts Talk in action

When my daughter entered public Pre-K, it took literally two minutes before a teacher's aide whispered to me that my daughter was "smart." This was after the teacher said, "Find your cubby!" and my daughter found the cubby with her name on it.

The command "Find your cubby" required the basic literacy of recognizing one's written name. My daughter could respond quickly to this command because she'd already been to a preschool that had her finding her name on a cubby every day. But the teacher's aide saw this and summed up the amount of "smarts" in her brain.

> **THINK / DISCUSS**
>
> How would you respond if a teacher's aide said this to you about your child? How about if you heard it said to another parent? I think I mumbled something like, "well, they're all smart . . . but thanks."

Misleading Smarts Talk claims are incredibly common. People blithely state that girls have less intelligence than boys in some fields, for example. While I worked at Harvard, our university president, Larry Summers, an economist, wondered publicly whether fewer women became scientists because boys were "innately" better at science.[1] Bus drivers told my grandmother she was "stupid" because she couldn't yet answer in English after immigrating as an adult, even though she could have answered in six other languages. People across the country call the kids who make it into college after eighteen years of interactions in opportunity context "the smart kids."

Sometimes we hear explicit Smarts Talk based on our membership in a group. Sometimes comments group children, just not explicitly. (A teacher at an all-Latino school just says matter-of-factly that "there are no gifted kids here.") And sometimes people make individualized comments that sum up your abilities, like "you're an art person, not a writer!"

Regardless, how someone talks about your "abilities" affects what happens next.

THINK / DISCUSS

Imagine you are writing your autobiography. Can you recount some moment in your own life when someone told you something about your abilities or intelligence that either fueled your success or dragged you down?

Now imagine that that person was saying the same script to another young person. You overhear it. How would you react?

Researcher Ray Rist famously observed such a process over several years. A kindergarten teacher learned a few bits of information about her incoming students' families and prior siblings. Then, as she noted her students' initial class behaviors, she quickly labeled some students as "fast learners" and others as "slow learners" and grouped them separately in the room. The "fast learners" were mostly kids whose families had more money. The teacher then taught each group differently, Rist observed: The students labeled "slow" and expected to fail "were taught infrequently, subjected to more frequent control-oriented behavior, and received little if any supportive behavior from the teacher." The "fast learners," whom the teacher expected to succeed, received "the majority of the teaching time, reward-directed behavior, and attention from the teacher." Over the year, the academic material offered each group diverged widely. And the children's subsequent teachers used their sense of "past performance" to continue to group the students even more rigidly as "fast" or "slow"—and teach accordingly. Over years, the students labeled "fast" did far better than the others.

Rist called this process a "self-fulfilling prophecy," where students labeled "fast" were taught so they succeeded and students labeled "slow" were taught so they failed.[2]

Examples like this demonstrate a key issue of Smarts Talk:

> The way people talk about your ability affects how they treat you and then, how you succeed—despite what is "in your head."

In Chapter 2, we started thinking about how everyday acts in the life of a child "snowball" into the child's outcomes over time. Your life is shaped by the opportunities you're handed, how others treat you, how you react to the situations handed to you, and how other people then react to you.

For some kids, early Smarts Talk sparks cumulative advantage over a lifetime as more opportunities to learn pile on. A student labeled "gifted" in elementary school is more likely to enroll in honors classes by high school, advantaging her for college admissions.[3] In Rist's study, students labeled "slow" experienced cumulative disadvantage in opportunities to learn, as instruction slowed and got less stimulating. (Teaching at Harvard, I often would ask who'd been put in "gifted" classes as kids, and nearly everyone would raise their hands. Most also said that after that elementary experience, they had then been scheduled into high-level classes through high school. One student noted that she'd ended up learning in the light-filled upper floors of her school while low-tracked peers did worksheets in the basement.)

So why do we talk so much about intelligence as just something you either have or don't have at birth, instead of talking more accurately about school outcomes and all skill sets as things developed in opportunity contexts over time?

Because pervasive myths about "smarts" are very old, very strong, and too rarely challenged.

To design communications for equity, we need to replace inaccurate scripted comments about young people's intelligence with comments based on facts.

So, let's start myth-busting. Hang on to a few key schooltalking strategies to communicate facts, rather than myths, about students' human potential:

STRATEGY   Actively reject the myth that intelligence is an easily measurable quantity of stuff "in the head." Say out loud that no student is "smarter" than any other.

STRATEGY   Talk about abilities as *grown* through interaction and collective effort, not something fixed inside students.

STRATEGY   Say out loud that no *group* is "smarter" than any other. Actively reject the myth that intelligence is distributed differently to "groups."

Let's go through these one by one.

Redesigning Smarts Talk

STRATEGY   Actively reject the myth that intelligence is an easily measurable quantity of stuff "in the head." Say out loud that no student is "smarter" than any other.

We have a bad habit in this country of saying who is "brainy" and who is "dumb."

One night I was with my children watching the video "Unpack Your Adjectives" from *Schoolhouse Rock*. Just as I was smiling along with the familiar tunes of the 1970s and my childhood, I hit this moment: http://www.youtube.com/watch?v=NkuuZEey_bs (at 1:25).

I'd watched the video countless times as a kid, but I'd never really seen that moment before. One student is at first labeled "brainy" and the other "dumb." After the "dumb" student on the left starts spouting equations, the labels get switched. Happy ending—the correct one is labeled "brainy."

Lesson learned: we *can* sum up a kid's amount of braininess.

So I had to explain the following to my kids, in my own words:

"Guys, there's no such thing as a 'smart kid' vs. a 'dumb kid.' 'Smartness' isn't even something we know how to measure. And everyone's intelligence can grow."

Let's get some of these facts straight.

We have no simple way to measure "intelligence."

Psychologists who talk carefully about intelligence make clear that intelligence is not some fixed "thing" in your head that "smarter" people just have more of and "dumber" people less of.

In fact, intelligence isn't a clear quantity of stuff in your head at all.

According to the American Psychological Association, psychologists really don't agree about how to measure intelligence.[4]

Many IQ tests refer to "general intelligence"—"g"—and give you a score quantifying how much "g" you have, often by giving you a test of logic activities or puzzles. In many schools, people use tests to quantify if a child "is" "gifted and talented" or not. But regardless of the test used, psychologists admit that human "intelligence" or "giftedness" is a phenomenon just too complex to be so easily quantified.[5] There are just too many versions of human skill and ability to measure someone's "intelligence" or "giftedness" with a simple number or summative word. Any such test only judges particular forms of skill as measured on a given day in a particular way.

My colleague Jeff Elman, an expert on children's cognitive development, noted: "Although there are a few who continue to believe in 'g' (as a hypothetical single measure), there are now more than a dozen theories, each of which argues for different kinds of 'intelligence.'" And even when people don't reduce intelligence to a number like "g," we still typically only measure some abilities in schools and not others. Your test scores or school grades are never a measure of your full skill set, just some of your skills as measured in particular ways after particular experiences. A math test assesses math skills you have been able to demonstrate on a particular test after a particular set of opportunities to learn a particular kind of math.

Like any label for a child, any measurement of a child's skill set is human-made. In an English-dominant country, for example, we often don't recognize bilingualism or multilingualism as skills deserving rewards, even as youth are acting skillfully as translators for peers or their entire families.[6] Instead, research shows, English learners are under-tested for potential placement in "gifted and talented" classes and disproportionately assessed as having disabilities because they are still learning English.[7]

As Jeff Elman put it to me, there also are highly useful life skills like "being socially adept, motivated, disciplined and organized" that we don't typically "associate with intelligence" and measure in kids. Robert Sternberg, who helped write the "Intelligence: Knowns and Unknowns" statement for the American Psychological Association,[8] suggests we should measure three forms of intelligence, even as only the first is typically measured in school:

* Analytical: "involves skills used to analyze, evaluate, judge, or compare and contrast"
* Creative: "involves skills used to create, invent, discover, imagine, suppose, or hypothesize"
* Practical: "involves skills used to implement, apply, or put into practice ideas in real-world contexts."[9]

Howard Gardner, who popularized the term "multiple intelligences," suggests we should recognize at least seven forms of intelligence:

* Spatial: "The ability to conceptualize and manipulate large-scale spatial arrays (e.g., airplane pilot, sailor), or more local forms of space (e.g., architect, chess player)"
* Bodily-kinesthetic: "The ability to use one's whole body, or parts of the body (like the hands or the mouth), to solve problems or create products (e.g., dancer)"
* Musical: "Sensitivity to rhythm, pitch, meter, tone, melody and timbre. May entail the ability to sing, play musical instruments, and/or compose music (e.g., musical conductor)"
* Interpersonal: "The ability to interact effectively with others. Sensitivity to others' moods, feelings, temperaments and motivations (e.g., negotiator)"
* Intrapersonal: "Sensitivity to one's own feelings, goals, and anxieties, and the capacity to plan and act in light of one's own traits"
* Linguistic: "Sensitivity to the meaning of words, the order among words, and the sound, rhythms, inflections, and meter of words (e.g., poet)"
* Logical-mathematical: "The capacity to conceptualize the logical relations among actions or symbols (e.g., mathematicians, scientists)."[10]

Many employers now seek additional "twenty-first-century" skills, like the ability to speak in public, work in groups, or navigate diversity. New academic standards ask children to persist through challenges and reason with evidence. Each new set of standards we come up with in education requires educators to find new ways to describe and measure the skills children have and are expected to develop. And adults worldwide have historically valued a huge variety of skills and accordingly asked kids to develop various skills to succeed in their community. If adults value skills in quiet observation and modeling, kids learn to do that more than asking for explicit directions.[11] If a community values organizing information in way X, a test asking people to organize it in way Y might seem ridiculous. As Sternberg has put it, "We have nothing even vaguely close to a 'tape measure' of intelligence," in part because people define "intelligence" itself differently.[12]

But remember this as we put new labels on kids' "intelligences": researchers demonstrate that we each have *many* abilities and skills under construction that are not measurable with a single number or in a truly objective way. It's more helpful to students if we recognize that we each are honing many different skills at various times.

While it's inaccurate to state that a person has only so much "intelligence," saying a person has *only one* form of intelligence is also inaccurate. We often talk inaccurately as if individual A has type A intelligence and individual B has type B intelligence: I'm musical, you're verbal. Howard Gardner has had his work misused in schooltalk, as teachers assert that some kids are "artists, not writers" or "math people" as opposed to "word people." Teachers have described groupwork scenarios where a colleague said something like, "You're a visual learner, you'll do the drawing!" and then helped the *other* children in the group learn to write well.

This inaccurate Smarts Talk can map dangerously onto Group Talk. Even while we all participate in multiple communities that support many kinds of learning (in schools, programs, neighborhoods, and homes), and while any one such community, like a family home, can support a wide variety of learning experiences (such as teaching kids to talk or listen to elders, fix an appliance, cook, or read), some educators dangerously decide that entire "cultures" are visual or into movement, not also analytic thinkers, or that some groups have "street smarts" and others "book smarts."[13] As Peter Murrell noted,

When we get to the place where we assign characteristics to groups, saying black kids are tactile-kinetic learners and white kids are abstract analytical learners, then we're engaging in the worst sort of stereotyping.[14]

So, inaccurate talk about "intelligence" falsely sums up how much "intelligence" we have, who has more or less of "it," or which single "intelligence" we have.

Intelligence isn't some objectively measured "thing" in our heads. We've ended up measuring some "abilities" in our schools and not others. And we each have many skills and abilities we hone over time.

> ## THINK / DISCUSS
>
> Do you remember how school adults measured your own intelligence in school? Do you consider that measurement inaccurate or accurate? Why?

Let's tackle that last myth-busting point: our abilities in any realm are not *fixed*, but *expandable over time*.

We also need to redesign our schooltalk to emphasize that abilities grow.

STRATEGY   Talk about abilities as *grown* through interaction and collective effort, not as fixed inside students.

How often do we talk inaccurately in schools as if our abilities are fixed, rather than expandable?

Our most well-known myth-buster on this is psychologist Carol Dweck. Dweck identifies two "mindsets" about intelligence and ability—one that doesn't help you succeed and one that does. If you have a *fixed* mindset, you believe falsely that talents and abilities are fixed traits. You fear you have a certain amount of talent in any given arena, and that's that; any failure must mean you don't have the talent needed. People with a "fixed mindset" become:

> Over-concerned with proving their talents and abilities, hiding deficiencies, and reacting defensively to mistakes or setbacks—because deficiencies and mistakes imply a (permanent) lack of talent or ability. People in this mindset will actually pass up important opportunities to learn and grow if there is a risk of unmasking weaknesses.[15]

If you have a *growth* mindset, you understand that talents and abilities "can be developed through passion, education, and persistence." You realize that through supported effort, you can get better at what you are trying; you seek out challenge and learn from mistakes. Na'ila Nasir notes that many sports coaches are good at communicating such a growth mindset: it's the idea that athletes become more skilled at hard stuff through practice.[16] Tapping science about our ever-developing brains, Jo Boaler urges a similar mindset about math: when we struggle through challenging problems, we learn.[17]

Educators can myth-bust by communicating to students as well as colleagues that no ability is "fixed": you can grow each ability if you practice. I have seen teachers successfully engage students of all ages in this discussion.[18] Here's a photo of my kids and me practicing growth mindset:

Source: Mica Pollock

I know a principal who says that his favorite word is "yet": as in, "you haven't mastered that, *yet.*" His school actually lets students retake exams until they can prove competency on specific expected skills.

Accurate Smarts Talk reminds people of all ages that growth in competency is possible.

And here's a key point to remember about "growth": skills grow when people are given the chance to develop them. You don't learn to play the piano unless someone offers you a piano to play; you likely become an even better pianist if someone mentors you. You get better at math when someone supports you to struggle through thought-provoking problems!

We can flip Smarts Talk myths by clarifying that no achievement is merely a natural outcome of an individual's inner "ability." Ongoing interactions in environments always shape what we can do. Every achievement is a *produced* outcome of our interactions *with other people* who offer opportunities to learn and develop.

> ### *Accurate Smarts Talk notes that abilities aren't just "in the head" (or the body!) but grown through interactions with others.*

Whether Julia is in that Advanced Placement class as a senior is not a question of her "smartness," but of how her learning experiences and opportunities got shaped over time. Did someone look at her, think "AP kid," and urge her to enroll? Even earlier in elementary school, was she labeled "gifted" or "fast," like the students in Rist's study? Did her parents call the school to insist she was placed in the "gifted" class or, later, in her first AP class?[19] What opportunities did she get in her early classes that helped her later on? What did she do in response?

So once again, we counteract harmful schooltalk—here, about innate or fixed "smartness" as achievement's ultimate cause—by describing young people's experiences in opportunity contexts over time.

THINK / DISCUSS

Can you think of a key opportunity to learn that shaped one ability you have today? What was an opportunity to learn that you wanted but did not receive? How did that shape your current abilities?

Do you ever mask that past process of learning, by talking about yourself as just "good at" or "not good at" a given skill set?

I like to use the movie *Slumdog Millionaire* as an example to demonstrate how our abilities are grown over time in interaction with others. Throughout the movie, the main character encounters various people who show him specific things, like whose face is on a specific piece of U.S. currency. By the time he gets to a high-stakes game show testing his trivia knowledge, he knows every answer (like whose face is on the currency) not because of innate genius, but because of an actual interaction in his life.

In her book exploring the formative experiences of black mathematicians, Erica Walker tells story after story about young people inspired and supported mathematically through a combination of chance meetings and active assistance from others. As a child, one mathematician got a slide rule from his uncle, who worked for a construction company. He learned trigonometry by reading the manual that came with it. He then glimpsed the applied math of engineering when he was stopped on the way home from high school by a local surveyor needing a hand; a teacher who gave him a college math book early inspired him to stay up all night solving problems. Another mathematician had a grandfather who encouraged him to think mathematically by giving him puzzles to solve. A third had a parent who taught fractions through engaging her in home construction projects. Others were invited into math camps paid for by NSF in the late-1950s Sputnik era.[20]

So, it's crucial to remember when we discuss ability that opening doors to opportunity to learn is key to developing any person's competencies.

We can also remember that competencies can be grown in all settings, including informal settings and homes.

Right around the time that Harvard president Larry Summers was wondering aloud whether girls weren't "innately"as skilled in science as boys, the first woman physicist tenured at Harvard told me she was convinced girls were more likely to become academic scientists if adults gave them access to stuff to take apart and put back together. She'd noted that adults typically gave such opportunities to boys, giving them opportunities to tinker with screwdrivers and mechanical objects in the garage and then calling them "natural" engineers and scientists.

Accurate Smarts Talk frames ability as *expandable if opportunities are provided.* And people will be more likely to provide each student access to opportunities if we remember that our abilities are grown in interaction with others. If we just think girls aren't likely scientists, why give them stuff to tinker with?

Here's another Smarts Talk problem: we often falsely assume that students don't have abilities just because we haven't seen them yet.

THINK / DISCUSS

As a child, did you have any skill that adults just never saw? Why didn't others get to see it? What were the pros and cons of having this ability stay private?

A great study by researchers Luis Moll and Stephen Diaz showed how class-room interactions influence the very abilities children can display. In a class-room, teachers asked Spanish-speaking students to read a passage in English and then define English vocabulary words taken out of context from the passage. Often, students had trouble defining the English vocabulary words out of context, so teachers concluded that the students didn't really understand English yet. But Moll and Diaz found that if the teacher asked students to retell and discuss the whole English story *in Spanish*, students could demonstrate deep comprehension of what they'd read in English. Moll and Diaz and the faculty then considered together how to design tasks so students could display their actual comprehension.[21]

Research has also shown that people who see children in one context sometimes see children displaying and honing abilities that people who interact with the children in other contexts have not seen. For example, researchers note that a child who is unable to pass math tests might be able to display the same math skills while baking a cake; another child might be able to read at home but get too anxious to do it on demand in a reading group, or remember phone numbers as needed but be deemed unable to remember facts and figures in school.[22] (Fred Erickson asks educators to spend half a day with just one young person to see how some learning experiences make students "light up" and participate and others make them "shut down."[23]) Researchers also point out how analytical, creative, and organizational skills young people might demonstrate in informal settings, like afterschool clubs, might not ever get seen in schools or tested on schools' tests.[24] Researchers also show that assumptions about who learns what at home keep us from understanding the full range of learning experiences children actually have. For example, old assumptions that low-income children hear few vocabulary words from their parents fail to see the full set of language interactions children actually have with their family members![25]

As an example of adults' failure to see or measure student skills from other contexts, Bud Mehan analyzed a placement meeting about one boy, "Shane," held as part of the Special Education evaluation process. The group was discussing whether Shane had a disability or not. Shane's mom tried to describe her son's abilities as seen at home; the teacher tried to describe his abilities as seen in class. But both descriptions were silenced by the psychologist's clinical assessment of his low performance on psychological tests. Shane, who started the meeting without a labeled disability, was labeled with a disability by the end of the meeting.

Mehan asks a jarring question: is Shane's disability truly just "between the ears," just a measurable thing inside his head? Or has it been co-produced by the people around him, through a series of descriptions of his "ability" level in which some voices are louder than others?

For Mehan and many other researchers, it's the latter. Mehan even has us thinking about how a simple piece of paper, like the psychologist's written diagnosis, can shape communications about a child's "ability" forever. Once Shane's diagnosis is written down officially, it becomes real—and for some, who he "is."[26]

THINK / DISCUSS

Can you think of one consequential meeting or piece of paper that shaped conversations in school about your own ability? What would you do if a child you know was about to experience the same thing?

Importantly, Mehan notes that despite the fact that Shane's disability label was produced in the meeting, words like "normal," "gifted," or "learning disabled" only characterize "intelligence in terms that place it inside the student." Regardless of Shane's full skill set, the final label "learning disabled" "naturalizes" the label as a summative descriptor of Shane's innate "abilities," he writes, "thereby masking the social construction work [like the tests and the IEP meeting] that generated the designation in the first place."[27]

So, accurate Smarts Talk emphasizes that *people, in interaction*, help shape both any child's current "abilities," and others' sense *of* those abilities.

To flip simplistic discussions of student intelligence, it's helpful to reframe even the most hallowed assessments of intelligence as *produced by people in interaction.*

Here are a few:

SAT scores are produced by people in interaction.

Popular talk about tests like the SAT continues to reinforce the false equivalence between scores and "smarts." An article that circulated widely on social media in early 2015 argued that your college major "is a pretty good indication of how smart you are." The author measured "smartness" by the average SAT scores of students pursuing different college majors.[28]

I emailed the article to a number of colleagues, who all felt that the article's Smarts Talk omitted all the interactions shaping someone's path *to* an SAT score. One colleague noted bluntly that SAT scores "reflect preparation, which in turn reflects access to training in skills that are measured by the SAT." Another noted that "research on U.S. parents' purchase of tutors for their kids, and access to societally valued activities—clubs, summer camps, museums, even people who help kids write college essays—provides insight into the U.S. version of parental influence on what we assume is inherent intelligence or 'smarts.'" Some colleges are questioning overreliance on the SAT in admissions processes, arguing that scores don't adequately demonstrate students' ability to succeed in the full range of skills college offers (nor measure students' full range of abilities) and instead say more about students' prior access to SAT-preparatory opportunities.[29] But too often, we fail to remember the lived experiences underneath any tested "ability."

To prompt more thorough Smarts Talk, I like to ask this simple question, pilfered from my graduate school advisor Ray McDermott: *who was involved in your SAT score?* On the day you took the SAT, it wasn't just the prenatal "aptitude" in your head sitting down to take that test as if your brain had been living in a jar. Rather, the SAT tested your *built ability* to succeed on that test as well as your experience of test taking at that moment. Indeed, research shows that if you tell people before a test that people from their "group" do worse on the test, test-takers do worse.[30] Even giving students food before tests can affect test scores. Instruction from experienced teachers particularly builds our ability to take tests—but only some students get experienced teachers.[31] And prepping for tests of course raises scores on those tests—as the many parents paying for SAT prep already know.[32]

Ironically, the SAT was originally introduced in part to broaden the opportunity to go to college—to show that a student had enough "scholastic aptitude" to attend the Ivy League even if he were not related to generations of Ivy League graduates.[33] But we've long framed it inaccurately as a measure of almost *innate* aptitude rather than a measure more precisely of built skill to succeed on SAT items.[34] As Howard Gardner noted to me, both IQ and SAT tests just "measure a certain combination of linguistic and logical intelligences needed for success in certain schools and on certain tests." And if the child's previous "real life situation resembles school/tests," the child is better prepped for the test and gets a higher score.

I never studied formally for the SAT, but the test makers used words I'd seen in books and asked me logic problems like ones I'd encountered in enrichment activities offered by skilled teachers. As an early reader supported by my mom, a college-educated woman who stayed home to raise me for the first years of my childhood, I had also taken initial tests successfully and received positive feedback on them, which built my confidence. My ability to take the SAT was also honed through spending my extra class time on those classic "SRA cards"[35] in elementary school, where I got praise and points for blasting through lots of cards with short reading passages and multiple choice questions.

THINK / DISCUSS

Who was involved in *your* SAT score? Make a brief mental list of all the folks who were involved in yours.

Remember back to Chapter 2: our test scores, grades, and college acceptance letters are all shaped by millions of everyday interactions with lots of people in opportunity contexts. Any test score is shaped by social interactions that occurred long before the test (did anyone around you use the vocabulary word used in that test question?), the construction of the test (does it measure all the skills you have?), and even interactions that occur during the test (how did your teacher introduce the test as it began?).

IQ test scores—or any score testing ability— are produced by people in interaction.

The American Psychological Association task force statement on "Intelligence: Knowns and Unknowns" clarifies that even IQ tests measure whether life experiences (including school experiences) have prepared someone for "the skills measured by intelligence tests." Sternberg argues that "often, intelligence tests measure skills that children were expected to acquire a few years before taking the intelligence tests."[36] As a renowned psychologist colleague put it bluntly to me in an email, "people think we are measuring something 'innate' when we give an IQ test. They forget that we are measuring the outcome of training (education, and life experience)."

Bud Mehan showed that even something as seemingly "innate" as an IQ test score could be shaped in the interaction between tester and child. IQ testers might lean forward after a child answered a question and raise an eyebrow. After that, the child would answer differently and his IQ score would change.[37]

Even when we talk about brain development—like young children's brain synapses developing due to early stimulation—we are talking about life experiences developing each child's human abilities toward doing specific things. If someone talks to you a lot using a large variety of words, for example, this leads you to have a bigger vocabulary, which helps you to impress people who value large vocabularies or to get higher scores on tests that test your vocabulary. This doesn't mean that you *are inherently more intelligent on some overall scale*. It just means you have developed a skill that someone values and is measuring. If your experiences keep preparing you for whatever is measured, you'll do better.

As Jeff Elman reiterated to me, any individual is born with their own set of genes (most human variation is at the individual level), and even tiny babies' skills (like the ability to focus on a stimulus) can be influenced by early experience. The brain always "incorporate[s] the effects of experience," and if what you're testing aligns with the baby's early experiences, she'll do better. Higher-vocabulary kids are not "smarter," nor more "language-rich" in some general sense; they're kids whose prior experiences gained them bigger vocabularies, and they then do better in schools that value vocabularies. Kids who read by third grade are not "smarter," but kids whose prior experiences led them to read by third grade; they then do better in schools that rely on reading. And no such built ability is then "fixed." Researchers show that any form of skill can grow based on interactions and efforts in your environment. As Jo Boaler points out, neuroscience shows that synapses keep growing throughout our lives if we get the chance to persist in learning something challenging.[38]

So we keep building our skills when we get the chance to! As researcher Josh Aronson notes, "Intelligence isn't a lump of something that's in our heads"—it's "a transaction among people."[39]

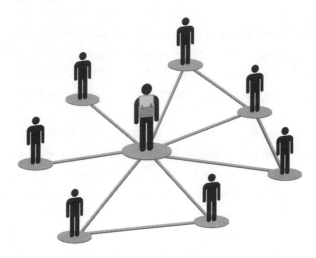

So if skills can be grown further through additional interaction and people have skills in all sorts of domains, why rely on tests of current skill measured once in single domains to limit access to "gifted and talented" classes, enriched coursework, or slots in college?

Many would argue that it's because the tools help us ration opportunity only to some.

In fact, anthropologists and historians have long argued that U.S. education has ranked people as more or less "smart" for this very reason: to ration opportunity.[40] When we frame intelligence or ability as something some people just have more of than others, we explain away any disparities in outcome and even opportunity as just the way of the world.

If you look historically in the United States, you actually can see people creating myths about entire groups deemed smarter than others in order to distribute opportunities to some more than others. So let's tackle that myth as a final script to flip in our Smarts Talk.

STRATEGY   Say out loud that no *group* is "smarter" than any other. Actively reject the myth that intelligence is distributed differently to "groups."

Think back to Larry Summers: Jo Boaler notes that "stereotypes about women and math are so strong that they're in the air all the time."[41] Research has shown that girls who identify with math get anxious and underachieve if their gender is highlighted as relevant before a difficult math test.[42]

Perhaps our deepest such myth is the lie that some race groups are smarter than others.

For several centuries, scientists calling themselves "white" imagined "racial" subgroups to the human race and presumed inner differences accompanied our exterior differences. A particular myth that a "white" race group was "smarter" seemed to justify giving "white" people more opportunities. Thomas Jefferson proposed in his *Notes on the State of Virginia* that black people, as slaves, were perhaps "inferior to the whites in the endowments both of body and mind"; his argument served to justify the slavery system, fundamental to the U.S. economy and his own household.[43] In *The Mismeasure of Man*, Stephen Jay Gould shows how scientists in the 1800s tweaked measurements of human skulls (e.g., by excluding smaller skulls or female skulls from a sample) to find "white" heads bigger and then claimed this skewed finding as evidence that "white" males were more intelligent. Into the 1900s, scientists then purported to measure "the interior stuff in brains" via intelligence testing, falsely calling intelligence a "unitary, genetically based, [and] unchangeable" quantity of stuff that varied across "races."[44] Others used such reports to justify Jim Crow segregation. As I put it in a short piece called "No Brain Is Racial," "in a cruel cycle, the notion that intellectual ability was distributed differently among so-called races was developed by white scientists through the eighteenth, nineteenth, and twentieth centuries to explain and justify a system of economic, social, and political inequality organized along racial lines."[45]

In the early 1900s, with many immigrants from Southern and Eastern Europe not yet deemed fully "white," people designed and used new IQ ("intelligence quotient") tests to sort children now entering public education in greater numbers into tracks for further education vs. preparation for manual labor. They also tweaked their tests to assert Northern European intellectual superiority and status and to argue for immigration restrictions.[46] For example, early testers went to Ellis Island to assess new immigrants and argued that "83 percent of the Jews, 80 percent of the Hungarians, 79 percent of the Italians, and 87 percent of the Russians were feeble-minded." ("Consider a group of frightened men and women who speak no English and who have just endured an oceanic voyage in steerage," imagined Stephen Jay Gould. "Most are poor and have never gone to school; many have never held a pencil or pen in their hand."[47]) Rubén Donato documents the similar use of intelligence testing in the early twentieth century to construct Mexican Americans in the Southwest and California as having "inferior natural capacities" to "whites." Mexican American kids attended segregated schools and classrooms that offered inferior educational resources; they were discouraged from going past elementary school so they could work in fields. Results on IQ tests justified those inferior resources and low expectations.[48]

Fast forward to 1969, the year the *Harvard Educational Review* published Arthur Jensen's widely read analysis of differences between black and white students' "IQ and achievement" performance. At the time, brief desegregation and resource investment efforts were just beginning, as lawmakers enforced the 1964 Civil Rights Act and enacted other federal laws. But Jensen proposed that "compensatory education" (additional supports for black students) had already "failed," in part because the students likely had less "ability" in the "cognitive" domain. John Baugh describes how in the 1970s educators reacted to African American Vernacular English (AAVE) as if it signaled lesser "intelligence" and even a need for Special Education assignment.[49] And in the 1990s, the authors of the popular book *The Bell Curve* again argued that poor people, disproportionately people of color, were poorer because they were less intelligent. Such arguments about race and intelligence appear cyclically in popular books, forcing the public again to muster evidence against these myths.[50] The last such book I saw was published and critiqued in 2014.[51]

I call the myth that *some race groups are smarter than others* "the hand from the grave." That's because it's like the end of so many bad horror movies: it never seems to totally die, no matter how many times you kill it.

But like the hero of any movie, we have to keep on stomping the myth, because it continues to have fundamental repercussions for children in schools.

Today, the hand from the grave pops up in small comments made about "smart kids" vs. "dumb kids" and in everyday actions treating kid X as smarter than kid Y. It pops up when children draw only white males when asked to draw "a scientist,"[52] and when college students or even professors quickly make comments about "the smart people" that assume only some students are "smart." It shows up when Supreme Court justices determining the fate of college admissions policies argue that black students just need "slower" classes.[53]

And sometimes, the hand from the grave slaps a student right in the face. This comment caught my eye in one online dialogue: "I'm a social work educator in a small Northern university. Every single First Nations student I have taught has been told by a teacher that they are dumb or that they will never succeed."

The hand from the grave can grip us despite our intentions: one colleague noted that "even while I *feel* I believe that all groups of kids have the same ability to learn, I sometimes hear words coming out of my mouth that don't align with that belief." Mahzarin Banaji studies "implicit bias," or mental associations that operate too fast for us to control or even recognize. Banaji times the seconds it takes you to literally click a positive word (like "love") on a computer after you've seen a face that looks "black" vs. one that looks "white" (www.projectimplicit.org). Banaji and colleagues have found that on computer tests, a majority of Americans—especially white people, but also people of color—associate "white"-looking faces more quickly with positive words.[54] As she told me via email, "the data in lab tests" also show the "association of white/smart to be stronger than Black/smart."

As Banaji noted to me, her "Implicit Association Test" (IAT) of racial attitudes shows generally that:

On the race IAT 70% of white Americans show white preference. About 10% show black preference and the rest are neutral.

On the race IAT 40% of black Americans show black preference, 40% show white preference, and 20% are neutral.

Racial biases about who is and is not a "smart" "type of person" have been programmed into our thinking for centuries.

And because Smarts Talk is so skewed toward old myths about intelligence, students from stigmatized groups unsurprisingly can fear that even universal struggles with achievement might expose some lack of innate ability in them. Research on "stereotype threat" by Claude Steele and colleagues shows that black students who worry about confirming pervasive stereotypes that they are innately less "smart" can get so plagued by worry that they actually depress their own test scores, often by checking and rechecking their answers and wasting time. On similar experiments, girls underperformed on math tests if an announcer said the test was designed to assess girls' innate abilities in math versus boys'. In one experiment, testers told white male students that "Asians" tended to do better on a difficult math test. This framing depressed the white male students' test performance.[55]

Steele and colleagues' work shows that if students trust that the people around them hold high standards for them and reject such myths about innate, group-based "intellectual ability," stereotype threat doesn't kick in. Dorothy Steele and colleagues call classrooms "identity safe" when students can rest assured that teachers and peers actively refuse false stereotypical views.[56]

But more typically, such myths persist because we let them. Consider the following scripted comments that many of us routinely nod along to or, fail to counteract:

"Asian kids are smart."

The "Asians are smart" script is a twist on the original hand from the grave, part of a larger racialized "model minority" myth built after World War II and immigration policy shifts in 1965 (when many of the Asian immigrants finally allowed to immigrate to the United States came professionally skilled) and particularly, to counter demands for black equality in the Civil Rights Movement.[57] We'll talk in depth about this particular myth in Chapter 4, as the same historical factors shaped scripted "cultural" claims about "Asians" that ignore Asian American diversity, experiences, and needs while denigrating other groups.

For now, we can plan to respond when people say "Asians are smart!" by saying no group is "smarter" than any other. The myth about "smart Asians" is dangerous for all students, including "Asians": in schools, many argue, Asian American students often don't get help they need because they're assumed to just "be smarter." As Vivian Louie notes, for example, "The Chinese American students I interviewed talked about peers who could not believe anyone Asian could fail a test and about teachers who never registered their academic struggles because Asian children are supposed to be the brainy, quiet ones who never need help."[58] One undergraduate in a class of mine talked to an "Asian" friend who recalled that in high school she "would always get treated with respect in the classroom," but "would not always get the help that she needed. Her educators would just assume that she could understand all of the material because she is Asian. She would feel bad because she could see the preferential treatment that she received from her teachers, while conversely other students were being treated poorly because of their racial identity." One Latino student talking to researcher Julio Cammarota recalled how "all eyes would be on me" when he entered honors classes he described as "majority Chinese":

So I would always walk into the class the first day, and the teacher would ask me . . . like that, "Let me see your program, just to make sure you're in this class." And I was like, "Yeah, I got this class." And they would be like, "You know, this is a difficult class—are you sure you can handle it? We do a lot of homework." Just like right there, they think that I can't do it.[59]

John Diamond and Amanda Lewis talked to black youth in the Midwest who experienced the same thing when entering mostly white honors classes.[60] Kevin Foster has talked to many black students in Texas who are stopped and questioned skeptically when walking through the hallways of their own mostly white honors programs. And crucially, students at my university who are not Asian American—particularly black and Latino students—have told me that after many years of "Asian" peers being framed as "smarter," some feared deep down that they actually weren't "smart enough" to succeed in classes with Asian American peers.

As we'll consider further in the following chapter, simplistic talk about "smart Asians" not only ignores wide variation in Asian American achievement and experience but, as usual, masks all of the interactions in opportunity context that produce any student's school outcomes.

Here's another scripted claim we nod along to:

"The kids in the gifted/AP class are smarter."

"Gifted" classes around the country (sometimes called GATE [Gifted and Talented Education], sometimes given names like "seminar") are disproportionately composed of white students and middle-class students but often naturalized as just full of "smart kids." Researcher Karolyn Tyson has studied majority-black North Carolina schools where the "gifted" class is exclusively white. As Tyson demonstrates, this is in part about parents who insist on GATE testing and placement, and in part about how old myths play out in educators' everyday decisions about who deserves such testing and placement.[61] A community group in New York City sent white, black, and Latino "testers" to schools as potential parents, asking school representatives about entrance to the school. White parents repeatedly were given material on gifted classes even if they didn't ask for it, and even offered tours and tips on admission. Black and Latino parents repeatedly were not offered gifted-class information. Some were told the classes or schools were full.[62]

When we truly inquire into the demographics of our opportunities, we often uncover how those demographics are made by people and not naturally occurring at all. "Gifted" classes are produced through referrals, testing, and placement processes that all rely on the presumption that some kids have more "capacity" than others. The website for my own kids' district long stated matter-of-factly that "gifted" children "possess a capacity for excellence far beyond that of their peers." Administrators often assign the most experienced teachers to "gifted" classes, compounding student advantage.[63]

Despite all the social interactions that create the demographics of "gifted" classes—and despite the fact that many tests involved are "using convenient, partial operationalizations of the construct of intelligence, and nothing more"—schools' and districts' very language for speaking of "gifted children" normalizes the demographics as innately justified. The *New York Times* wrote an article on the racial demographics of gifted classes in New York City as an exposé because so many people were taking these demographics for granted as normal.[64]

Inquiry into demographics is a key starting place for equity-oriented Smarts Talk. Karolyn Tyson suggests that educators ask, for example:

> What procedures are used for identifying and referring gifted students? Do some procedures or practices allow for the identification of a more diverse group of students? Do some procedures and practices inhibit the identification of a diverse group? What are the signs or indications of giftedness commonly used at your school? What instruments does your school use to assess giftedness?

Such inquiry can lead to deeper questions educators can ask themselves:

> . . . Do you tend to assume that children from black, Latino, or low-income families do not have as much family, community, and peer support for academic endeavors as children from other families and therefore should not be expected to realize high levels of academic achievement? Do you assume that enriched instruction will be of little or no use or value to these children?[65]

Some equity efforts focus on informing more parents about how to access "gifted" or advanced opportunities.[66] (The College Board estimates that many students who might have done well in AP coursework never enrolled in it.[67]) As Tyson puts it,

School personnel often complain about parents who demand that their children be placed in the gifted program or advanced classes, or who push for a particular service that is believed to provide educational benefits, even when the children do not meet the official criteria for inclusion. . . . Understandably, these parents want the best for their children; the difference is that they believe they are entitled to the best and they usually have the means to find ways to obtain it.[68]

And still other equity efforts question the very idea that "gifted" opportunities should be reserved for a few. Tyson advises us to ask perhaps the ultimate equity question:

> If that child were yours, what would you want her school experience to be? What kind of an education would you want for her? How would you want her teachers to see and treat her? Would you allow her to be overlooked for an opportunity to experience a high-quality, challenging curriculum? Would you make sure she has access to the best education available?
>
> . . . If you saw every child as your own, you might consistently think of aptitude as something to be developed and attempt to develop it in all of your children, not just a select, privileged few.

Let's say you looked out at an undergraduate engineering class in 2011, for example, as I did, and saw two women in a sea of men, and very few black or Latino students. Do you assume that girls, or black or Latino boys, are just less innately able to be engineers? Or do you ask someone what's going on? Colleagues and I helped start a campus initiative leveraging university resources to help more kids get prepared for STEM majors.

As another example of such inquiry, Amanda Datnow and colleagues worked with a district to disaggregate their data on placement in high schools' college preparatory classes. Through this inquiry, the district realized that:

> Asian students who scored at the basic level on the state tests had double the chance of being in college-preparatory courses than Latino students who scored at the same basic level. This data analysis led district leaders

to reexamine their class placement procedures and expand access to college-preparatory courses.[69]

Instead of talking about who is "smart," it's much more accurate to say that the kids in college-prep, "gifted," and AP classes are the kids whose supporters made sure they got there. While writing this book, I got an email from a colleague (in this case, an upper-income black woman) asking for information about programs for "gifted" *three-to-five-year-olds* where we lived. Access to colleagues with knowledge about such programs, plus the clout and energy to find and shepherd an application, is key to getting in to such programs—that is, if we insist on reserving such opportunities for a limited few.[70]

If left unchallenged, myths about "types of kids" also seep inside children labeled "gifted" or "advanced," who can come to think they are naturally "smarter" than the kids in other classes.[71] For example, I've heard students try to explain why they are in classes like "GATE" or "seminar." They often say that someone noticed they were "smart" and recommended them. And as Karolyn Tyson notes, advanced coursework follows: "regardless of their level of achievement, students who are identified as gifted are more likely to describe themselves as 'smart' or 'intelligent' or to enroll in Advanced Placement (AP) and honors courses in high school."[72] As adults offer enriched learning opportunities only to some, students gradually decide they are either naturally one of "the smart kids" or they're not—and motivation is threatened if they decide the latter. Some choose not to risk advanced courses.

Tracking by presumed "ability" creates social tensions, too, because young people sort themselves even as they are getting sorted by others. As students see achievement patterns forming around them—who's in gifted, who is in AP—students start to shape their friendships and styles around the demographics of their classrooms.[73]

When such tracks are racialized, myths about race and intelligence get reinforced for youth as well as educators. As one black student in a majority white class said anxiously to a researcher colleague, "If I am in a class like where there are a majority of white students, sometimes, for me, I won't feel as smart."

To counter such pervasive myths, some schools refuse tracking altogether and put all young people in single high tracks designed to carefully support every student toward college.[74] Many call such efforts to spread rigorous instruction to all students the critical fix for U.S. education.[75] Educators can stomp myths individually as well, by insisting on high expectations for every student. As a starter, sociologist Sam Lucas suggests that every time we see an individual student we don't know, we might *actively refuse* automatic assumptions about how that "type" of student might achieve; teachers can then set forth to investigate and address the past experiences and current needs of individuals.[76] Joshua Aronson urges similarly that educators cultivate an "insatiable curiosity" about individual students to counteract programmed assumptions about who will achieve how.[77]

Researchers also urge that as educators challenge Smarts Talk myths in their own thinking, they must stomp down the myths with youth—for example, by inviting in contemporary professionals and local "ordinary heroes" who are as diverse as the nation or neighborhood is and can broaden everyone's expectations about youths' potential. (Meira Levinson cautions that educators should go beyond just retelling the story of extraordinary historic achievers, which risks conveying unintentionally that only one child in a million will achieve something important.[78])

Teaching history is another essential way to stomp down Smarts Talk myths. One great resource for such myth-busting Smarts Talk with young people is Theresa Perry's book *Young, Gifted, and Black*, designed to help educators support black students in a society where too many observers expect black underachievement.[79] I think aspects of these Strategies can be used in an education community of any demographic, including to counteract gendered or other racialized myths. I also think other students need to hear much of the same information. The key is to actively stomp down each myth that presumes some types of students are smarter than others.

Perry argues that educators need to "communicate a counternarrative about (students') intellectual capacity" and to deliver to students a strong, explicit "message about intellectual competence."[80] Perry calls specifically for educators to recount the historic African American quest for education through self-funding schools, self-teaching literacy, insisting on public education and access, and producing scholarship, to "forge the identities of African American students as achievers, literate, and a people with a rich intellectual tradition."[81] Smarts Talk about how people from all communities have contributed and continue to contribute to human knowledge is essential, even as we clarify that not everyone has benefited equally from formal schooling and university. Carter Woodson, a historian of black education who started Black History Month as Negro History Week in 1926, hoped such history would someday be common knowledge, but we still learn little in schools about many communities' intellectual traditions and contributions, in the United States and globally.[82] My students taught me at age twenty-two that the early Maya helped invent the concept of zero, while professors introduced me to African learning traditions; I was in my early forties before I learned that people in India helped invent the decimal system and Islamic mathematicians, algebra.[83] Many programs focus on closing such knowledge gaps with youth far earlier. The Alaska Native Knowledge Network insists on recovering and regularly sharing, with youth, Native contributions to "the global knowledge base,"[84] while Navajo community leaders running math camps in Arizona made sure that youth came to see mathematics knowledge as indigenous to their community, not external to it.[85]

Yet such inquiry into the facts of universal "smarts" is threatening to some: for example, state lawmakers passed a law to shut down the Mexican American Studies program in the Tucson, Arizona, public schools for teaching young people about the intellectual heritage of Latinos in America. Opponents argued the program was anti-"white" and even prohibited youth and teachers from teaching Mexican American history and literature in class.[86]

Many emphasize that to support young people in such a world, myth-busting also requires supporting students to develop fierce belief in their own (ever-expandable!) intelligence *as* a member of any social group falsely stigmatized. Lisa Delpit suggests that teachers supporting African American children need to explicitly help "provide the emotional ego strength to challenge racist societal views of the competence and worthiness of the children and their families."[87] Na'ila Nasir argues that schools successful in helping students forge a "positive sense of themselves as African Americans and as students" explicitly discuss "how to psychologically manage being stereotyped."[88] As one student in Tucson put it after learning more about Mexican and Mexican American history, "to know who you are and to be proud of who you are . . . just, like, gives you power to do better for yourself—to keep learning, want to keep doing things."[89] Patricia Gándara describes how "a guiding principle" of the Puente Project in California "is that it is crucial for young Latinos to analyze their own educational situation as Latinos. Without a critical perspective, students run the risk of internalizing and acting out the racist stereotypes they see all around them."[90] A Native teacher designing science curricula around local Indigenous knowledge in Utah told mentor Bryan

Brayboy that after years of denigrating interactions in a boarding school, she was determined to teach Indian students that they could "be smart and Indian at the same time."[91] Janie Ward suggests a four-step model for "black children and parents to resist racist notions about ourselves": "See It," "Name It," "Oppose It," and "Replace It."[92]

The Young COBRAs in Austin, Texas, cocoon African American students one period a day with African American mentors for conversations that insist critically on achieving together as "brothers." Director Kevin Foster explained to me the program's commitment to improving on typical Smarts Talk. As we close this chapter, I want to share his description in full as an example of flipping Smarts Talk scripts:

At a recent large youth track meet, there was a problem measuring the times of all eight runners in one of the heats. As a result, the heat would have to be re-run later in the day. The athletes and crowd present were predominantly African American, yet also quite diverse, with a noticeable critical mass of Anglo, African American and Latino participants. At the height of confusion an exasperated parent stated, "See, this is what happens when WE run things, it's a mess. Black people can't run nuthin." Another African American parent calmly but resolutely turned to him and said, "Hey Brother, no. We don't talk like that here. That's not us. Please keep that sort of talk to yourself." It was a noticeably uncomfortable moment for many parents present, but one that came with nods of agreement, and perhaps even relief, as the elder African American spoke up in implicit defense of positive talk about ourselves over negative.

As uncomfortable as it may be to some, the reality is that African Americans have been taught for centuries that we are "less than" in areas related to competence, intelligence, organization and management, even as we are imagined as excellent as athletes and entertainers, and notorious as drug dealers or in other forms of criminality. Another set of stereotypes surround our Latino students as drug dealers, baby makers, and likely gang members. Against this backdrop, one of COBRA's core tenets is *Critical Consciousness*. Our group understanding is that there are many widely broadcast images that can come to define us, and that it is up to us to discern which images will help us become successful community contributors and which ones are traps that are part of what Carter G. Woodson called *Miseducation*. We seek Critical Consciousness as the portal to our most important tenet, which is to *Define Yourself for Yourself.*

As an example of critical consciousness in action, in one session we have students call out the things that society expects of black males. Typically an unholy trinity arises—Athlete, Entertainer or Criminal. Next, we ask the students what is a most likely path for black male success. The two most common answers are music industry and professional sports. Finally, we give the students a task. They are to find out how many black doctors there are in the U.S., how many black lawyers, how many black CEOs, as well as how many African Americans there are in each of the major professional sports in the U.S. The sports stats are available at NCAA.org and the other stats are available with less than ten minutes of Internet searching. The results routinely shock the students. While there are tens of thousands of doctors, lawyers and CEOs, the number of Black professional athletes number in the hundreds. In the case of basketball, there are a few dozen job openings per year. How can it seem like there are so many more black athletes than doctors and lawyers, when that clearly is not the case?

The conversations that flow from this exercise are typically animated and go on for a few weeks in chapter meetings; they carry into the halls of the schools. There are many takeaways for students, but among the biggest is that society—through its ubiquitous megaphone outlets of television, radio, print media, social media, politicians and others—can lead students to accept lies about what paths they should take if they aspire to material success and an ability to give back to their families and communities.

We ask students, in the spirit of Malcolm X, Martin Luther King, Carter G. Woodson, W.E.B. Du Bois and others: *who taught them* the misguided, improbable and often self-defeating notions of who they could become? We thus prime a critical consciousness and an ability to separate societal common sense ideas from healthy good sense ideas. Students are then equipped to ask and answer for themselves: "What is important to me, and absent media images preaching to me, *who do I want to become?*"

When young people say how much they appreciate hearing such messages stated explicitly, it shows they are all too rarely said aloud. I once gave a talk for first generation college-bound young people, largely from Spanish speaking families, who were visiting our university with their parents. Afterwards, a student noted in their school newspaper how important it was to hear a simple comment I'd made in the middle of offering advice for becoming "a leader":

> As I discovered the educational life at University of California San Diego, I realized that we can do and become anything we desire, if we dedicate ourselves. As I heard a speech from Dr. (Pollock), a university professor, she inspired me with the words she said. She said "no person is better than any other person, and no group is smarter than any other group."

As Geoffrey Cohen describes, educators can stomp intelligence myths every day by conveying trust that students will reach very high standards through ongoing, supported effort. On assignments, for example, educators can accompany "critical feedback" with "an explicit, two-step message: a reference to high performance standards and a personal assurance of students' capacities to reach those standards."[93]

Beyond stomping myths every day, educators also need to offer the daily supports students need—what Ron Ferguson calls offering "high help," in combination with "high perfectionism."[94] And to fully stomp intelligence myths, the curriculum itself needs to actually be challenging. Theresa Perry argues that "to tell students that they are smart and to repeatedly teach content that is not intellectually challenging affirms that in reality the students are not seen as smart or intellectually capable."[95] Carol Lee adds that "simply telling people they can accomplish a task without providing them with explicit support for doing the work the task requires . . . is not likely to inspire someone who sees herself as failing."[96] In schools where students have been under-challenged for too long, we also can't just ignore any skill deficiencies that have been produced.[97] Principals and administrators "detracking" schools—putting everybody together in high-level classes—note that after low-level classes have made work slower and more boring, students don't only need to be told that their talents can grow. They also need extra supports and time to pick up skills they still need.[98]

Smarts Talk for equity insists on necessary opportunities to grow necessary skills.

Communicating toward equity means actively counteracting the myth—all day, every day—that some young people or some groups are naturally "smarter" than others. Every student and all groups of students need opportunities to keep on learning.

Before tackling the Action Assignments and additional **THINK/DISCUSS** questions, you might debrief personally or with others:

THINK / DISCUSS

> Which information mentioned about intelligence in this chapter has been new to you? Which information has even felt questionable given your own prior knowledge?

> Which of the information here has felt personally difficult to hear? What does this help you realize regarding the difficulties of Smarts Talk?

> Which of these facts should we talk about more in schools (with whom?), as we consider how to have "high expectations" for all young people?

> How prevalent today is the old lie that some race groups are smarter than others?

> How does that lie show up in schools today? Has the "hand from the grave" affected your own life?

> What "low expectations" for some "types of kids," and "high expectations" for others, have you encountered in your own life?

> What's one initial way you might want to counteract these myths for young people today?

ACTION ASSIGNMENTS

1. Try using an idea or a piece of information from this chapter to begin a conversation with someone you know about their concept of "smartness" or "intelligence." Do they think about intelligence as a fixed quantity of stuff "in the head"? Do they know that in reality, no group

is "smarter" than any other? Where did their ideas about "intelligence" come from? Report the experience and your reflections on the following questions:

> How did the interaction go? What in the conversation went well, or what do you wish had gone differently?

> Do any of the ideas shared by your conversation partner make you fundamentally question how to talk about "intelligence" or "smartness"? Why?

> If you could change one thing about the conversation about intelligence or "smartness" in an education setting you know, what would you change? How might you start to go about this? What would be some Core Tensions of that effort?

2. Do #1 again, with someone in a school community you know and could actually improve.

3. Try to turn one gold nugget idea or fact from this chapter into a #school-talking tool that lots of other people could learn from. For example, create a poster or PowerPoint slide, short video, or other multimedia image publicly sharing that gold nugget quote or idea. To accompany your main message, create a brief user's guide of five related information points or ideas from this chapter that can help users be more fully informed about the issue at hand and have a productive conversation sparked by your tool. See Chapter 1, pages 65–66, for more instructions.

Here is an example based on a poster design by a UC San Diego student:

ALL STUDENTS ARE *SMART*

THEY EXPRESS IT IN A VARIETY OF UNIQUE & DIFFERENT WAYS

4. In person or via the Internet, find an educator or young person who you feel is schooltalking for equity in their Smarts Talk. Document (with permission) and share (#schooltalking) some example of their work—a photo, a video, an image, a quote from them, or something they have produced.

More schooltalk scenarios

THINK / DISCUSS

How would you now respond to these real comments framing young people's ability? Practice responses to each at the Try Tomorrow level. Then name a Principle or more general Strategy and Core Tension behind your thinking.

> Student, after class: "This is where all the dumb kids go."
> Teacher, in car: "In the academic decathlon, they get all the smart kids and we get all the losers."
> Student, in class: "You really think if we had more resources it would make us smarter?"

THINK / DISCUSS

Can we envision a world where every young person can be called "gifted" or "brainy" or "smart"? Why or why not? What will you do or say the next time you want to describe a child as "smart"? End by naming a Principle or a Core Tension behind a general Strategy for using the word "smart" in a community you belong to.

THINK / DISCUSS

Was there any ability or skill you had when you were younger that adults in school never saw or measured? Consider the pros and cons for you. Now, can you think of a young person you know who has a skill that is not recognized by his or her school community? What are the consequences for that young person? Would you design some way for the student to communicate (demonstrate) that skill in school? Consider a Principle or Core Tension behind your thinking.

THINK / DISCUSS

What's one adjustment you might make to how people in an education community you know measure or discuss student ability and skill? Name a Principle and Core Tension behind the adjustment you propose.

THINK / DISCUSS

Often, we label elementary school reading or math groupings innocuously ("the bluebirds" or "the yellow group") but then call them "ability groups." Research indicates that support groups should be flexible rather than permanent—students should move out of them when they've moved forward in a given skill area.[99] I sometimes explain that a reading group "is a group of kids with reading skills measured in a particular way at a particular time." What's your take: would you call these groups "ability groups" or use some other phrase? Consider a Principle and Core Tension behind your response.

THINK / DISCUSS

What pieces of paper or online records in schools shape communications about a student's abilities? Consider one such document you saw recently (a referral to a program; a transcript; a note between teachers) and its consequences for a young person. Would you change the document's communication in any way? Name a Principle or Core Tension behind your idea.

THINK / DISCUSS

Would you ask students the question "who was involved in your SAT score?" as they prepared for the SAT? Why or why not? Consider a Principle behind your decision, and a Core Tension of such Smarts Talk.

THINK / DISCUSS

Have you encountered the myth that one's accent or dialect says something about one's "intelligence," perhaps when people mock a particular way of talking when playing "stupid"? Power relations affect how speech styles are valued and devalued, and as a result associated with "smarts."[100]

How might you respond next time someone suggests inaccurately that someone's accent or dialect signals something about his or her intelligence? Consider a response at the Try Tomorrow level and a Principle and Core Tension of such Smarts Talk.

THINK / DISCUSS

In her research for *Unequal Childhoods*, Annette Lareau learned of one African American middle-class family who had a daughter who fell just below the Gifted and Talented Education qualifications on her school's assessments. The family paid for a tutor and hired a psychologist to conduct the exams again. After the mother insisted that the school admit the girl into the program, the school did.

You are a new administrator hearing this story from a parent who wants the same process for her child. How will you respond? Role-play talking through the situation at the Try Tomorrow level. End by pinpointing a Principle and Core Tension behind your comments.

THINK / DISCUSS

I know some parents in New York City who have refused to place their children in "gifted" programs even when they "got in." One parent explained to me that she didn't want her child in an opportunity that excluded others.

If you were a parent and your child were offered a test for "gift-edness" in a school community you know, would you have him or her take it? Why or why not? How might your decision depend on the range of opportunities offered in your school system? Name a Principle and Core Tension behind your response.

Now think: If your child took the test and did not score well, would you tell him or her the results? Would you tell him or her the results if she scored as "gifted" on such a test? How would you phrase either comment? Name a Principle and Core Tension behind each Try Tomorrow response.

THINK / DISCUSS

You are a teacher. Several colleagues just proposed that your school merge the curricula and students from the "gifted" classes into all classrooms, ending the "gifted" program. Parents of students in the "gifted" classes are furious. Other teachers have suggested that a better solution is to test everyone every year for "gifted" class placement.

You have been asked to give opening comments on this issue at the next faculty meeting. What will you say to assembled colleagues? At the Try Tomorrow level, practice commenting on the options before you. Then, name a Principle and a Core Tension behind your comments.

THINK / DISCUSS

Which communities' intellectual contributions and histories are discussed and not discussed in a school you know, and what are the pros and cons of this standard Smarts Talk? Could you broaden the conversation to explore more contributions from more communities? What's one learning experience you might add to that school community to get started? Name a Principle and Core Tension behind your idea.

THINK / DISCUSS

You are about to tutor a group of young people assigned to work with you for remedial help in math. It's your first day on the job. What might be your opening comment as you frame the task of achieving for your students? Would you explicitly tell students some of the key facts about intelligence from this chapter, or utilize any Smarts Talk Strategy? Would the demographics of the students affect your comments? Consider a comment at the Try Tomorrow level, and a Principle and Core Tension behind any Strategy you propose.

THINK / DISCUSS

Ivette Sanchez observed math teachers that colleagues deemed highly effective with Latino students.[101] She heard consistent growth mindset comments like "Let's tackle this problem!" and "Si se puede!" A workshop I went to based on Carol Dweck's work suggested that rather than praise students for being "good at" something (which suggests fixed innate skill), adults might always emphasize the possibility for growth, such as "You're becoming much better at skill X through your hard work!" Dweck also emphasizes that growth requires not just more work, but ongoing trial, error, and adjustment. Geoffrey Cohen also notes that pure praise doesn't fully flip Smarts Talk myths. In fact, "excessive praise can backfire,"[102] as students stop believing in the incessant compliments.

What's one sentence you might say to a young person you know to send a message about gaining competence in some academic domain? Role-play it at the Try Tomorrow level, and consider a Principle and a Core Tension of such Smarts Talk or a general Strategy for it.

THINK / DISCUSS

At OCR, I reviewed a district where schools that served low-income students of color offered few or no AP classes. Administrators in some of these schools said that no one was ready to take such classes, so it wasn't worth the limited money available to offer them. But more classes offered can mean more classes taken. In an agricultural area east of San Diego, I saw the children of farmworkers and service laborers line up to take summer AP classes because so few were offered during the school year.

What would you say if you worked in such a school and a colleague said to you, "we don't have advanced opportunities because our kids won't be able to succeed in them"? Practice a response at the Try Tomorrow level. End with a Principle or Core Tension for this Smarts Talk situation.

THINK / DISCUSS

You are a university admissions officer. You see an applicant who has excelled in her grades and scores despite centuries-old myths about her potential as a "type of person." Might that person bring particular strength to a campus? Will you recognize this in reviewing the student's file? Consider a Principle and Core Tension behind your response.

Chapter 4

Culture Talk

Every claim about group or individual experiences in schools needs to be fueled by inquiry with and about the people mentioned.

"Chapter Goal:"
Go from shallow to deep. Reject simplistic claims about other "cultures" in schools and start exploring people's real experiences in specific contexts. And invite any speaker to do so too.

This chapter asks you to combine all of your tools from previous chapters.

Have you been in a conversation lately where a speaker made a quick overarching claim about someone's "culture" and its orientation to education?

How about these common scripts?

an opinion →

* "Asian parents care about education, so Asians achieve highly."
* "Latino and black parents don't really care about education, so their kids don't achieve."

Such "culture" claims are fundamentally misleading schooltalk, though many people seem to feel quite comfortable making such claims publicly—particularly when describing people other than themselves.

Such claims harm when they keep us from knowing, respecting, and supporting actual young people.

As we discussed in Chapter 1, it's one thing when people strategically summarize a "group" experience in their own community, to navigate a world of "groups"—as long as they don't denigrate others in the process. Ideally, longer dialogues explore a range of experiences in more depth; Part 2 will invite such deeper exchanges into school.[1] This chapter worries first about quick, underinformed claims people make about culture "groups" as if we know a lot about *other* people's everyday lives and behaviors, even when we don't.

Such claims involve all of the schooltalking scripts we've engaged in the past few chapters. Underinformed claims about "groups," about lives in opportunity contexts, about how achievement happens—all of them are buried in quick summative comments about how other "cultures" achieve.

And such claims often violate all our Foundational Principles of equity-oriented schooltalking (page 8), particularly the need for accuracy.

Even while knowing little about people's *actual* lives, that is, speakers often describe "a culture's" everyday behaviors in schools as internally uniform, ignoring diversity within the group. And we talk routinely as if each group lives in a bubble that simply "achieves" on its own due to group-specific "attitudes." We also make simplistic causal claims about school achievement that ignore everyone and everything *outside* the group.

I call these scripted culture claims "shallow" because they are simplistic and contain too little data,[2] even as they become what Gloria Ladson-Billings calls "omnibus" explanations for everything young people and families do and experience.[3] Such claims are dangerous not only because they distort our sense of people, but because they make getting to know actual people seem unnecessary. Such claims also *distance* speakers from those we describe as if "they" are fundamentally other "types" of human beings, rather than complex people trying to thrive in specific, often shared contexts—just like "us." And in schools, such claims overlook the many opportunity factors and people involved in student outcomes, including educators themselves.

Such claims thus block us from understanding young people's real experiences and strengths, and supporting their actual needs.

We've seen throughout Part 1 that to redesign schooltalk for equity, we first must recognize scripts that distort people. Then we set forth to learn and share accurate information about actual people. So with young people in mind, let's continue our efforts at more informed schooltalk, fueled by facts!

A "culture" is a regularly interacting group of people that comes to share some experiences, norms, and behaviors.[4] We all actually belong to multiple "cultures" that shape our behaviors. Gutiérrez and Rogoff describe this as participating in various communities of "practice" to various degrees.[5] A neighborhood, a family, a peer community, a school community, a nation—each might be a regularly interacting community of practice or "culture" partially shaping our everyday experiences and behaviors.[6] Sometimes we speak of "youth culture" (behaviors shared and shaped by people younger than "adults") or, about "school culture" (the norms and everyday practices shaped in a particular school community). Most often in education, though, we speak as if people participate in single racial/ethnic/national -origin communities as their only "cultures"—and then we sum up others' "cultures" simplistically. *Deep* experiences in racial/ethnic/national-origin communities are indeed often primary shapers of our histories, families, and lives and demand *informed* attention. Equity-oriented schooltalk *also* always recognizes that each person belongs to and interacts across many dynamic and complex communities, as a first guard against oversimplifying people. Research on "intersectionality" clarifies that we each are negotiating multiple group experiences simultaneously, including experiences of gender, sexuality, citizenship, language community, and economics.[7] Author Chimamanda Ngozi Adichie calls for all of us to move from "single stories" that mask people's complex and multifaceted lives, to a habit of seeking more robust understandings of other human beings' lives, experiences, and strengths.[8]

THINK / DISCUSS →

What cultural communities might you say you "belong to"? Which of those cultures are predominant in shaping your behaviors and experiences? Can you think of one example of how you participate in multiple such "communities of practice" at the same time? Which such communities do you wish had been better recognized or understood in your schooling experience?

Here's the problem with *shallow* Culture Talk: much talk about racial/ethnic/national-origin (or class) "cultures" in schools just sums up communities' *assumed* behaviors, experiences, norms, or values based on too little information, and then uses those assumptions to quickly explain people in the community. This happens particularly when people are describing "cultures" they don't "belong to"—and these claims *block* further learning. Indeed, as a teacher educator, Gloria Ladson-Billings noted that the new, mostly "white, middle-class, monolingual, Midwesterner" teachers she was working with made lots of "cultural" assumptions about the low-income students of color they were meeting—while they didn't see themselves as "culturally" shaped at all.[9] Unable to see students *or* themselves clearly, they blocked inquiry into improving their own work.

THINK / DISCUSS

Are there common claims about "cultures" made where you live or work that you suspect are underinformed? Who makes these claims, about whom? Are these claims framed positively (e.g., groups said to "study a lot" or "care a lot" about school) or negatively (e.g., groups said to "misbehave" or "not care")? What consequences do those claims have for young people?

Inviting more exploration into real experiences in specific contexts—including educator-student interactions, in the schools we share—is often the key to flipping shallow "culture" scripts. To replace shallow comments with more informed claims, we strive to learn about people's real everyday lives rather than *imagining* those lives. We remember that all people, not just some people, are individuals shaped by experiences in complex and worthy communities. And to question how schools might support every student *from* every community, we strive to learn from and with people themselves, rather than make reductive claims about others from a distance.

As we'll see in Part 2 of this book, such deeper learning about and with the individuals and communities who share education settings can happen in doable ways every day, as just part of what educational communities do to support all young people.

But this chapter first makes the case for how essential such learning is. We'll get prepared for the first step: *reacting* to shallow Culture Talk about "other cultures" rather than just letting it pass.

I'll suggest these strategies for taking shallow talk deeper:

STRATEGY   Challenge nouns. (Insist on exploring variation and complexity inside any community named.)

STRATEGY   Challenge verbs. (Insist on exploring the complex experiences masked by quick causal claims about any "culture's" behavior regarding schools.)

STRATEGY   Emphasize that no group lives in a bubble. (Insist on looking at group members in ongoing interaction with people *outside* "the group.")

STRATEGY   Remember that human beings share behaviors across cultural groups. (Don't imagine "cultures" as overly different—instead, learn more about shared experiences as well as different ones.)

Each strategy reacts to scripted claims with a call to inquiry.

Shallow Culture Talk in action

Consider the following examples of shallow Culture Talk captured by researchers. In each case, a quick claim or assumption blocks learning about and with real people:

1. A white counselor tries to celebrate diversity by putting up a poster of a Native American in ceremonial dress in his office. In a career counseling appointment with a Navajo student, he points to the poster and comments that "the more traditional Navajos" have "such a simple and pure life. We should have left them alone." The counselor makes no gesture to learn more about the complex daily life of the Navajo student in front of him. The student leaves feeling totally misunderstood, saying, "That picture isn't us!" He does not return for career counseling.[10]

2. In a conversation with her professor, an educator in training immediately assumes "cultural" difference shapes her students' behaviors:

"The black kids just talk so loud and don't listen," said one teacher education student. I asked her why she thought they spoke so loudly. "I don't know; I just guess it's cultural." I then asked if she thought they were talking loudly because they were black or because they were kids. She paused a moment and then said, "I guess I've never thought about that."[11]

3. A social studies teacher assigns her students to read a front page article about Iraq and then overhears her kids saying things about "Arabs" as inherently violent. The teacher looks anxiously at one Arab American student, ignores the comment, and moves on to the next current events topic.[12]

In each case, initial efforts at deeper Culture Talk would ask people to *keep learning about* real people's complex experiences in real places (including in their own schools!) rather than just talk quickly (and often inherently negatively) about "groups."

Even some training on "culture" for teachers propagates shallow Culture Talk, through making quick claims about "groups" rather than urging people to learn about people's lives in any depth.

For example, I met one Boston teacher who shared a quick tip she'd just learned in a workshop on cultural competence: that her Haitian students would likely defy her authority due to their "culture." She felt more prepared for conflict with students thanks to the workshop. But she had no plans to learn anything from or about her students to complicate that vision, nor any plans to assess the consequences, for them, of her own reactions to them in class.

Similarly, Doug Foley describes a workshop in Iowa where white teachers learned that their Native American students would always be "silent," as a "cultural" thing. Having "learned" this notion of human difference, teachers stopped trying to invite students into conversation and stopped ever asking individual students who were sitting quietly how they were doing. When Doug asked this question of students, he found that some were quiet because they felt isolated or bored, some because they were shy, some because they were struggling with something, and some because they were really annoyed with how their teachers framed them. And some actually weren't that quiet.[13] As Angelina Castagno and Bryan Brayboy also indicate, a deeper "cultural" training would invite educators into a process of *learning from and with* local Native American students and adults, including about past educational experiences and experiences needing attention in their own classrooms.[14] Instead, shallow Culture Talk blocked learning that could improve relationships and instruction.

Particularly for educators working in communities where they didn't grow up, as Christine Sleeter points out, research suggests that ideally, learning about supporting any population of students doesn't occur a priori in a workshop—it occurs through educators' own ongoing community- and school-site inquiry and reflection with the actual people they are serving.[15] Because training instead often offers educators quick "tips" on "cultures" rather than encouraging ongoing learning, training actually sometimes prompts us to feel as though we have no more to learn about the people described, and no more questions to ask about our own behaviors, either. We might leave feeling satisfied that we "learned something about Group X" with just a small time investment, but we risk misunderstanding the complicated young people and families we support—and missing a chance to work together on improving school experiences.

I once saw well-known author Ruby Payne lead a summer Harvard Graduate School of Education workshop on "class" and schools for a diverse crowd of teachers and administrators. Her workshop was full of quick claims about the "culture" of "poverty," like the following:

* "You walked in here and you knew I was middle class. Talk to your neighbor. How did you know that just by looking."

* "In poverty, you have a few things but no material security. After a few generations of that, your decisions are made on three things—relationships, survival, and entertainment."

* "I don't know if you know this, but in poverty one of the rules is 'to be a real man, a real man doesn't push paper.'"

Some educators appreciated this rapid preparation to interact with children and families "of poverty" and lined up for her autograph, but I was pretty appalled by how few facts we requested from Payne. Nobody questioned any of Payne's claims. Instead, we literally nodded along to claims as if they were facts.

I noted that Payne would make a claim and ask a question about a child "in poverty," like "His mother never forgave him for going away to college. Why, do you think?" Then, she'd say, "Talk to your neighbor." We'd have a minute or two to brainstorm explanations with a stranger next to us. Then, she'd pull people back to the full group by repeating, as if fact, a claim about a sentence long. She told us that for poor people, relationships were always more important than school; a slide stated that "middle class" people prioritized "work," "achievement," and "material security."

[handwritten margin note: not all of them]

While Payne was trying to engage issues of class, income, and schooling, I didn't leave prepared to *learn* much of anything from actual families about their diverse relationships, financial situations, ongoing school experiences with educators, or thoughts about college in a joint quest to support specific children better. Instead, I walked away with negative shorthand about the static behaviors of people "in poverty" and tips on how to interact with "them." As Paul Gorski notes, there is no "culture of poverty," just a wide range of experiences of poverty and wealth: "I learned growing up among my Appalachian grandma's relatively poor people [that] there is as much diversity of values and dispositions among poor people as there is between poor and wealthy people."[16] In a critical review of Payne's published writings, Richard Valencia notes similarly that "a communal mindset among the poor simply does not exist."[17]

Inviting more informed and respectful understanding of real people's complex experiences, rather than letting shallow claims stand, is similar to acting like a self-critical anthropologist—a committed learner who humbly learns more from and with fellow humans about their *actual* experiences in various contexts, rather than accepting assumptions from afar about how humans live. I emphasize self-critical because poorly executed research also makes shallow claims about types of people prematurely. Early anthropologists sometimes summed up groups too quickly (often from a distance), overlooked individuality, and even ranked communities as more or less complex.[18] Today, anthropologists honor people in both familiar and unfamiliar settings by assuming that all humans are equally complicated and valuable, and by taking time accordingly to learn about people's everyday lives.[19] To an anthropologist, *everyone,* including herself, is shaped by experiences in complex communities of practice worth understanding. And crucially, skilled anthropologists who study U.S. schools also remember that people don't live on separate planets. Anthropologists of U.S. education see all of us as negotiating a shared society, even while attending carefully to our different experiences in it with the goal of improving schools.

We don't have to feel like formal "researchers" to be learners: this basic commitment to respectful, personal learning alongside equally complex and valued people in often-shared situations is essential to being an educator, too. The goal is to keep learning how to support the real young people one serves. This is why teacher educator Gloria Ladson-Billings, herself trained in anthropology, asks teachers to flip shallow claims by spending time with young people in their communities as a key part of their training, to see youth as multifaceted and successful and to learn how to *keep on* learning to support them.[20] It's why anthropologist Fred Erickson asks educators who too easily sum up "other cultures" to "become ethnographers" of their own school and classroom interactions, as well.[21] Educators thinking more like self-aware anthropologists recognize that they, too, not just kids and families, are shaped by experiences in various communities. Rather than assume difference, they explore actual experience. They learn to consider their own "backgrounds" simply as training in communities of practice, not as inherently preferable or "the norm." And they learn to think critically about their own responses to students and families—and to always evaluate their actions' consequences for kids.

To begin the respectful inquiry that counters shallow claims, we actively counteract a tendency to sum up "other people" by continually asking humbly what we still need to learn. This is particularly important when considering groups we don't "belong to," but it's even important when observing familiar communities. Think to yourself: what routine assumptions do you make about what people do or "care about," without actually knowing or asking? When I teach anthropological methods to educators, I ask them to observe people in a K–12 or college setting and then reread their notes "like Martians," asking self-critically what they have assumed and judged about people's behaviors. I've seen hundreds of educators realize how easily they've described students as "disengaged," for example, with almost no evidence of those students' personal experiences of classrooms. Often, the words people realize are most packed with assumptions are the words they use the most in their work.

Now imagine someone making a claim about an entire "culture's" orientation to school.

Shallow claims about other people's lives need to be challenged with an invitation to inquire—with the goal of better seeing (and respecting, and supporting) actual complex people.

So let's explore some Strategies for inviting inquiry from ourselves and others. As an example, let's try responding to a classic shallow culture claim together:

"Asian parents care about education and so Asians achieve highly."

People in schools nod along to that one all the time, distorting views of "Asians" and non-Asians alike. I want to share how I myself started to go deeper on claims about "Asian" achievement.

An effort to take Culture Talk from shallow to deeper

When I started working at UC San Diego, whose student body was recently recorded as 46 percent "Asian,"[22] I started to hear the script above a lot—from people explaining the campus and in my own head. I realized that even after many years of studying race issues in U.S. schools, I hadn't asked nearly enough about the vast variety of Asian American experiences in those schools. (Here's a group of young people from UCSD demanding deeper   knowledge: http://generasian.org/post/40576467821/18mr-ucsd apsa-i-am-not-your-model.)

In the months before I would explore these issues with students in my own classes, I turned to one source as a starter—the work of researcher Vivian Louie, who has explored a variety of Asian American community experiences with schools on the East Coast. I read a particularly useful chapter she'd written and then emailed her a few questions.[23] I also branched out to read additional secondary sources, including reports published by community organizations (see endnotes).

In this effort to inquire, I started with a first Strategy for taking culture claims from shallow to deeper:

STRATEGY   Challenge nouns. (Insist on exploring variation and complexity inside any community named.)

A noun in a sentence is often where the shallow claim begins. In many claims about "cultures," not only do we forget that people share all sorts of practices across cultures and that we each belong to many "cultures." We forget there is internal diversity within every group we name. This blocks learning about actual kids.

So my first question about the typical shallow claim "Asian parents care about education and so Asians achieve highly" was, where's the evidence that all "Asians" achieve highly?

Think back to Chapters 1 and 2: claims require disaggregation when they're too general to describe an experience or a need. To support young people, we can seek to describe nuance with more precise nouns (and adjectives) *even while* describing any aggregated patterns that people experience. It can be useful starter information to say that almost half of the students getting college degrees via UCSD are "Asian,"[24] even while many other UCSD students are not and countless Asian American students never make it there. It's also crucial to clarify (as I did by asking our campus data staff) that one-third of the undergraduate students who recently self-identified as "Asian" on UCSD forms were international students, based on their visas. Similarly, it's factual starter information to say that only 12 percent of Latinos over age twenty-five in California have a college degree, according to recent data,[25] and that Latinos in California disproportionately attend high-poverty schools that also offer limited access to AP or honors classes—while Asian Americans in California disproportionately go to better resourced schools with white kids, despite many exceptions (see Chapter 2). But it's not sufficiently precise to say that "all Asians achieve highly"—or that Latinos "don't achieve." "It's a constant struggle to educate others, including Asian Americans, about the diversity within the community," said one organizer reacting to overstated claims about "Asian" achievement in 2012. "But we are not a monolith. We have needs."[26]

Vivian noted to me that immigrants moving to the United States from Asia have been "bifurcated" into rich and poor. Those here for generations (before, or despite, exclusion laws) "have had some upward mobility and assimilated." Newer immigrants have included both economically stable professionals (coming, e.g., from East Asia and India), and the very poor, particularly Southeast Asians who "come under refugee resettlement assistance programs." Many of the poorer children struggle in under-resourced schools in low-income neighborhoods. A notable slice of Asian immigrants come undocumented (e.g., from China and India), even as many others come with documentation inviting high professional skills.[27] Exploring the lives of the many Asian students struggling through community colleges further complicates views of exclusively high achieving "Asians."[28] And this information from a student services professional recently flipped a script for me: a significant number of the undocumented students she was supporting were Korean.

Vivian's work also breaks down other overly aggregated claims about "Asians" by looking more closely at the varied economic situations families encounter. For example, she points out that recent Chinese immigrants in a dense new immigrant neighborhood of Boston are not living the same lives as middle-class, third-generation Chinese people in New York City's wealthy suburbs, nor achieving as highly on average. Low-income Chinese Americans working in lower-income food or garment industries cannot pay for the extras that higher-income Chinese Americans in suburbs can, and often do not "achieve" as highly either. Vivian pointed out that variety in school achievement also exists within families that share the same general economic situation. Vivian grew up in New York City's Chinatown and in Queens, New York, with parents who worked in the garment and restaurant industries. Her brothers didn't go to four-year college, while she went on to Harvard. She was the outlier in their immediate family.

So you can always ask people to rethink their nouns. Again, the solution is to keep asking when claims are precise enough and when they are not—because imprecise claims leave us unequipped to support young people properly.

Even a claim about an average pattern needs precision to be accurate. And even if a "cultural" community on average *experiences* something shared doesn't mean that community's "culture" *causes* the experience.[29]

So let's get to the verbs.

STRATEGY   Challenge verbs. (Insist on exploring the complex experiences masked by quick causal claims about any "culture's" behavior regarding schools.)

Big, static claims about what entire "cultures" *do* regarding schools—particularly, claims by people who don't consider themselves part of the group described—can keep us from seeing real people, because in reality, actual complex people respond in a variety of ways to specific situations they encounter in specific contexts. Skilled researchers committed to improving schools strive to make more nuanced claims about what people in any community do and experience regarding schools. Stacey Lee explored how Asian American students had a wide variety of reactions to specific schools, teachers, and peers;[30] Gil Conchas noted how specific K–12 school programs shaped Latino youths' various reactions to specific schools;[31] Contreras and Contreras investigated how specific college supports affected *which* Latinos made it to bachelor's degrees;[32] Prudence Carter learned from black youth how *some* youth attached to specific schools and teachers as they forged school identities, while others didn't; Pamela Perry learned from white youth struggling with a range of "white" identities in schools.[33] All these more nuanced claims about young people offer ideas for improving student supports. Big comparative claims about how entire cultures handle school mask all this nuance.

In shallow Culture Talk, verbs also often contain simplified, *comparative* explanations of people's actions and outcomes that we can challenge with an invitation to inquiry. For example, the verb "care" commonly appears in scripted claims about *which* "cultures" "care" about their children's education. While "caring" about young people is obviously a critical thing to do, the real problem is that comments about *which groups* "care" are almost always paired with explicit or implied claims about which groups purportedly do "not care," as in:

"Asian parents care about education and so Asians achieve highly."

"Latino and Black parents don't really care about education and so their kids don't achieve."

The verb "care" in these phrases blocks learning. It both presumes parent motivations and offers a shorthand *explanatory claim* that simply explains school achievement as the result *of* those presumed motivations. Such claims imply that the whole group is lining up in a function hall hearing instructions from leaders, or imply that kids just achieve based on what parents presumably tell kids at the dinner table. In addition to their implied or explicit rankings of "cultures," then (which often subtly position "white" people as the norm), the key problem with such "cultural" claims is one we've seen before in this book: *they overlook all the interactions and other players involved.* No child gets vaulted to the graduation stage through parental motivation alone. Suggestions that they do belie the full set of interactions in opportunity contexts that add up over time to students' outcomes, and stunt educators' efforts to *improve* those interactions in partnership with students and families.

For starters, I call such verbs "blobby" because they murk up the action described. What does "caring" about "education" actually look like, and where's the evidence that some parents don't care about it? Research shows that all typically functioning parents hope for their children's success. There is no evidence that any group "cares more" in any absolute sense. Educators need to explore how various parents play out their caring as they interact with their children and other adults in a given context.[34] We often judge "caring" after tallying who comes to school-day events, overlooking the parents who are caring by working many hours to pay rent or buy food and clothes, or by driving, cooking, and talking to children about their lives.[35] Even when parents critique a given schooling experience, they often demonstrate how much they care about the education experience for their children,[36] but we rarely sum up such behavior as "caring." Shallow Culture Talk thus masks parents' actual efforts to support their children. Deeper Culture Talk insists on learning from those efforts.

Shallow Culture Talk verbs also often reference a timeless, vague present ("Asian parents care . . .") rather than more precisely describing actual experiences in actual places. Gutiérrez and Rogoff offer a thoughtful suggestion to improve on such static verbs: we might speak of children's or families' experiences or behaviors in the past tense ("Armenian families in this community often have experienced X") rather than in the timeless present so often used for Culture Talk ("Armenians do X"). They argue that this requires people to cite information actually observed, rather than "too quickly assuming a timeless truth" to any claim.[37]

THINK / DISCUSS

Can you think of any culture claim typically stated in the timeless present in an education community you know, that could be stated more precisely in the past tense to describe something people have actually experienced?

Beyond challenging simplified verbs like "care" when they keep us from really seeing people's behaviors, how else can we go beyond shallow claims about who "cares" and doesn't "care" about school and how that "caring" "causes" student achievement?

STRATEGY   Emphasize that no group lives in a bubble. (Insist on looking at group members in ongoing interaction with people *outside* "the group.")

Whenever we talk about education outcomes, we need to hang on to the idea that no group achieves in a bubble. Consider earlier chapters: school achievement is always the result of people interacting in opportunity contexts shared in some way with people outside as well as inside "the group," including educators. Analyzing those interactions is critical to improving schools: if educators don't discuss those interactions, we can't support the young people we're describing. So let's take a bit more time on this strategy.

I use two images to convey the idea of pursuing deeper, more informed claims about any "group's" interactions in context (including with folks outside "the group"). I call the first "peeling the onion" and the second, "cutting open the paper towel roll."

An onion image demonstrates that any story has many layers under the surface. Shallow culture claims often just describe and purport to explain the surface of a phenomenon, by explaining, in isolation, a single observed action just involving people inside a group. At the high school I taught at and then researched, for example, people often pointed out privately that black students were disproportionately wandering in the school's hallways. To explain that phenomenon, they then quietly blamed black students and families for "culturally" not "caring enough about school." To peel that onion—that is, to go deeper to understand why kids were in the hallway— once I became a graduate student researcher, I asked students themselves what experiences had them in the hallway (boredom and overreactive discipline by teachers topped the list); I observed in others' classrooms how (predominantly white) teachers disproportionately ejected black students into the halls; I saw how security guards habitually let these students wander, often for hours; and I learned from the non-black students who typically went off campus to cut class rather than wander in the halls until they were noticed.

I could have done all of the same things as a teacher. By broadening the analysis to include people beyond black hall-wanderers only (like school adults!), I was just looking more accurately at group members in ongoing interaction with people *outside* "the group" and so, recognizing interactions that needed attention. (Researching similar dynamics through conversations with both students and adults, Diamond and Lewis found that black students in a suburban school were routinely stopped in the hallways by adults and overdisciplined—another version of school adults shaping students' fates, and one similarly requiring attention.[38])

I also call such more accurately inclusive analysis "cutting open the paper towel roll." Let me explain what I mean.

We noted in Chapter 3 that people often explain student achievement reductively as just a result of what's assumedly in a child's head, ignoring the child's interactions in a context with many other people. There were lots of people involved in your SAT score, even while you might not always credit them! To illustrate this, imagine looking through a cardboard paper towel roll at a child's head. You can't see anything but the head. (When I teach, I usually demonstrate this on a student with an actual paper towel roll to make my point.)

In scripted culture claims like "Asian parents care about education and so. . . ," people look through a paper towel roll at a given "culture" and explain student achievement as just a result of assumed activity inside the group. For deeper analysis, we expand the group that we are analyzing. Imagine cutting open your paper towel roll with scissors so you can see the fuller context around young people and families, like suddenly seeing all of the other folks involved in black students' wandering the hallways at my school. It's another version of cleaning our lenses—this time, so we can see and discuss interactions with multiple actors that affect young people's school achievement. Sometimes we open the paper towel roll to see and discuss people interacting in broad opportunity contexts, as we did in Chapter 2; we'll do that again momentarily. Sometimes we open it to see and discuss consequential interactions inside schools, particularly with educators themselves.

Inside schools, kids don't achieve in a bubble: all the people in our Foundational Image (page 10) react to them. And not only do adults often frame some children as "smarter" or more likely to succeed than others, as we've seen; school communities also reward children for doing things "correctly," and "correctness" is determined by the adults in control of schools. If you know how to raise your hand at the right time and give a particular type of desired answer expected by a teacher, you get rewards.[39] A big Standard English vocabulary or the ability to read is typically rewarded in U.S. schools, but you don't tend to get rewards if you come to school reading a lot of words in Portuguese. Middle-class teachers tend to give more points to "isn't" than "ain't" in a typical classroom, even while "ain't" might get a teenager more points with his peers.[40] And there are often racialized, classed, linguistic, and gendered patterns to *who* gets punished or rewarded in schools, in part because teachers disproportionately grew up in whiter, more monolingual, and financially resourced communities of practice and public school students disproportionately don't. Educators tend (even unconsciously) to reward children whose behaviors look like those valued in the homes (cultures) the educators grew up in and the schools (cultures) the educators successfully got through. Fred Erickson notes that other "gatekeepers" to education opportunities—like school counselors—often offer those opportunities more readily to students whose behaviors signal a shared "background" with the gatekeeper.[41] Lewis and Diamond found that even in a homogeneously middle-class school, educators particularly disciplined black students wearing baggy clothing that was merely *associated* with "urban" youth.[42] Shallow Culture Talk blocks attention to these educator reactions. Educators going deeper *question* their reactions to children, and ask *why* some communities of practice should be valued over others when this punishes so many so unnecessarily.

Going deeper, Lisa Delpit points out a broader "culture of power" operating in schools: "those who are in power" in society have more power to determine which behaviors (and which children) get rewarded with school success.[43] Ray McDermott opens the paper towel roll even further, asking educators to question a larger cultural assumption that only some can "achieve" and some must "fail."[44] And I'd remind us that all the schooltalk scripts we've been analyzing—and the opportunity contexts we've considered—operate each day in U.S. schools as well, shaping the ways educators respond to young people every day. Educators pushing past shallow Culture Talk about students and families in isolation seek to support *all* communities' children by analyzing their own actions as part of "the actual interactions among actual people in shared opportunity contexts that contribute to children's school achievement over time."[45]

Deeper Culture Talk points out that parents have consequential interactions outside the bubble, too. Not only can parents with more money buy their children more opportunities, as we've seen; in a snowball of cumulative advantage, parents whose prior experiences already align with educators' more easily prep their kids for school rewards. For example, Annette Lareau argues that middle-class parents who have themselves been relatively successful in schools tend to train their children purposefully in behaviors that they know will get rewarded by middle-class educators. (She finds this across race lines.) As one example, a predominantly upper-middle-class school system near where I live warns parents to send their children to kindergarten already knowing their alphabet. Parents who prepare kindergartners accordingly help them show up with a real advantage. College-educated parents can then more easily prep their children for rewards from colleges, too.

Schools give "points" to particular child behaviors; some parents, knowing this, can prepare their children to get those "points." So, equity-minded educators opening the paper towel roll *with parents* often focus on discussing "the culture of power" with them directly, by discussing how to navigate access to things like AP, reading programs, parent-teacher meetings, or preschool.[46] Crucially, in all such dialogues, equity-minded educators simultaneously respect the childrearing and home learning parents are supporting already, and the skills youth are building at home.[47]

Researchers also urge that educators open the paper towel roll with students, for example by critically analyzing which behaviors get them "points" in which settings. For example, Prudence Carter points out a cultural issue worth analyzing with youth and educators alike: educators often react to youths' "non-dominant" dress or speech styles inaccurately, as if they signal lesser potential or a non-academic orientation. Carter urges educators instead to learn more about the styles students value and to "engage students in explicit conversations about how different cultural currencies—languages and dialects, codes of conduct, mannerisms, and physical presentations of selves—pay off in various communities." Through this deeper Culture Talk, children and youth can feel encouraged to become powerful "multicultural navigators" who are "fluent in different cultural and stylistic codes" and can tap each style for "situational use" where it is "advantageous."[48] For their part, educators thinking more deeply about the value of all cultures' practices can also welcome more community skill sets into schools, as a resource for all (see Chapter 7): Django Paris and H. Samy Alim argue that the ability to navigate *many* "cultures" is the skill set that will pay off most in our diverse society.[49] Relatedly, Angela Valenzuela urges educators to think of their work as adding school-specific skills to students' existing repertoires rather than as a process of "subtracting" the skills and behaviors students come in with.[50] This both-and, rather than either-or, approach to succeeding across a blend of equally valued community *and* school "cultures" pervades many researchers' (and communities') advice for educators working to respect all "cultures." In essence, educators invite community strengths and knowledge into the building.[51]

In sum, claims about achievement as a result just of culture-specific parental or youth "caring" mask how student and parent experiences in schools are forged in ongoing interactions with schools' and educators' systems of "points." While culture scripts often train educators' eyeballs on others only, then, educators have to look critically at *their own* reactions to students and parents in order to support children. Eugene Garcia tells a story about one such consequential interaction that affected his family deeply. His Spanish-speaking mother brought his sister to school on the first day, and the monolingual teacher asked Eugene's sister what her name was. "Ciprianita," the sister replied. The teacher tried unsuccessfully to pronounce the name, then asked, "Can I call you Elsie? It's my favorite name." Eugene recalls that to his sister, that moment "represented the moment when she was told to leave her full self at home"— and to Eugene's mom, it marked the end of happy visits to the school. Eugene's communities of practice then diverged rather than combining. At home, Eugene recalls, his mom always emphasized the importance of education. But the incident permanently strained her relations with *that school*, by devaluing her family's most basic practice of naming children. She stopped coming to the building.[52]

So, imagine colleagues at school then noting Eugene's mom's absence from Parents Night and saying, "Latino parents just don't care about school." They'd be overlooking the interactions actually keeping her at home—and missing a chance to learn how she supports her children.

Shallow Culture Talk blocks learning that could improve schools. One key for educators engaging in deeper Culture Talk, then, is to always recognize how learning more about families' and students' experiences outside *and inside* their schools could improve their own work with students. As Ray McDermott puts it, "breakthrough occurs when we realize that 'their' situation is 'ours' as well."[53]

To lay groundwork for talking with parents, students and colleagues about improving interactions across communities of practice, anthropologist Fred Erickson asks educators to document, for one day, every time they enter a different "social situation"—and to consider critically how the speech styles, power relations, and expectations of each setting affect them. (Erickson also asks educators to remember the norms of a family dinner in their childhood household, to consider another community of practice that shaped them.)[54] Educators then can better consider critically how (and why) they privilege particular behaviors in the classroom situation they control, and how they might welcome a broader range. Dorothy Steele and Becki Cohn-Vargas ask teachers to question their own culturally primed reactions to any student's behaviors in class, by asking *why* some behaviors make them "uncomfortable" (and whether they should) and what they might learn from students instead:

* "Do any of [this student's] learning behaviors make me uncomfortable? For example, do I feel she is too loud or too quiet?"
* "What assumptions am I making about the reasons for her behavior?"
* "Are there any alternative explanations that I have not considered?"
* "Am I making similar assumptions about other students' behaviors?"
* "How can I respond differently?"[55]

Before assuming "cultural" difference, educators also can question scripted paper-towel-roll assumptions about the "culture"-specific "reasons" behind students' behaviors, by remembering that students too are complex individuals who "behave" in school in ongoing interactions with many other people—and by considering how they might not yet understand a student's interactions with school adults.

And in *Why Race and Culture Matter in Schools*, Tyrone Howard suggests that educators can ask themselves "Questions for Understanding Student Culture" like these. The questions again really emphasize educators' own need to learn more about (rather than assume!) specific students' experiences across various communities of practice, while considering their own:

* What are the expectations and experiences my students have had with school?
* What are the factors that shape students' understandings of school?
* What do I know about my students' home and community life?
* How can I learn more about my students' home and community life?
* Who are the individuals that influence my students most?
* What are the tools, skills, and practices that students use to navigate their homes and communities?
* What are the contexts that seem to motivate my students to learn?
* How do my students express themselves in different settings?

✳ What are the topics, issues, and themes that generate high levels of student engagement, effort, and interest?

✳ What are the cultural practices that seem to be most common among my students? How and where were they acquired?

✳ What, if any, contradictions or tensions seem to exist between the cultural practices and traditions that my students bring to the classroom and the practices and traditions that I operate on?[56]

The goal of all such questions is deeper learning about real, respected lives: to encourage educators to learn more about (and build on) young people's experiences in various communities, to consider their own such experiences, to avoid any premature assumptions about a young person's "cultural practices," and to consider their own reactions to young people as extremely consequential.

In schools of any demographic, inviting such deeper inquiry about people's actual experiences is always the key to schooltalk that helps educators *see* the actual young people and families they're paid to support. And at some point, we have to actually engage with others in the deeper learning. An initial commitment to learning is the key: in their "Leading for Diversity" study, Rosemary Henze and her fellow researchers highlighted school administrators who had promoted "positive interethnic relations" and helped make schools "safe places where students and staff were respected for their diverse backgrounds."[57] Each leader modeled efforts to learn more deeply from and about the complex communities they were serving. One elementary principal in the D.C. area, a white woman, spoke of the importance of simply responding to a black parent's invitation to join her on a neighborhood walk. Appearing publicly as a willing and respectful learner opened "the doors" to ongoing learning experiences with individuals and in the community that she could tap to improve her school:

[The parent] popped in and said, "Want to see the neighborhood?" and I'm ready to say to her, "Does it look like I want to see the neighborhood?" (laughter) I want to unpack these boxes. I said, "Yeah, I would like to." and I'm thinking, God, make it quick. Well it wasn't going to be quick. That was the best move I ever made. Because by virtue of me being with her and being seen that first time, that's why all the doors opened the second time when [I went out for another neighborhood walk].[58]

Similarly, Gloria Ladson-Billings recalls a transformative moment in her own teaching as a new black teacher in a white Irish American neighborhood in Philadelphia: she went to a funeral for a student's parent and stayed to talk and eat. "The word spread through the community that I had honored and respected them," she recalled. "Things turned almost on a dime."[59]

Each of these inquiries began when people expressed a basic willingness to respectfully learn more about and from the complex people they shared schools with, in order to better support students. We'll pursue such learning in the rest of this book, as something educators just do daily to support young people! But to conclude this chapter, let me finish sharing my own much more preliminary effort to learn—to tackle that classic Culture Talk claim, "Asian parents care about education and so Asians achieve highly." In my case, initial inquiry tapping secondary sources and a researcher friend just got me started in learning; it just set the stage for ongoing learning with specific students, families, and teachers where I live and work. That is, my initial inquiry (which first peeled the onion on some broader experiences shared by many individuals in opportunity contexts) did not unearth the full "range of experiences had by Asian American children in schools,"[60] nor introduce me to the complex individuals in my classes (see Chapter 6). I share it simply to demonstrate how *acknowledging* one's own need to learn—and then seeking even slightly deeper knowledge about everyday lives in real places—can *begin* a process of correcting shallow culture claims about how "groups" behave in relation to schools. You'll see me using all three of our strategies so far—learning to get more precise with nouns and verbs, and struggling to clarify how no one achieves in a bubble. Let me just start to tell a story of people struggling to thrive in a shared nation, through interactions with people outside the group. Many students in my own classes—Asian American and not—have said they valued learning the same initial information, as it started to deepen shallow views of "Asians" that had affected them all.

Peeling the onion/opening the paper towel roll on shallow claims about "Asian achievement"

As usual, thorough schooltalk requires some history. As I asked her to talk through the "Asian achievement" script with me based on her work learning from students and families, Vivian reminded me by email that most

Asians were excluded from the United States for generations through the exclusionary immigration laws we first mentioned in Chapter 1. But those few Asian Americans (primarily East Asians) already in the United States could now "make some gains, albeit in very restricted fields." And after World War II, Vivian noted further, "the opportunity structure opened up for many except blacks"; second- and third-generation Asian Americans became more integrated in workplaces and housing. Vivian then pointed out a key year shaping today's opportunity context for "Asians": 1965, when U.S. immigration policy finally lifted restrictive quotas favoring Northern and Western European immigrants and opened up more immigration to the United States from many different parts of the world, including Asia. Some new Asian families came poor, as refugees or undocumented immigrants. Also arriving for the first time were "a lot of highly educated, highly skilled folks" from Asia, as Vivian put it (particularly East Asia)—because U.S. immigration policy privileged skilled workers.[61]

I found that Wikipedia actually stated this history pretty clearly, so I'm citing it with Vivian's blessing:

> The Hart-Celler Act of 1965 eliminated highly restrictive "national origins" quotas, designed, among other things, to restrict immigration of those of Asian racial background. The new system, based on skills and family connections to U.S. residents, enabled significant immigration from every nation in Asia, which led to dramatic and ongoing changes in the Asian American population. As a result of these population changes, the formal and common understandings of what defines Asian American have expanded to include more of the peoples with ancestry from various parts of Asia. Because of their more recent immigration, new Asian immigrants also have had different educational, economic and other characteristics than early 20th century immigrants. . . .
>
> Asian American immigrants have a significant percentage of individuals who have already achieved professional status, a first among immigration groups.[62]

Vivian indicated the need for even more specific nouns: in the aggregate, even when new Asian immigrants tended to arrive without much actual *savings*, more individuals tended to come with higher levels of *schooling* and with lower rates of immigration-related family separation—in comparison to many Latin American immigrants, for example.[63] Vivian described this class complexity carefully this way, specifically comparing the Chinese and Dominican immigrants' experiences she'd explored:

> This is not to say that Dominicans who have migrated to the United States are not diverse in social class origins. . . . Nor do I mean to suggest that the Chinese enclaves are absent poverty and inequality when both are clearly present. . . . It is to say that the middle-class professional stream is not as pronounced among the Dominican migration and that Dominican enclaves here certainly do not have the kind of transnational and ethnic wealth as the Chinese enclaves do.[64]

Vivian helped me get still more precise with my nouns and verbs, by peeling another layer of the onion regarding some Chinese immigrant experiences specifically. She pointed out that wealthier Chinese people have often extended a hand to poorer Chinese who arrive, by steering new arrivals toward neighborhoods with higher-performing schools. As Vivian explained by email, this happens through "the parents' social networks with fellow Asian immigrants or even more distant second-generation kin—at work, through the ethnic media, e.g., newspapers, radio." While the Dominican families Vivian met "also [had] social capital from their parents," their U.S. relationships linked them to a more "homogeneously poor community" less connected to well-resourced schools.[65] Parents also navigated the U.S. systems they encountered in part based on the school systems they attended in in their native countries. Vivian found in her research that while some Chinese immigrant parents in Boston told new arrivals about finding the best public schools, for example, many Dominican parents in Boston shared information about the best Catholic schools because in the "DR," Catholic schools offered the best opportunities to learn.

Through concrete experiences in immigrant information networks, Vivian argues, Chinese families' children often end up *less likely* to attend the under-resourced schools disproportionately serving black and Latino students and more likely to attend better-resourced public schools with white students. (More precisely, Vivian pointed out, some families come to live in more affluent communities near or among whites, while other families do not have the financial resources to live in these areas but learn how to access those better-resourced schools.) Even while many Asian families stay living in low-income communities, she argued further, *in the aggregate,*

Asian immigrants now are often less residentially segregated in high-poverty areas than other "non-white" immigrant groups, and this has implications for schooling and "overall group resources." This isn't about "caring" more or less: through specific interactions in the segregated U.S. context (see Chapter 2), many immigrants from the Dominican Republic end up living in lower-income communities and attending less-resourced schools.

Vivian opened the paper towel roll further for me, pointing out that the connections immigrants keep to home countries matter. For example, she noted that even if families in U.S. ethnic Chinese communities are poor in the U.S. context, Chinese investors from abroad and "well-to-do Chinese American investors" are helping to shape and reshape banking and other institutions affecting many of those families, including funding language/ test preparatory schools or other neighborhood resources for kids. *East Asian* economic growth thus means more transnational investment in U.S. ethnic Chinese communities (and, of course, helps produce more "Asian" international students from China able to attend universities like mine). In the Dominican cases Vivian explored, "the transfer of wealth tends to be one-directional," with families' extra wages sent back to the Dominican Republic rather than "large flows of capital" coming from the home country to the U.S. to build businesses here.[66]

Vivian peeled another layer via email, noting that the test-prep schools or language academies that exist in various Chinese American immigrant communities (sometimes funded by wealth back home or investments from middle-class Chinese Americans who do not necessarily live in those communities, she noted), "don't exist just because of some Asian 'pushing' thing"—that scripted notion of Asian "caring." Instead, they get created because parents try to apply strategies from their prior context to the new. "Even though there is a big deal made about how Asians in Asia prize education," she wrote, "the systems of education in Asia are very stratified—they are very tracked, with entrance based on examination scores (particularly national exams to get into university). Your score determines where you get admitted into. Cram schools (themselves stratified by quality) help students prepare for these exams." So, she explained, many Chinese adults arrive in the U.S. having already successfully weathered "highly stratified national systems of education where only a limited number of folks get into university, based on an examination system"—that is, competitive, test-driven schooling like the United States'.

No group "achieves" in a bubble: "Asian" children then encounter schools'

and educators' preexisting systems of racialized stereotypes, scripts, and
"points." Vivian noted to me that "Asians encounter different expectations
when they *get* to school because of preexisting 'model minority' myths." She
writes that while Asian American children often encounter educators who
expect them to be "on it" and "naturally quiet," for example, Latino children more often encounter teachers who expect them to be disengaged.[67]
Because of such scripted educator expectations, Vivian noted via email,
some Asian American children may be placed more often by educators in
high opportunity programs within schools—including the few such opportunities available in low-income neighborhood schools, when they attend
such schools. (Simultaneously, Stacey Lee points out, Asian American kids
not in such programs can get framed as "bad kids."[68])

"Model minority" myths are shallow claims with particular force. They
started brewing after World War II and then 1965, as observers purport-
ing that "Asians" just "worked harder," "cared more," or were "smarter"
not only ignored the fact that other immigrants on average had arrived
less professionally skilled but also continuously positioned "Asians" as
"profoundly different" culturally from other groups then organizing for
more civil rights. "The purposeful ways in which Asians were heralded for
their success was a direct attack against African Americans in their outspo-
ken quest for equality in the 1960s and against a critique of institutional
and structural racism," argue Ng, Lee, and Pak.[69] "Model minority" claims
also masked actual barriers for Asians. For one, they masked internal economic diversity: as Vivian noted, for example, even while "working-class
'Asian' immigrant families might get information about and access to the
better public schools" from other parents, language barriers often mean
that "working-class parents also cannot go into schools to intervene on
behalf of their children (and are not that effective if they do)." Vivian
also noted that many working-class immigrants cannot really help children with schoolwork *except* through ethnically run cram schools set up
by others in their communities, which kids can attend "only if they have
the financial resources." Wesley Yang and Margaret Chin each point out
further that many immigrant parents also can't offer dinner-table access
to knowledge or habits that might be rewarded in the careers young people try to access *after* schools, nor network their children to the leaders
already running organizations. After disproportionate college level academic success and initial employment, Yang and Chin each note, "Asians"
in the United States often aren't rewarded with top jobs or management,

instead hitting a "bamboo ceiling."[70] And in Mia Tuan's terms, Asian Americans even get positioned as "forever foreign"—not "American," no matter how long people have lived in the United States.[71] Indeed, Ng, Lee, and Pak note that in the highly racialized United States, any narrative about "Asians" and education—like this one, perhaps—risks reinforcing that "foreign" positioning.

All these barriers and experiences are ignored in shallow claims about "model minorities"—as are the complexities and layered identities of each individual "Asian" child.

Now think about being a young person who has to encounter myths of his or her "model minority"-ness in school. Asian American students in my own classes have asked an important question about such Culture Talk: are such myths actually less harmful than racialized myths about one's likely "disengagement"?

Shallow claims oversimplify actual people and block the learning crucial for informed student support. All families and all youth are complicated people forging responses to specific opportunity systems, actual schools, and educators in real time. Parents from all "groups" are struggling to support kids through an often harshly skewed system of "points." As Vivian summed up, "There's a huge structural situation real people navigate. And we need to learn about that."

Vivian ended our email exchange with a particularly memorable point about viewing complex people in context. She noted that any "pushing" by the "Asian" parents who disproportionately arrive highly educated or middle class is actually not exclusively "Asian." "We expect middle class parents to push their kids (to keep class privilege), right?" she said. "Those practices might look different depending on context, but they have the same goal—pushing the children towards the success the parents have already experienced."

That's the final thing we tend to forget in shallow culture claims: how in many fundamental ways, humans just aren't that different.

> STRATEGY   Remember that human beings share behaviors across cultural groups. (Don't imagine "cultures" as overly different—instead, learn more about shared experiences as well as different ones.)

Everyone works to survive or support their children in a given opportunity context, using skills from the other contexts they've experienced and whatever connections they can get. All parents and kids navigate an educational system easier if they can access critical resources or tap opportunity information from others, or leverage their own related experiences. People who do not show up at well-resourced schools with such aligned experiences or prior successes "may be just as motivated, full of hope, and willing to push," Vivian said; the question is whether next experiences in schools and opportunity contexts then support students toward success.

So let's conclude with a basic call for learning. To *more accurately see* complex young people and their families, simply questioning any shallow claims about young people and families is the first step. Actually setting forth to learn more about specific people's experiences in specific (often shared!) places is the next (see Action Assignments)—particularly if we don't "belong" to the communities learned about, but even if we do. In communities we're less familiar with, respectful learning from and about real people in order to improve student support doesn't require exhausting individuals as unpaid "teachers" on entire communities through ongoing personal queries. Indeed, for some grounding, we can learn a lot first from secondary and primary sources created by people who have labored already to tell thorough stories about individual and collective experiences past and present. To go deeper with any group of individuals, we can set forth respectfully to learn informally by spending time with the adults and young people around us. One teacher in my class admitted that "I have heard, time and again, teachers talk about how certain groups of students have less support at home. I feel that *I* need to have a deeper understanding of the communities my students come from." She planned to finally walk across the street to a tutoring program run by a community organization, to begin to learn simply through meeting tutors and parents at pickup.

And critically, truly deep learning about any people's experiences inside and outside schools is continuous: quick shortcuts, especially with communities we don't yet "belong to," actually avoid depth and don't help. For example, Leisy Wyman and Grant Kashatok (respectively white and native Yup'ik educators with deep experience in rural Alaska) point out that educators need to build sustained learning relationships with various students and families, and go beyond just quickly asking one person in a community to describe their whole community. Any given individual is herself not fully informed about everyone else's experience, and "insiders may also feel insulted when they are asked to provide quick, oversimplified portrayals of their own communities."[72] (In classrooms, such "spotlighting" asking an individual to speak for all often harmfully assumes "group" knowledge: as one student told researcher Dorinda Carter Andrews, "I guess they [teachers] assume just cuz we're Black that we know everything about Africa."[73]) Teresa McCarty urges educators and students to move beyond simplistic ideas about "Native Americans" by reading community narratives and inviting community visitors to class; simultaneously, she cautions that "teachers can help students understand that they should not expect one person to be representative of all Native Americans, or to be the expert on everything Native American." As Joseph Bruchac puts it, "there are so many stories, as many as the leaves on trees."[74] In every school, we can remember that every family and every student leads a complex, ongoing life across multiple communities of practice: in "The Danger of a Single Story," Chimamanda Ngozi Adichie emphasizes similarly that each individual inside every community has many layered stories worth learning about.[75] Christine Sleeter suggests similarly that teacher preparation experiences need to go beyond "eye opening" quick exposures to new community settings (which actually can reinforce stereotypes), to ongoing learning about specific people's everyday lives in those settings and in schools.[76] And I debated a key issue once with a group of multicultural education experts sensitive to educators' time constraints: can an educator ever rest satisfied with *prior* deep knowledge she's collected about young people? If you've taught many Samoan students or seventh graders, for example, can you just feel confident in your knowledge about "Samoans" or seventh graders? Folks in the room emphatically said no. Equity-oriented educators *keep* learning about specific young people's ongoing experiences in and out of schools, so they can keep honing their own efforts and respond as things come up. As Jacqueline Jordan Irvine puts it, "responsive teachers" *continually* "modify their knowledge and training" by continuing to learn about the actual students in front of them—as well as "by devoting attention to classroom contexts and individual student needs and experiences."[77] If learning about individuals, school experiences, and community realities isn't continuous, research has shown, educators risk reverting to scripted ideas about "types of people."[78]

So, how do we make education communities places where people learn routinely and continuously about the experiences and needs of the complex, valuable young people they serve, in order to continually improve their own supports to students?

That's the goal of the rest of the book.

Part 2 sets us on this overall schooltalk redesign task:

Help people routinely get informed about the experiences young people are having and the supports specific young people need to keep developing their full human talents. Then, insist that young people get those supports.

We will call this designing schooltalk infrastructure for equity.

ACTION ASSIGNMENTS

1. Ask a young person or colleague to consider a "cultural group" that they have thought or talked about in their own work or school experience. Consider together some typical claims about that "group." Then ask yourselves: were those ideas shallow, or deeply informed? What did you truly understand about the experiences of the people in question, inside and outside of schools? What information would you need to learn to have a deeper, more informed conversation?

   Together, brainstorm one step you or they might take to start getting to know members of a particular community you feel underinformed about, slightly better. If you are a teacher, it might mean asking families or youth one question about their experiences in schools (including with you), or meeting a family on their "home turf." If you work in another aspect of the profession or are a student, it might be going to one community event or meeting, or simply having a conversation with an individual. It might mean reading a narrative or seeing a film made by members of the community as a starter. Just remember that each person is a multifaceted individual who belongs to multiple communities of practice, just like you do!

   Don't assume that a quick glimpse of a community is a substitute for ongoing learning, either; it may in fact reinforce shallow thinking. Wyman and Kashatok suggest ongoing learning through "many channels." For example, teachers hoping to improve their work with students can just start a learning process with home visits ("teachers should explain that they want to learn more about their students' backgrounds in order to become better teachers" and "present themselves as learners ready to appreciate the strengths found in everyday practices," not position themselves like "tourists fascinated with 'exotic' customs"). (As one example, Fred Erickson asked educators to imagine life inside a student's local home, then go visit it and meet actual people—and finally, to compare their assumptions to their actual experiences. Erickson found that after thoughtfully visiting and debriefing, educators started to replace "one dimensional," deficit-focused views of families with "multidimensional" views of actual "people" with "hopes and concerns, ideas and opinions."[79]) Wyman and Kashatok also suggest that educators can learn by attending "community events that are open to outsiders," after checking in with someone who is running or attending the event; by starting to learn a local language; or by participating in local activities like sports teams or choirs. Their full chapter in *Everyday Antiracism* offers great guidance on "getting to know."[80] Wyman added to me via email that any effort to "get to know" a community needs to consider community vulnerabilities—like anxieties about documentation and deportation, and exposure more generally—and slowly build trust. (We'll explore these issues further in Chapters 6 and 7.) And remember—"getting to know" any community member might mean learning more about their interactions with folks "outside the group," including with you.

2. Try one of the options you brainstormed above. Then, discuss:

> What were the barriers you expected to encounter in this initial or small effort to "get to know" members of this community?

> What did you learn in your initial effort, about people's actual complex experiences? Did you learn anything about individual experiences, or about people "belonging" to multiple communities of practice simultaneously? Did you realize anything about your own experiences, or notice gaps in your knowledge base?

> How might personal interaction, versus written "sources" or films on the community, help you and *not* help you understand actual people? For example, a Latina educator in one of my classes watched a film about Navajo communities and had this reaction:

> > "This documentary film does provide a good background on this history and some of the Navajo people's cultural and

spiritual beliefs. However, clearly the film itself is limited in scope and is not made by the Navajos themselves, despite numerous first-person narratives. Given the great variability within groups, I would never assume that the film captures my current students' "culture(s)." . . . I will continue to educate myself by looking for work coming out of the community itself. Rather than make any assumptions about my Navajo students based on any film representations, I think that simply having a conversation individually with each one of my students would give me more insights about their actual life experiences and how I could support them in my classroom."

> Think: what's one thing you could do to learn a bit more about the experiences of people in this community, without taxing people from the community as unpaid "teachers" for you?

> How would you start to shift any typical conversation about this community where you work, if needed? What is one aspect you would improve on first, and why?

3. Think of a simplistic claim someone has made about a "cultural group" or community of practice you belong to. Think to yourself: what information or personal story would you share with that person to help them pursue deeper understanding? Would you "open the paper towel roll" to help them see your interactions (or your parents') with anyone outside "your group"? Would you demonstrate to them how multiple communities of practice "intersect" in your life? Would you invite them to some learning experience along with you?

4. Try to turn one gold nugget idea or fact from this chapter into a #school-talking tool that lots of other people could learn from. For example, create a poster or PowerPoint slide, short video, or other multimedia image publicly sharing that gold nugget quote or idea. To accompany your main message, create a brief user's guide of five related information points or ideas from this chapter that can help users be more fully informed about the issue at hand and have a productive conversation sparked by your tool. See Chapter 1, pages 65–66, for more instructions.

For example, how about these posters:

See Me: We all "contain multitudes."
—Walt Whitman

See Me: Learn the history that brought us
each here to this shared room.

See Me: Get to know me before you explain
my achievement, my motivation, or my parents.

The real poster series mentioned in the chapter is online here: http://generasian.org/post/40576467821/18mr-ucsdapsa-i-am-not-your-model.

5. Find an educator or young person who you feel is schooltalking for equity in their Culture Talk. Document (with permission) and share (#schooltalking) some example of their work—a photo, a video, an image, a quote from them, or something they have produced.

More schooltalk scenarios

THINK / DISCUSS

Think about someone you know who often repeats a scripted claim about a "culture" he or she does not seem to belong to. At the Try Tomorrow level, how would you challenge a noun or verb the person typically uses, "peel the onion" to help him or her see people in context, or invite the person into a learning experience that might help him or her rethink that scripted claim? Practice a response or invitation in a role-play with a friend. Consider a Strategy and a Core Tension behind it.

THINK / DISCUSS

In an email one day about "Asian Americans" at the University of California, my colleague Susan Yonezawa modeled how to challenge a noun—to describe diversity within a "group" while considering average experiences of opportunity. She first acknowledged that in many cases Asian Americans tend to access more-resourced schools also serving white students. She then said that "describing 'Asian American' demographics is also complicated":

— Japanese Americans are the most integrated (with white people) of all ethnic groups—Asians or otherwise.
— Chinese Americans are an extremely diverse group all by themselves—with families here for five generations versus newcomers.
— South Asians are often counted as Asian but are among the highest educated and wealthiest of the Asian subgroups due to immigration policies.
— Asians are more integrated (with white people) than Hispanics or blacks, but there are still many southeast Asians and Filipinos in "low-income" schools.
— Vietnamese are a mixed group with those arriving in the first two waves demographically differing from those coming in waves 3 and 4.
— Filipinos are often counted separately—but not always. Which makes comparing data on Asians difficult.
— Asians are often in multi-generational and multiple family households, which can mask poverty by allowing their families access to more successful school systems. But when they apply to college, they (deservedly) get the low-income points on applications.
— Finally, lower-income Asians are often employed in the small business economies—think Cambodian doughnut shops, Vietnamese nail shops . . . making a true measure of income difficult.

All this complexity exists *while* as an aggregated group, she repeated, Asian American families tend to go to school more often in higher-resourced environments with white students.

(continued)

Susan concluded, "we say that Asians are 'overrepresented in UC,' with many of the spots at elite UC campuses. But what if we counted each (sub)group separately [looked at "Japanese American" vs. "South Asian" vs. "Filipino" vs. "Vietnamese" enrollment, for example]? Would we still think of Asians as overrepresented?" (Remember too that a third of the undergraduates labeling themselves "Asian" in UCSD's records are actually international students.)

What do you think of this effort to challenge a noun? When might we speak of a lump-sum group like "Asians," and when should we "disaggregate" those claims for more precise discussions of specific experiences? Consider a Principle and Core Tension behind your responses.

THINK / DISCUSS

Where you live or work, do people ever make shallow claims about their own "culture's" everyday behaviors in comparison to other "cultures'"? Is it possible to make such comparative claims without implicitly denigrating one of the "groups"? For example, some of my Filipino tenth graders used to describe "Filipino culture" as a group that "cared about education"—always in contrast to other communities in the school.

Consider a Try Tomorrow for responding to a student's comment about their "own" culture as preferable to others'. Then consider a Principle and Core Tension behind your response.

THINK / DISCUSS

Look back to page 170, to the example of the counselor summing up local "Navajo" life as "traditional," "simple," and "pure." If you were this counselor's colleague and overheard the remark, what's one initial thing you might say to him to encourage him to learn more about the complexities of local Navajo life, or about the individual student in front of him (including the student's experiences in the school)? (For example, Donna Deyhle points out that "the Internet, Ivy League and community colleges and universities, multicultural global communities, and advice from grandparents are all parts of young American Indian men's and women's ways of being in the world today," and that "there are over 500 different American Indian nations, speaking hundreds of different languages."[81]) Consider a response at the Try Tomorrow level. Then consider a Principle or a Core Tension of the situation.

THINK / DISCUSS

Look back to page 184, to the example of Eugene Garcia's mother.[82] Now consider: you are a teacher. Parent Night has just occurred, and many parents, including Eugene's mother, were missing. In the lunchroom, a colleague is commenting that a particular community was absent because folks from Group X do not "care." How might you prompt that colleague to inquire more about the situation? Consider a response at the Try Tomorrow level.

Now consider: how might you start to learn more about experiences with the school, from specific parents you saw missing from Parent Night? Consider the pros and cons of various questions you might ask when approaching a parent. Then pinpoint a Principle or Core Tension behind each suggestion.

THINK / DISCUSS

Thea Abu El-Haj notes that Arab and Arab American experiences are often either caricatured or never mentioned in U.S. classrooms. She urges teachers to think more critically about how groups are both represented in and absent from school curriculum.[83]

You are a teacher in a community where few Arab American families live, but where people say a lot of disparaging things about "Arabs." What's one way you might support students to learn more about the varied experiences of Arab Americans, locally or nationally? Would you invite someone in the community to come to class? Start to learn via more secondary sources, like books, reports, or community-made media? (As an example, Teresa McCarty urges educators to move beyond typical simplistic representations of Native Americans in schools through "engaging students in a complex exploration of Native American experiences." Teachers can have students "read autobiographies of Native people" or "work by American Indian writers, historians, storytellers, and performers" and "compare these accounts with media depictions"; teachers and students can research "Native nations and organizations" to find "indigenous teaching resources" like http://www.oyate.org, especially Oyate's *Teaching Respect for Native Peoples*. McCarty also urges teachers to "invite community members to discuss their own life experiences and perspectives with the class," seeking references through "community-based American Indian centers, institutions of higher education with American Indian or Ethnic Studies programs, and tribal museums and education offices."[84])

Consider one Strategy for getting started in learning about local Arab American experiences, and a Principle or Core Tension behind it.

THINK / DISCUSS

Books, films, and other media can give us glimpses into complicated human lives. (Christine Sleeter notes that regarding such materials, students sometimes want to look into "mirrors" to learn more about their own communities, and sometimes through "windows" to learn about unfamiliar experiences.[85]) But in schools, as Sanjay Sharma notes, it's often too easy to watch a film about "another culture" and then make simplistic comparisons of how "cultures" live, often by making cultural practices seem static and timeless ("Hindus are vegetarians"; "this is how Muslims pray") rather than constantly negotiated by people. As an example, Sharma asks us to think of a teacher showing *Bend It Like Beckham* to students.[86] A shallow conversation-starter about the movie might be, "Aren't you glad that parents here don't arrange marriages for their kids like Indians do?" To go deeper, a teacher could note that some, but not all, Indian or South Asian families arrange marriages; point out that the whole family is struggling over "arranging" a marriage in the movie; emphasize how the family represented in the movie is both British and South Asian simultaneously; or, connect to a common human experience ("Have you ever struggled with your family over who to date, just like the character in *Beckham*?").

Imagine that you are a substitute teacher in a classroom where the teacher has left a film and a simplistic question for students to engage. (Choose a film you've seen and a likely simplistic culture question about it.) At the Try Tomorrow level, consider one question you could ask students to prompt deeper inquiry, a Principle or more general Strategy behind it, or a Core Tension of this Culture Talk situation.

THINK / DISCUSS

Geneva Gay notes that for many of us, "mass media is the only source of knowledge about ethnic diversity . . . unfortunately, much of this 'knowledge' is inaccurate and frequently prejudicial."[87] Consider: what's one "shallow" understanding of a community of people you've developed based on the media? Consider one initial action you could take to pursue "deeper understanding," and a Core Tension of your proposed effort.

THINK / DISCUSS

Kathy Schultz and Doug Foley each ask educators to refrain from judging students in their classrooms in too-quick "cultural" terms (like "students from [group X] are quiet!") and instead, to ask students more about their own experiences in classrooms.[88]

You are a teacher. How would you learn more from several students who have been silent in class? (One university-level educator told me that, "As a teacher, I have learned that no groups of learners are quiet or shy just because of their first language and the supposed culture from which they come. How have I learned this? Over time, I noticed groups of learners hanging out together on breaks having boisterous noisy discussions in their first languages. These groups often included some of the learners who were the most quiet in my classes.") Consider the pros and cons of various ways you might learn from the silent students in your class. Then name a Principle and Core Tension behind each of your ideas.

THINK / DISCUSS

Consider Prudence Carter's argument (page 183) that educators often punish youths' "non-dominant" dress or speech style. Now consider one "non-dominant" behavior (dress, speech style, appearance, musical taste) of a young person you know, that seems to clash with school expectations. Imagine that you are a staff member advising the student.

> What's one thing you might say to value the young person's "non-dominant" behaviors while explaining how people in power give "points" to familiar or "dominant" behaviors? Role-play one response.
> What's one question you could ask the student so you start to learn more about the style the student clearly values?
> Would you approach educators at school to ask them to reconsider their typical reactions to students? What would you say? Role-play a question you might ask.

Consider a Principle and Core Tension behind your thinking on each.

THINK / DISCUSS

You are a teacher who hopes to visit families' homes, to begin a conversation with them about supports they feel are needed for their children. (We'll consider this Strategy further in Chapter 7.) One educator (who described her family as Puerto Rican) recalled to me that teacher home visits had been great for her as a child: "my teachers never gave us the feeling they were blaming parents or the 'culture' for differences in behavior or learning issues. In fact, I recall feeling a great deal of pride when my teachers came to participate in our home life. They didn't visit to tell us what we were lacking or doing wrong. They came to get to know us, to share information, to sometimes even eat and drink with us."

You are a teacher asking students' parents if you can make a home visit. You have written a letter to go home with all families, and you plan to ask a bilingual colleague as needed to help with translation.

> What is the first sentence of your letter?
> What is the first thing you'd say in person to begin the home visit?

Name a Principle or Core Tension behind each initial effort to "get to know" families.

THINK / DISCUSS

In "service learning" efforts in schools and universities, often, more privileged individuals attempt to help young people they wouldn't typically encounter.

I've talked to teachers who fear that some service learning can reproduce underinformed or even condescending notions about types of people, if young people don't get to know the people they are "serving" in a real way. Some have claimed that the height of condescension is "voluntourism": people traveling briefly abroad ostensibly to help others, but primarily to enrich themselves.[89] (Author Chimamanda Ngozi Adichie also notes that we often grow up with underinformed, often negative "single stories" about the communities other youth come from—until we start actively looking for more robust and complicated stories of experiences, strengths, and achievements. To demonstrate her point, she recalls assuming as a relatively wealthy child growing up in Nigeria that the "house boy" who helped her family was only "poor" and to be "pitied"—and without any skills worth knowing or admiring.[90])

Imagine that you are a teacher, trying to set up a visit to a local community organization that supports refugee families. What's one conversation or interaction you would want to ensure your students have with youth at the organization? Name a Principle behind your thinking, and a Core Tension of the situation.

THINK / DISCUSS

At the high school where I taught, the new principal put all staff on a bus to tour a local housing project where some of our students lived. We drove around looking at buildings; we never got out and talked with anyone. Then, we came back to the stage of the auditorium and debriefed by lamenting the living situation of our students and the lack of resources in their neighborhood. I remember feeling like we'd actually learned almost nothing.

If you were a principal reorganizing this experience, what's one conversation you'd want your staff to have with people in the community visited? Describe a conversation you'd want to pursue and how you'd set it up. Then consider a Principle and Core Tension behind your thinking.

Part Two
Designing Schooltalk Infrastructure →

Part Two Goal:
Design schooltalk infrastructure for equity. Help people routinely get informed about young people's experiences and the supports specific young people need to keep developing their full human talents. Then insist that young people get those supports.

Let's continue to lay a new foundation for equity effort in education by redesigning the basic ways we talk about and with young people in schools.

Part 1 equipped us to *flip scripts*—to counter common misinformation about young people generally with more fact-based talk. That way, we can better see actual young people and start to support them more effectively.

In Part 2 of *Schooltalk*, we're going to design ways that school communities can routinely inform each other about supporting the specific young people they serve.

We will call this designing *schooltalk infrastructure* for equity.

Starting to design schooltalk infrastructure

Look at our Foundational Image on the next page and think of an education community you know—or a young person you care about. Start thinking about something people need to discuss to support that young person, but often don't.

For example,

✳   Have you seen teachers who can't access critical information on students' school progress, don't routinely share it, or rarely talk thoroughly enough about students' skills and achievements?

✳   Are students able to talk with caring supporters as needed, about pressing issues in their lives inside and outside of school?

✳   Do parents and school staff discuss ideas about opportunities young people could access in the local opportunity context?

If you considered some communication necessary for student support and then designed a way to routinely enable it, you'd be designing *schooltalk infrastructure* for equity.

In Part 2, we'll start to ask these *infrastructure design* questions with equity in mind:

To support the full human talent development of every student and all groups of students (equity) in an education community you know,

>   Who in this school/classroom/community needs to communicate what information to whom? (How often? When?)

>   What are the barriers to needed communication, and how could those barriers be overcome?

>   What channel (face-to-face conversations, paper, technology) might allow necessary communications to occur?

For example, perhaps a newly designed report card could help multiple educators, families, and students to discuss new ideas for supporting students' progress. Maybe a weekly journal activity could invite students to tell teachers more regularly about consequential events in their lives in and

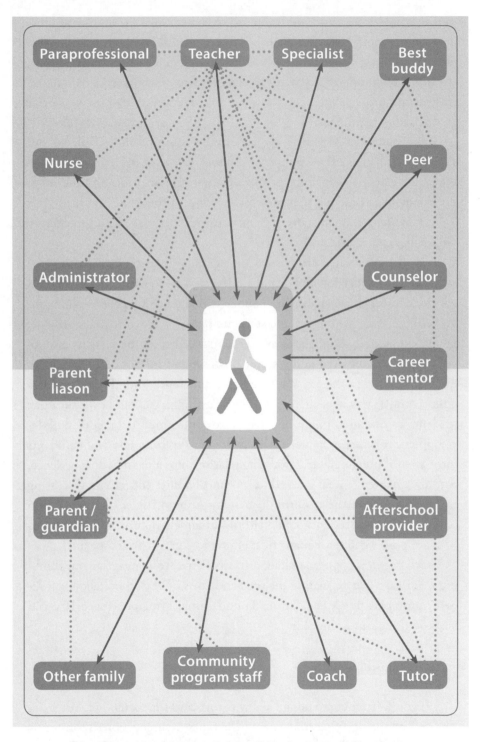

The Foundational Image of *Schooltalk*: A sample of the people who help shape a young person's fate in school every day

out of school, so adults could respond. Maybe a new listserv or standing coffee hour could help administrators communicate routinely with parents about improving opportunities for young people. Like adding new pipes or wires to a building to carry water or electricity to new places, schooltalk infrastructure helps people *routinely* share information needed for *supporting specific young people better.*

Think about embedding a pipe between some of the people in our Foundational Image that *routinely transmits some necessary information* between these people—enabling people to better support students' progress or development (Data Talk, Chapter 5), respond to their ongoing lives (Life Talk, Chapter 6), or improve the opportunities they access (Opportunity Talk, Chapter 7).

Treat the next three chapters as one gradual inquiry into inviting the schooltalk necessary for supporting students. We know that by shifting this everyday information-sharing in schools—and by getting people talking together about supporting specific students better—we won't necessarily get people addressing all of the improvements needed to the systems around young people, nor even address every issue raised in Part 1. But we'll get quite a lot done in three chapters. By critically rethinking the typical Data Talk central to schools, Chapter 5 will get us thinking about how educators, students and families might better monitor and support students' skill development together. Chapter 6 will invite new information from students into schools, potentially transforming relationships and student experience. And by Chapter 7, we'll have educators and families collectively discussing transformations to the opportunity systems around students. Each shift in schooltalk "about students" could afford fundamental improvements to student support—and buoy many next efforts to support young people.

As we start to design schooltalk infrastructure, we'll engage all our thinking from Part 1 in evaluating the pros and cons of any schooltalk improvement proposed. Look back at our Foundational Principles (page 10), and keep on using our Equity Line!

For example:

* If you were going to design a new report card that could help teachers, administrators, students, and parents each get more informed about students' skill development and school progress (Data Talk),

how might you ensure the data doesn't label students in ways that harm them, omit important information, or misrepresent what they can do?

✳   If you think a journal activity could help teachers better understand and respond to young people's experiences (Life Talk), how might you invite deeper understanding of those experiences without making students feel forced to share, or exposed?

✳   If you think a listserv or coffee hour could support more inclusive communications between staff and parents about improving the opportunities available for students (Opportunity Talk), how might you handle it when less wealthy parents, parents without computers, or parents who speak other languages still don't get information or don't get heard?

Note that for the first time we're considering the *channel* people use to communicate about and with young people, with equity in mind. People in schools can communicate face-to-face (a parent-teacher meeting, an in-class dialogue, a faculty meeting), on paper (a bulletin board, a journal, a data printout, a poster); or by using some technology (a text message, a listserv, an online data display). Channels will let people talk as needed in some cases, not in others. So start thinking: which channels might help and *not* help share specific information necessary for supporting young people?

The goal of Part 2 is to continue to catalyze your ongoing efforts as an equity designer. This book will have succeeded if, long after you're done reading, you stay in the habit of questioning what is said and not said about young people anywhere—and of inviting the schooltalk necessary to support them.

So first think about what needs to be discussed to support young people in an education setting you know. Then, consider how to get it discussed. We'll consider other designers' efforts. And while thinking critically, set yourself free to imagine. In the conclusion of the book, we'll Action Plan for improving schooltalk for equity in a real place you know.

Chapter 5

Data Talk

If we're underinformed about young people's skills and talents, we can't support their development in necessary ways.

Chapter Goal:
Help key people routinely get necessary information about specific students' progress and development, so they can use that data to support young people.

We said throughout Part 1 that seeking more accurate information about young people is key to equity effort. If you don't know even basic things about students, how can you support them?

Let's continue to design schooltalk for equity by tackling a foundational infrastructure problem for the folks in our Foundational Image (page 211): keeping accurate track of students' skill development and school progress.

Data Talk!

Accurate Data Talk about young people—even about the basics—is rarer in schools than one might imagine. How are students doing in chemistry? Many teachers don't keep track of which students are struggling or succeeding with which concepts, often because they have too many students to monitor. Who passed Algebra II in summer school? I've seen students wait for months to get credits logged by district record-keepers while college application deadlines loomed. Many parents, low-income and immigrant parents particularly, don't get to see or hear critical information about their children's school progress.[1]

Conversely, parents often don't get to weigh in on the skills they see in their kids—or the skills they hope their kids will develop. Teachers often have no idea what their students can do after school or at home (who can speak multiple languages or use math in home construction?), or how they do with other teachers. Program staff often have no idea how students do when they move between school and afterschool program or from one school to the next, because each program keeps its own records and educators rarely talk in person across sites. Beyond reviewing limited data on individuals, many educators never analyze school data patterns in any detail—like who's being placed in "gifted" programs, AP, or Special Education, and who isn't, and why.[2] And students all too rarely get asked to say anything about their own achievement or skill development, including experiences in classes their skill development outside of schools.

So day after day, the folks in our Foundational Image need critical information from and about young people to make informed decisions about supporting students' progress and development. And often, such information is not readily or reliably shared. Our lenses for seeing students remain dirty; our understanding of students remains shallow rather than deep; many students "fall through the cracks," unseen and unknown.

Ready to design Data Talk for equity?

Start thinking about a young person you care about in an education system you know. *Who* in our Foundational Image most needs to see and discuss *which* information about this young person's progress and development, in order to support him or her? More precisely:

To support the full human talent development of every student and all groups of students (equity) with our Data Talk, we must ask:

> Who in a school/classroom/community needs to communicate what information to whom? (How often? When?)

> What are the barriers to needed communication, and how could those barriers be overcome?

> What channel (face-to-face conversations, paper, technology) might allow necessary communications to occur?

We will work on two design activities in this chapter to pull our thinking together. Make a document with two sides. On the left, make a Data Wish List—a list of the *types of information about young people's progress and development* that you think the people in our Foundational Image need to know and share in order to support young people. On the right, describe an Ideal Data Communication for each item—a *plan to routinely communicate that item on your Data Wish List.* Who will tell whom about that information? How and when? Will they communicate online, on a piece of paper (like a paper report card), or face-to-face?

These lists just get you started; the next chapters will expand our thinking further, and you can update your lists long after you're done reading this book. We'll start by considering basic school data educators keep "on" student achievement, and expand gradually to broader data from students themselves. And as you'll see, there aren't always clear answers on which information on student progress is necessary or who should have it in hand—or even what forms of progress everyone is hoping to see. As usual, being a designer of schooltalk for equity requires ongoing questioning about which schooltalk helps and harms.

Data Talk in action

One college student-athlete told me about an active weekly review of his basic school progress that he felt had been critical to getting him through high school. Student-athletes had to maintain GPAs to stay on sports teams, so coaches made sure each player received a weekly grade and attendance report and comment page from a teacher. Each student was put in a mandatory study hall with a tutor if he or she got off track, to work on specific things noted on his or her report. My student felt this infrastructure for habitual Data Talk linking student, teacher, tutor, and coach helped him greatly, "because it was such a frequent analysis and evaluation of my progress that if I ever fell behind, I would get the help I needed in order to succeed." In talking through the situation with his old high school friends, my student realized that non-athletes had been jealous of the intensive monitoring and support athletes received. Other students had had to keep track of their own grades and standing. And if they fell behind, they said, no one reached out to them to pull them back on track. They felt that more frequent monitoring and support of their progress would have helped them, too.

These young people were calling for better *infrastructure* for monitoring and then supporting students on a regular basis—for more habitual communication between various people, including students themselves, about how students were doing in aspects of their development and next steps that might support them.

Many researchers emphasize that educators need such ongoing information on student progress in order to make informed decisions about supporting each student the next day or week.[3] Other researchers emphasize that educators need to give such running feedback and response to students themselves. As Na'ila Nasir notes, it's the kind of feedback a caring coach gives a player: concrete feedback on specific ways they might improve and grow, wrapped in a stated commitment to support success.[4] Improving on specific dimensions toward high expectations becomes just part of the work of growing.

And of course, the various supporters in students' lives also need to talk actively to one another and with students about which young people need which supports from whom to develop specific skills and grow next talents.

So the key design question of Data Talk arises: *who* needs to share *which* data on student progress and development with *whom, how,* to support students? And we have to grapple with a gnarly Core Tension about circulating information (data) inside any education community:

CORE TENSION   Just "more" talk about "more" data isn't always good.

I've seen many examples where more data could have negative consequences for young people. For example, I visited administrators in one Massachusetts district who showed me a new expensive online data system they'd developed. They proudly demonstrated a data view that could show educators stats on students at the click of a button. To demonstrate the system's potential, they offered examples of immediate access to discipline data. Each example showed a black student with a suspension record displayed right next to his face. My immediate thought was how such decontextualized data seen by more people could actually prompt a harmful response to students as "problems," if this was all the data educators saw or what they saw first.

In the first district where my children went to school, the district briefly required classroom "data walls" that publicly displayed students' (anonymized) test scores to all children and parents. Parents revolted, arguing that even if names were taken off of scores, such out-of-context public information stressed and demotivated children rather than motivating them. The district stopped displaying this data publicly.

I met distressed teachers in Chicago who had been told by leadership to literally stick test scores on their kids' chests, as stickers. Teachers feared that sticking test scores on children—making "more" data seen by more people—would humiliate them. And I've talked to other teachers whose "data talk" with colleagues consisted primarily of teachers looking at such scores, then lamenting that students would never do better.

What's the equity lesson in each of these examples?

Beyond the obvious Principle of discussing all students as people with potential, one lesson is that data has to be more *fully contextualized* to be helpful. Decontextualized facts like discipline records or scores on single tests, just circulated more widely, can risk distorting the view of a child. Scripts percolate on unabated: with too little information in hand, we reinforce false assumptions that some kids are about misbehavior or that test scores represent students' "smarts." Or, we overlook all the others involved in the suspension or the score!

Another lesson is that *who* sees data matters. Test scores just shared with more viewers may not help a young person, even while such information in a thoughtful teacher's hands could help target at least some instructional supports. Discipline data in the hands of someone who doesn't know a student could be harmful if people don't learn more of the backstory, versus such data in the hands of someone who knows the student well.

And a final lesson is to think critically about *which* data we're sharing more widely. One student considering these examples thought that "test score data should never be shared among the other students. But hobbies and talents should." Many educators reading this chapter have decided that the key was moving beyond single sources of data "on" students to multiple sources helping educators improve *their own work* with students—even as people continued to debate *which* data sources to use while reading the next two chapters!

So, as we design Data Talk for equity, we need to consider carefully *what* information *which* people really need in hand to respond more knowledgably to students. For example, what data would help educators more fully contextualize a test score or respond to a discipline record on a child?

Let's start a Data Wish List.

Create a Data Wish List

Researchers of "data use" in education suggest that inviting educators "to contribute to a 'data wish list' can encourage them to think creatively about what kinds of data could help them get a better picture of their students."[5]

So, on the left side of a document, start to *make a list of the types of information about young people's progress and development* that you think the people in our Foundational Image need to know and share in order to support them.

Think outside the box. Such information may include whether a student is passing algebra or how a student is doing on algebra concepts this week. But it also might include information on how he is experiencing the math class or doing personally today, what he likes to learn, or what he does and can do outside of school. Don't limit your thinking as an equity designer.

In beginning this Data Wish List with me, educators from both K–12 and higher education have suggested they'd appreciate information such as that below in order to improve their work with students. This is just a small sample to get you started on your own Data Wish List. In their own words, educators said they wanted:

* The ability to add backstory—e.g., on attendance—and have it actually be right next to the numerical data.
* The ability to look qualitatively at schools and students rather than just by aggregated numbers.
* More assessments created by teachers than by the state or district.
* More qualitative data from students themselves.
* More surveys on kid experience, including student interactions with school staff.
* More info on what's going on with the student.
* More interviews and focus groups, getting input on the class or school from young people who aren't typically included.
* Observations of students as data, along with reviews of student work, to show what students can do already and what they still need to work on—and which materials teachers might need to teach differently.
* Stories about students—like specific things students say in class

about a given subject, to demonstrate their understanding of the subject.

✳ Input from students on how they experienced interactions in class.

✳ Not just judgmental commentary about teacher or student, but productive information—meaning, information helpful to serving the child. For example, strategies that helped a child already, or obstacles in the way of helping the child.

✳ A student data management system that gives a full picture of a child, not just a reduced set of numbers and red-flag issues.

✳ Information on who was (and wasn't) already offered which classes, programs, and other opportunities to learn.

✳ More from students themselves about their interests, talents, and lives. Information from parents, too.

District leaders I worked with recently said they could support students better if they had the following forms of "data" on both K–12 students and college students, even though none of it was formally collected in their systems:

✳ Students' extra-curricular activities (whether they were involved in athletics, school government, yearbook, band, service learning);

✳ Students' work status (if students are working part time; if so, how many hours a week; do they work at or outside the university once in college?);

✳ Family status of students (e.g., teen parenthood, etc.);

✳ Eventually, students' career and employment outcomes.

The Action Assignment at the end of this chapter will ask you to ask students or other adults what data they think are key to share in schools. You might do that Assignment now to shape your thinking. One high school student noted to her teacher conducting the Action Assignment that "data communicates grades but not what's going on in the students' lives." Another student called for "asking students about their learning"; teachers have wanted student input on specific teaching efforts. One teacher suggested reviewing the work students produced for other teachers, to get a broader sense of students' skills. Researchers also point out that asking families about their own hopes for their children provides a key form of data, so that a high bar for student development is set together. McCarty and Lee note, for example, that a key goal of Indigenous education efforts is to serve "the needs of Indigenous communities as defined by those communities," developing locally valued talents and knowledge in addition to the standardized skills expected by all.[6]

THINK / DISCUSS

Which forms of data listed above would you add to your Data Wish List? What data do you immediately see as missing from this list, that you'd want to add to your own?

Your Wish List might focus on monitoring individual students' progress and needs. You might also design ways to monitor the progress of every *group* of students in a school. You might vote for less data on a given issue, rather than more! And remember, this is just a starter—this can remain a living document that you revise over time.

Design Ideal Data Communications for each item on your Wish List

On the right side of the document where you are making your Data Wish List, envision an Ideal Data Communication for each item—a plan for people to *communicate* that item on your Data Wish List. Think about our infrastructure design questions here. Who would share the information with whom, how, and how often? What barriers to sharing would they have to confront? (E.g., data not stored in an accessible place; people unable or anxious to meet to talk.) And what channel would you use for the information-sharing? (You could imagine an in-person conversation about how a student is doing; a communication using a phone or the Internet; or a communication using a piece of paper, like a paper report card, a comment in a notebook, or a note mailed home.)

These are important decisions. How people decide to collect and share data about students' progress and development shapes what people learn and discuss about young people and about their own efforts to *support* young people. The words used on a report card summing up a child's progress; the categories organizing a portfolio of student work; or the questions teachers ask colleagues in a conference each shape routine conversations about how students are doing and what adults might do next to support them.

Start making your Data Wish List and considering your Ideal Data Communication of each item.

To get started, let's recall some big issues from Part 1 of this book, to think about designing Data Talk with equity in mind.

Thinking critically about Data Talk for equity

Look back at our Foundational Principles of schooltalking for equity (page 8).

Now start to think: which numbers, words, and stories do you think are essential to collect to helpfully describe young people's progress and development?

First, remember our quests to "clean our lenses" (Chapter 2) and "go from shallow to deep" (Chapter 4) in any schooltalk about young people. In any Data Talk, we can treat all data as only partial information on a child— as a conversation starter rather than a final word. And to care for young people, we can get in the habit of seeking more thorough information about any number or word summing up young people too quickly. Fiarman and colleagues call this "digging into data."[7] Researchers point out similarly that while Data Talk needs to name initial patterns in student "achievement," the real work begins when people talk in detail about how they could contribute to specific aspects of students' learning and progress.[8]

So, now think critically about a test score on a wall. System leaders often seem to like summative numbers more than words as descriptions. Yet Larry Cuban points out that every number circulated as "data" still has to be interpreted, requiring more information about what's going on with young people, educators, and schools.[9] (As Linda Darling-Hammond put it, teachers reviewing student work as data commented on how much they'd learned about student thinking [and necessary changes in their instruction] from such information, compared to what they'd learned from "a two or three digit score."[10]) A district administrator posted this note to a public listserv I belong to:

"We are overwhelmed by vendors pushing complex mega-/meta-systems that compile multiple quantitative indicators, but we are not so good at systematically investigating, analyzing, and applying the results [and] the human piece (the stories etc.) are not being systematically collected or analyzed at the school or district level."

This administrator added,

"We (school and district administrators) have clearly embraced the need to examine data and make evidence-based decisions, but I think we often forget that anecdotal information, observations, perceptions, discourse, narratives etc. are data too."

As one teacher in my class noted while considering the example of test scores stuck to children's chests in Chicago, "In some ways, adding qualitative (narrative) record-keeping to the written record about young people is essential. Otherwise, the *only* thing that 'sticks' is a number about a young person." And as we saw in Chapter 3, we've been describing student skill or "ability" with misleadingly simple numbers for centuries.

However, we saw throughout Part 1 that quick words labeling or explaining children don't inherently clean our lenses either. A label "at risk" placed by a child's name on a spreadsheet, or the summative label "SPED kid," can harm if it comes to stand for an entire, complicated young person or emphasizes presumed deficits rather than students' myriad assets.[11] What's perhaps most dangerous is if any number or word stands as the primary description of the child, instead of starting a deeper conversation about what the child currently needs and can do and who in a shared opportunity context will do what to support him or her further.

As usual, "larger, more complex stories" are key to schooltalk supporting young people.

STRATEGY   Use any data as a conversation starter on student supports, not as a complete representation of "the whole child."

Conversations need to start, of course: I've seen people sit anxiously on data about very serious student struggles and fail to mention it at all, much less "dig in" to it to design solutions. At the school I taught at and then studied for *Colormute*, people kept data private when they weren't ready to debate and address the causes of patterns that implicated them. They anxiously refused to discuss, much less act on, data like racial patterns in suspension, "F" lists, or dropout rates. So folks muted Data Talk altogether: they let many problematic patterns just stand as normal, and they missed the chance to share ways to assist students, improve pedagogy, or improve relationships between students and themselves.

As we discussed throughout Part 1, however, helpful Data Talk regarding any individual or group of students has to be thorough—to tell a larger, more complex story about how valued young people are doing and what supports they currently need from whom. Further, data has to be *used* to actually improve opportunity. As Datnow and Park put it in their call for "data *use* for equity," "in many schools and districts, the enthusiasm for data-driven decision making has produced volumes of data that are never actually used to inform, much less improve, classroom instruction."[12] (Many educators have told me that conversations about "data" in their schools typically just rehashed how students were failing, instead of considering what adults in the room could do to improve learning opportunities for students.) Everyday Democracy creates templates asking school and community stakeholders of all ages to help people move beyond naming "achievement gaps" to planning together to address their causes.[13] "Improvement science" efforts engage educators in sketching the causes of outcomes using tools like "driver diagrams" and "fishbone diagrams," to pinpoint specific components of complex systems to tackle first.[14] Colleagues and I produced a guide to talking through patterns in school discipline as a key component of student achievement in schools.[15] Datnow and Park gathered "data protocols" designed to support groups of educators to move beyond naming failures to pinpointing and addressing student learning needs.[16] Ilana Horn urges that small groups of teachers focus discussion on how they could help students understand specific concepts, rather than summing up kids as "fast" or "slow."[17] With equity in mind—and buoyed by a deep commitment to young people—each Data Talk effort seeks to talk thoroughly, specifically, and proactively about addressing all students' needs and strengths and supporting all students' ongoing development.

Sharing data at all to start such analysis is step one. A high school teacher described getting brief "notices" about students only after high stakes decisions were made about them: "Often, administrators send notices of students who are dropped to adult school because they are absent. Then, teachers might ask administrators to reconsider because they have information on why students are missing." One student described how as an office assistant in high school, she'd hear the secretary calling parents of "students who were in trouble" and referencing "old yellow slips" on discipline incidents kept "in a manila folder for each student, filed away in a filing cabinet in the office for almost no one to see." As a student, she said, "I found [it] unfair that the student's situation wasn't being fully relayed." Another student recalled that in her own school experience, "There was very little effort for staff, teachers and parents to get together and try to figure out what was causing behavioral issues with the student." Instead, teachers wrote short words like "defiant" on referrals and sent students to the office.

There is an untold human story behind each isolated snippet of data—each yellow slip, brief phone call, and quick referral. As equity designers we can help data get shared, to even start telling those stories. But we can also make sure our conversations about data are thorough—and focused on specific ways of supporting each student better.

We've also seen that understanding and addressing patterns involving groups of students requires peeling the onion on initial information—going beyond surface patterns to deeper understanding. One administrator "peeling the onion" on a school's failing math grades found that a single teacher was failing most of the students; the administrator then started rethinking his own role in providing professional development to math teachers. Deeper conversations about discipline patterns go beyond initial data on who is suspended to detailed analyses of how educators can support students more effectively.[18] As noted in an earlier chapter, Datnow and Park watched one district investigate their data patterns for equity by looking beyond the surface outcome data (who was in AP) to see how students *ended up* in AP. Educators soon found:

> Asian students who scored at the basic level on the state tests had double the chance of being in college-preparatory courses than Latino students who scored at the same basic level. This data analysis led district leaders to reexamine their class placement procedures and expand access to college-preparatory courses. Rather than relying only on students' grades and their own professional instincts, teachers were also asked to support placement recommendations with other forms of student achievement data, including data from various assessments the students had taken. This more holistic approach resulted in a greater number of students [and more Latinos, Datnow notes] being placed into college preparatory classes.[19]

Data Talk for equity moves beyond shallow or complacent descriptions of students or their outcomes to considering, in more detail, whose actions affect students' outcomes and how the various people involved in student outcomes can take next steps to support every student's success. It seeks thorough analysis of specific actions by both adults and young people that could improve students' school experiences, offer critical opportunities, and meet student needs.

Now that we've started to remind ourselves of some key ideas from Part 1, let's jump into our role as equity designers and start to evaluate some real efforts to shape Data Talk infrastructure for equity. Equity design is an ongoing process; many of these designs were first attempts by me, with flaws I can see only in retrospect. **THINK/DISCUSS** questions will ask you to evaluate the pros and cons of each design effort. As usual, I suggest you read them all but tackle the questions most pertinent to you. Keep adding to your Data Wish List and considering your Ideal Data Communication of each item on your list.

Evaluating Data Talk infrastructure design efforts with equity in mind

I helped design Data Talk infrastructure of various kinds as a leader of the OneVille Project, a large community project in Somerville, Massachusetts, between 2009 and 2011. OneVille was at root a collective equity effort, with the goal of linking members of a diverse community in collaborations supporting every child's success. Specifically, the project explored how technology might help connect folks in student support.[20] As one project, we ended up designing several online data displays to enable more informed Data Talk. I want to consider the pros and cons of that work in equity terms, asking if our designs would have shared necessary (and sufficiently thorough) information with the right people, through workable channels.

I need to preface this discussion by noting that the data displays ("dashboards") I show here actually didn't get used in Somerville, because we ran out of grant money to finish what turned out to be a huge programming job. Our dream goal was to create open source software that could be available free to any district, but we never got there. We made the code publicly available on wiki.oneville.org. (Several years later, Code for America started working on a similar project in the city.)

We designed this Data Talk infrastructure to handle several structural cracks inhibiting informed Data Talk. In the district at the time, administrators who wanted to view various data about multiple students kept in the school district's Student Information System (SIS) had to send data requests to a central data person and wait for him or her to organize the data and send it back out in viewable form. Teachers wanting to see basic patterns on their classroom at a glance lifted data from the SIS by hand into their own Excel spreadsheets, a cut-and-paste process that consumed valuable hours. Administrators also told us of time wasted in meetings as staff flipped through multiple printouts to find basic data.

So, with the goal of enabling more easily informed Data Talk, a district administrator, several principals, teachers, and parents, and a few students weighed in with a lead teacher advisor on designing these data views to enable what one called "one-stop shopping"—the ability to see different kinds of basic student data at the same time, in a single display. Administrators could see a schoolwide view like that below; teachers would see this same data just for the students in their own class.

OneVille Admin Dashboard

Home Student Example Planning

Students Example Grade/Class

Grade 6

Name	G	Homeroom	Abs	Tardy	Home Language	Y @ H	MAP Math Δ	MAP Reading Δ	Ward	ELL	MEPA	Has IEP	Afterschool
	♀	HEA 316	9	12	English	6	+2 (223 => 225)	+4 (233 => 237)	5	Yes	R18 / W18	No	Comm Schl
	♀	HEA 313	13	5	Spanish	6	+7 (225 => 232)	+6 (159 => 165)	4	Yes	R30 / W17	Yes	Mystic
	♀	HEA 301	2	11	Portuguese	2	+9 (187 => 196)	+6 (247 => 253)	5	Yes	R27 / W14	No	Mystic B&G
	♀	HEA 219	4	13	Spanish	4	+12 (163 => 175)	+4 (201 => 205)	5	Yes	R16 / W28	No	
	♀	HEA 301	5	8	English	4	+6 (156 => 162)	+17 (184 => 201)	5	Yes	R13 / W28	Yes	Mystic B&G
	♀	HEA 105	0	1	Spanish	2	+13 (223 => 236)	+7 (185 => 192)	3	No		No	B&G Comm Schl
	♂	HEA 200	7	16	Spanish	1	+4 (247 => 251)	+11 (228 => 239)	6	No		No	B&G Comm Schl
	♀	HEA 219	3	6	Spanish	5	+5 (181 => 186)	+1 (237 => 238)	3	Yes	R12 / W23	No	B&G
	♀	HEA 219	7	9	English	5	+9 (224 => 233)	+0 (232 => 232)	6	Yes	R24 / W24	No	
	♀	HEA 200	8	10	English	2	+8 (178 => 186)	+1 (217 => 218)	3	Yes	R12 / W20	No	B&G
	♀	HEA 316	1	6	English	6	+3 (233 => 236)	+6 (187 => 193)	2	Yes	R19 / W11	No	Peabody
	♀	HEA 301	3	12	Creole(Haitian)	2	+7 (235 => 242)	+9 (156 => 165)	3	Yes	R14 / W27	No	B&G Comm Schl
	♂	HEA 200	15	10	English	1	+30 (217 => 247)	+3 (204 => 207)	1	Yes	R25 / W11	No	B&G
	♀	HEA 105	17	5	English	2	+5 (199 => 204)	+15 (252 => 267)	3	Yes	R14 / W23	No	B&G
	♀	HEA 313	9	1	Spanish	3	+2 (195 => 197)	+4 (212 => 216)	1	Yes	R25 / W13	No	B&G Peabody
	♀	HEA 105	3	6	Spanish	1	+0 (223 => 223)	+4 (162 => 166)	7	Yes	R27 / W19	Yes	B&G Peabody
	♂	HEA 316	0	1	Spanish	6	+24 (211 => 235)	+5 (180 => 185)	7	No		No	Mystic
	♂	HEA 105	4	16	Spanish	2	+1 (211 => 212)	+5 (240 => 245)	7	Yes	R11 / W27	No	Peabody
	♂	HEA 105	1	3	English	4	+3 (156 => 159)	+27 (236 => 263)	6	No		No	B&G
	♀	HEA 200	5	6	Creole(Haitian)	1	+11 (258 => 269)	+15 (259 => 274)	6	Yes	R13 / W17	No	B&G
	♀	HEA 105	0	7	Spanish	5	+2 (207 => 209)	+6 (248 => 254)	4	No		No	Peabody
	♀	HEA 313	8	5	English	1	+11 (160 => 171)	+27 (150 => 177)	3	No		No	

Look at the display above and consider your Data Wish List. Educators had asked for the ability to see, in one view, the following data from the district's SIS: students' name, gender, homeroom, recent absences and tardies, home language, years at the school, growth in score since the latest standardized math and reading assessments (MAP), which ward (neighborhood) of the city students lived in, whether students were classified as an English learner (ELL), an ELL-specific assessment score (MEPA), whether students had an Individualized Education Plan (IEP) as part of the Special Education process, and which afterschool program students were enrolled in. (That last item was on the district's Data Wish List, as each program entered its own data in its own database, not the district SIS. So, the afterschool data here is a placeholder.) The dashboard said nothing about discipline/behavior records, because an advising district administrator thought attendance was a better measure of student behavior—and because discipline records were kept on hundreds of slips of paper that administrators felt were too laborious to enter into the district database.

THINK / DISCUSS

* With equity in mind, what data on this spreadsheet view would you add to your own Data Wish List?

* Is there any data you would delete, or discuss in person only rather than display online?

* What do you think of the labels for "types of children" used on this data display? Is any "type of student" label you see problematic? (Think back to our Strategies from Chapter 1: we can question which labels enable student support and which get in the way.)

* How might you use any data shown to catalyze a deeper discussion of meeting a student's needs?

* Might having this data available "at a glance" online actually inhibit deeper analysis? For example, one educator reviewing this dashboard years later argued, "I think we (educational leaders and student advocates) should be prepared to ask good questions and then go *get* the data we need to respond to them. We shouldn't need a set of clicks and drop-down menus."

Now consider that our programmers designed the dashboard to let users not just *see* students' "group" labels (e.g., "ELL") but also to *sort* children by "group" (e.g., to see students from particular home language groups who also had heavy absences). That's because educators wanted to be able to check quickly for patterns. One principal wanted the dashboard to let her sort quickly for who had an IEP, for example, so she could see who might require special assistance on a standardized test day.

THINK / DISCUSS

As we saw in Chapter 1, "sorting" students into "types" also enables group comparisons. *Which* group comparisons through "sorting," if any, would you enable as part of your Ideal Data Communication? What concerns do you have about such sorting?

Since this is a black and white book, you can't see that the display also color codes students in particular situations. We designed that feature to help people quickly flag pressing student needs. We colored students yellow when they were approaching a danger situation (e.g., racking up excessive absences), green when they were doing fine on that measure, and pink when they were definitely in the danger situation (e.g., too many absences to pass a class). Why pink? As designers concerned about harmful labeling, we thought people might have a more positive conversation about a young person if a specific "risk" situation were notated as "pink" rather than the classic "alert" color of red. But in the end, people didn't know what pink color-coding meant! In a later version we turned the alert color back to red.

Similar data infrastructure increasingly is being created to flag students likely to encounter "problems." For example, an NPR story described online "early warning" systems in various states, flagging middle school students as statistically likely to fail to graduate from high school later based on current performance. Interviewees described both the utility of predicting who might struggle and their anxieties about framing young people negatively as likely to fail.[21] The National Black Child Development Institute, for example, resists framings of black students as statistically "at risk," questioning how such "deficit"-focused shorthand sees children through dirty lenses: "the prevailing discourse about Black children . . . overemphasizes limitations and deficits and does not draw upon the considerable strengths, assets and resilience demonstrated by our children, families and communities."[22]

As part of your Data Wish List or Ideal Data Communications, would you somehow "alert" educators about students in specific "risk" situations? Would you do anything to also emphasize students' "strengths, assets and resilience" or otherwise mitigate potential harms of the "at risk" frame?

If you facilitated a meeting about a student with some flagged "alert," what's one thing you might say to frame the discussion to be helpful to the student, rather than harmful?

In the next version of the dashboard, we added more data educators said they wanted—more test results (e.g., basic results from DIBELS, an early reading test), and more detail about IEP status ("no IEP," "partial inclusion," "full inclusion") rather than just Yes or No.

Would you add any data on your Data Wish List to enhance the second display below? Why or why not?

As you look at that example of a data display, now think bigger about communicating for equity.

THINK / DISCUSS

If you were a teacher discussing any item on this display with other teachers, what's one question you might ask to push Data Talk beyond potentially shallow analyses of student achievement? For example, would you insist on exploring more evidence behind any term or number used here to describe a child? Would you invite any other people into that discussion? (As a starter, some teachers have suggested immediately that they'd invite colleagues into a much more detailed discussion of students' skills than the test scores here would afford—and push discussion way beyond supporting math and reading!)

Now consider this Data Talk example I've experienced. You are in a faculty meeting. Someone has sorted this data by language group and school absences, and he notes that students from Haitian Creole–speaking homes are disproportionately absent from school. He says, "Those kids need motivation. Let's have a pizza party." What could you do to invite colleagues into deeper inquiry about the data pattern, before assuming that student motivation was the problem?

I held an initial discussion about student support with a subset of Haitian parents living in a nearby housing project and shared the attendance pattern with them. They raised several issues for educators to consider and address. Some kids were signing in tardy and then anxiously going home to avoid a detention for lateness. Parents also revealed, through interpreters, that they actually couldn't understand the language of notices sent home and weren't quite sure if the current starting time had shifted. Some low-income parents (both Haitian and white) then admitted they didn't feel that the teachers thought well of them. One told a story of a child referred to social services for a stain on their clothes, making the mom distrustful of school staff and wary of making appointments to discuss student performance. Given these dynamics, no parents had shared these experiences with the school.

Think of a data pattern mentioned once in an education community you know. What question, asked of whom, might get people to "open the paper towel roll" on that pattern, to consider the factors, actors, and interactions involved in it and specific actions educators might take to support students? How might you start to get that sort of deeper information in an education community you know?

Are you updating your Data Wish List and considering your Ideal Data Communication of each item?

Let's now also start to consider our first infrastructure design question in more detail. *Who* should share and see which data items on your Wish List?

Who needs to share which information with whom?

Consider an item on your Data Wish List: should all the people in our Foundational Image who know the young person have access to it, or not? Why?

Various communities are busy trying to link data across K–12 schools, community colleges, and universities, across schools and community programs, or even across housing, criminal justice, or health care systems in addition to schools. Such projects can spark critical conversations about opportunity contexts outside and inside schools. They also always end up debating who really should see which data in order to support young people.

Laws offer some answers, of course. Under the Family Educational Rights and Privacy Act, also known as FERPA, anyone can see a school's anonymized or aggregated data (e.g., schoolwide test scores by race), as long as the group of students isn't so small that individuals can be recognized. Parental consent is needed for sharing student school information that is personally identifiable by name or identifiers like social security numbers. Non school-based student support programs (like afterschool or tutoring programs), or research partners, can get a school's or district's permission to see such identifiable student-level data.[23] Only school staff are allowed automatic access to the entire Student Information System—including staff who don't know children in more depth or like particular young people. Educators encouraging deeper data conversations thus have to decide who is encouraged to review which data on whom.

Data Talk designers need to consider when school staff helpfully learn which non-school information, too. Chapter 4 urged us to "get to know" family lives outside of school; the next chapters will explore this further. But for now, consider: for example, who at school should know if a child has asthma or parents who just got divorced? Is it helpful if an educator learns more about a student's arrest record? At OCR, I had one case where a school resource officer searched a student's house for drugs while visiting the student's house for truancy, blurring the boundaries of school and police data. While there, he even checked the student's dad's criminal record and ended up arresting the father.

THINK / DISCUSS

Which out-of-school "data" should which school people have access to in order to support young people? Start to consider this question for your Data Wish List.

Beyond legal rules, Data Talk designers must also debate which personal student data is appropriately requested in schools at all. Since national surveys of youth show that LGBT students are disproportionately bullied and harassed as well as suspended and expelled from schools,[24] for example, researchers are debating whether schools might collect students' sexual orientation self-identifications along with race and gender identifications to keep track of these potential disparities—and how they would even do this.[25]

> **THINK / DISCUSS**
>
> Consider one data form that you would exclude from a data spread-
> sheet viewable by many school staff, and why. (Consider that
> backers of the Racial Privacy Initiative in California [Chapter 1,
> pages 72–73] argued that the state should not record public school
> students' racial identifications at all.)

And how can necessary people seeking to support students get the complex individual backstory on any student's situation?

Disability rights law insists that a support team convene regularly to discuss ways of supporting each young person deemed as having a "disability." Proposed interventions are written down on an Individualized Education Plan. I've often heard educators say that it would be ideal if this sort of individualized review and planning could occur for every young person—which requires decisions about which information-sharing supports individual students.

So let's critically evaluate some Data Talk infrastructure that could help people share and discuss data about individuals. To support the full human talent development of every student, who should share which information with whom?

Individualized Data Talk for equity

In many diverse districts, for example, parents often don't really understand how their students are doing on basic school or district progress markers—like grades, test scores, and credits for graduation or college eligibility. Taveras and colleagues describe a group that designed paper printouts of parent-friendly individual student data for teachers and parents to discuss in person.[26] In other schools, public "data talks" help larger groups of parents understand the tests used to assess their children.[27] Which data get reviewed in such gatherings with parents is itself a question for equity designers. One high school teacher recalled arguing with her principal over reviewing students' credits for graduation (the principal's preference) vs. the higher bar of their college readiness (the teacher's preference).

Parents, of course, aren't the only ones who need to see data on individuals: tutors, afterschool supporters, and even teachers often have trouble sharing information on their work with individual students because time isn't built into the schedule. As a teacher put it to me once of her own school, "having conversations about individual students becomes very difficult because teachers from different disciplines do not ever have a chance to dialogue about the individual needs and strengths of the students." As Data Talk designers in the OneVille Project, we thought that an individual data view online might at least help student supporters get some basic regular updates without having to meet in person each time.

At the time, parents could see their child's grades, tests, and attendance directly in the district's online student information system if they could remember their passwords. But many parents who weren't regular computer users had a hard time understanding the way the system displayed data, and the data there also was only in English, while Somerville's other main parent languages (of a total of forty-two) were Spanish, Portuguese, and Haitian Creole. Our initial goal (advised by a teacher, an administrator, and parents) was to try to create a more multilingual, family-friendly presentation of individual student data for parents and students. After making the basic individual-level views, we were going to translate each view's interface.

This was the first "individual" view a user would see. The photo (a placeholder) would be of the student's teacher, here "Mr. W.":

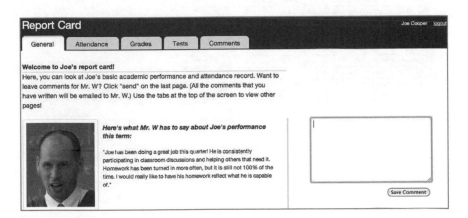

Let's continue to evaluate the pros and cons of this Data Talk infrastructure with equity in mind. Might it enable necessary communications about supporting individual student progress and development, or not?

For one, we designed this data display to let educators *comment in their own words* on a child's performance and growth. Typically, paper report cards were printed from a report card database that "opened" for brief, character-limited comment a few days before each quarter's report period ended; the teacher could choose premade assessments for each student ("meets standard consistently," "sometimes meets standard," "not meeting standard") and select from a list of prewritten qualitative comments. Our teacher co-designer wanted to write his own personal comments for every child detailing at more length what a student was doing well and needed to work on. So we designed the dashboards to allow this. (See the overall quote "Joe has been doing a great job . . ." above, which would supplement the more typical report card view below.)

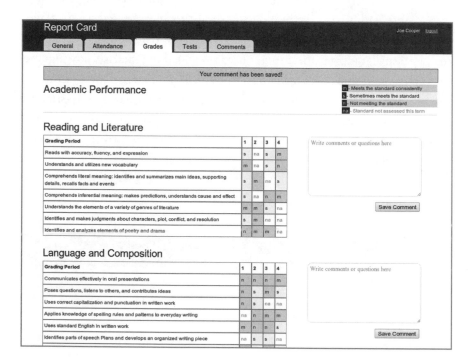

THINK / DISCUSS

What issues of a child's progress and development would you most want teachers to comment on in their own words? Why? How would you hope teachers would share that commentary (online, on a piece of paper, in a face-to-face meeting)?

Which issues of a child's development would you be fine with educators summarizing with simplified labels or words like "meeting the standard"? Why?

Data Talk designers also need to consider whether descriptions of students' progress and development are detailed enough. Some have pointed out, for example, that letter grades "are so imprecise that they are almost meaningless."[28] On her Data Wish List, one teacher looking at the report card view above echoed "the need to zoom in to a finer grained analysis of what students really need." One educator worried to me that counselors in her own district used simplistic data to place students into AP classes or advanced/remedial math, rather than reviewing students' progress in sufficient detail. "You should see the triplicate form counselors use to determine what classes kids should take next year," she noted. "Simplistic labels are everywhere. When I challenged it and offered an alternative, you'd have thought I was suggesting revolution."

As with most schooltalk for equity, finer-grained analysis can enable more informed support and care for students' ongoing progress toward high expectations—if educators insist on deep belief in every child and evaluate their own efforts with equity in mind. Researchers of equity-oriented Data Talk often suggest that educators press beyond quick summations of student performance to pinpoint what specific students can currently do and not yet do—and then, what adults can do next to improve instruction and other aspects of student support.[29] One principal who helped improve a large struggling high school in Massachusetts recalls focusing such Data Talk on what educators could do to support students, asking, "What are we teaching, how are we teaching it, and how do we know the students are actually learning it?" Dialogue also focused on immediate possibility rather than impossibility: "We are not likely to get any additional staffing or resources, so what resources do we have now that we can use more effectively?"[30] Similarly, a math teacher once told me that the key to Data Talk for equity in math was to "focus on specific errors that a student makes and try to help the student overcome those errors as a growing mathematician" rather than "form an overall image of the student as a kind of mathematics learner." Gutiérrez and Rogoff argue relatedly that rather than try to quickly sum up what kind of "learning style" a child has, it's critical to focus discussion on considering a specific "course of action or assistance that would help ensure student learning."[31] Researchers also argue that teacher "feedback" straight to students ideally helps students pinpoint, "What knowledge or skills do I aim to develop? How close am I now? What do I need to do next?"[32] In such feedback, Hattie and Timperley sum up, "Specific goals are more effective than general or nonspecific ones."[33] One elementary teacher told me of her use of daily paper "exit slips" to "uncover," from students, "what students know, what they don't know, their misconceptions, and their confusions," so she could pinpoint which students needed "reinforcement" from her on what and who was ready to move on. Amanda Datnow described the most promising use of data she'd seen recently: a math teacher sat with small groups as students solved math problems, took notes on specific students' misconceptions, and returned the next day ready to respond to each one.[34]

In each case, Data Talk for equity pursues detailed and insistent discussion of next moves to develop students' talents, meet students' needs, and offer specific opportunities to learn. One educator reading this chapter designed a sample sentence to help colleagues (who typically lamented students' reading) plan for actions they'd take to support students in literacy: "This student can already (*identify specific literacy skill*). He/she needs (*identify specific literacy need*). Providing the opportunity of (*teacher activity to support the specific need*) will support growth in literacy. We will monitor growth through (*data*)."

THINK / DISCUSS

If you were going to rewrite one sentence you've heard used to discuss students' progress, how would you rewrite it?

THINK / DISCUSS

Choose one or more items on your Data Wish List. Now consider: *how often* should people share information on that dimension of student progress, at what level of detail?

Researchers and educators often suggest that the less *frequent* or *immediate* the update, the less actionable the information it provides. MCAS, Massachusetts's basic skills test (on our spreadsheet view above), was a summative test administered once in the spring to assess skills gained that year. As one Massachusetts school district explaining a third-grade MCAS test to parents suggested, "The scores your child received will be mailed to you during the fall of [the following] year. Your child will be in fourth grade by the time any of us see them."[35] Datnow and Park write of the need for "*ongoing* feedback regarding student mastery" as well as detailed feedback, highlighting a school that assessed student progress weekly and flexibly re-taught students who needed a specific form of help at the time.[36] To support students' individually paced growth, middle school educators I know replaced summative, quarterly letter grades with regular, finer-grained discussions with both students and parents of students' development toward specified "learning targets." They asked students and teachers to reflect together on students' skill development every two or three weeks and sent the reflections home for parents to read and comment.[37]

There's another thing to notice about that detailed skill report regularly engaging students and, finally, parents in commentary. It's related to the comment box on the right of each individual online view we designed. Each infrastructure allowed viewers to communicate back!

I realized in designing our data views that much Data Talk is one way. That is, educators often ask parents, students, or other adults just to view information on student progress, not comment on it. As one teacher in California put it to me, "This data is not really even explained to the students, and conversations are never had with parents about the realities and potential of their children." Hattie and Timperley note that educators also often just tell students how they are doing overall, rather than engaging students in more powerful dialogue about "Where am I going? How am I going? and Where to next?"[38] (Teachers have pointed out to me that educators, too, often just "get data" from their district or state, without discussion of how they might best respond to it.) Researchers also point out that while adults routinely view data on students' performance without talking to students, students also can be asked explicitly to weigh in on what they understand and don't—and on the teaching strategies and classroom interactions that assist them.[39] Great teachers seek such input all day in class!

Regarding out-of-class discussions of student progress, the contributors to *Data Wise* suggest overall that any data conversation should "ensure that the conversation includes multiple voices rather than just the usual ones," to deepen understanding of students' needs and strengths and help educators plan more productively for improvement.[40] In designing our dashboards, we realized we could design an opportunity for people to communicate *with* the teacher and others about students' progress and development.[41] I pushed for the inclusion of a comment box on each view that would invite users to add their own commentary and input.

For example, this next data view might invite a conversation about a single student's attendance, enabling people to start to peel the onion on the story behind the data.

We also included a mechanism encouraging people to continue the dialogue with the teacher by phone, via email, and then as needed in person.

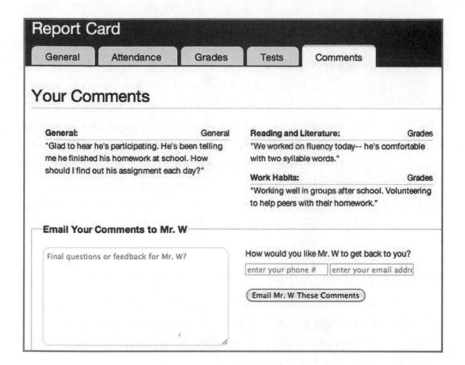

This is how infrastructure design can reshape the conversation about young people.

But keep thinking critically about this design.

An open invitation to speak more about a child—like a blank comment box—wouldn't ensure *helpful* commentary. One could imagine viewers uploading underinformed or derogatory comments about a student's culture or intelligence with a click, for example.

THINK / DISCUSS

Would you put a specific question or prompt above the comment box to invite helpful rather than harmful talk about the young person? If so, how would you word it, and why?

Equity designers also have to consider the *channel* used to discuss any data on a child. The designing teacher felt strongly that even if an online interface were multilingual and inviting, only some parents would actually feel comfortable weighing in on anything until a relationship was built face to face. He wanted to have parent-teacher meetings in person first, and then encourage people to access updates or join conversations via the dashboard.

Some parent advocates in the community, themselves bilingual, dismissed the idea of expecting any online conversation between teachers and new immigrants, even a multilingual conversation. Later, though, we talked to immigrant parents who welcomed the ability to readily see or comment on their child's school data on their own time, even if some were going to have to be shown how to see it via technology or assisted by a neighbor to type or translate exchanges with teachers. For parents, discussing student progress in person required a personal appointment with a teacher, time off from work, and for many, scheduling with staff for in-person interpretation—all infrastructure potentially more onerous than figuring out the technology. We'll engage these issues more in Chapter 7.

> **THINK / DISCUSS**
>
> Consider one piece of information on your Data Wish List that you think would usefully be discussed with someone online, and one you think should not be discussed online. Why, in each case? Does it matter who is communicating with whom?

Online conversation could also potentially broaden the group that could share any update on a child, creating more decision points for equity designers. We dreamed initially that our individualized data display might be designed like Facebook, to allow multiple educators, family members, mentors, and youth to make suggestions the others could see. Yet our teacher designer felt strongly that viewers' comment box comments should go to him only. He felt concerned, for example, that parents able to "reply to all" might criticize him to many people at once, rather than give constructive criticism to him first. So, we designed comment box comments to go directly to the teacher's email. Ironically, our final programmer finishing the dashboard instinctively linked the comment boxes to a publicly viewable string of comments that anyone discussing the student could see.

> **THINK / DISCUSS**
>
> How might you invite multiple perspectives on some data on your Data Wish List? How could you begin a group conversation about that data to make discussion most helpful to students? Give an example.

Equity designers also have to consider how much information on a young person to archive. For example, many educators worried about students' successful transition between grades and schools argue that it's essential for the receiving teacher to see prior records on a child. Yet other educators find getting "the folder" from prior teachers particularly problematic because students are quickly framed as "kinds of kids" before next teachers even meet them. As we've seen, initial surface information on children can lead to underinformed expectations, then treatment, then actual achievement. So, should new supporters see *old* information on a young person? On what issues should students get "clean slates" when they meet new supporters?

THINK / DISCUSS

Consider an item on your Data Wish List: should adults who don't yet know the young person see it or not? Why? (One college student considering this question decided that "once reaching college, data from high school should not be available; the student should be working on a clean slate." How about in earlier grades?)

So with equity in mind, let's consider one outer limit of Data Talk: young people and supporters able to check constantly online on the "points" given students on assignments and tests, in an anxious quest to increase scores and grades. As an equity designer, how would you feel if such Data Talk were enabled for a young person you know?

Many would agree that the problem in that last example isn't the frequency of information about student progress—it's that the data discussed frequently are only points, scores, and grades. Researchers argue that tests, for example, particularly high-stakes standardized tests, have long eclipsed other forms of data on student progress, particularly educators' own review of student work.[42] In the early 2000s, one Texas principal lamented to researchers that "the parent conference time that we used to spend getting to know parents and talking about what we knew about their kids, from their progress in previous grades, turned out to be talking about taking a test and then talking about the results of that test."[43] To many, such single measures of "progress" just skim the surface of a child's skills, or even mask them; researchers call for more thorough and varied measures of student development instead.[44] (See Chapter 3.) And increasingly, calls for "multiple measures" even extend beyond the skills typically measured in schools: as leaders of one Albuquerque school working to build on local indigenous community knowledge argued bluntly, "defining students by test scores and grades" alone just felt deeply reductive. For example, "standardized tests do not assess students' levels of wellness, the strength of their cultural identity, and their commitment to their communities."[45]

So, does your Data Wish list yet include sufficiently varied forms of information on student progress and development?

In fact, there's a whole realm of data about young people that we haven't even engaged yet—what students themselves say they can do, like to do, and do, in and out of school.

So, let's finish this chapter's Data Talk design brainstorm by considering the pros and cons of asking students themselves to communicate a broader range of their own developing talents, skills and abilities. We'll call this Talent Talk.

Supporting students' own Talent Talk as part of Data Talk

In Chapter 3, we saw that inside schools, the information shared about young people's abilities is often more reductive than robust.

> **THINK / DISCUSS**
>
> Can you think of one skill you have developed (or had as a young person) that nobody in school knew you had? (Would they not have expected you to have that skill? Why?) How, if at all, would you have wanted to share this skill with others in school?

> **THINK / DISCUSS**
>
> Were you ever invited in school to comment on the full range of skills and talents you wanted to develop further? Which skills and talents would you have focused on?

Remember that gold nugget quote from John Dewey from the introduction, about how supporting any student means developing "the full and ready use of *all* his capacities"?[46] And the delegates in Charleston after the Civil War who demanded "the right to develop our whole *being*, by all the appliances that belong to civilized society"?[47]

With equity in mind, many argue that we need more robust information about young people's *current* range of talents and interests so we can think bigger about developing their *potential* human talents and interests via schools. As a teacher working with Sonia Nieto put it, too often with students "we never ask them who they are and where they want to go."[48]

So which information on young people's growing skills and interests, from which domains of life, should adults know about in order to support them more effectively? And what infrastructure would let students add that information to the conversation about them in schools?

Inviting Talent Talk from students themselves

Many researchers suggest ways of asking students to share a broad range of skills they value in themselves or want to develop further. Moll and González suggest that educators head to homes to learn about the skills students are busy honing in everyday family life—their household "funds of knowledge"—so they can tap these daily "funds" in classroom curriculum bringing academic subjects alive. (After such a visit, for example, some Arizona teachers built a lesson around the economics skills a Guatemalan family used while running a family candy business.[49]) Wyman and Kashatok suggest that teachers go see local youth in community spaces that demand additional skills, like church choirs or community center programs, to begin to glimpse a broader range of skills valued by youth as well as community adults.[50] Rich Milner similarly advises educators to visit places where students are displaying skills they might not get to demonstrate in class, to build a shared sense of student potential:

> **Attend extracurricular activities featuring your students.** It means something to students when teachers take time out of their schedules to visit an activity they are involved in. I shall never forget the time my third-grade teacher attended my football game at a city park. Needless

to say, I played at my highest capacity that game, and I remember feeling a great sense of pride that my teacher had supported me in this way. In the third-grade classroom, I remember putting forth more effort after this experience and looking at my teacher with an intensified level of respect.[51]

At home, in jobs, and even in leisure time, students might be using skills or pursuing skills that people in schools never associate with them—and demonstrating potential along many dimensions. When we recognize young people displaying a broad range of talents and skills, researchers note, we and they are more likely to act as if they have more to offer—and students don't have to make false choices between school and personal identities, either.[52] Peers can benefit from such information too. One undergraduate clearly remembered a day in high school when he'd seen recent immigrant students he'd rarely talked to in class show major skill and confidence on the soccer field. The new information made him realize how little understanding he had of these classmates' "lives and circumstances"—and he set forth to learn more.

I developed an assignment when I taught high school summer school that asked students to explain in detail in a ten-minute class presentation something they already knew how to do well. One student who was annoyed with me most days in class proudly explained to us in her presentation how exactly to run a food stand at her job at a local football stadium. I had no idea she had this responsible role outside of school. The assignment changed our relationship because it fostered more mutual respect. It was also my first glimpse into inviting students to describe their own developing talents.

Encouraging students to share their range of talents and interests doesn't actually take that much work at this point in the twenty-first century. Today, young people are describing themselves all the time through social media, for example. How and when should we harness that digital infrastructure to enable young people to show more of what they like to do and can do?

In the OneVille Project, teachers, students, and community supporters spearheaded an online portfolio (ePortfolio) project at the city's high school, inviting students to document on a simple personal website their own developing skills, learning efforts, and talents inside and outside of school.[53] Our goal was eventually to link that information to the dashboards' more typical Data Talk—as Henze and colleagues put it, to enable "conversations where numbers, names, pictures, and narratives come together" to "find faces and names of students abstracted in numbers" and more fully describe "the contributions, skills, and intellectual strengths of a student."[54] Other schools combine portfolios with verbal "presentations of learning," or hold quarterly, student-led, face-to-face dialogues with educators and parents on specific study skills, academic skills, and social skills students are working to develop.[55] Such Data Talk efforts are designed to let students describe their own progress (and desired progress) on a wider range of dimensions than tests or grades allow.

In Somerville, teachers, administrators, and students wanted to move beyond an initial portfolio tradition of students' best class assignments (chosen by teachers) kept in a locked cabinet. In comparison to paper folders, they reasoned, online portfolios could enable more documentation of student skills (videos, links) and allow students to communicate their skills to more supporters (mentors, admissions officers, employers). Students were invited to use any media to show their skills, to document skill in both "twenty-first century" categories and traditional school subject categories, and to document out-of-school skills as well. So a student could upload a physics assignment to show "creativity," upload a history assignment as evidence of skill at "acquiring and evaluating information," show a photo of himself leading the soccer team or a classroom project as evidence of "leadership," or describe babysitting efforts or a community program role as an example of "responsibility."[56]

Over two semesters of afterschool design sessions, dozens of students and teachers tested ways for students to communicate what they could do in and out of school. Student portfolios presented in a spring 2011 community expo shared "videos of students narrating their original poetry, solving math equations, doing physics, and learning to skateboard; interviews with teachers evaluating students' negotiation skills; photos and commentary on students' original art and work experiences, including their skills in engineering, carpentry and dress design; and class assignments students found particularly valuable to their learning."[57] See the project website for a video of these presentations (http://wiki.oneville.org/main/Eportfolio).[58]

As one student described in her presentation, an ePortfolio allowed her to "show all of the sides of who I am, in one place," and to communicate "little cool things about me" as well as evidence of "being a good student." Her example shared various aspects of her life in Brazil and now: designing dresses, loving chemistry, and dyeing her hair blue. Another student's draft portfolio shared his ability to design and engineer projects out of wood, do strange art with Photoshop, draw cars, and do physics assignments.

> **THINK / DISCUSS**
>
> What is gained when a student gets the ability to show himself or herself from such multiple angles? Are there any negatives?

Participants named several key factors in inviting students into Talent Talk. One critical aspect was naming broad categories of skill and ability that the school would value. Young people also were motivated by choosing their own best work for showcase, in conversation with adults who encouraged students to believe their work was worth showcasing. One student, a Spanish speaker, described how transformative it was to feel encouraged by teachers to post her original poetry online; it was her first time sharing it with anyone at all. Participants also said that an anticipated teacher, peer, and potentially public audience was key to inviting students' Talent Talk. At times, students agreed, adults had to stress how much this audience believed students had skills in progress and wanted to see those skills.

> **THINK / DISCUSS**
>
> At the Try Tomorrow level, what's one sentence you could say to encourage a young person to recognize and share skills he hasn't yet shown others, or skills that she values in herself and wants to develop?

Finally, adult participants also argued that asking students to reflect on their own talents helped students "articulate the best ways they learn" and helped adults individualize attention to student interests.[59]

Adult participants argued the following in a presentation on the project:

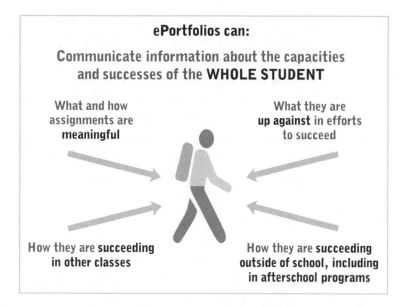

ePortfolios can:

Communicate information about the capacities and successes of the WHOLE STUDENT

What and how assignments are **meaningful**

What they are **up against** in efforts to succeed

How they are **succeeding** in other classes

How they are **succeeding** outside of school, including in afterschool programs

Of course, equity designers inviting Talent Talk need to contend with some Core Tensions. Inviting and listening to students' self-descriptions takes time and often money; a week of school spent making holistic student portfolios or a whole day spent on students' presentations can seem to some a week or day not spent building academic skills, and to others a critical investment lifting students' confidence or transforming adults' understanding of students. Some people fear diluting a focus on school skills by allowing out-of-school talents into the conversation; others frame tapping students' out-of-school competency for classrooms as one of the most important things a teacher can do, as it helps students connect what they can do already to the school skills they are expected to build.[60] And as with all schooltalk, designers need to consider when to praise the skills students currently have and when to push them to go further, emphasizing everyone's potential for growth.[61]

THINK / DISCUSS

On your Data Wish List, would you take school time to invite students to document and discuss their out-of-school skills? Why or why not? (How about a broader range of their in-school skills?)

But if we want our Data Talk to pursue equity, inviting Talent Talk from young people can help counteract distorting ideas about young people that limit what we support young people to do. As we've seen throughout this book, scripts program us to *not see* young people's full range of skills and talents—or even to imagine such talents. Being mis-seen and mis-described daily as a human being *without* talents and potential contributions is a point of pain for countless young people. As one student who had dropped out of school in tenth grade due to excessive suspensions told researcher Marcia Caton, "Many of my teachers were not aware of my strengths because they did not spend time getting to know me."[62]

Seeing young people incompletely and inaccurately blocks educators from fully valuing young people and connecting to them; it keeps young people "confined to a box" of stereotypes and misinformed reactions;[63] it blocks young people from developing "identities that they choose for themselves, rather than identities that society or peers expect of them";[64] and it constrains us from fully committing to developing students academically.[65] If we design Data Talk to share a more complete range of information about what young people can do, are learning to do, and love to do, counter-stereotypic learning about young people[66] can happen every day.

Getting more fully informed about young people of course requires attending not just to students' developing talents, but to students' ongoing lives in real time—struggles as well as triumphs. Through seeking a "personal bond" with her pupils, Gloria Ladson-Billings noted long ago (citing researcher James Comer), "the teacher ceases seeing his or her students as 'the other' and addresses students' psychological and social development along with their academic development."[67]

So how, and *when*, should people talk to students about which aspects of their personal lives and needs?

Figuring that out is the challenge of our next chapter.

ACTION ASSIGNMENTS

1. Finish your Data Wish List for now, plus your Ideal Data Communication of each item. What information about student progress and development do you now most care about sharing with whom?

2. Consider one typical way that data on student progress is displayed, accessed, discussed, and used in an education community you know and actually might be able to improve. Analyze the pros and cons of that approach with one adult and one student, asking each person:

In that education community, what typically is communicated and not communicated (by whom) about how students are progressing and developing, and what adults might do next to support students?

How and when do students get to communicate about their own progress and development? Are families brought into the dialogue? Consider together the pros and cons of the standard practice.

Finally, ask about one way they think this DataTalk might be improved.

Report on how the conversation goes. What did you think of their suggestions? Were there some Principles or Core Tensions embedded in them?

If you now were going to change one thing about Data Talk in that setting, what would you change first?

3. Talk to someone else about one suggestion on your Data Wish List/ Ideal Data Communications document. Explain each aspect of your infrastructure design idea:

> Who in a school/classroom/community needs to communicate what information to whom? (How often? When?)
> What are the barriers to needed communication, and how could those barriers be overcome?
> What channel (face-to-face conversations, paper, technology) might allow necessary communications to occur?

Then ask: what tweaks would they make to your infrastructure with equity in mind? Name any Core Tensions of Data Talk you encounter.

4. Try to turn one gold nugget idea or example from this chapter into a #schooltalking tool that lots of other people could learn from. For example, create a poster or PowerPoint slide, short video, or other multimedia image publicly sharing that gold nugget quote or idea. To accompany your main message, create a brief user's guide of five related information points or ideas from this chapter that can help users be more fully informed about the issue at hand and have a productive

conversation sparked by your tool. See Chapter 1, pages 65–66, for more instructions.

Here's a poster I'd like to make:

**If you don't know how I'm doing,
you can't support me to grow.**

5. In person or via the Internet, find an educator or young person who you feel is schooltalking for equity in their Data Talk. Document (with permission) and share (#schooltalking) some example of their work—a photo, a video, an image, a quote from them, or something they have produced.

More schooltalk scenarios

THINK / DISCUSS

Think of a number, word, or phrase you've heard used lately to describe a child's school progress. (Or, think of a number, word, or phrase once shared to describe *your* progress.)

What additional information, from whom, might you add to that number, word, or phrase to assist a young person? How would you get it? Name a Principle and Core Tension behind your suggestion.

THINK / DISCUSS

Have you ever seen people fail to discuss and address a conse-quential data pattern regarding many young people? If you were a teacher facilitating a faculty meeting, what cautions would you urge as people started to discuss that data? For example, might you ask people to pursue a thorough conversation about causation, analyze their own roles in the pattern, or emphasize possibility rather than impossibility? Role-play one Try Tomorrow suggestion for starting a discussion about the data pattern you have in mind. Consider a Principle and Core Tension behind your suggestion.

THINK / DISCUSS

Can you think of an example when a failure to "disaggregate" data along some dimension can hamper efforts necessary for equity? A friend told me about one district that decided to lump English learners, low-income students, and Special Education students into one category of "historically underperforming students" whose performance they would monitor in the aggregate under a grant. When my friend asked the superintendent about the choice not to monitor students in race-group terms, the superintendent said, "We just didn't want to deal with that one."

If you were an educator in this district, would you insist on a conversation considering specific subpopulations in your school? If so, how would you begin that conversation in a helpful, rather than harmful, way? For example, one leader recalled a strategy for comparative Data Talk: "When I discussed achievement gaps, I did not compare the performance of one subgroup with another. I compared each subgroup with the standard of 100%. For example, if the state reading assessment pass rate for our white students was 90%, and the pass rate for Hispanic students was 80%, I presented the achievement gap for white students as 10% and the achievement gap for Latino students as 20%. Thus, we needed to close gaps within every group in the district. The community seemed to buy in to this approach."[68] Consider a Principle and Core Tension behind your own idea for starting a dialogue about any specific subgroup "data" you have in mind.

THINK / DISCUSS

What might be lost if administrators pore over data patterns without input from teachers? How about if teachers pore over data without input from students and parents? Name one shared conversation you'd find particularly necessary in an education community you know, and a Principle or Core Tension behind your suggestion.

THINK / DISCUSS

If someone wanted to understand your own current progress on something you're trying to learn, what information would they most productively review? Who else, besides you, might they ask for input? Would you feel comfortable about those people being asked for input on your progress? Why or why not? Name a Principle or a Core Tension of such Data Talk.

THINK / DISCUSS

Most tech-based data tools in schools require substantial financial investment by districts, prohibitive for some and a large risk if the technology doesn't work for people or the company folds. I've also seen districts that have built and installed very expensive new data systems but didn't pay for enough staff to learn how to use them.

Should schools and districts spend a lot of money on online data tools? Consider a Principle and Core Tension behind your response.

THINK / DISCUSS

Have we unnecessarily replaced face-to-face or paper-based communications with newer online communications about student progress in schools? Brainstorm the pros and cons of any tech-oriented Ideal Data Communication on your Data Wish List. Might you "blend" that communication with in-person or paper-based communications? Name a Principle and Core Tension behind your thinking.

THINK / DISCUSS

Can you think of one type of skill that a school community you know could reward publicly, but doesn't? For example, Django Paris and H. Samy Alim[69] and Ted Hamann[70] each frame multilingualism as a critical life skill that is rarely rewarded explicitly in schools. If you were a principal, would you reward student multilingualism? Some other skill? Name a Strategy for rewarding typically uncelebrated skills in schools, and a Core Tension of doing so.

THINK / DISCUSS

When should students be in charge of describing their own growing skills and talents? When should educators? (Would you feel more confident in students judging their "softer" skills, like their relational skills or abilities to speak in public, as opposed to their "harder" skills, like the ability to solve linear equations? Why?) Consider a Principle and Core Tension behind your answer.

THINK / DISCUSS

Which categories of skill would you track in schools if you were in charge?

Look back to Chapter 3. If you were Robert Sternberg, you might invite examples of students' "Analytical intelligence," "Creative intelligence," and "Practical intelligence." If you were Howard Gardner, you might invite examples of students' "Spatial" skill, "Bodily-kinesthetic" skill, "Musical" skill, "Interpersonal" skill, "Intrapersonal" skill (understanding oneself), "Linguistic" skill, and "Logical-mathematical" skill. And if you used the verified résumé adapted in the OneVille ePortfolio project, you might invite examples of students' skills in "Creativity," "Listening," "Responsibility," "Teamwork," "Working with Cultural Diversity," "Interpreting Information," "Negotiation," and "Acquiring and Evaluating Information," as well as in traditional school subjects.[71]

Consider several categories of skill you think people should track but typically don't in an education community you know. Name a Principle and Core Tension behind your suggestions.

THINK / DISCUSS

One university admissions officer told me that with huge numbers of applications, there was no time for reviewing documentation of student skill in multiple forms. So beyond short personal essays, the school prioritized more quickly reviewed and quantified measurements of skill—tests, course completion, and grades.

Should students' more thorough self-presentations matter more in college admissions? Consider a Principle and Core Tension behind your response.

THINK / DISCUSS

Should more holistic Talent Talk ever trump typical measurements of skill? What if a college applicant's SAT math scores aren't great but he can design fabulous engineering projects, and he wants to be an engineer? What if an applicant to journalism school can write amazing op-eds convincing public audiences, but she failed English 12?

Here's an interview with Sternberg himself, arguing that additional documentation of students' skills should perhaps supplement typical assessments but not supplant them: "A video can measure creativity, initiative and practical skills in a way a typical standardized assessment does not," he argues, but it is not "a substitute for a high school transcript."[72]

Name a Principle and Core Tension of allowing evidence of students' broader talents to ever trump scores and grades.

Chapter 6

Life Talk

⊙ **PRINCIPLE**

We need to make it more routine, not rare, to invite dialogue with students about their ongoing life experiences.

Chapter Goal:
Enable Life Talk. Design ways supporters can communicate with young people as needed about things young people are experiencing and supports they need.

Look back at our Foundational Principles on page 8 and our Foundational Image, reprinted on the next page.

Put together, all the previous chapters have suggested that these people need to get more informed about students' lives, experiences in opportunity contexts, developing talents, and current needs so they can help offer necessary opportunities and supports.

We've just talked about enabling more informed discussion of students' progress and development (Chapter 5).

So how about just talking to students on a regular basis about how they are doing in life?

In this chapter, we'll start designing infrastructure for Life Talk—for helping the folks in our Foundational Image to communicate more routinely with young people about their ongoing experiences, situations, and needs, so that folks know *from* students what's going on with students and offer supports on the spot.

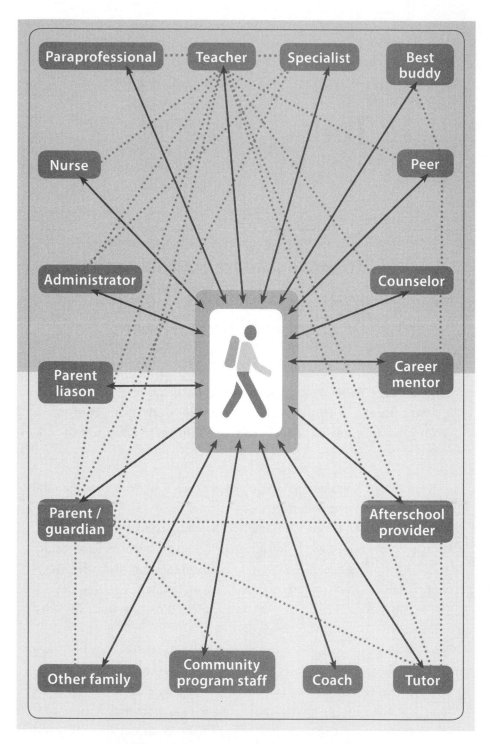

The Foundational Image of *Schooltalk*: A sample of the people who help shape a young person's fate in school every day

This might sound obvious to you—adults need to talk with young people about how they are doing in life in order to support and care for them. Similarly, Blankstein and Noguera argue that "the starting point for working towards the goal of excellence through equity is creating a community where the needs of each student are thoroughly known. . . . By knowing our children—how they learn, what motivates them, what challenges they face, and so on—we are better able to create an environment in which all students can get what they need to succeed . . . students can be part of this process, and spaces can be provided so that they can tell us what they need to be successful."[1]

Yet in most schools there seems to be little time to talk to young people about their ongoing lives. As one teacher put it bluntly, "With 187 students, I just do not have time to fill in all the holes about each individual student." University students of mine put it even more bluntly: "Too many students, too little time." And regardless of staffing ratios, many educators don't think it's their job to get to know students personally.

So, in this chapter, we'll both hang on to and debate the key Principle above: *should* educators routinely invite dialogue with students about their ongoing life experiences, as part of caring for students in schools? If so, how? If you don't work in schools, no problem: consider the Life Talk needed to support any young person you know.

Life Talk in action

Various education reform efforts focus on designing ways for adults to support students through regular conversation about their lives. For example, "personalization" efforts in schools often focus on creating situations where young people can talk more easily and regularly to adult supporters, individually and in smaller groups. As Yonezawa, McClure, and Jones sum up,

> Most efforts to foster strong relationships and personalize schools focus on new, smaller organizational structures and programs that make it easier for teachers and students to spend time together—individually and in small groups—and to get to know one another. These range from advisory programs and small learning communities within large schools to autonomous small schools. . . .

The idea is that educators get to know their students well—not just their abilities and learning styles but also their interests and motivations—and they use this insight to design more effective individualized instruction and guidance.[2]

Making time for talking to students (individually and collectively) about their everyday lives is core to other movements in education. For example, widespread calls for "culturally responsive" teaching ask teachers to continually learn about both the community lives and the "individual student needs and experiences" of the complex students in front of them; teachers then can teach to engage the specific students in the room.[3] As Kenneth Zeichner notes, such "responsive" teachers hone the ability to "learn about the special circumstances of their own students and their communities and the ability to take this knowledge into account in their teaching."[4] Geneva Gay suggests that teachers learn about, then build on, students' experiences in local communities as "filters" for engaging students in any subject;[5] Jeff Duncan-Andrade urges educators to engage the "real material conditions" of students' lives in class; Brayboy and Maughan call for "contextualizing what is being learned and tying it to the actual lives of the children."[6] Christine Sleeter suggests that educators can "interview their own students to find out what they already know, or believe they know, about the main idea for the curriculum. Usually these interviews reveal a combination of prior experience and knowledge that can be built upon, inaccurate assumptions, and questions students would like to explore."[7] And Carol Lee sums up that "neither teachers nor students come into the space called the classroom as blank slates." Instead, each brings "both their individual characteristics and priorities" and experiences "from community life" that educators can draw on when teaching, through tapping familiar images, words, or experiences from students' lives to link directly to the academic task to be accomplished.[8]

All such learning requires talking with young people about their experiences in and out of schools. As Bryan Brayboy put it to me, educators need to "build relationship with their students, their students' lives and their histories."[9] Many youth themselves call for educators who welcome such dialogue.[10] Researchers frame the informed "alliance" and "positive, caring relationships" forged through such dialogue as critical to student success. As Nasir writes of successful student support programs, "students and teachers consistently alluded to spaces, formal and informal, where students could raise and discuss personal issues and struggles with their teachers," almost like family. Through respectful mentoring and listening in such discussions, adults supported students emotionally and socially as well as academically—as "whole people."[11]

Many school reformers note that there are dire consequences if adults *don't* connect more personally to students. For example, Yonezawa and colleagues argue that "almost one-third of U.S. high school students fail to graduate," with dropout in part a consequence of "the widespread feelings of anonymity, irrelevance, and disengagement that students report, especially in large urban high schools." "There is a tremendous personal and societal loss associated with these feelings and the resulting failure to thrive academically," they add. "Personalizing schools can help stem this loss by engaging students and making schools not only relevant, but places where they can feed 'their hunger for support and connection.'"[12] Others emphasize that students of all backgrounds who feel alienated from suburban or rural schools, too, need personal "connections" with supporters;[13] that young men crave supportive relationships no less than young women do;[14] that LGBT students need supportive educators to welcome their actual "lives, stories, contributions and existence" into school life in order to feel safe and connected to schools;[15] that students experiencing deep stressors of poverty particularly need educators to engage, not ignore, those stressors; and that even college students still need personalized support relationships with supporters who listen to how students are doing, advise on next steps, and express belief in students' ability to make it.[16]

Researchers also note that the benefits of such support relationships aren't just for students. "Teachers report greater passion for their students, for teaching, and for their content area when they know their students as individuals, take a personal interest in them, and set high expectations for them."[17] Educators implementing "student voice" or "restorative" practices also find that getting students' input on the schooling experience can improve both schools and their own teaching.[18] And as a colleague who spent many years teaching in a rural community put it to me, "Getting to know students as members of particular communities, and getting to be known by community members as someone with a reputation for caring, can be deeply rewarding."

So here's a deep equity question to think with first as we set forth to design Life Talk: who gets to get known in school, and who doesn't?

In a graduation slide show for a 6–12 school I know that graduates every one of its seniors college-enrolled—all low-income students of color—

educators show baby pictures through graduation pictures for every student alongside student quotes, conveying loving attention to each student's personal development in the community over many years. It's the core of schooltalking for equity: treat every young person from every community as if she or he matters.

Yet such personalized care is far rarer for students in other schools. One teacher I know realized that in his large suburban high school, he and his colleagues were simply less likely to ever get to know their students personally, particularly their students of color: "In talking about white students, conversations in schools are on more of an individual scale," he said. And as I noted working at the Office for Civil Rights, the predominantly middle-class parents who intervened to secure support for students with labeled disabilities were in essence securing ongoing individualized conversations about students' school experiences and needs. Low-income students and students of color labeled as having disabilities were more often put in understaffed Special Ed classes without such personalized attention. And no law demands such intensive personalized conversations about students not labeled with disabilities. As one new teacher put it of her school crowded with low-income students of color,

> My mentor, my co-intern, and I are all guilty of lumping students together, and not taking account of the particular needs of particular students that arise out of many meaningful differences—in socioeconomic status, previous schooling experiences, immigration status and amount of time spent in the U.S., to mention just a few. . . . More precise talk about specific students and their needs would at least allow us to begin personalizing our support for each of them.

We've seen throughout this book that such a commitment to deeper, more informed understanding is key to equity-oriented schooltalk. But even if students are lucky enough to have educators who want to take the time to consider individual and community experiences, a major structural crack still requires our attention as equity designers: personalized attention is often a goal unmet because there are so many individuals to get to know.

Educators in well-funded private schools might have tiny classes (one school advertises a student-teacher ratio of five to one).[19] Less-resourced public elementary schools in my area have some classes nearing thirty or thirty-five students, and middle schools have classes approaching forty.

Sometimes half of those students are recent refugees from war zones speaking many languages; all bring individual situations, strengths, and needs. Secondary teachers in understaffed schools are often each working alone to get to know every one of their 180 students. While the American School Counselor Association recommends a ratio of one counselor for every 250 students,[20] student-counselor ratios in many high schools in our area approach six hundred to one, and one thousand to one was recently calculated as the average across K–12 schools in California.[21] Just picture *one thousand students* in the middle of our Foundational Image, all competing for time to discuss their lives and college applications with that one "Counselor." As one California teacher put it to me, in her school, which served many low-income students learning English, "Students used to meet with counselors every time they earned a credit, and it was an opportunity to chat and check graduation status with the counselor. Now, they are lucky if they see a counselor at all."[22]

So in many cases in schools, getting more and more frequent human support per student seems key. As Carol Lee writes, even "difficult life circumstances do not in themselves inhibit learning; rather, it is the nature of supports available that influence whether rigorous learning takes place: supports for coping with loss, for resisting negative influences, for persisting in efforts to learn when the tasks are difficult and appear on the surface abstracted from everyday life . . . schools need to be supportive communities for students as well as teachers."[23]

This is where you come in as an equity designer.

While we press to get more educators funded to support young people, can we simultaneously *design school time* to enable more supportive Life Talk? And once adults and young people get the chance to talk, *what might they actually discuss* to be most helpful to young people? As Rich Milner puts it, "I rarely, if ever, hear practitioners contest the idea that relationship building is a critical aspect to their success with students in any classroom or school. The question, however, is how do teachers and other educators build those relationships?"[24]

There's no single right answer for "how." I know educators who arrange advisory periods where one teacher meets the same thirty students twice weekly for seven years.[25] Others run lunchtime mentoring groups where students talk to a caring adult who shares their gender or racial-ethnic community. Others assign an adult to "adopt" an entire grade for a year. Others ask adults to build more student support talk into their role (e.g., asking a dean of discipline to spend more time chatting informally with students; starting class with "circle time" engaging third graders personally). Others have tried one-to-one texting or even interviews to make time to talk to each student.[26]

Educators who *arrange repeated time* for students to talk with supporters about their lives and needs are creating infrastructure for Life Talk. Life Talk opportunities mix information-sharing and relationship-building. Sometimes, information-sharing leads to relationship (a young person reveals a struggle or success at home, then feels closer to his teacher) and sometimes relationships lead to information sharing (after getting to know a teacher in advisory, a young person feels ready to talk about college).

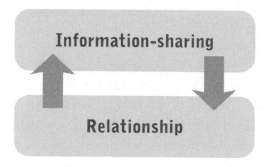

And in every case, as we'll see, support depends on what people actually say.

We'll work on two Design Activities throughout the chapter as a way of collecting our thoughts about enabling the Life Talk we think is necessary for equity in schools.

Design Activity 1: While you read this chapter, collect infrastructure components for an Ideal Student Support Calendar

Consider this: if you were going to design an Ideal Student Support Calendar to structure a student's typical month, what communication opportunities would you schedule on that calendar? Who from our Foundational Image would you gather, how often, to talk about which domains of students' experiences? Via *which channel* would you support them to communicate? Print yourself a blank calendar and start designing, asking our infrastructure design questions:

To support the full human talent development of every student and all groups of students (equity) with our Life Talk:

> Who in a school/classroom/community needs to communicate what information to whom? (How often? When?)
> What are the barriers to needed communication, and how could those barriers be overcome?
> What channel (face-to-face conversations, paper, technology) might allow necessary communications to occur?

February

Sunday	Monday	Tuesday	Wednesday	Thursday	Friday	Saturday
1	2	3	4	5	6	7
8	9	10	11	12	13	14 Valentine's Day
15	16 Presidents' Day	17	18	19	20	21
22	23	24	25	26	27	28

For example, depending on the age of students you might schedule in an advisory hour linking one teacher weekly with thirty students, face to face, to discuss the nuts and bolts of college preparation (especially if the students' parents have never been to college). You might design quarterly meetings for each student with a local mentor, to discuss career interests and needed skills. You might decide that a coach should head into study halls once a day to talk proactively to specific students about achieving their potential. You might design a monthly dialogue about school discipline, office hours where a small group could reach a teacher or tutor online each afternoon, or a weekly meeting in person for each student with a peer "cocoon."[27]

Designing school calendars is a moment with major equity implications in schools. As one educator put it to me, every "master schedule" distributes a limited number of staff to young people on limited time. Another principal says that if you want to know a principal's "values," look at the master calendar to see which supports have been scheduled, when and for whom.

Figuring out who spends time with whom, for what purpose, is essential equity work.

And what would you want people to talk about once they got connected?

Design Activity 2:
Mock up an Ideal Student Support
Conversation that can occur during one
or more of the slots on your calendar

This is critical. Once you have time scheduled on your calendar for a supporter to talk with a student, *what communication with a young person would be ideally supportive?* Remember, some talk harms. So, get specific: zoom in to envision an actual exchange between a student and a supporter. In any "slot" on your calendar, how would a supporter flip a script, try to learn more from a young person, motivate a youth struggling through a snowball, or just listen?

You'll see exchanges throughout this chapter that will give you some ideas!

Designing your Student Support Calendar and Ideal Student Support Conversations for equity will require thinking about questions from earlier in the book. For example, on your calendar,

* Would you schedule in a group-specific peer support group (what Gándara calls a "cocoon"[28]) at any time during your calendar month, and with whom? For example, might you invite immigrant students, Asian students, freshmen, athletes, Vietnamese speakers, boys, into a support group just with others in that "group"? Why or why not? If so, would you prioritize a mentor from that same "group"? And what would you hope they'd discuss while together? (Chapter 1)

* Will you schedule in particular time and attention to kids struggling with acute problems, or will you give all students the same minutes of student support each week or month? And what's the most supportive thing a supporter could say to a student struggling in an opportunity context you have in mind? (Chapter 2)

* How often will you convene explicit conversations about a young person's school progress? What aspects of his or her skill development

would you consider the highest priority to discuss? And once together, what words or phrases would you use to convey belief in students' strengths and human capacity to develop skills, as you discussed any student's current abilities? (Chapters 3 and 5)

✳   Would you build time into the school month or week for educators to learn more from young people's families? And once together, what questions might you want people to ask to invite dialogue on students' or families' experiences inside and outside of school, without prying? (Chapter 4, discussed more in Chapter 7)

Throughout, even as you dream big about ideal student support communications, you'll also have to consider a pragmatic issue of designing schooltalk for equity: time. There are only so many minutes in a school day, and a lot to get done. Which Life Talk, with whom, is worth those precious minutes?

> **CORE TENSION**   How can any necessary student support communication happen without draining resources from other precious needs?

Keep your eye on the prize of enabling *necessary* communications *when needed* (not just "more").

So let's start to work on our two Design Activities with equity in mind. First, start to collect ideas for "slots" you might schedule on your Ideal Student Support Calendar, so that students have a chance to talk in necessary ways with supporters. Then, consider an Ideal Student Support Conversation for some of those slots. What would you hope people would discuss once together?

Let's consider suggestions from other designers. **THINK/DISCUSS** questions will ask you to evaluate the pros and cons of their designs with equity in mind.

Enabling Life Talk with equity in mind

Equity designers have proposed Life Talk infrastructure in many forms, ranging from quick classroom assignments that invite (not force) students to discuss some incident in their lives to more in-depth activities that invite students into extended dialogue. Such efforts invite conversations with young people more regularly than rarely, affording a deeper understanding of (and response to) whatever students want to share about the ongoing experiences shaping their lives.

As an example, Sonia Nieto suggests that educators create case studies of individual students through informal interviews. She encourages educators to first ask themselves: to support students better, "what most interests you about young people? What do you most want to know?" Then, with permission from students, educators can sit down with young people one on one in a "get to know you" interview, conducted inside or outside of school. In full case studies that Nieto has asked educators to produce for professional development, educators conduct multiple interviews (with guardians' permission), review secondary sources for more general community information (including community history), and write up anonymized "cases" on student lives to gather their thoughts. Nieto explains that in a case study, "The students are described within a variety of settings—home, school, community, and city or town in which they live—because, by looking at each of these settings, we gain a more complex pictures of their lives" as younger children and now, "including their thoughts about how schools might be improved so that more young people could succeed academically." Nieto suggests that educators ideally interview someone from a different "background" than their own. She also notes that the "interviews themselves" can be "empowering for the students," who feel more heard and better known.[29]

In these snippets from a case study, Nieto demonstrates the level of knowledge that educators can strive for through combining one-on-one interviews and secondary sources:

James Karam is 16 years old and a junior in high school. His dark eyes are serious but animated when he speaks. He thinks he has a big nose and jokes that it is one of the characteristics of being Lebanese. Poised between childhood and adulthood, James is that pleasing combination of practical, responsible, wise adult and refreshing, spirited, eager kid. His maturity is due in no small part to his role as the "responsible" male in the household. His mother and father are separated, and he is the oldest of three children, a position he generally enjoys, though he admits it can be trying at times.

James is Lebanese Christian, or Maronite. His father, whose heritage is Arab, was born and raised in the United States. . . . In a participant-observer study of the Arab community in this city three decades ago, it was reported that the first Arab settlers arrived in the 1890s from Lebanon. . . .

James went to a Catholic school from kindergarten until third grade, but he has been in public school ever since. Although he was held back in third grade because his family moved out of the state and he lost a good deal of school time (this still bothers him a lot), James is a successful student who has given much thought to his plans after high school. He works at keeping his grades high so that he can get into a good college and is fairly certain that he wants to be a mechanical engineer. His real dream, however, is to be a professional bike racer. . . . James is fluent in both English and Arabic. He has never studied Arabic formally in school, but the language is important to him, and he means to maintain it.[30]

THINK / DISCUSS

Would you schedule a case study "interview" on your Ideal Student Support Calendar at any point in a student's school year, as an intensive effort to "get to know" a young person? Why or why not?

Many educators I know who have read Nieto's work on case studies have agreed with her emphasis on knowing young people more fully, particularly when young people are struggling and might have input on improving their school supports. Nieto argues that "students who do not succeed academically can too easily become casualties of educational systems that cannot 'see' them because their problems remain invisible."[31] Getting to know individual students can also catalyze deeper understanding of students' experiences in communities[32]—and locate community adults already supporting and mentoring young people in ways youth value.

But every educator considering such Life Talk approaches has then raised the same Core Tension. How can an educator learn about young people's complex lives and thoughts in this much detail in the middle of a very busy school day, month, or year, if she doesn't have *time* to sit down with each student for an extended case study interview? And some teachers have then asked an even more fundamental question about Life Talk: is it really teachers' place to get to know students this much?

Many researchers and teacher educators argue that this *is* a teacher's job. Rich Milner suggests pointedly that "teachers sometimes spend infinite amounts of time talking about students to their colleagues or to students' parents but minimal time actually talking to students themselves." Milner suggests that for starters, teachers simply "engage in conversations with students themselves to learn from and about them."[33] Gloria Ladson-Billings asks teachers "to interact with children and adolescents in non-school settings" in order to get to know them, particularly "in places where they are likely to be experiencing success—community and neighborhood centers, clubs, teams, and afterschool activities."[34] As she writes of several successful teachers later profiled in her book *The Dreamkeepers*, "it was common for the teachers to be seen attending community functions (e.g., churches, students' sports events) and using community services (e.g., beauty parlors, stores)."[35] During 2015, as repeated examples of excessive discipline meted out to students of color filled the news, Ladson-Billings posted this more basic suggestion publicly on Facebook:

I taught school in Philadelphia for 10 years and 3 years in E. Palo Alto. In those 13 years I "suspended" ONE student because he was a danger to himself and others. All other "suspensions" were me requiring students to spend MORE time with me, not less. Thus, I picked them up early each morning to attend school. I ate lunch with them and I drove them home late in the afternoon. Two things invariably happened. One, no one went through more than one suspension. Two, over our 2–3 days of intensive interactions we actually got to know each other better and recognized our individual humanity. I have never suspended kids for doing kid things—talking out of turn, not completing assignments, cursing, and petty fights. My role as a teacher was always to show them alternatives to solving problems and maximize the time they spent in school.

THINK / DISCUSS

Start to think: on your Ideal Student Support Calendar, would you schedule in time for any of the people in our Foundational Image to interact more with students in non-classroom and even non-school settings? Why or why not?

But many educators still grapple with a key question about Life Talk: how much time should people take to talk specifically about students' lives, especially if their main job is to teach a subject?

Much of the field wrestles with this Core Tension. In professional development ("PD"), for example, we often divorce professional development on "diversity" or on building relationships with students from PD on "math" or "science" or "reading." And in "diversity"-focused PD, I've found, someone almost always will argue that attending to relationships with students in a "diverse" society is "taking time" away from the real goal of teaching "content." For example, someone might say, "If you really want me to do equity work, let me just focus on teaching math!" Some even anxiously caricature "diversity"-related effort as a rejection of all content (like math), in favor of fraught conversations "about race" all day with students in classrooms.[36]

If you were to draw a Venn diagram of that common "let me focus on teaching content!" argument, it would look like this. That small slice in the middle is the time when it would make sense to consider students' everyday lives during math class, for example.

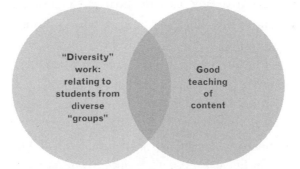

But to many in our field, "good teaching" means teaching content successfully *to* students in a diverse and inequitable world, which requires relating successfully all the time to the complex human beings in one's room:

This new Venn diagram suggests that teaching any subject requires some human relationship, and that human connections with students can *lead to* successful engagement with "content," not just exist as some separate part of the work.[37]

But how much time should be taken in schools to get to know young people "personally" remains up for debate for many.

THINK / DISCUSS

Do you have a gut feeling about the Venn diagrams above?

Other researchers suggest that efforts to "get to know" students in order to successfully teach them don't always have to be quite so time-consuming or even so explicit. Ben Rampton suggests that just by stopping to listen to youth interact informally outside of class or after school, teachers can start to learn a lot about students' complicated identities and lives.[38] One teacher I know called it essential and "doable" to "meaningfully interact with every student at least once during every class period." And as Carol Lee notes, while teachers ideally "come to know each student and the life circumstances that student brings with him when he enters a classroom," "all students do not require the same level of monitoring" at all times; often, precious time can be spent on students currently most acutely in need of attention.[39]

So let's continue to design slots for your Ideal Student Support Calendar and collect ideas for the Ideal Student Support Conversations in those slots. Look back at our Foundational Image (page 258). Think about a young person in the middle that you care a lot about. To support him or her, *who* most needs to be talking to *whom*, about *what*, and *when?*

Student support ratios: To support young people, *who* needs to be talking to *whom*?

Support communications can come in various sizes, ranging from one-to-one communication to small group communication (like a routine gathering with several students and a coach), to a classroom-size dialogue (a home-room, a math class), to a grade- or school-wide communication (e.g., a principal holding an assembly with all seniors), to a neighborhood- or community-wide communication (e.g., a dialogue about youth experiences in a shared town) or, even, perhaps, global communication (like a student discussing his feelings online via a blog). We might consider each "layer" in this image a support group that needs to talk about and with a young person in order to care for him or her.

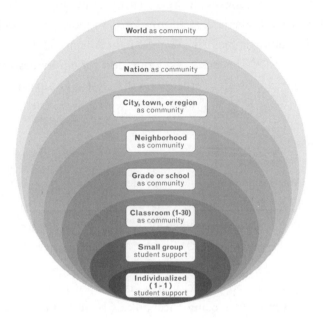

A student support relationship in any such "layer" requires both talking to young people and listening to them. One student described "the impact of communication as a two way stream—listening when someone talks, and talking as someone listens."

Let's start to explore a few examples of student support communications at each "layer," thinking critically about pros and cons for equity.

The world as community

Efforts to support youth in media-making often invite youth to speak to "the world" about the issues affecting their lives.[40] Online formats then enable response from the world. Many in education are increasingly excited about the idea of students sharing ideas online using social media, blogs or online chats, and getting responses from peers or mentors anywhere, anytime.[41]

Of course, research suggests that online, youth often get support from people "like them" along demographic, experiential, or interest-based dimensions. Youth often talk online to peers who share race and class demographics, as when white students talk mostly to white students. Yet many youth also deepen fundamental skills through online dialogues about shared interests (think programmers talking to programmers).[42] Researchers note too that online connections with peers sharing a circumstance (e.g., LGBT youth) offer many students critical emotional support—even as in-person alliances *across* demographics (like Gay-Straight Alliance clubs) can offer essential supports too.[43] This raises a key question for equity designers: when should youth get support from others who share some group experience, and when should they cross "group" lines to talk with new people?

> **THINK / DISCUSS**
>
> On your calendar and in your Ideal Student Support Conversation, will you link students with peers or adults who are "like them" or *not* "like them" along some key dimensions? Which dimensions? Why?

Questions of privacy and publicity arise as well for equity designers. For example, some schools are using Facebook as basic infrastructure to keep connected to graduates across "the world," but students might not share post-graduation struggles. Other youth-support organizations use private Facebook messaging or text messaging for more targeted one-to-one support instead.[44] Researchers also say that while online communications with "the world" enable support at all times, "Familiar practices of making friends—gossiping, bullying, and jockeying for status—are reproduced online" and perhaps increased, due to these communications' "publicity" and "always-on" nature.[45]

> **THINK / DISCUSS**
>
> Would you schedule in any *fully* remote group supports on your Ideal Student Support Calendar, where students and their supporters don't have to meet in person? On what issue, between whom? Why or why not?

Schools usually require some adult supervision of students at all times when they're on school grounds. Still, if you had no constraints, would you schedule in any time on your Ideal Student Support Calendar when students would talk to one another for support (online or in person) without any adult present? Why, or why not, to discuss what?

A region, city, town, or neighborhood as community

On your Ideal Student Support Calendar, would you schedule a community dialogue focused on young people's local experiences? Some organizations invite young people to discuss city- or town-wide issues in school auditoriums, community centers, or school board meetings; some such dialogues focus on listening to youth, while others prompt intergenerational sharing. Organizations like Sacramento Area Youth Speaks (https://vimeo.com/135921332) and Teen Empowerment (www.teenempowerment.org) sponsor youth poetry slams, dialogues with families or police, and speak-outs on issues affecting local schools and neighborhoods. Across the country, practitioners of "youth participatory action research" work with young people to investigate issues of local concern (school resource patterns, segregation, policing), then share research findings publicly (see also Chapter 2).[46] Some designers invite city-wide, multilingual dialogues on community or school district improvement with youth online, even via games (www.communityplanit.org).

On your Ideal Student Support Calendar, would you schedule any time to discuss youth experiences at the level of region, city/town, or neighborhood? Why or why not? What issues would you most like to see young people invited to discuss in a public forum, and who would you want to listen to them? (Would you prioritize intergenerational dialogue, or presentations where youth speak and adults listen?)

Grade or school as community

Some schools design infrastructure for schoolwide or grade-specific Life Talk. Pope and colleagues describe "Challenge Success" teams (including an administrator, a counselor, one or more parents, and two or more students) that regularly review indicators of "student stress and well-being" schoolwide, then report results.[47] One 6–12 school, Gompers Preparatory Academy in San Diego, organizes lunchtime tables so that no student eats alone but always has peers from class to talk to. The director routinely gathers an entire grade (or sometimes, a gender group within a grade) so he and other adults can talk with a segment of the school about college-prep behavior. Another administrator adopts the entire eleventh grade as his grade of focus for a year. He reviews student attendance and homework completion daily on a Google form filled out by teachers, allowing him to approach individuals whenever they need supports on specific things.

> **THINK / DISCUSS**
>
> This video by Gompers educators starts to explain their schoolwide Life Talk communication efforts. Which of these elements might you incorporate into your Ideal Student Support Calendar, or choose not to incorporate? Why?
>   See http://www.gompersprep.org/culture.

> **THINK / DISCUSS**
>
> On your Ideal Student Support Calendar, would you schedule in ways to dialogue with students on schoolwide issues? On what issues, and how?

The classroom as community

Much student support communication in schools happens at the classroom level—schooltalk in a group averaging, say, thirty people.

So, what Life Talk would you want to make sure occurs in a group of that size? Milner urges teachers of any subject to:

Encourage classroom discussions that let students be the center of attention. Teachers should not always be at the center of discussions but should allow students to share events and experiences from home and their community. Students should be allowed to share whatever information they feel comfortable discussing.[48]

THINK / DISCUSS

On your Ideal Student Support Calendar, how often would you afford time for full-class discussions on events and experiences important to students? Does it depend on the subject area?

Educators balance Life Talk and content talk differently in every classroom to support students. Some center discussions of content around issues of interest to students; some talk briefly about personal lives before class or as class begins. Some glue to students' lives occasionally during discussion of content (e.g., connecting familiar life experiences to a novel or a chemistry concept). Some glue content to local lives as often as possible; some interrupt class as needed to engage issues eating at youth. Some educators take time out of class for structured Life Talk whenever conflicts arise. In a restorative justice "circle," for example, a class or small group gathers to hear from all sides about a recent conflict or to explain and evaluate recent behaviors affecting the others; participants commit to improvements on all sides and make a return to class more productive.[49]

In classrooms, Life Talk of any form for equity ultimately enables rigorous work as well. A class filled with conversations about the weekend but no rigorous engagement with content can't be an equity-oriented classroom. Researcher Ilana Horn notes that successful math teachers she studied discussed students as "learners of mathematics" as well as "worthwhile human beings," for example, not only as the latter.[50] Hattie and Timperley argue that to support school progress, teacher feedback to students about specific strategies for improving schoolwork is more helpful than pure "feedback about the student as a person."[51] Castagno and Brayboy note that "caring" is "a necessary but not sufficient quality of effective teachers for Indigenous youth"; the ideal "warm demander" expects excellence as well.[52] As Yonezawa et al. note, "Increasingly, we suspect that healthy relationships matter most when they are used as a conduit for enhancing student engagement and curricular mastery."[53] At the same time, many note, a classroom that focuses exclusively on discussing subject matter while ignoring consequential events shaping students' lives and moods is also not an equity-oriented classroom.[54]

Jones and Yonezawa suggest that educators also can invite student input on the school or classroom experience itself, via student research groups or focus groups (others have used student surveys). When convening focus groups, educators can participate, or sit quietly and listen: "Often, educators listening to diverse students discuss teaching and learning reconsider their own assumptions and beliefs about students' capability and motivation."[55] Students in focus groups have called for higher standards ("your teachers accept the work that you've done instead of telling you that you could do better, that you should do better"), or critiqued lax due dates ("they'll have a deadline and if the students won't reach that deadline he or she will extend it, and keep extending it, extending it, extending it"). "It really bothers me when teachers are not hard on you," one student summarized.[56]

Others engage youth in research on school climate or discipline; educators and researchers alike work with youth to research other students' input on effective teaching practices, as well, then hold professional development sessions where young researchers share their perspectives on teaching practices with teachers. At one session organized by Nicole Mirra and colleagues, students even engaged additional teachers in reacting to the students' own presentation style, modeling questions like "How does ('talking at you') make you feel," and "Can you give us some examples of how you would like to be engaged?" "We ask you not just to leave here, but to leave here and reflect on how you teach and learn," one student concluded. "Teach as if you were teaching yourself."[57]

So educators increasingly are asking students to weigh in on their schooling experiences. As Makeba Jones put it to me, however, "to embark on focus groups (or youth-led research) as an educator, you need to know your limits. Before you decide to do focus groups and ask for their honest opinion, you have to be prepared to take it. And if you're not ready, you have to do your own work to prepare."

How about this Life Talk infrastructure: Lorna Hermosura, a trained counselor and former Upward Bound leader, created edMosphere, a tech tool that lets students privately tell teachers and counselors how they are doing in daily one-minute check-ins. To begin class, students click icons that match how they are feeling that day. Teachers see a dashboard showing every individual's response. They can follow up in person with anyone sending a distress signal.

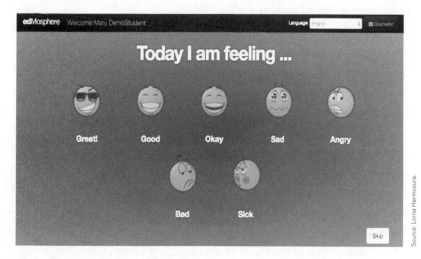

Source: Lorna Hermosura.

Such infrastructure need not be digital: Makeba Jones described one math teacher with "large classes, 40 students each" who invited students to write to her three times a week for ten minutes, via paper notebooks kept in the classroom. "Over time, kids got comfortable; they could comment on things they were experiencing at home," Makeba said. "They knew they had this one-to-one relationship with her through writing."

Other infrastructure routinely convenes a classroom of students for Life Talk specifically. Yonezawa, McClure, and Jones provide a description of "advisory" classrooms designed "to be the one place where students feel they have at least one school advocate. Advisory teachers are to get to know their charges over a long period of time and become the person the students go to for advice and support regarding academics, social and emotional needs, and postsecondary information":

> [A teacher] might also lead an advisory course with 20 or 25 students in it, with the charge of getting to know each student individually regarding their academic strengths and their socio-emotional needs as adolescents. . . . The teacher might keep his or her advisees for several years, seeing them through until graduation (or even beyond). If a student gets in some sort of academic or behavioral trouble, the teacher might easily walk down the hall . . . to discuss the matter with other teachers and compare notes, records, and even prior assignments completed as they pool their knowledge formally and informally to better serve the student collectively.[58]

As anyone who had a pointless "homeroom" in high school knows, however, an advisory slot isn't *inherently* helpful in equity terms; it has to actually provide needed supports. (I recall gathering weekly based on alphabetized last names, to hear announcements that we could have read in a bulletin.)

So what might an *equity-oriented* advisory caring more fully for students look like? Educators at the Preuss School in San Diego have designed their school's grade 6–12 advisory program over many years and now consider it a crucial aspect of their student support infrastructure. Teachers stay with a single advisory class for seven straight years, meeting an entire class period like any other class. Advisory class is used for supplementary help on academics (e.g., all teachers focus on time management, organization, and literacy; math teachers send problem sets into advisories for peers to work on together). Advisory is also used for college preparation (e.g., the counselor uses advisory time to help with financial aid forms or host college reps; teachers use advisory to help students prepare for the SATs, seek scholarships, and write résumés and personal statements). Advisory also supports one-on-one conversations about how young people are doing personally. Advisors say that issues shared privately with them range from advisees' personal struggles with depression, family poverty, or immigration to adolescent issues with girlfriends or boyfriends, plus ongoing personal successes. One advisory teacher told me the relationship creates "a family—I feel more at home with this group than any other." As two Preuss teachers put it when sharing their advisory model, advisory "supports a diversified student body *through* high level curriculum" by providing "a sense of belonging and inclusion they so desperately need. And we all know that when that happens, learning happens."

THINK / DISCUSS

Watch this video Preuss educators made about their advisory model. Would you schedule an advisory on your Ideal Student Support Calendar? How often? Ideally, what would people in your advisory talk about? See http://preuss.ucsd.edu/current-students/university -prep.html.

Small group student support communications

What could happen if every young person had a "support team" in school—a small group to talk to as needed? Support "teams" are required as part of disability services; many schools convene other support teams when students need them. Mark Warren describes one school's as-needed "pupil rescue team": "when a child has a problem," a team including "a learning specialist, social worker, and health-care professional" would meet, discuss the child's needs with his/her teacher, and follow up with informal updates.[59] Other educators use small support teams to avoid unnecessary suspension and expulsion, as adults ensure that students don't get into trouble and that other adults don't overreact to minor behaviors.[60]

Schools structure academic "team" relationships, too. When I taught high school, four teachers (math, science, English, social studies) shared 100 students in a group we called a "house." We met weekly to discuss individual student issues and needs. "Team" members who knew students more deeply could then help other colleagues question underinformed schooltalk. One middle school assistant principal described the benefit of such conversations to researcher Gilberto Arriaza:

> I try to let [teachers/colleagues] see what I know . . . I tell them: "Do you know that this student's father was killed in a gang shooting and stuff, that the kid is in a foster home and has nothing, not even uniforms?" I do it when I have an opportunity, when we have a conversation. I hope once teachers know about the student they [have labeled], that they will investigate. They usually say, "Oh, I didn't know that."[61]

Students were not present at these "team" meetings, however (nor were parents), and students also typically had no choice over who was included on their support team. As in the example above, we also tended to talk much more about youths' struggles than about their successes or strengths.

THINK / DISCUSS

On your Ideal Student Support Calendar, would you convene a support team to routinely discuss young people? If so, consider:

✳ *Who* would you put on any student's support team? Would the student get to choose any members of their team? If some students have closer relationships with security guards, school office staff, or older peers than any teacher, why not bring them on a "team" as a critical supporter? As one student told researcher Gretchen Brion-Meisels, "The secretary or the nurse are the only two people in my whole school that I can trust."[62] (To consider this, you might recall: who would you have put on your own support team as a younger person, to discuss your well-being and needs?)

✳ Would students be present at discussions? How about parents?

✳ *How often* would the team meet? Would team members check in proactively with students, meet on a schedule, or convene as needed? (The strategy of "intrusive advising" has mentors or supporters checking in proactively one on one with college students, for example, rather than waiting until the student asks for support.)[63]

✳ Would you ask the team to focus on students' positive experiences and strengths, in addition to students' needs and struggles?

✳ Finally, *what channel* would support team communications? That is, would you only have the "team" talk face to face? Might they use some technology? Why? (I knew a teacher who, at parents' request, used an email string to update a large team of supporters regularly on the experiences of a student they were all concerned about.)

Take a minute to update your Ideal Student Support Calendar and consider your Ideal Student Support Communications.

And how about this Core Tension of convening any support team to talk: not everyone assigned to support young people is actually supportive of them. As one teacher noted to me of a student needing support, "In the teacher's lounge at lunch, the math teacher constantly talks about how lazy this student is." She wondered: Would it be helpful or not helpful to have a "team" conversation of any kind that included this teacher? But what would happen if this teacher were excluded from team conversations about how to support the student?

THINK / DISCUSS

If some people assigned to be a student's supporters are not actually that supportive, should they be included or excluded from conversations about supporting the student?

Have you been considering your Ideal Student Support Conversations—what supporters actually *say* in any of the slots on your calendar? Let's start thinking about that at the level of one-to-one support conversations.

All of your schooltalk thinking actually comes together in this question. Imagine that you are preparing any of the supporters in our Foundational Image to talk with a young person you care about, in one of the slots on your calendar. *What's one conversation you would want those people to have?*

Individualized (one-to-one) student support communications

In some ways, one-to-one communication enabling informed support for each student's specific needs is the holy grail of schooltalking for equity. It's also the most precious communication resource in resource-starved schools.

And of course, just having a one-to-one discussion doesn't ensure support. The conversation actually has to be supportive.

CORE TENSION   Making space to talk is crucial, but it isn't enough. It matters what you say!

The key is to keep asking yourself our guiding question:

Does this communication help support **equity** (the full human talent development of *every* student, and *all groups* of students)? Or not?

NOT supporting each/all students' talent development   SUPPORTING each/all students' talent development

To complement the many examples of adult-student talk already in this book, I went looking for researchers' favorite documented examples of one-to-one (or small group) Life Talk to jog our thinking. Here's one conversation between two African American students and a track coach, which researcher Na'ila Nasir considered particularly supportive. Nasir argues that the coach provided seamless personal support *while* students were doing the hard work of developing a skill, helping young people to be their "social selves" *and* "learners" at the same time.[64] She also points out that unlike many classrooms, the support exchanges had an important "lightness"—a playfulness "not viewed as a problem for players completing the work."[65] See what you think:

> **Coach:** Michelle what do you want to be when you grow up?
> **Michelle:** A pediatrician.
> **Coach:** A pediatrician? So we're gonna have a pediatrician and an obstetrician?

Michelle: Yep.

Coach: Maybe you guys could go into business together—Candice can deliver the babies and you could take care of them once they get here. OK. That's cool. Why do you want to be a pediatrician?

Michelle: 'Cause I have a way with kids.

Coach: You have a way with kids? Do you take care of them when they're sick? You give 'em, like, Tylenol? What's the grape stuff?

Michelle: With my little sisters, I used to—

Ella:—give the baby codcine. [*She laughs. The coach laughs too. There's more conversation about the medicine.*] What's your nickname? What's your nickname Michelle? [*There's more talk about nicknames. The coach plays around with nicknames for her.*]

Coach [*returning attention to the practice*]: You ready to do this one, Michelle?

Michelle: Yep.

Coach: Whenever you ready, Ell. [*Ella runs, but the timing is off and they miss the handoff.*]

Ella: I'm tired and I can't run no more!

Coach: That was right there.

Michelle: I got out that time.

Coach: Yeah, you got out two steps too early. One step too early and you'd be fine. Y'all were right on pace to get it right here. Right here Michelle would have had it in full stride. Let's try it again. [*Ella expresses frustration and walks back to her starting place.*] I know. I know. If you're that tired, then get it right. [*Returning to chat*] What you wanna be when you grow up Ella? [*She doesn't answer for a moment.*]

Ella: A hustler.

Coach: Did she say a hustler? A hustler, no we don't want that, Ella.

Ella: Brett Favre. [This is a joke, as Brett Favre is a white professional football player.]

Coach [*pressing*]: Do you want to be a business person?

Ella: I want to be an entrepreneur.

Coach: What do you think you're good at selling?[66]

What aspects of this exchange, if anything, would you include in your
Ideal Student Support Conversation? In which slot on your Ideal
Student Support Calendar would it take place? Why? (Could this
exchange with a coach occur between teacher and students? Why or
why not?)

A next favorite Life Talk example came from Leisy Wyman's long-term participatory work with youth and adults in a Yup'ik village in rural Alaska. A
coach asked players to pause, listen, and strengthen after one youth showed
his frustration at losing a sports event. Words in italics below are translated
from Yup'ik. By referencing youths' everyday lives in the community, the
coach emphasized that youth were already strong:

> Just because somebody beats you, you don't *get angry. You are not to
> get mad.* . [. . .] . . *If someone* beat*s you,* you're not taking first place in
> tournament, and you get beat in a tournament, don't get mad, don't
> show it. . . Work harder. . . . *That's what you should do, we are not to
> get angry,* don't *pound* the floor. . . . . We are supposed to do that, we
> should learn. *No one will ever live without ever getting* beat*en.* . . [. .
> .] All through life . . . like in hunting. *So then wherever if you have a
> breakdown of your snow(mobile),* it's part of life, learn from accidents,
> *that's the way it is.* Working hard *all the time is the way to learn.* Work
> hard, even in education. *You guys have to do your* homework *all the
> time.* . . . *You know,* don't quit on anything.[67]

What aspects of this exchange, if anything, would you include in your
Ideal Student Support Conversation? In which slot on your Ideal
Student Support Calendar would it take place? Why? (Could an adult
with less experience in students' communities, or someone who
didn't speak students' native languages, participate in such Life
Talk? Why or why not?)

Researcher Rich Milner pointed me to this favorite example of Life Talk he'd once observed. He describes a teacher, "Mrs. Shaw," who always "attempted to cultivate relationships" with students. Here, Mrs. Shaw's ability to reference background knowledge on the spot helped her calm down a young person deeply stressed over an in-school suspension, or "ISS":

Christine: Miss Shaw, fill this [the assignment sheet] out. They [the administration] put me in ISS. [Tears started to flow.]

Ms. Shaw: Christine, what's going on?

Christine: I just don't like her [referring to one of her other teachers].

Ms. Shaw: Well, Christine, you will meet a lot of folks in your life you don't like. You've got to learn to work with people you don't like. It's going to be all right, though, because you are smart, and you've got to let that situation roll off your back.

Christine: I knew you were going to say that, but I still don't like her. . . .

[As Christine still looks deeply distressed:]

Ms. Shaw: OK, Christine, sit down. Just hang out here with me for a while. You don't need to go to ISS in this state. How is your sister doing? You know I have taught all your older sisters, and you all are smart girls. What would your sister Tonya say if she saw you all upset like this?

Christine: She would tell me to calm down.

Ms. Shaw: Exactly. Just shake this situation off, Christine. It is so not the end of the world. You will bounce back from this. How is Tonya doing?

Christine: She is fine. She just got married.

As Milner recalls,

By the time Ms. Shaw finished posing questions to Christine about her sister and reassuring her that she was indeed "all right," Christine had calmed down. In fact, by the end of her exchange, Christine looked like a completely different person. . . . When I talked with Ms. Shaw about the interaction, she said she worried that, had she allowed Christine to leave her room in the state she was in, she would have run into even more problems. She felt responsible for Christine and invited her to hang out in her room until Christine was in a space to move forward.[68]

THINK / DISCUSS

What aspects of this exchange, if anything, would you include in your Ideal Student Support Conversation? In which slot on your calendar would it take place? Why? (What else would you add to this conversation to make it ideally supportive? For example, could Ms. Shaw have asked what landed Christine in the suspension situation in the first place? What sorts of exchange between the *other* teacher and Christine, or between the two adults, could help Christine further?)

Tiffany Lee quoted "Darren," a Lakota teacher who explicitly positioned himself to students as family. Darren explained to students that "he was not only their teacher, but that he wanted them to view him as an uncle." Lee highlighted his effort (and non-Native teachers') at deeply respectful, family-like relationships or *k'é*. Darren explained, "It was hard for them to kinda think of like, 'Dang, I have an uncle here,' or something like that, you know?":

> But then like that, I said, "You guys are family as well in this class. You guys are gonna treat each other— you guys are gonna care for each other. . . . I was like, "I want you—if somebody is being hurt, if somebody is being called names, I want you guys to stand up for them because that's your responsibility." We talked a lot about responsibility in a society, to care for each other, and . . . then we got into all the virtues that we have, you know, respect, wisdom, sacrifice, generosity.[69]

THINK / DISCUSS

What aspects of this exchange, if anything, would you include in your Ideal Student Support Conversation? In which slot on your Ideal Student Support Calendar would it take place? Why? (Can any educator position himself or herself as "family"? Why or why not?)

Finally, researchers emphasize the critical importance of students and educators planning toward both academic and social goals, asking: "Where am I going? (What are the goals?), How am I going? (What progress is being made toward the goal?), and Where to next? (What activities need to be undertaken to make better progress?)"[70] In a chapter called "What a Coach Can Teach a Teacher," professors and high school teachers Jeff Duncan-Andrade and Ernest Morrell describe building such goal-focused Life Talk into a basketball program they ran for girls. Both had already engaged students in classrooms through literature, popular culture, and social science on educational inequality; in this excerpt below, they described developing a "powerful counter-narrative to urban school failure" through additional Life Talk with youth as basketball coaches. They recalled the importance of three one-to-one "reflective meetings" per student per year, where they asked questions like this to prompt students to consider their own strengths and goals:

Basketball
>   What are your strengths as a basketball player?
>   What are the areas you need to improve as a basketball player?

Academics
>   How would you describe yourself academically?
>   What are your strengths and weaknesses?
>   Why do you feel this way?

Future goals
>   What you want to accomplish this year as a player? How will you do it?
>   What do you want to accomplish this year as a team? How will you do it?
>   What do you want to accomplish this year as a student? How are you doing?
>   What are your long-term goals for yourself (five years, ten years, twenty years)? How will you accomplish them?

"These meetings were part of a year-long process of self-reflection that helped participants focus their energies on specific goals," Duncan-Andrade and Morrell recall, adding that "our experience as teachers and coaches allowed us to identify potential in students that they often did not see in themselves. . . . Students and coaches alike left these meetings with clear goals and concrete steps to achieve those goals, a process that one student," Ada, "pointed out is rarely experienced by students in urban schools":

You got me to think about where my life was going and what I wanted out of it. I know that most of the kids I knew never even thought
about that at all. When I'd ask them stuff, they would just say, "I dun-
no." But you got me to think about my future . . . all the planning we
do, it made me feel like I was together.

The coaches also helped each student develop a personalized plan for pursuing specific goals. One student secured extra tutoring and summer accel-
eration to bridge from her athletic prowess to academic success. Another
student, less athletically inclined, developed her leadership on the team and
focused on advanced classes. After analyzing potential responses to educational inequality in their own community, students started a basketball
camp that focused on supporting other youth through navigating local adolescence. The discussion and pursuit of "hard-to-reach goals" was the key.
As one student summed up,

The most helpful part of this program was the conversations that you
had with me. When we would meet and we would talk about what you
thought I could do, I really started to believe in myself. Sometimes,
it felt like you believed in me more than I believed in me. This was a
dramatic change for me. Before I didn't even see a reason for coming
to school. I think because I didn't have any goals.[71]

THINK / DISCUSS

What aspects of this exchange, if anything, would you include in
your Ideal Student Support Conversation? Why? Might you schedule
time for such "goal-setting" dialogue on your Ideal Student Support
Calendar? (How familiar with the local opportunity context must the
adult already be to support such dialogue?)

Here's a last set of examples for equity designers to consider—one-to-one
Life Talk via technology, in this case via text message.

In the OneVille Project, I and a graduate student colleague, Uche, worked
with two teachers at an alternative school, Ted O'Brien (high school) and
Maureen Robichaux ("Moe," middle school), to formally pilot the use of

one-to-one text messaging in everyday student support. This was at the suggestion of students, who had argued that if we wanted to set up anytime supports for them, we should try the simplest and most available way to reach them: texting. (Note: just between 2006 and 2010, the percentage of teens using text messaging rose from to 51 percent to 72 percent.[72]) Both teachers were excited to test out texting's possibilities; at the school, students were often absent and on the brink of dropout. With the goal of designing a full "support team" eventually, we decided to first try simply allowing one-to-one texting when needed between students and a key type of supporter—their teacher.[73]

As equity designers, we invited both teachers' nearly forty students into the pilot as co-researchers. We got signed permission forms indicating that participating adults would monitor the texts for safety and explore the utility of text messaging for student support. Students and adults together brainstormed ground rules for using the channel, including the following:

✳ Don't expect a text back before 8 a.m. and after 10 p.m.;
✳ No inappropriate language;
✳ No sharing of anyone else's business.

We used Google Voice, a free web-based phone and text-messaging service that provided teachers new phone numbers to share with students and recorded all of the texts in teachers' Google inboxes. In weekly discussions over doughnuts and in focused data analysis meetings reviewing anonymized texts, Ted, Moe, and student participants joined us in analyzing the student support that was possible and not possible via the channel.

Teachers and students chose anonymized examples like the following as examples of useful support conversations.

Most obviously, participants noted, texts could reach students even when they were absent. For example:

8:15 p.m. Teacher: Worried about you!!
8:16 p.m. Student: im feeling much better now I will deff see u tmr (:
8:17 p.m. Teacher: Good we miss you!! Can mom right a note for the
    last 2 days

8:18 p.m. Student: she called [School administrator] today telling him I was out sick not truent

8:19 p.m. Teacher: Good..see you tomorrow..and glad your feeling better!!

8:24 p.m. Student: thanks

THINK / DISCUSS

What aspects of this exchange, if anything, would you include in your Ideal Student Support Conversation? Why? (Would you insist that your Ideal Student Support Communication not have misspellings or slang in it, or would you not care? Why? Notably, several teachers at the mainstream high school had refused to pilot texting, saying such "anytime" support would be infantilizing and would encourage improper English.)

THINK / DISCUSS

While almost all students who wanted to text had phones and texting plans, not all had consistent access—some lost phones, ran out of minutes, or changed numbers. If some students can't afford a channel for communication, does that mean that the teacher shouldn't use the channel?

Moe sent some "wakeup texts" before school to middle school students she was concerned about. For example:

7:00 a.m. Teacher: Like I said, you need to get it from him. Be on time for school today

7:00 a.m. Teacher: You're doing great

7:01 a.m. Student: I will and u woke me up .thanks

7:03 a.m. Teacher: You're welcome

What aspects of this exchange, if anything, would you include in your Ideal Student Support Conversation? Why? (What are the pros and cons of an educator being able to contact a student any time, anywhere for support, and vice versa? Ted noted that one-to-one support texts, in theory, could expand communication time exponentially. He also noted that a text could deepen a relationship in seconds, saving school-day time, and that, as with any student support strategy, you could just choose when to communicate as a texting teacher and when not to. For example, Ted said he wouldn't be trying Moe's "wakeup texts," explaining, "I'm trying to put more responsibility on the high school student—I'm shying away from the pre-school conversation.")

Students pointed out this exchange as an example of Ted's student support via text:

7:19 p.m. Student: Hey I dont think im going to come to school tomorw im wicked sick

7:44 p.m. Teacher: Have a glass of o.j. and drink water often. Get some rest, and you'll feel great in the morning, ready for school

7:58 p.m. Student: Ive been doing that all day and it hasnt helped one bit

9:31 p.m. Teacher: Lets have a good full 1/2 day tomorrow

9:46 p.m. Student: I dont know if im goin to school tomorw

9:49 p.m. Teacher: You haven't been putting consecutive full days together, push yourself to improve, you can do it!

What aspects of this exchange, if anything, would you include in your Ideal Student Support Conversation? Why? (Is there any point where adults offer "too much" help? Terrence Roberts, one of the "Little Rock Nine" who desegregated Central High School in Little Rock, Arkansas, recalled the power of being advised to become "the

(continued)

CEO of his own education."[74] Are any of these an example of babying keeping a student from growing into his or her own "CEO," or is this monitoring just part of a supportive educator's job?)

Participants pointed out how these exchanges about school absence turned into deeper conversations about grades and behavior:

9:30 a.m. Teacher: Everything ok?
10:39 a.m. Student: Ted?
11:02 a.m. Teacher: Yup
11:05 a.m. Student: Everythings alright I guess im gonna b in tm .. Is there anything I can do to put my grade up for your class
11:06 a.m. Teacher: Be on time tomorrow, we'll talk then.

10:12 a.m. Teacher: You need to be in school way more my friend
10:13 a.m. Student: Ok ?
10:14 a.m. Teacher: Everything ok?
9:22 p.m. Teacher: You left early today, then I saw you down the street at dismissal. I'm quite concerned about your behaviors the past month, we should sit down and talk some time this week

THINK / DISCUSS

What aspects of these exchanges, if anything, would you include in your Ideal Student Support Conversation? Why? (Could students get too dependent on text-based communications, and neglect to interact verbally or face-to-face? As one student put it to a teacher via text,

No don't call. I feel comfortable texting. I think it's better texting. Cuz I'm gunna break down and cry if I hear your voice. Let's just text.

At the same time, we found that in many cases texting didn't supplant face-to-face conversation. As here, we saw many texts used to prompt or schedule a face-to-face dialogue.)

Participants noted how informal and humorous texting exchanges could be:

2:38 p.m. Teacher: [Student,] do you still have the math book I gave you for homework? If you do let me know and [teacher] too

2:59 p.m. Student: Ya I do

3:27 p.m. Teacher: Use it!

3:31 p.m. Student: Ok. I will

7:47 a.m. Student: I just left my house right now so I'm going to b late

7:48 a.m. Teacher: And I need to know this?

7:49 a.m. Teacher: Hurry up!

7:49 a.m. Student: Because I don't want you to worry

7:51 a.m. Teacher: You miss school regularly silly goose

7:54 a.m. Student: I came in all this week and collected points

7:55 a.m. Teacher: Get here, we can celebrate

7:58 a.m. Student: Hahaha okk I'm on cross street now

And participants said examples like this demonstrated how students and teachers used text to "bond":

8:20 a.m. Teacher: Hey is your mom coming in

8:21 a.m. Student: Yah bro waiting for her that's y I ain't in school my G G=grandma lmao ur old

8:23 a.m. Teacher: Not funny....lol

8:24 a.m. Student: Ii hate the fact u don't apritiate my jokes

8:24 a.m. Student: -_-

8:26 a.m. Teacher: But I appreciate you:-)

8:31 a.m. Student: Ahhh good made my morning

8:32 a.m. Student: =)

8:32 a.m. Student: Lol jk jk idc

8:33 a.m. Teacher: Awwwww

What aspects of these exchanges, if anything, would you include in your Ideal Student Support Conversation? Why? (Are educators losing authority in these conversations? Teachers and students said that texting exchanges invited student-teacher relationship in part by temporarily putting teacher and student "on the same level" to talk. Yet as Moe noted, "the relationship" could also then snap back almost "like a rubber band" to teacher-student hierarchy back in class. Teachers also noted that they still insisted on school-appropriate behaviors in their text messages, even if they did so informally. Both students and teachers also pointed out that no "inappropriate" texts were ever sent. Instead, teachers mused that students were unusually polite: Ted noted that "the language that the kids are using to thank and what they do verbally is surprising. It's refreshing to know that they have that capability.")

In the texting pilot, we saw support on school expectations ("Be on time tomorrow") mix seamlessly with personal support ("did you have fun?" "you're a smart kid"; "you can do it!"), greased by texting's classically light banter ("You better be in tomorrow!!! Lol"). But this Life Talk wasn't just about texting. As Ted noted, "in some ways, it comes down to someone paying attention to them." Just responding to a text, as one student said, "shows you appreciate the person and you're thankful they helped you out." Moe noted that students "appreciate (Ted) taking time out of his own private life to send these texts." Ted agreed that students' own texts to teachers could also "show a level of investment": "Even if [the text is] not school related, the student is checking in, making that contact, when they don't have to." The exchanges thus built relationships that students said made them want to come to school at all. Moe noted that some students she texted to wake up still came late, but that the same students were now contacting her privately during rough times in their lives, one even just to make contact during a drug rehab placement. "Success for a depressed student in a sense is the engagement itself," she noted. "Even having this exchange." As participants put it, texting was just another way of actively "worrying" about the other—and being "here for you." Life Talk helped forge the "trusting relationships" that Angela Valenzuela calls "the cornerstone for all learning."[75]

Of course, making time for one-to-one Life Talk via any channel raises some obvious Core Tensions that equity designers have to consider. One is time: should teachers be *paid* for communicating with students outside of normal school hours, or is communicating outside of the school day part of a caring educator's job? Another is safety: should educators ever be "alone" with students to talk one to one? Many educators are counseled never to have one-to-one student support conversations with young people in person because of potential sexual harassment allegations; one elementary teacher told me she was afraid to even give an upset student a hug. Crucially, Ted and Moe felt that having all exchanges documented in a running record actually protected teachers as well as students. Texting aside, ensuring student safety is a top priority of Life Talk requiring ongoing consideration.

Another Life Talk issue equity designers must consider carefully is privacy. Laws require that educators share, with authorities, information youth reveal about child abuse, for example. In several cases, Moe shared texts with a depressed or self-destructive student with the principal, to catalyze student aid in a moment of crisis. But Ted wondered about "honor[ing] the kids' sense of privacy" in more typical situations. Texts legally could be requested by parents at any time, of course, but Ted wondered of typical situations, "Which communications should go to parents? Which to kids? Which to both?" As one student who had a destructive relationship with her mother put it, she was now up for texting teachers but not for having her mom know her school-related "business." And as one young person told researcher Gretchen Brion-Meisels, "most times you can't really find a trustworthy person in school": a teacher who "let out too much information about you" told in confidence could break "trust" for future communications, such that "you don't feel comfortable talking to them."[76]

Additionally, what if students feel forced by their supporters *to* share? One teacher noted that when he asked his students personal questions for the Action Assignment ending this chapter, "When asked about their lives, students began by looking around to make sure nobody was listening in and trying to hear what they were going to say." To him, they seemed deeply uncomfortable about sharing "aspects of their private lives with those around them." Every effort at caring Life Talk indeed must navigate the line between "supporting me" and "being too much in my private business"; the effort to learn in order to support students can't be confused with an insistence that students reveal. As Hiro Yoshikawa points out of undocumented students, for example, many students put their families at risk if they share critical facts about their lives with anyone; other individuals just want more privacy.[77] One undergraduate told me that when a sibling of hers died, teachers helped her by promising to be there to talk if she needed it, not by prying into how she was feeling. With equity in mind, educators have to invite contact with students without forcing it.[78] Many educators prioritize connecting young people as well to additional community members they can talk to and learn from.[79]

Chang and Conrad suggest that adults follow young people's leads when *they* open the door to deep conversations, by just asking open-ended follow-up questions.[80] Some researchers and youth organizations give students cameras to take pictures of their own neighborhoods and lives outside of schools, so that they provide a "window" into their own lives on their own terms. Like photographic self-portraits, invitations to write poetry, then share it—or make and share art—can let young people speak as they wish (and from multiple standpoints) about what's going on in their lives (and going well) and also what they hope to change.[81] (Datnow and Park describe educators who learned more about students' experiences of disengagement in school without asking them any questions—instead, by spending a whole school day with them.[82])

Some young people also might resist sharing when asked about their lives, out of fear that their answers will somehow be misunderstood and deemed "deficient." Researchers argue that when inviting students to share, educators have to explicitly convey that stories beyond the educator's own experience will be valued. As one example, Thandeka Chapman tells a story of a white teacher matter-of-factly asking all students to draw their family tree. Some students responded with pride, while others, several black students specifically, got anxious and didn't respond. Chapman asked these young people afterwards why the activity had backfired. Students revealed that they had a lot to say if they felt their answer would be valued:

> When I spoke informally to several of the African American students outside class, they articulated extensive family trees and stories about family reunions and origins from various southern states. . . . I asked [Deron] why did not he write or verbally share the story he had told me about his granny. He shrugged his shoulders and quietly said, "I only know one side of my family."[83]

Black students in a focus group told researcher Dorinda Carter Andrews that some teachers even derided students' everyday lives: "they make fun of you if you don't live with your mom," said one, while another described an incident where a teacher imitated a black student and said, "I'm from the hood; ain't you from the hood?" Such hurtful interactions made students reluctant to tell any teachers much about their *actual* lives. As one student put it, "We cannot trust the teachers with our personal business. They will . . . talk negatively about us to other students and teachers."[84]

So, educators can remember that students may have experienced hurtful Life Talk previously in schools. Educators often need to be patient when building relationship, to overcome students' distrust after past experiences of disrespect.[85] And rather than stay limited by their own sets of experiences, norms, and values, researchers suggest, teachers can invite and *explicitly value* a full variety of stories—without forcing them.

Finally, equity designers also have to consider when and how adults usefully share their own lives with young people. Life Talk for equity is often two-way, so that "students are not the only ones who are asked to share." As Pueblo youth in the Southwest told researchers Lee and Cerecer, "Teachers know all about us, our families, our lives and yet we don't know much about them." Students wanted teachers, too, to share something about "where they live, or how they grew up."[86] As teachers, Julio Cammarota and Augustine Romero asked youth to write "I Am" poems to initiate student voice; the pair wrote "I Am" poems too, to share themselves "as people."[87] Heather Pleasants urges that educators individually ask themselves, "'What can I do to help the kids better understand me?' as well as 'What can I do to understand these kids?'" and then build some classroom experiences around sharing their out-of-school passions.[88] Other researchers urge adults to share their own family stories or professional journeys with students (while valuing different experiences), and to share their own experiences managing a world plagued by stereotypes and scripts.[89] As one youth put it, "I feel like if adults listen to kids more and kids listen to adults more, then there could be a better relationship as a whole."[90]

What sort of "sharing" from adults about their lives might you particularly include or discourage in your Ideal Student Support Conversation, or build in to your Ideal Student Support Calendar? Give one example.

And here's a final Core Tension of Life Talk. Sometimes, a tiny bit of information about a student's life (e.g., "so and so's father has been arrested") can lead to all sorts of assumptions and, in the end, harm. So the previous chapters' goals of seeking more complete understanding of young people must hold as we design in two-way Life Talk between youth and their supporters—even as we work not to pry.

ACTION ASSIGNMENTS

1. Finish designing an Ideal Student Support Calendar that organizes time for students to talk with various supporters over a month. Ask our infrastructure design questions:

    To support the full human talent development of *every* student and all groups of students (equity),

    > Who in a school/classroom/community needs to communicate what information to whom? (How often? When?)
    > What are the barriers to needed communication, and how could those barriers be overcome?
    > What channel (face-to-face conversations, paper, technology) might help necessary communications to occur?

    Now, explain to one adult and one young person one or more of the key components you put on your Student Support Calendar. Talk through the pros and cons of your ideas with them.

2. Finish mocking up or describing an Ideal Student Support Conversation that you would hope might happen in one of the slots on your calendar. For example, you might consider specific student support sentences linked to prior chapters of this book:

> How might a supporter help a young person critically analyze a label others use to describe him or her? (Chapter 1)

> How might someone listen and respond most helpfully to a young person in the middle of a "snowball" in a specific opportunity context at a precarious moment that could go positively or negatively for him or her? (Chapter 2)

> To support a young person worried about his or her skills or talents, what's one phrase or response that might help bust a myth about intelligence? (Chapter 3) How could an adult give a young person supportive feedback on improving a specific skill? (Chapter 5)

> How could a supporter help a young person communicate an actual family or community experience, to challenge others' underinformed claims about his or her "culture"? (Chapter 4)

If you don't have a young person in mind, consider an ideal student support communication that could have supported *you* more effectively at a critical point in your life.

Show your Ideal Support Conversation to a young person or adult and get their input. Then, debrief: what did you learn about Life Talk from this conversation?

3. Consider when and whether students in an education community you know get to communicate with supporters about their personal needs and situation. Ask one student and one supporter from the education community: what are the pros and cons of such standard practice? How might this typical communication be improved?

Then, debrief: what did you think of their suggestions? Were there some Core Tensions embedded in them? Would the ideas suggested actually work?

4. Try to turn one gold nugget idea or example from this chapter into a #schooltalking tool that lots of other people could learn from. For example, create a poster or PowerPoint slide, short video, or other

multi-media image publicly sharing that gold nugget quote or idea. To accompany your main message, create a brief user's guide of five related information points or ideas from this chapter that can help users be more fully informed about the issue at hand and have a productive conversation sparked by your tool. See Chapter 1, pages 65–66, for more instructions.

5. In person or via the Internet, find an educator or young person who you feel is schooltalking for equity in their Life Talk. Document (with permission) and share (#schooltalking) some example of their work—a photo, a video, an image, a quote from them, or something they have produced.

More schooltalk scenarios

THINK / DISCUSS

In supplementary activities for their book *Identity Safe Classrooms,* Dorothy Steele and Becki Cohn-Vargas suggest various Life Talk strategies for building trusting relationships between adults and students. Which of these examples would you recommend teachers utilize or adapt, and why? Consider any Core Tensions that might arise:

Try a quick daily check-in at the beginning or end of each day. One easy way to start is to greet each student as the students enter the classroom at the start of the day. Focus your observation on two students who might benefit the most from this closeness, and document any changes in their behavior. What did you observe?

. . . Try instituting a get-to-know-you activity in which each student is the focus for a week. Have the student bring in pictures, artifacts, family members, instruments—anything that reflects who the student is and what the student cares about. You could begin the process by being the first to "present" yourself so that students see you as a person and possibly see similarities between you and them. What did you try? What did you learn from this activity?[91]

THINK / DISCUSS

A principal and staff team developed "Testify Tuesday," a weekly morning activity that, as the principal describes,

> Permits the students to share with their peers and their teachers positive or not so positive experiences that they have experienced during the previous week. . . . In addition, the activity addresses any concerns students, teachers, and the administrators might have regarding any situations that may have arisen during the week, and the team works to resolve anything deemed problematic to the success of the students.[92]

Would you schedule a Testify Tuesday on your Ideal Student Support calendar? Why or why not? How would you shape the "sharing" talk in the event? Name a Principle and Core Tension behind your thinking.

THINK / DISCUSS

Kevin Foster describes how his Young COBRAs meetings supporting black youth in Austin, Texas, follow a Life Talk structure "that was completely student conceived and initiated":

> Back in 2006, when we were still just a small informal group of 12 African American boys who met weekly, we (a local professor and the school principal) took the kids on a field trip to the university campus. At the end of the day, the boys attended a meeting of SAAB or Student African American Brotherhood. SAAB opened every meeting with Venting, where students "got stuff off their chest," as the President described it. They would quickly recount instances or circumstances from the past week that bothered them and that they were dealing with. After that they would "do Accountability." Students would stand up and hold themselves accountable for their actions, especially areas where they felt they needed to do better. Next, they would "do Celebrations," where they would acknowledge one another or

(continued)

share with the group something they were proud or happy about. This was a college student organization of predominantly African American males who came to Thursday evening meetings in shirts and ties and were clearly "about business," but also clearly identified with African American culture and identity. Upon meeting the next week, the SAAB meeting that ended the day was all the kids could talk about. "Dr. Foster," one student offered, "no offense to how you talk to us, but can we run our meetings that way?" That was back in 2006. The structure of Venting, Accountability, Celebrations, and then discussion of activity is how all chapters run their meetings to this day.

Would you utilize this structure of "Venting, Accountability, Celebrations, and then discussion of activity" in any slot on your Ideal Student Support Calendar, or in your Ideal Student Support Conversation? Why or why not? Name a Principle or Core Tension behind your thinking.

THINK / DISCUSS

One principal described an effort to enable Life Talk about a national issue affecting local young people's emotions and concentration.

On the day of the decision about the Rodney King case, we had an email fan out [from the district office] that you cannot talk about Rodney King in school. It's too dangerous. If students raise their hands and want to talk about it, you are to tell them no. If you can't handle it in the classroom, you're supposed to send those kids out, or call for an administrator. Basically, a news blackout.

As the principal explained to researcher Rosemary Henze and team, "the school did not follow this order from the district. Instead, it shut down classes and had a facilitator come in and work with students to make sure they could get their stuff out in a safe place." As the principal explained, "for me, there's the difference between a pent up, we don't dare, it's too dangerous to talk about this and they could get out of control [situation]—versus if you don't talk about this, it's dangerous and will be out of control."[93]

What's your take on this educator's decision about inviting Life Talk? How would you have handled the situation as a principal? (And how would you apply your thinking to discussions of local events more regularly affecting students?) Name a Principle and Core Tension behind your reasoning.

THINK / DISCUSS

What's your take on this Life Talk from a fairly famous mentor? Would you incorporate aspects of it into your Ideal Student Support Conversation? Why or why not?

You don't do things alone. Nobody does things alone. Everybody always needs support. For a young man like you, you should never be too afraid or too shy to look for people who can encourage you or mentor you. There are a lot of people out there who want to provide advice and support to people who are trying to do the right thing. So you'll have a lot of people helping you. Just always remember to be open to help. Never think that you know everything. And always be ready to listen.[94]

Chapter 7

Opportunity Talk

Talk so opportunities to learn get shared widely (and to meet needs), not just with some.

Chapter Goal:
Enable Opportunity Talk. Design inclusive and ongoing dialogue about increasing and spreading necessary opportunities to learn.

Throughout this book, we've been considering which schooltalk supports the full human talent development of every young person and all groups of young people.

At root, equity effort requires offering all young people opportunities they need and deserve.

So, to end this book, let's consider how to get necessary people into the discussion of necessary opportunities, so more opportunities actually get to young people.

Opportunity Talk

Basically, equity designers keep asking: Are people communicating so necessary opportunities get to all the young people who need and deserve them? And are all the people who need to be included in Opportunity Talk actually included?

We've considered many ways that schooltalk shapes opportunity for students. In this chapter, we'll focus on designing schooltalk that *includes* critical stakeholders in young people's lives—specifically families, the influential adults most directly connected to young people and often excluded from Opportunity Talk about them.

As we'll see, Opportunity Talk for equity is a two-way street: it involves getting information "out" to all stakeholders and input "in" on improving opportunities for young people. But typical Opportunity Talk (e.g., with families) often only includes people who are already included. Opportunity Talk *for equity* brings more voices into the conversation—which gives educators new ideas and more resources for opportunity effort. If we can figure out how to include all families in school Opportunity Talk, for example, we secure particularly powerful partners in the joint effort to get opportunity to students. And we learn how to include others on our Foundational Image, too. In fact, my own efforts to include all families as key resources in Opportunity Talk have given me ideas for including all kinds of other people not on our Foundational Image who also can help improve opportunities for young people—university folks, district administrators, industry people, and more. At the end of this chapter, I'll invite you to keep thinking about sparking Opportunity Talk with other stakeholders in children's lives, as well.

But let's focus first on including families, the folks too often excluded from dialogue about improving opportunities for the young people they know.

Opportunity Talk in action

Look at our Foundational Image (page 10) and think about an educational community you know. When someone in that community has information or an idea for improving or creating opportunities for young people, do others listen to it—or even get to hear it?

Any community—a school, a neighborhood, a city, a region—could ideally be an education community, one big network working together to offer opportunities that can develop local young people's talents. But often the network goes underutilized, like a city at night with half of the bulbs gone dark. Instead, folks normalize situations where students don't enjoy all the opportunities that a region, a community, or even a single school has to offer.

So, the most important effort to reshape opportunity provision in an education community may be getting more folks to ask which current opportunities are sufficient, and which are not:

Does this action or situation help support **equity** (the full human talent development of *every* student, and *all groups* of students)? Or not?

NOT supporting each/all
students' talent development   SUPPORTING each/all students'
                                                talent development

That's the point of our Equity Line. Itself a schooltalk tool, the line asks folks to *routinely evaluate* which actions and situations in schools (and education communities broadly) support young people sufficiently, and which don't. In its call to develop all children's full human talents, it openly invites both evidence about students' current needs and diverse "value judgments about what [a] child needs to succeed."[1] And it also raises the bar for what we expect for young people and from the adults around them. I've personally used the Equity Line to ask teachers to consider the equity implications of their everyday ways of disciplining students, teaching math, or using technology; to invite students to assess the opportunities available and accessed in their classrooms, schools, and neighborhoods; and to encourage families to evaluate whether the opportunities in their children's lives live up to their dreams for their children. I've used it at the university level and in community settings to talk with colleagues about how they might help get more opportunities to students, and to families and educators too. Basically, the equity line invites a running conversation about getting essential opportunities to young people, and it helps us have lofty goals for what those opportunities might be.

So if I could display our equity line on every wall in America as my schooltalking act of choice, simply to keep people considering the opportunity consequences of every action and situation for young people, I would do it.

But the second problem with typical Opportunity Talk is that discussions of opportunity don't include or listen to all the people in the community with ideas and energy for getting opportunities to young people.

Research on "social capital" (the resources in any community) and on "social networks" (who knows whom in any community) shows that educators often don't even share with one another the ideas and expertise they have about improving opportunities for young people.[2] Fostering such Opportunity Talk between educators is critical work (and a core goal of this book!). But regarding families, research shows that families with fewer connections to wealth and to local institutions particularly get left out of crucial forms of opportunity offered by schools and organizations, because they're left out of the opportunity dialogue.[3] Sometimes, people simply don't receive information about opportunities because it comes via a channel they don't access (like a listserv) or in a language they can't speak or read. Sometimes, education communities only include a subset of families in Opportunity Talk because they only forge relationships with that subset. And sometimes, members of education communities don't feel invited or comfortable to request more information about the opportunities available or needed, or to share ideas themselves. Or, the folks inside education communities only listen to the families in the community who already talk the loudest![4] Such structural cracks in Opportunity Talk then disadvantage children from less-included and less-listened-to families, who won't access the institution-based opportunities circulating. Schools also don't benefit from the knowledge, improvement ideas, and connections to learning opportunities that everyone, including families themselves, might be able to provide.[5]

So, if we want to tap everyone's ideas, energy, and connections to opportunities so more young people develop their potential, we have to design Opportunity Talk to reach and listen to everyone who needs to be included. As a friend, Ana María Nieto (who studies parent empowerment), once mentioned to me, equity designers trying to "include" parents specifically need to think about parent communication as a two-way exchange. While ensuring information gets "out" to all who need it, designers also need to consider how to get input in from all who could give it. "School issues usually get defined by those who have louder voices," Ana said. "We can think about concrete ways to help bring the voices of those who usually are not heard to the forefront."

The most obvious cracks in Opportunity Talk to start with are situations where critical opportunity information just never makes it "out" to all the people who need it—families particularly, but also youth themselves. For example, colleagues interviewing low-income youth in San Diego found that many didn't have sufficiently frequent or positive relationships with counselors and so got college information primarily from relatives and friends who had not been to college themselves. Youth were often "left on their own to figure out how to use those facts to help them navigate university application processes," and they often made life-altering missteps. Around the country, some youth never take the SAT, and so can't go to university, just because no school staff ever told them they could get a fee waiver. Some don't hear they need to fill out the FAFSA or pay a housing deposit and, come fall, find college prohibitively expensive.[6] Many families never learn in time that math preparation will be critical to children's college success, and so they accept situations where students don't get the skills or even the classes that they need.[7]

In contrast, some children keep getting opportunities from schools and local institutions because their families already know about them—and in many cases, because their families also contribute to shaping them. College-educated families in our area access, insist on, and help create opportunities for their kids (and sometimes, for their kids' classmates and teachers) to tap local universities, museums, nonprofits, and industry so their kids can program robots, see Nobel laureates, attend tech camps, secure lab internships, create models with engineers, hear lectures from professors, and more. And inside schools, too, such parents more accustomed to demanding opportunities for their children tend to insist that their children get the best opportunities—into top teachers' classrooms, GATE or AP classes, targeted special education supports or afterschool programs, and more—and to demand more conversations about improving opportunity further.[8] Such families also often share that opportunity knowledge only with other college-educated families they know in their schools and neighborhoods—particularly, research shows, with the families that share their "group" along race or language lines.[9] On the soccer field, at birthday parties, on listservs, or during school governance meetings, already-advantaged parents routinely get even more information about accessing school programs, camps, scholarships, enrichment opportunities, top teachers, and more. And research shows not only that such parents get more school opportunities but also that such parents routinely dominate school improvement discussions, too.

In the Massachusetts school where I enrolled my daughter in kindergarten, I learned a lot about typical Opportunity Talk through talking to other parents. For example, Opportunity Talk from school to home often failed to reach parents who spoke languages other than English or who rarely used technology. As one egregious example, many recent immigrants who lived in a housing project a few steps away from the school told me they didn't know how to get kids into a magnet program inside their own school. The magnet program, which enrolled my daughter, required simply checking a box on the common paper form during the school registration process, but you needed to understand what you were checking and why. The magnet program was disproportionately composed of middle-class white students and, secondarily, the second-generation kids of more established immigrants. Low-income children from the next-door housing project, many of them first-generation immigrants, were most often assigned automatically to the school's "Neighborhood" program based on home address.

Input in from these parents on improving the school's opportunities for young people was also limited. Magnet parents communicated far more often with teachers and school administration about improving the school. I saw just how stark this communication divide was some months into a controversial decision-making process about merging the school's magnet program with its Neighborhood program. I walked around the housing project talking to Neighborhood parents about the upcoming decision; many hadn't even heard the issue was up for debate. In contrast, middle-class parents in the magnet program had been debating the issue for months. A magnet program listserv carried invitations to parents to attend school board meetings in person, and magnet program parents were then the ones who showed up to those face-to-face meetings. Magnet program parents also dominated attendance and conversation at a weekly, English-based "coffee with the principal," where school information was distributed and discussed.

All this meant that lower-income, immigrant parents in our school weren't getting information on opportunities for their children, nor on school decisions or programming. They also weren't giving their input to the school on broader questions of improving opportunity for young people, nor sharing their own knowledge base or connections with the school. Parents also weren't building friendships across program lines or language lines (nor with educators) because they never spent any time together.

This wasn't particular to our school at all.

As we saw in Chapter 4, families of all income levels, from all communities, share any information they can find on navigating opportunity systems. (Families in all communities also provide various opportunities to learn at home, even while some families can purchase more opportunities than others.[10]) But research shows that already-advantaged parents' information about (and then demands for) educational opportunities inside and outside of schools are part of many children's "snowballs" of cumulative advantage. That is, parents who argue confidently that their children should have access to institutional opportunities they know to demand are more likely to gain access than parents who don't.[11]

Such opportunity-advantage is based in large part on access to information and relationships with people who control opportunities already. But because U.S. education so often rations opportunities only to some, broader sharing and inclusion can also be limited by fear that more opportunity for "others" means less opportunity for "us." As researcher John Diamond put it to me of such dynamics, "So much of inequality in schools is about people wanting what's best primarily—if not exclusively—just for their own children." Lewis and Diamond researched a Midwestern middle-class suburb and found that white middle-class parents tended to "opportunity hoard" rather than share—to keep within their "group" both information on accessing "advanced" opportunities, and the opportunities themselves.[12]

Dream big here: as we've said from the beginning of *Schooltalk*, every community benefits from the development of all children, not just some. What would happen if we tapped the voices of all the folks in and around our Foundational Image, sharing and dreaming up ways to share more opportunities with more children? What if instead of accepting the seemingly limited opportunities available, people together actually insisted on *more* high-level classes, more "gifted"-style learning opportunities, more resources for teachers, and more staff to provide individualized attention, and figured out ways to tap local resources for additional opportunities to learn? What if people clued in others to the vast learning opportunities available in local communities—opportunities to tap the skill of local mentors, showcase local careers, or enrich the skills and knowledge of everyone as citizens of the world? What might schools look like if we actually included everyone in ongoing Opportunity Talk about every way to improve opportunities for children?

Could we actually make more opportunities to go around?[13]

Here's where you come in as an equity designer. If we want to share opportunities widely and tap the potential contributions of every stakeholder for our schools, we have to caulk structural cracks that keep some people in the dark and out of the conversation. And if we design schooltalk infrastructure to help fully include more people in productive Opportunity Talk, we can indeed make more opportunities to go around, because we get more people seeking, finding, demanding, and creating opportunities for kids.

A first step is shaping all conversations in schools *to* focus on the pursuit of opportunity for more children, asking,

Does this action or situation help support **equity** (the full human talent development of *every* student, and *all groups* of students)? Or not?

NOT supporting each/all
students' talent development

SUPPORTING each/all students'
talent development

But a next key effort is to design Opportunity Talk infrastructure that *gets more people* considering together how to get more opportunities to young people—that taps more stakeholders' energies for improving opportunities both for the children they already support, and for children in general.

So, let's start to consider ways of enabling inclusive Opportunity Talk that gets more opportunities to more children, focusing our design energies particularly on overcoming barriers that exclude some families. Keep thinking about how efforts to include all families can inform efforts to include other key stakeholders in our Foundational Image, including more educators and youth themselves. (And finally, families of course include relatives of all kinds. I'll sometimes call family members "parents" for short. At times, I'll use the broader phrase "community members" to indicate that these Opportunity Talk strategies can include folks beyond families, too.)

Design an Opportunity Talk Inclusion Plan

As you read through the rest of this chapter, create an Opportunity Talk Inclusion Plan for an education community you know. It's basically three lists side by side—three columns on one document. Be sure to leave yourself sufficient space to write in each column.

Ask our three Infrastructure Design Questions in turn:

> In the first column, ask yourself: **to pursue equity, who in this school/classroom/community needs to communicate what** *opportunity-related* **information to whom?** (How often? When?) Consider necessary information out and input in. Like, "More parents need to know about afterschool options in the community," "math teachers and families need to discuss necessary precollege coursework," or, "families need to share their take on supporting the homework we've been assigning."

> In the second column, consider barriers to the needed information-sharing. Ask: **what are the barriers to needed communication about improving opportunity, and how could those barriers be overcome?** (E.g., "We haven't typically discussed community programs at family events," "math teachers don't have time in the school day to meet with parents to discuss precollege course options," or "not all families with ideas about the homework feel comfortable sharing their ideas at parent meetings.")

> In the third column, ask: **what channel (face-to-face, paper-based, or technology-based communications) might allow necessary communications about improving opportunity to occur?** ("Handout, phone message, and email home in Spanish on tapping local afterschool options," "stipend staff to hold school-family Math Night on precollege courses," "face-to-face dialogues with small groups of parents about their family's experiences with the homework.")

Ready to design Opportunity Talk infrastructure for equity? Let's first consider a number of examples from other designers to get us thinking. Then, we'll think through key barriers to Opportunity Talk. Keep updating your Opportunity Talk Inclusion Plan.

Info out, input in: Starting to explore examples of Opportunity Talk infrastructure

Equity designers in schools across the country are designing infrastructure that helps get opportunity information out to community stakeholders, and input in from them. Participatory efforts engage community members themselves in design or in evaluating existing infrastructure's pros and cons. I've collected some such efforts here to get us thinking. Many focus on including families specifically, but they could be used to include other stakeholders too.

Info out

Equity designers nationwide are testing many channels for getting opportunity information out. Communities are experimenting with **digital bulletin boards** where people can read scrolling info about community events for children, **paper bulletin boards** placed at playgrounds and supermarkets, online **community calendars** sharing out events submitted by the community, multilingual **hotlines** allowing anyone in the community to record and post voice memos on events for young people, **paper calendars** sent home for those without reliable Internet access, and **online chats** for public Q & A about opportunities for young people. Some schools are using **online social networks** or **listservs** to share opportunities, or **group text messaging** for one-way blasts.[14]

In schools, info-out infrastructure also can support Opportunity Talk with one family at a time. Some teachers team up with community members for **home visits** to discuss school strategies (like reading techniques) or curriculum, and to build relationship with families. Some schools appoint a **parent contact** to give each new parent a call. Some send **advisory teachers to homes** to meet each new family. In many schools, a bilingual **family liaison** is a key infrastructure resource offering families and students face-to-face referrals to food banks, immigration services, mental health or medical services, and counseling. Such liaisons also invite families to social and informational events.[15]

The great book *Beyond the Bake Sale* is essentially a giant list of potential Opportunity Talk infrastructure components. Here's one mini-list below. Note how many efforts at full "partnership" between schools and families invite two-way communication, rather than just one-way:[16]

Partnership School

All families & communities have something great to offer—we do whatever it takes to work closely together to make sure every single student succeeds.

Building Relationships
- Family center is always open, full of interesting materials to borrow
- Home visits are made to every new family
- Activities honor families' contributions
- Building is open to community use & social services are available to families

Linking to Learning
- All family activities connect to what students are learning
- Parents & teachers look at student work & test results together
- Community groups offer tutoring & homework programs at the school
- Students' work goes home every week, with a scoring guide

Addressing Differences
- Translators are readily available
- Teachers use books & materials about families' cultures

- PTA/PTO includes all families
- Local groups help staff reach families

Supporting Advocacy
- There is a clear open process for resolving problems
- Teachers contact families each month to discuss student progress
- Student-led parent-teacher conferences are held 3 times a year for 30 minutes

Sharing Power
- Parents & teachers research issues such as prejudice & tracking
- Parent group is focused on improving student achievement
- Families are involved in all major decisions
- Parents can use the school's phone, copier, fax & computers
- Staff work with local organizers to improve the school & the neighborhood

Full partnership moves beyond getting information "to" families and community members to also engaging people in dialogue and relationship. As Andrea Dyrness puts it, "How many times have we facilitated or attended parent meetings in which we never hear parents' voices? When our preoccupation with communicating information has left no time for parents to discuss, share, or reveal themselves? . . . If we invite parents into a dialogue about their own questions and goals for their children, we open up the possibilities for meaningful exchange and collaboration within the school."[17]

So what infrastructure helps get *input in* on creating more opportunities for young people?

Input in

Remember Karolyn Tyson's advice to ask that key equity question, "If that child were yours, what would you want her school experience to be?"[18] **Community dialogues** can invite important Opportunity Talk (in small or large groups, dependent on people's comfort level), on the opportunities people envision ideally for young people. For example, the Alaska Native Knowledge Network urges educators to foster "extensive on-going participation, communication, and interaction" with "community personnel," particularly elders, to invite reactions to school programming and discussion of the skills and knowledge that community members hope schools will offer their children. Often, such dialogues—and **reports** by community organizations, sharing community perspectives in writing—have demonstrated that community members dream of a "both-and" approach, in which a school serves as a hub for sharing both community expertise and standardized school knowledge.[19]

Other equity designers invite more routine opportunity dialogues, such as "**weekly parent coffees** as a chance for parents to discuss concerns with each other and the principal," **open conversation sessions** between families, staff, and administrators, **workshops for parents and students** on key school information, and **parent academies** focused on questions like, "How do I know that my child is learning?"[20]

Designers have found that **dialogues focused on supporting parents to learn about a school** can also evolve into **dialogues supporting school personnel to learn from parents** about ways to support their children. In one Oregon town, as Ann Ishimaru describes, community leaders began organizing events for Latino parents, starting with Spanish-based workshops that helped parents build relationships, "understand their rights and the public education system," and strategize how to advocate for their children in conversations with educators and other parents. Then, over time, indigenous Mexican mothers "who had been timid and afraid to talk in the group prior to the training programs" soon started facilitating the programs for other parents. Eventually, district and school administrators started sitting down with the parents to learn from them about supporting the increasing numbers of local children learning English. "I didn't know virtually anything about ELLs, but I knew I could be a learner, and I needed to learn about the community's needs," said one elementary director.[21]

As Opportunity Talk infrastructure, other school communities design in-person **community meetings** where families and community supporters talk with educators about local issues affecting students' daily lives in schools, including local safety or transportation issues; **school surveys** (on paper or via technology, anonymous or with names) that tap parent and student input on school improvement without people having to speak in public; and "**neighborhood walks**" and "**house meetings**" to "build and strengthen relationships between school faculty, families, and community members."[22]

Some Opportunity Talk infrastructure takes tips explicitly from **community organizing** and organizes dialogue around analyzing, then solving, high-priority problems that are common issues of concern. A middle school parent-teacher group that Mark Warren studied in Texas engaged parents and teachers in addressing the highest-priority joint concern: closing down "a store near the school that sold alcohol to underage students." Then, the group focused together on homework skills and afterschool programming.[23] Similarly, **youth-focused dialogues** or efforts to **include youth as participatory researchers** during or after school bring in youth voices on high-priority opportunity issues, ranging from making teaching more engaging or discipline more fair to out-of-school opportunity issues like jobs, policing, or transportation. One youth organizing group I know in Boston started with the cost of bus passes for getting to school, because that issue engaged the most youth in a common opportunity discussion.[24]

Families and youth around the country also are engaging with other local researchers in **community-led research on improving opportunities for young people**.[25] As Elaine Simon and colleagues demonstrate, for example, parents in New York City teamed up with a community organization to research their school systems' opportunity gaps and press for specific resources from district and state decision makers. Parents first researched, then demanded, more open access to "gifted" courses in the city. Then, they researched and demanded smaller classes, new teacher hires, more professional development opportunities, improved facilities, and new libraries, school buildings, and tech equipment. As one organizer put it, publishing public reports and crowding into school board meetings to demand opportunities benefited everyone. "As a membership-based low-income organization that works in low-income neighborhoods, not for one single moment [have we] ever separated schools and community. . . . Members have been students, do have kids, continue in education, schools are in their neighborhoods, there is no separation."[26]

In a **parent-led research** project in California, parents interviewed other parents to hear their opportunity suggestions and then presented findings to other parents and staff. Parents recommended smaller class sizes, "progress visits" where educators discussed student progress with parents (particularly regarding students learning English), more substantive communication to parents "in appropriate language" of "any information related to the education of our youth," and additional personnel to support students—all recommendations that could be helpful to educators too.[27]

Designers are finding that including families in **two-way Data Talk** also enables dialogue that pinpoints necessary supports for young people. Texas schools profiled by Mediratta and colleagues held **routine data analysis meetings** where parents analyzed schoolwide data and strategized with educators on what to do about it.[28] Taveras et al. document meetings engaging parents in analyzing school assessment results in New York.[29] Schools that invite outside community members to see **student presentations** or host **internships and other community-based learning experiences** also invite two-way discussion of the skills students might develop further.

Home visits designed to tap families' knowledge also can tap resources for enriching classroom curriculum—what Luis Moll and Norma González call tapping local funds of knowledge. For example, "Hilda," a teacher, interviewed parents in home visits and started to understand that there was a vast local expertise base in construction. Then, Hilda "invited parents and other community members who worked in construction to share their expertise with the children. Some parents talked about their tools and explained how they used numbers and measurements in their work. Others spoke about their work methods and told how they solved problems." Through tapping local expertise through nearly twenty parent and community visits that semester, Hilda also "began to establish a social network for her classroom. The parents and community members she worked with became what Moll calls 'a cognitive resource for the class.'"[30]

So, that's a lot of ideas for two-way Opportunity Talk! But any such effort still is likely to encounter some key inclusion barriers, unless we design our infrastructure to address them.

> **STRATEGY** The real key to designing inclusive Opportunity Talk is to evaluate barriers to necessary communication in diverse communities, and to test ways of transcending those barriers with equity in mind.

So let's consider some barriers that typically inhibit fully inclusive Opportunity Talk in diverse education communities, particularly with families. Keep adding to your Opportunity Talk Inclusion Plan! (Pay attention to detail: an effort to include everyone in Opportunity Talk might still leave somebody out.) And as we'll see, just getting parents (or youth, or other community stakeholders who care deeply about young people) together in the same place with educators to talk isn't enough. (Gloria Ladson-Billings recalls asking teachers frustrated with parents who didn't come to school events, "Suppose you arrive at school tomorrow morning and every African American and Hmong parent in this school is here. What would you have them do?"[31]) The goal of Opportunity Talk is not just to get people in the same space but to focus a mutually respectful dialogue on concrete ways of improving opportunity for students.

And as we'll see, building *trusting and respectful relationships* is a key task of fostering such truly inclusive Opportunity Talk. As with Life Talk, such relationships lead to essential information-sharing, and respectful information-sharing can lead to more trusting relationships. So, equity designers need to consider barriers to relationship and to information-sharing, pursuing inclusive Opportunity Talk each step of the way.

Crucially, community members who have experienced such barriers habitually will have particular expertise for co-designing improved Opportunity Talk infrastructure. So keep thinking about how any of the infrastructure "components" on your Inclusion List could be co-designed with those you seek to include.

Barrier: Tech access and skill

Think of the listserv sending parents notices about meetings to decide the fate of the school. As noted above, many schools are turning to technology to help people share school-related information, enabling inclusion if people don't have time to gather in person. But adding tech doesn't automatically include.

> **CORE TENSION**   Adding tech channels can at times widen
> communication inequalities rather than caulk structural cracks—for
> example, if some of the channels expected for communications aren't
> fully accessible to everyone.

Not having a tool at all (a computer, Internet access, or reliable computers and Internet) is the most obvious communication barrier for many families and students and what we often call the "digital divide." In 2015, researchers reported that "82.5% of U.S. homes with school-age children have broadband access," but that "5 million households, with school-age children, do not have high-speed Internet service at home," and, more specifically, that "low-income homes with children" (disproportionately black and Latino families) "are four times more likely to lack broadband vs. middle/upper-income families."[32]

There are more complex tech inequalities, too. For example, money affects how many data minutes you can pay for on a phone as well as the speed of a broadband connection. On a closer read, cheap plans enabling broadband access "for all" sometimes provide slower communications for some. A schoolwide listserv requires new parents to get email accounts as well as access to computers. Old computers surf the Internet too slowly or can't open particular documents. Someone waiting to use a computer at the library might access information days behind everyone else, logging on to find an opportunity missed. Someone waiting to share a computer at home has less time to access information than someone with their own computer. And baseline skill is needed for basic access: in communities where I have lived, some parents didn't know yet how to use a mouse.

Accessing opportunity online involves yet more complexities. As a superintendent described to me, many low-income families in his district were very resourceful in sharing time on single devices or accessing the

Internet via taco shops, libraries, and cafes. But research also shows that even if you have a computer you might not use it to access a full range of opportunities. Some online programs are expensive or require extensive free time. Research suggests that the wealthier you are, the more you find, access, and complete robust learning opportunities online—that people with more functional devices, faster Internet, more tech skill and time, more money, and more knowledge about what's available online can access more and deeper opportunities to learn.[33]

So, to get started in overcoming such barriers in many communities, organizations are not only refurbishing computers or running computer centers but also broadening Internet access and teaching foundational tech skills, supporting more people to access a full range of opportunities online. Other efforts at inclusive Opportunity Talk rely on common denominator technologies like phones.[34] Because technology changes so fast, our main task as equity designers is to *keep asking* how to tweak tech-based infrastructure to be inclusive.

Take a minute to update your Opportunity Talk Inclusion Plan.

Barrier: Lack of translation, particularly for families

Did you know that parents have a civil right to translation and interpretation of key school information that affords their children an equal opportunity to participate in school? Including all members of a school community often requires figuring out infrastructure for translation of written material and interpretation of spoken words.[35]

In the OneVille Project, a group of parents, including me, together explored and designed infrastructure enabling Opportunity Talk across language groups in our multilingual school community. (The district had forty-two home languages recorded at the time; our school's families spoke three languages other than English in significant numbers.) We called ourselves the "Parent Connectors." Our quest was to figure out how to "connect" our English-dominant school to the many parents who spoke Haitian Creole, Portuguese, and Spanish, particularly by tapping the bilingual skill of local parents. We also wanted to tap more parent input on improving the school and to build relationship across divides of class as well as language. You can read about our full set of infrastructure design efforts here:

wiki.oneville.org/main/Summary:_Schoolwide_toolkit/parent_connector
_network.[36]

As equity designers critically evaluating existing communications, we noticed all sorts of barriers. At the school, for example, each school robocall home was recorded in four languages on one recording (English, Spanish, Portuguese, and Haitian Creole, in that order) in an effort to reach most parents. But in talking to parents, we realized that many machines cut off before Portuguese- or Haitian Creole–speaking people received the long message in their language. To respond, bilingual Parent Connectors learned to record targeted robocalls in one language at a time. We got the principal's permission to use the school's robocall system and learned how to select speakers of a given language in the school database. Then a Parent Connector would speak the message, and it would get sent only to parents who spoke that language. We were co-designing Opportunity Talk infrastructure for equity!

As I described in a 2013 article "It Takes a Network,"[37] we parents learned, through trial and error, how to design Opportunity Talk infrastructure of various kinds:

> We began with the face-to-face parent dialogue strategies of Reading Nights, sharing literacy strategies across both programs' kindergarten classrooms and a Special Education K-2 classroom; multilingual coffee hours, in which parents took the time to translate to and from the principal in four languages so that all parents could both listen and speak; and parent issue dialogues about the integration decision facing the school. In this, we soon realized the extent of a commonly known problem: language and tech access barriers, and related barriers of relationship, kept many low-income and immigrant parents (predominantly, speakers of Spanish, Portuguese, and Haitian Creole) from being equally informed about and included in school events, school improvement efforts, and educational opportunities. An English-dominated listserv had long enrolled only some parents, and many not on it were unaware of key issues facing the school community; many handouts streaming home were only in English. While many English-speaking parents emailed teachers and administrators regularly for personalized attention, some immigrant and low-income parents felt they tried at length and in vain to reach their children's teachers or administrators. . . . After meeting in multilingual coffee hours and

Reading Nights, bilingual parents and several staff focused from 2010 forward on designing the Parent Connector Network, an effort to tap parent bilingualism in parent information efforts. In the "PCN," bilingual volunteer parents ("Connectors") started making phone calls to recent immigrant parents to explain important school information, hear parents' questions about the school, and introduce themselves as generally available to help. Several also began to translate key school wide information onto a prototype open-source hotline that a MIT technologist, Leo Burd, designed for free at the suggestion of parents brainstorming how to reach parents not yet on the Internet. Burd also developed the hotline further to allow parents to leave phone messages, to be relayed to school staff by a hotline monitor. Connectors also convinced the school to support a part-time bilingual Parent Liaison at five hours a week to coordinate Connector calls (and hotline translation), run the multilingual coffee hour, and help schedule [professional] interpreters for parent-staff meetings. In 2011–12, parents and staff were testing the entire infrastructure model and considering holes in it. . . .

Diagrams of our efforts, plus a video of Parent Connectors, can be found on the project website: http://wiki.oneville.org/main/Summary:_Schoolwide _toolkit/parent_connector_network.

THINK / DISCUSS

Which of these infrastructure components, if any, would you include in your Opportunity Talk Inclusion Plan, to share which necessary information? Which would you not? Why?

You might be thinking: that's a lot of work! Over time, we indeed would have streamlined these many components to those that worked best. But just remember that translation of key school information is a parent's civil right, requiring every school to figure out how to handle it. Civil rights law does generally recognize that a school likely can't translate every piece of information for the many languages in its community. So the school is allowed to triage and translate the most important information for the most demographically represented language groups. (All parents have the right to have a trained interpreter present at high-stakes and student-specific events like a disability services meeting.) Interpretation also facilitates input in from parents to educators.

But many educators don't fulfill or actually know these translation and interpretation rights—or necessarily agree with them. One educator I know started a school for refugees because so many disability services meetings she saw in her first school system failed to offer parents interpreters. As another teacher put it to me, "I believe that some of our colleagues and parent leadership may feel that we do not have a responsibility to provide translation or native-language services—that if you want to be a part of the American school, you should learn English." Others argue that teaching families English is the most critical support, with translation and interpretation rights just essential in the meantime.

I also have seen how in starting to analyze language barriers to participation in Opportunity Talk, educators start to notice how often typical schooltalk prevents full parent participation. One teacher reviewed her school's website and noticed how it said the following on almost every page, even on a page asking parents to join a committee to advise on supports for English Learners: "For more information, contact the office." "There is no contact information and all text is in English," she noted, adding, "There is no actual information about a committee in existence and whether there are actual meetings."

If left unaddressed, language barriers can complicate various well-meaning efforts to "include." *Beyond the Bake Sale* offers this ideal situation defining a welcoming school:[38]

---

3. Front office staff are friendly—recognize visitors right away, provide information easily, and answer the phone in a way that makes people glad they have called.

☐ **Already doing this**   ☐ **Could do this easily**

☐ **This will take time**   ☐ **This will be hard**

Now think about a parent walking in to a school building who needs some information about an afterschool program. He does not speak English and is unable to converse with the friendly secretary at the front desk, who does not speak his language and is asking in English what he wants.

How to design for inclusion? Some schools handle translation by asking staff on campus who speak a given language to call homes, interpret for parents, or translate written documents as part of their job. This strategy builds relationships between staff and the families they reach and, in theory, avoids the costs of hiring additional liaisons: as one teacher in a class of mine put it, "Based on budget constraints, I don't think my principal would pay someone to do this job." But beyond giving more often-unpaid duties to bilingual staff often not formally trained as interpreters, this strategy also relies on those staff being available to interpret whenever and wherever they are needed. A parent liaison I know who speaks Haitian Creole once needed help on the phone to explain a child's injury in Spanish. The school relied on a few Spanish-speaking staff, but she couldn't find any of them to help her.

So, in addition to hiring bilingual liaisons, equity designers try various other infrastructure designs to handle additional translation needs. Some districts formally train and pay bilingual parents as translators and interpreters, even to learn highly specialized vocabulary to interpret at confidential disability services meetings. Others train and employ bilingual youth to do interpretation at public events. Those interpreting student-specific information should be trained to do so: educators sometimes rely on students themselves to be "language brokers" for their own parents, which can get particularly fraught when students have to interpret sensitive information about their own progress. When school districts rely on free online translation tools like Google Translate for all translation efforts, such translations are often strewn with errors. (To experience this, go to translate.google .com and paste in a long passage written in a language you do not know [you might find one at www.onlinenewspapers.com]. Click and translate it to English.) Others pay for interpreters to wait at public meetings to support parents; for efficiency in this resource use, they also have to try to ensure that parents from all language groups know about these meetings and feel actively invited to attend them. I know one principal who innovated the use of walkie-talkies at back to school night, allowing him to call for on-demand interpretation for parent-teacher conferences. Yet his strategy accommodated a tradition of parents approaching teachers for on-the-spot conference scheduling—one that disadvantaged parents who couldn't show up in person, or wait, or were afraid to ask. In the Parent Connector effort, we noted that parents particularly needed Connectors' interpretation help in the morning, when they had quick questions of teachers that could be answered immediately. But Parent Connectors themselves had to get to work!

Given how many of these strategies rely on multilingual skill, many designers point out that education communities (and young people today!) might be best off when young people and adults hone multilingual talents. Many say that rather than thinking of a multilingual school as an inherent "barrier" to communication, the focus should be on supporting education communities to become and remain multilingual.[39] And to bring these multilingual (and multicultural) skill sets into schools, many urge bilingual youth to become educators one day themselves!

See how every structural crack in inclusive Opportunity Talk needs ongoing analysis and attention? Take a minute to update your Opportunity Talk Inclusion Plan.

Barrier: Money

Infrastructure like cell phones or computers costs money. But there are other money-related barriers to inclusive Opportunity Talk. For example: when do people spending time supporting others into Opportunity Talk need to be paid? Many schools rely on volunteer labor, like appointing Room Parents to send emails or make phone calls to other parents. Women in particular donate an enormous amount of such labor for free. How equitable is this, and where's the limit?

In the Parent Connector project, Connectors—both middle-class and low-income women—spent many hours communicating with parents via phone and in person, translating information, and planning events. In the end, we realized we needed at least to pay a coordinator to organize all the work Connectors were doing, and that a sustainable program should either pay lead Parent Connectors for some of their work or hand some of it to paid liaisons. One program Mark Warren studied paid parent leaders $1,200 per year (circa the early 2000s) for two hundred hours of work to engage other parents. Warren noted that:

This is a significant amount to many parents. Although unpaid volunteering has been the paradigm for parental involvement in school, LSNA defends the necessity of paying stipends to encourage involvement and to bring in a broader range of people than would otherwise participate.

At the same time, Warren notes a Core Tension: having to fundraise to pay parents to work in the school "is a constant struggle that saps the time and energy of some organizing staff."[40] Schools that arrange budgets to hire professional parent liaisons often have staff build relationships with more volunteers who pitch in with lower levels of time commitment. But under-resourced school communities often struggle with paying for staff to facilitate Opportunity Talk at all.

THINK / DISCUSS

When should the people helping to connect opportunities to schools and people to opportunities be paid? How about the people spending all day building relationships between parents and schools? Consider a Principle and Core Tension behind your answer.

A barrier related to money is time.

Barrier: Time

Time to participate in Opportunity Talk is a major barrier requiring attention in infrastructure design. At my daughter's first school, one Brazilian parent didn't even have time when he wasn't working to come in to post a sign, saying he hoped to pay another parent for help picking up his daughter. Yet schools often prioritize face-to-face dialogues with parents. When should people actively call in, log in, or physically come in to get or share opportunity information, and when might information be exchanged via a backpack note, handout, or text or call that people receive more passively? More specific equity design questions abound:

THINK / DISCUSS

Consider a form of opportunity information you consider important in a school community you know. Should communications on that issue always be pushed out to reach people where they are, or should people be expected to actively come find certain information? (For example, should parents be required to come physically to school to talk to teachers about needed opportunities and supports for their individual children, even if they have trouble fitting in the time because of work or childcare?)

THINK / DISCUSS

Should principals or teachers be expected to head into communities or homes to talk about/hear ideas for improving opportunities for young people? Should they be paid to do it? (I remember how odd and rare it felt for a principal in my daughter's first school to walk down to the local housing project to meet with parents on a weekend. Typically, he expected parents to come up to the school to meet with him during the week. Was he wrong?)

THINK / DISCUSS

If some form of essential opportunity information needs to get to parents, students, or others in an education community, when should equity designers prioritize the speed, public access, and potential money saved through tech- or paper-based communication, and when should they prioritize the potential relationship gains of a face-to-face meeting?

As usual, further, *more* communications aren't always inherently good: educators using technology to communicate instantly with families and students are increasingly overwhelmed as people communicate back one by one, sometimes taking up time that could be used for supporting many students and families at once.

One principal told researchers that extensive face-to-face conversation with parents actually could save time in additional communications, noting that "because we've talked so much to each other, we don't need to write so many memos for this or that." But the principal also noted another thing that "talking" had achieved: relations of trust, and comfort with getting input in as well as information out. "The parents know that it's safe to talk, to ask questions, and to probe and push the teachers' thinking," the principal added. "And vice versa—parents know that it's OK for the teachers to push their thinking because that's the environment that we've set up."[41]

So, how do we "set up" environments where people feel safe to talk, ask questions, and "push" each other's thinking on improving opportunities for young people? The schools I've seen get into the most trouble with Opportunity Talk—with parents particularly, but also between educators—are actually those that resisted people's dreams of more opportunity for all as somehow inherently threatening, rather than as input from valued partners on the joint task of educating young people. Such communities get consumed by distrust, a major barrier to Opportunity Talk.

Barrier: Distrust

Many researchers argue that improving opportunity in school communities fundamentally requires improving relationships for "trust and cooperation."[42] Working at OCR, I saw schools implode due to distrusting relationships that impeded productive effort to improve opportunity. Parents or teachers who launched OCR complaints typically felt that administrators had dismissed their initial requests for more student opportunity, often specifically because they didn't understand or validate their experiences across lines of race, gender, language, and disability. And administrators typically dismissed these complaints because of a fundamental lack of trust as well. Distrust simmered in silence or exploded into raging arguments, blocking collaboration.[43]

Some researchers suggest that school improvement is impossible unless those who share a school community trust each other.[44] Educator-educator collaboration requires building trust; so does collaboration with families. Engaging families as equally valued partners in the work of supporting children is key: as Mark Warren writes, for example, especially when parents and educators' experiences differ across lines of race, class, or prior education, a parent might initially seem to educators to lack "the status and education to collaborate as an equal with her child's teacher. Efforts to build trust and to foster meaningful collaboration among principals, teachers, parents, and community members need to confront these power inequalities. If they don't, reform efforts can be derailed by mistrust and unresolved conflicts."[45] Researchers and community-based organizations alike argue that forging equal-footing relationships through respectful learning and listening is key to building trust for productive Opportunity Talk.[46] For example, Tiffany Lee emphasizes building "trusting relationships between educators and community members" through educators' efforts to honor community languages;[47] Paul Gorski calls "building respectful, sustainable relationships with low-income families" "The Mother of All Strategies: Committing to Working *With* Rather than *On* Families in Poverty."[48] Framing families as true partners in student support, and respecting the knowledge they hold, is critical: the Alaska Native Knowledge Network emphasizes that if "all forms of knowledge, ways of knowing and world views [are] recognized as equally valid, adaptable and complementary to one another in mutually beneficial ways," educators and parents can forge "a high level of complementary expectations between home and school."[49]

Researchers also argue that the key to counteracting distrust is sometimes for people to explicitly acknowledge prior distrust—and then, get to know each other, actually listen to each other, and explicitly value each other's contributions and potential.[50] Over time, as Warren puts it, "all the adults that children know also know each other and coordinate their actions . . . when teachers and principals build trust with each other and with parents, they can develop a common vision for school reform and work together to implement necessary changes in the school."[51]

So, equity designers have to keep thinking: what gatherings, activities and dialogues—between families, between staff, and between families and school staff—help people who share a school start to build more trusting relationships? One Portuguese-speaking parent working on the Parent Connector Network argued that to start forging important relationships across us parents, we really just needed a party with a little tequila! Regardless of your take on her suggestion, she was on to something important about the need to bond.

Research suggests that adults who share a school can build trust and mutual respect through new efforts to partner in opportunity provision. In the Parent Connector efforts, I personally experienced how the ongoing effort of organizing events for the entire grade started to bring a very diverse group of parents together, even more than simply coming to the events. Parents also told us they came to events not just because a robocall invited everyone, but because a peer who spoke their language invited them via the robocall to join in discussing how to improve things for everyone's children. Community organizers seeking actively to unite parents also often invest first in relationships with key community members who might be catalysts for involving others in Opportunity Talk. In schools profiled by Mediratta et al., community organizers "used a process of individual meetings (called one-on-ones) to identify people with leadership potential who could mobilize others in efforts for change." "These meetings, along with small-group sessions (house meetings), also served to build relationships among people based on a deeper understanding of each other and to identify issues of concern that could rally larger numbers of community members."[52]

THINK / DISCUSS

In an education community you know, who might you "invest" in as a potential connector to others? How might you find people who wouldn't immediately come to others' minds as potential leaders, as in through "one-on-ones" or smaller dialogues?

A more extensive effort to build trust between parents and teachers, led by an initial small group of dedicated parent designers, was documented by Andrea Dyrness, who spent many months learning from and with a group of Latina mothers in Oakland, California, who called themselves "Madres Unidas." At first, many Latino/a parents at the school felt "they were often not present at the table when decisions about reform were being made";

they were talked about, not to. (Citing bell hooks, Dyrness considers how so often in schools, "people of color are spoken about, rather than invited to speak as experts of their own experience." As hooks described this dynamic, "'No need to hear your voice when I can talk about you better than you can speak about yourself.'"[53])

"Much of the parents' frustration stemmed from the failure of school professionals to recognize their ability to discuss serious educational issues," Dyrness recalls. "The mothers pointed out how many times they had been asked to crowd school board meetings and [school reform organizing] actions, when the bodies of parents had been critical to win concessions from city officials. Within the school, the mothers discussed how parents were invited 'to organize things for parties,' but never to plan an academic program" with educators. One mother noted that it was just parent "bodies," not voices, that teachers seemed to want in schools, beyond a "complaint box" that educators never seemed to open.[54]

During meetings around a kitchen table between the small group of mothers, "relationships of trust allowed the mothers to retell experiences they had had at the school and debrief painful and frustrating meetings in the company of supportive friends."[55] The mothers then interviewed other parents about the inclusion they hoped for at the school and presented their findings and reactions to the full school staff. In this meeting, Dyrness argues, the Madres sought to model a different kind of communicative style, based on *confianza*, or trust, and equitable relationships. They chose to speak "personally" to educators in sharing their findings and to ask the teachers reflection questions, like these:

* What are the consequences of leaving out some families? How does this affect our community?
* What does it mean to have parent leaders in the school?
* How can we value the voice and vote of parents?
* How does it affect parents when their decisions are not respected?
* How do you feel when you are heard? How do you feel when you are not heard?
* What does it mean to have equality between parents and teachers?
* How do you define communication among staff at the school? How do you define communication with parents?
* What are the advantages of getting to know and understand the different cultures of our community?

＊ What does it mean to have trust (*confianza*) between school staff and parents, and what are the consequences of mistrust?

＊ What factors affect the ability (or inability) to have good communication among parents?[56]

The meeting led to new Opportunity Talk infrastructure at the school, including a new parent center where parents could come together informally and in workshops and share stories. "Created with the support of three teachers in the fall after the parents' research [presentation], the parent center was intended to be a 'second home' for parents in the school." The mothers also began to serve on key school committees, specifically to help educators design supports for English learners and to weigh in on teacher hiring. "As Madres Unidas repeatedly reminded school staff, 'We're not here to criticize. We're here because we want something better for our children,'" Dyrness writes.[57]

THINK / DISCUSS

What's your take on the Opportunity Talk process Dyrness documented, of frustrated parents interviewing other parents about their concerns and hopes, then presenting findings to teachers? Would you put a similar process on your Inclusion Plan? Why or why not? (How would you shape your process to build trust between parents and educators as the Madres intended? For example, if you were a parent, what might you say to open a meeting with educators where you presented your concerns and suggestions? Which questions above might you use, or adapt?)

Educators have also found that they can build trust with both families and students through the infrastructure of home visits—specifically, if they approach home visits as opportunities to learn from and bond with parents and students, rather than only get school information "out." When I asked Norma González for a good description of a home visit that successfully tapped a family's "funds of knowledge," she recommended this teacher's description of visiting her fourth graders' families for the first time.[58] I think it's worth citing in detail, as the educator carefully overcame an initial teacher-family power differential by listening respectfully to parents as sources of knowledge rather than just talking at them. The teacher's effort to listen also catalyzed more informed Life Talk and even deeper Culture Talk, Smarts Talk, and Group Talk.

Anxious about invading family privacy by asking to visit, the teacher, Elizabeth Schlessman, still decided to try it. She scheduled home visits through catching parents at school, by phone and at games, and by sending notes home suggesting times. ("The note stated that the visit would last 10–15 minutes, and that the family did not need to cook, clean, or prepare anything for the home visit.") Then she started her visits—which became two-way dialogues and relationship builders.

"While conversing on couches, at kitchen tables, soccer game sidelines, and front porches, I learned how much I still had to learn," Elizabeth describes. "I learned that Jesús and Ale had been next-door neighbors their whole lives. I learned that Alberto's family spoke Tarasco, an indigenous language of the Michoacan region of Mexico—which I hadn't realized, despite teaching two of his older brothers in previous years. I learned that quiet José was the responsible oldest of five, and that Carolina's family was thinking about moving back to Mexico. I learned that Diego's mom was too sick to work, Antonio's yard was full of trees, Erica's family had a garden, and Luis' mom spoke a secret language."

Most activities for parents at the school were driven by one-way talk at parents, she noted. "My hope was that home visits would create space to listen," she recalls. "I remember Erick's dad standing on the front porch, asking, 'Do you have any questions to ask me?' When I assured him that my purpose was to introduce myself and learn more about his hopes for his son, the conversation opened up." Having viewed herself only as a teacher of native Spanish speakers, Elizabeth also learned that many of her families actually spoke a variety of indigenous languages as well and valued these skills in their children. She found that the home-visit question, "Do you speak other languages?" became "pivotal as it turned parents into experts and me into learner."

"By far, the most powerful outcome of home visits was trust," she concluded. "Meeting parents at their homes instead of on school turf seemed to create a willingness to call, visit, and communicate during the school year." Parents also started to contribute new learning opportunities to the classroom: "Ana Maria's mom came to teach the class how she designs and embroiders a *huipil*; David's mom came to reading workshop to work one-on-one with students." Home visits also provided new personal resources to draw on in class: "there was something almost magical about being able to exchange a meaningful look with a student and refer to home visits—Ale's pet care responsibilities or Jesús' homework routine—in the middle of teaching." From her home visits, Elizabeth also learned to craft assignments inviting students to share their lives. "When I think I'm done learning, that I have a good enough label or assumption to work with, I stop asking questions," she noted. "Home visits taught me humility. They taught me to wonder."

Such efforts to build relationship and trust with families also can start with single conversations inside schools. In a piece entitled "Cultivating the Trust of Black Parents," for example, Beverly Tatum urges educators to use their parent-teacher conference time in part to build trust, for example by acknowledging to black parents that relationships between parents and educators are *not* always trusting given the negative experiences many black students have in schools (and, Tatum argues, in "white-run schools" particularly). Teachers can also ask parents how they are experiencing the school and then listen, rather than immediately resist what they hear. Listening to learn can be the key: Tatum notes that even a teacher accused of bias can stay engaged by "ask[ing] sincerely, 'Help me understand what I did that made you think so.'" "An invitation to enter into dialogue rather than a rush to defend oneself goes a long way in cultivating trust even in the midst of a difficult interaction," Tatum advises.[59]

THINK / DISCUSS

On your Opportunity Talk Inclusion Plan, what's one conversation you might add to start to build trust between a teacher and a family member, or between two other key types of supporter in our Foundational Image (page 10)? Where and when would you want the conversation to take place, and what's one thing you'd hope either party could say or ask when starting the conversation? (How could you learn from people what trust-building efforts they'd most welcome?)

Trusting relationships have to be built through explicit efforts to support young people collectively. They don't just happen if we show up in the same schools.

In efforts at inclusive Opportunity Talk, equity designers also have to decide: *who* gets invited to participate in *which* Opportunity Talk? I've attended many efforts to bring people together around improving opportunities for children that forgot to invite some key actors to the table. A meeting with K–12 leaders on designing pathways to careers didn't include industry leaders; a neighborhood improvement initiative invited leaders of afterschool organizations but not teachers. During any conversation, considering which community members are invited to talk and listen (when) is also important. Some of the most productive Opportunity Talk I've participated in has asked typical guardians of opportunity—like college professors—to *not* talk first and instead, to listen to those with new ideas about supporting students (like K–12 teachers). Yet not everyone will agree on who most productively talks and listens. At Reading Nights in the Parent Connector effort, we encouraged kindergarten parents to share their own tips for engaging their children in reading; some middle-class parents would have preferred tips from reading professionals.

THINK / DISCUSS

If you were going to convene a public dialogue on an issue of importance in an education community you know, who would you invite to speak (when) and who would you ask to listen or ask questions? Why?

The middle-class parents' reactions—which implied that some people were more worth listening to than others—indicate another barrier to inclusive Opportunity Talk. Beyond initial inclusion, people need to feel empowered, welcomed, and comfortable to speak up in communications once they have basic "access" to them.

Barrier: Unequal voice

In many parent-focused events in schools, the "choir" of already-empowered parents often comes and dominates conversation, while others don't come or don't speak. As one teacher I know described parent communication where she worked, "When I really reflect on it, there are certain families that monopolize time and resources and others we barely see"— "too much access" for some parents and not enough for others.

This is a question of voice and empowerment as much as access. One high school teacher noted to me after doing this chapter's Action Assignment that at his school, parents who "have heard little from the guidance counselors at the middle school and feel oblivious to the workings of education as they move into high school" felt inadequately empowered to ask questions even when given guidance counselors' email addresses. Parents had told him this was because "they feel that they do not know how to *word* questions in emails." Inviting equal voice in Opportunity Talk through honoring all voices and questions takes proactive effort in most communities. As Lewis and Diamond show, even in communities where everyone is middle class, educators tend to listen more to parents who already demand opportunities more confidently.[60]

Inclusive Opportunity Talk also won't automatically happen if you get everyone enrolled on a listserv, even though enabling universal enrollment often is a crucial first step. The same people may talk at length, and some likely still won't feel comfortable. With a schoolwide listserv, the Brazilian dad without time to come to school during the day could (in theory) have posted a request for help picking up his daughter. But getting help via the listserv required him not just to find and use a computer and potentially get someone to translate a message for parents who didn't speak Portuguese, but also to feel comfortable posting the idea.

Inviting equal voice via any channel also takes proactive effort. In the OneVille Project's multilingual coffee hour effort, we had to consider multiple aspects of supporting parent empowerment to speak: when to schedule the multilingual coffee hour, how and where to post multilingual signs inviting people, what food and drink to bring to make people feel comfortable, and which language to talk in when at the event. We also actively tried to build equal-status relationships at the events through inviting stories about everyone's dreams for our kids. To include all voices, I learned talk tools like parent leader Consuelo's "yarn ball" activity, where each speaker tosses an unspooling ball of yarn to someone else as an invitation to speak. The yarn ball unfurls to leave everyone connected in a web. ("Talking piece" strategies in restorative justice "circles" similarly invite all voices. "Chalk talk" activities invite people to silently write responses to others' ideas on a common sheet of paper, inviting all voices without forcing any speech.) We also explicitly invited participation from all guests to start every coffee hour, emphasizing often that we'd love to hear from people who hadn't spoken yet, and we made sure to give people sufficient time to talk and have information translated. A moment of equal "voice" in my mind was when a parent spoke at length in Spanish for the first time to explain a suggestion to the principal while English speakers waited for translation, just like Spanish speakers typically did.

Think back to Chapter 1, though: sometimes we assume falsely that people who share "group" experiences will naturally bond in Opportunity Talk and feel comfortable to speak. One teacher told me how in her district, fifth-grade teachers were brought together to share ideas about teaching, but the group didn't automatically gel; a colleague noted in response that "teachers want to talk to people with whom they share philosophies. You don't want to just talk because you all happen to teach fifth grade. You also want to talk to people with whom you are aligned." I've seen educators more successfully "align" with colleagues by inviting everyone more explicitly to dream together of needed improvements for students. Similarly, we might assume that parents will immediately "bond" just because they're all parents, but at times we need to actively bond people through proactively addressing common concerns about young people and inviting equal relationship. And to communicate about fraught issues particularly, people may need even more trusting relationships—and at times a smaller group-only "cocoon." One principal noted that low-income Spanish-speaking parents in his school wanted to talk first just to other low-income Spanish-speaking parents about serious issues of poverty affecting their children, not (yet) to school administrators who had set up parent gatherings for the purpose.

And indeed, some educators anxious about including families in Opportunity Talk long for an educator-only "cocoon." One teacher I know spoke of colleagues "talking straight through back-to-school night so no powerful parents ask questions that cut you down." She said the same teachers feared that immigrant parents would ask too many questions if supports were there for them to talk. In order to move beyond parent meetings that are really just about educators "giving directions" toward real dialogues on improving opportunities for students, she said, "teachers need to feel supported that nobody will hurt *them* if they open up the door."

Anyone in the room should be able to ask, of any suggestion made:

Does this suggestion help support **equity** (the full human talent development of *every* student, and *all groups* of students)? Or not?

NOT supporting each/all students' talent development   SUPPORTING each/all students' talent development

People invited to figure out *together* how to support *every* child, as key people shaping students' fates, are more likely to talk productively about what each can do to create more opportunities for young people. And many stakeholders will need to be assured that the others in the room want to support *them* to support young people, not just critique their attempts to do so.

As we've seen throughout this book, just getting folks in the same room won't ensure an equity-oriented dialogue. But the potential gain of inviting more stakeholders into joint Opportunity Talk is vast. For just a moment, imagine an educator and a parent together at the center of our Foundational Image (page 10), aided by the others to support young people collectively. And now, imagine applying everything in this book to schooltalk with others *outside* the Foundational Image, so they, too, help secure the opportunities students need and deserve.

All of the Strategies in this book can help with the actual conversation. But Opportunity Talk has to be actively invited with equity in mind. It won't happen naturally in schools.

As I've written elsewhere,

Expecting partnership in education without actively enabling communications between partners is like expecting a network of bulbs to glow without a power cord. It takes a network to raise a child; the tiniest break in the network dims the bulbs. The design question is how to light the network up.[61]

Take a minute here to update your Opportunity Talk Inclusion Plan. Now let's go learn from others.

ACTION ASSIGNMENTS

1. Share your Opportunity Talk Inclusion Plan with a young person, parent, or educator you know. Get their input on several of your suggestions,

considering an education community they know. Engage our Infrastructure Design Questions with them:

To support the full human talent development of every student and all groups of students (equity),

> Who in a school/classroom/community needs to communicate what (opportunity-related) information to whom? (How often? When?)
> What are the barriers to needed communication, and how could those barriers be overcome?
> What channel (face-to-face conversations, paper, technology) might allow necessary communications to occur?

Debrief after talking with them. What's one improvement to Opportunity Talk you now find most compelling?

2. Try to turn one gold nugget idea or example from this chapter into a #schooltalking tool that lots of other people could learn from. For example, create a poster or PowerPoint slide, short video, or other multimedia image publicly sharing that gold nugget quote or idea. To accompany your main message, create a brief user's guide of five related information points or ideas from this chapter that can help users be more fully informed about the issue at hand and have a productive conversation sparked by your tool. See Chapter 1, pages 65–66, for more instructions.

3. In person or via the Internet, find an educator or young person who you feel is schooltalking for equity in their Opportunity Talk. Document (with permission) and share (#schooltalking) some example of their work—a photo, a video, an image, a quote from them, or something they have produced.

More schooltalk scenarios

THINK / DISCUSS

Look at www.skooltopia.org as infrastructure for circulating parents' own opportunities to learn as well as local organizations'. Consider pros and cons. Now brainstorm five other ways of tapping community skills, talents, and connections in an education community you know. Name a Principle and Core Tension behind your thinking.

THINK / DISCUSS

Many educators make school listservs one-way (parents can't respond) to avoid conflict. What does your gut say about making a listserv multidirectional so school community members can contribute to Opportunity Talk, not just get announcements? Consider a Principle and Core Tension behind your gut reaction.

THINK / DISCUSS

If you were a school administrator, how would you address the civil rights provision to provide every parent who speaks a demographically common language other than English with translation and interpretation services to access core opportunity information at the school? (What would you do as a school administrator if a small group of parents who speak a more rare language asked if they too could have an interpreter available at school events?)

And for your inclusion plan, would you prioritize hiring new staff who speak the school's main languages, asking current bilingual staff to talk to parents, formally training staff or parents as confidential interpreters, engaging parents as translators of public information, or some other Strategy? Name a Principle and Core Tension behind each of your reactions.

THINK / DISCUSS

Think of an education community you know. What's one activity you might encourage to help people who share that community to "bond" and build trust? Consider a Strategy and a Principle or Core Tension behind your Strategy.

THINK / DISCUSS

Imagine you are the head of a school's PTA. Consider how to prepare for and run a dialogue inviting family members to join a discussion with educators on their educational hopes for young people at your school. Without forcing it, how might this dialogue support parents to share both experiences they've had, and experiences they'd like to have? Could you invite input in smaller-scale ways or even anonymously, if parents don't feel comfortable talking in a group? (How could you learn from parents what sharing mechanism they'd find most comfortable?) Name a Principle behind each aspect of your plan, and a Core Tension of it.

THINK / DISCUSS

Think back to the Madres in Andrea Dyrness's narrative (pages 331–333), who felt that a school comment box collected parent and student input but never addressed it. You are a principal who has to decide what to do with a) your school's comment box and b) lists of parent suggestions made at the last coffee hour. How could you ensure that suggestions for improving opportunities are not just made, but addressed? Name a Strategy for responding to suggestions, and a Principle and Core Tension behind your idea.

Conclusion

Schooltalking for Equity, Long Term

You've been thinking like an equity designer throughout this book. Now let's plan for improving schooltalk in some way you care about personally, in a place you know.

Think about an education setting that's familiar to you. It may be where you went to school, a place you work now, or a place that affects young people you know. Or maybe now you want to bring this book's thinking to another location where people talk about young people and about education—a school board, a newspaper, a nonprofit. Maybe you'll take the learning from this book to your talk with superintendents, professors, or politicians in a broader education community. Take it anywhere in your life where schooltalk might be shifted to support young people better.

Look back to pages 7–10, at our Equity Line, Foundational Image, and Foundational Principles.

Now ask yourself these design questions about that place and its people.

To pursue **equity** (the full human talent development of every young person and all groups of young people), what schooltalk improvement is necessary? More specifically, perhaps:

> Who in this school/classroom/community needs to communicate what information to whom? (How often? When?)

> What are the barriers to needed communication, and how could those barriers be overcome?

> What channel (face-to-face conversations, paper, technology) might allow necessary communications to occur?

This book's seven chapters fleshed out seven foundational domains of schooltalking for equity. Start to envision just one improvement to schooltalk that's needed to support young people better in the setting you know. Or start to look for people elsewhere who seem to have that aspect of schooltalk figured out. Either way, you need an Action Plan!

Your Action Plan can pursue one of three ways to improve schooltalking for equity. Regardless, the first step is to consider the implications for students of some schooltalk situation that exists now. Then take these steps:

✳ **Hypothetical.** You flesh out a **hypothetical** improvement to schooltalk, in detail. (You analyze the equity pros and cons of an improvement you ideally could implement in the setting.)
✳ **Exploratory.** You **explore** something someone else is trying. (In person or via a secondary source, you explore the work of other equity designers who are redesigning schooltalk in some way that could be adapted to your own setting.)
✳ **Real.** You **try** something in your setting and **document** what you do so that others can learn. (You dream big, but you start trying to improve schooltalk in a tangible way, yourself or with partners. Then, you share out what you learned.)

I've helped people imagine, explore, and test many schooltalk improvements they write up as Action Plans. For Hypothetical plans, some review a school's needs and decide that support groups where older students mentor younger ones could be useful, or that the school could really use monthly conversations among Asian parents of special needs students. Some start to design potential workshops about intelligence for use at a university or in an elementary school; some envision messaging to share via social media. Some create protocols helping teams of teachers to talk more productively about supporting students' growth in particular subjects. Others imagine redesigning a report card's language in a particular way, or starting a regular conversation with administrators about securing necessary opportunities for students in a district. One teacher I know hoped to innovate Twitter use at his high school to "push" out information about college opportunities and eligibility requirements, calculating that his school had 3,200 students and five guidance counselors—a 640-to-1 ratio, he noted. ("Guidance would have to meet with four kids a day to see you once in a year.") He was also investigating a "super reduced cell phone plan" he'd heard was available for students who qualified for free lunch.

In Exploratory plans, people have investigated other equity designers' efforts, using social media, research articles, or in-person visits. Some have reviewed others' efforts to engage youth in dialogue about experiences with school discipline or about opportunities in their schools and neighborhoods. One teacher explored the OneVille Parent Connector project further online and then brainstormed the related idea of a welcoming "buddy" for every new parent at her school, "a parent who speaks your language."

And for Real plans, other educators have fully tested their own schooltalk improvements for equity, then documented their efforts' pros and cons for others to learn from. I've worked with teachers who have tried specific tech tools for supporting students to express their thinking to teachers or peers, and documented their efforts' pros and cons for students.[1] Still others have documented their advisory models as mechanisms for Life Talk.[2] Still others have tested take-home journals for communicating with students, or tried a new way to share critical opportunity information with parents. These folks wrote up their efforts to share.

Each design effort—hypothetical, exploratory, or real—starts to steer everyday schooltalk toward equity by analyzing and envisioning a needed improvement, exploring someone else's efforts, or actually trying out some needed communication in an education community. Ideally, we document our thoughts and "ahas" so we can share them.

So, consider some communication needed in a real place—some typical talk you feel is harmful or underinformed, or some absence of necessary schooltalk. Identify a schooltalk problem that gets in the way of the full human talent development of each student and all groups of students.

What will you do about it?

Sample Action Plan Template

Follow this template for writing an Action Plan.

Intro:

Describe the general schooltalk issue you're concerned about in your specific setting. Why are you tackling this communication issue specifically? In a nutshell, what schooltalk improvement feels needed for equity, and why?

Body:

A. **Consider in detail the current schooltalk situation in the setting you know.** Use our Equity Line to evaluate the implications for young people of specific aspects of the existing situation. Ask:

Does this communication help support **equity** (the full human talent development of *every* student, and *all groups* of students)? Or not?

NOT supporting each/all students' talent development   SUPPORTING each/all students' talent development

B. **Describe your vision for what improved schooltalk might look like.** To pursue equity in that place, what schooltalk improvement do you suggest? More specifically, perhaps:

> Who in this school/classroom/community needs to communicate what information to whom? (How often? When?)
> What are the barriers to needed communication, and how could those barriers be overcome?
> What channel (face-to-face conversations, paper, technology) might allow necessary communications to occur?

C. **Then, talk through your proposed improvements to schooltalk in detail.**

Hypothetical: Walk through your schooltalking improvement idea in detail. Use our Equity Line to question the pros and cons of each aspect of your proposed redesign. (Ideally, to help you think, briefly consider the pros and cons of someone else's related effort—a local effort or an effort elsewhere.) Name some likely Core Tensions of your efforts.

Exploratory: Review, in detail, an example of somebody else tackling your schooltalking issue in a seemingly useful way. (Ideally, if possible, contact the designer personally or go see the effort in person.) Consider in detail: what do you learn from their example about tackling the schooltalking issue of your choice? Could aspects of their effort be adapted to your setting? Do you have thoughts about what might not work? *Note: if the work isn't already public, get permission from the "designer" reviewed to document and further share their work. Ask if they want to be named or their contact information included.*

Real: Try an actual improvement. (Ideally, before you get started, briefly consider the pros and cons of someone else's related effort—a local effort or an effort elsewhere.) Then, talk humbly through how it went. With necessary permissions from participants, share documentation of the consequences or implications for young people of the schooltalk improvement you attempted. Use our Equity Line to question the pros and cons of each aspect of what you tried. Name any Core Tensions of your efforts.

Conclusion:

Summarize what you've learned about this schooltalking issue and raise questions for future inquiry. Based on the hypothetical pros and cons you've considered or the evidence you've collected on a specific schooltalk effort, what schooltalking improvements might others want to try? And what do you need to learn more about, in order to address this issue even more successfully in the future? Discuss, and finally reiterate why the schooltalking issue you're tackling is so important.

Add a **reference list** of tools useful to your own thinking, so others can find them. If you want to, share your contact information so others can contact you to learn more.

Action planning: Some overall advice

Here's some overall advice as you get started.

* Prepare to imagine, explore, or test one schooltalking improvement in real detail rather than many improvements at once. Do you think your setting might benefit from an annual assembly on talking about intelligence? Explore exactly what's harmful about current Smarts Talk, and then consider the wording of specific statements you'd want made at the assembly. Do you want to hold a dialogue for youth and educators exploring resource patterns across a district, or experiences of immigrants in the community? Consider an opening question that would invite people to share without feeling forced, and a follow-up question you could have ready in case people make shallow claims about student achievement or other "cultures." Do you want to explore those parent meetings for Asian parents of students with special needs because you sense they are typically excluded from Opportunity Talk? Explore what's missing from some current parent events, then zoom in to consider the meetings you would hold, considering who should be invited, how translation might work if needed, and how children might be talked about in these meetings. Do you want to try convening a "support team" that meets face-to-face (or online as needed) in a setting you know, to discuss individual students' needs and strengths? Take care in monitoring whose voices get included in discussing which aspects of students' lives and achievements. Name any Core Tensions that arise.

* In addition to the examples in this book, I suggest you include some exploratory review of related efforts by others even if you do a Hypothetical action plan or Real action plan. That way, you'll always seek out examples of others tackling your issue in a useful way.

* When pertinent, also cite and discuss any ideas or information you have collected from others' efforts. This way, you'll share helpful resources with other people.

✳ An Exploratory or Real Action Plan will be most useful to you and others if you collect any evidence you can of the benefits (or lack thereof) to young people, with permission from anyone you document—e.g., student writing that helps make the case for a form of Life Talk, informal interviews with adults or students evaluating some effort at Data Talk or Inequality Talk, etc. (Sometimes evidence on something that did not work is the most powerful data of all.) If you have any faces or names in your documentation, make absolutely sure to get permission to use them. For children and youth shown, named, or centrally involved in any test of a schooltalk solution, parent permission will be required.

Design research in education—often called action research when educators do it—involves trying an innovation and documenting effects, often tweaking an effort until benefits occur or are shown not to. It then involves telling the full story to others so they can support young people more effectively. As a teacher I know put it, equity-oriented educators actually "test" efforts all the time. Here, it's a question of actively evaluating the pros and cons for young people of anything you're observing or trying, collecting evidence on these pros and cons as you go, and then documenting how the whole thing went.[3]

When possible, invite students, families, and colleagues into your design effort as co-designers, either to get advice on needed improvements to schooltalk or to help test a design.

✳ Whether your Action Plan is hypothetical, exploratory, or real, ideally share your #schooltalking ideas, examples, or efforts in some form that can be circulated without you having to be present (a video, a PowerPoint, a blog post).

Staying an equity designer and sharing what you learn

We too rarely learn from other equity designers! In education, we often reinvent the wheel in every community. In one sense, every community needs to buy in to its own plan, and envision efforts to fit a specific setting.

Excitement to innovate also sometimes relies on feeling like we are "first" at designing something. But not everyone has time to experiment together from scratch. To spread innovation, we need to learn from others about efforts that support young people, and adapt others' efforts—and personalize them—to where we live and work.[4]

In education, we also see an increasing desire to move from just naming problems to also trying and sharing solutions. This is the turn to *design*—and for us, it's *equity* design.[5] Even as we learn from others, it is up to each of us to design solutions to specific equity problems in specific places.

That's why this book's goal has been to invite you, along with the folks in our Foundational Image, to step forward as designers of equity effort in education today.

First, we started questioning all communications in schools, with equity in mind. Then, we started to consider needed schooltalk improvements in real places. Schooltalk redesign is just one foundational form of equity effort, and it's an endlessly available one—because regardless, one thing we do all day already is talk.

Whether you improve communications or some other everyday action or situation in education, being an equity designer means questioning the situations that exist and crafting improvements with equity in mind. You don't have to start big; start where you are and with something you can immediately improve. Seek out others who have also found that issue critical and ask them what they're doing.

I know elementary educators who have started to rethink their habits for listening to students in their own classrooms, and then tried starting class with a simple dialogue circle. I know teachers venturing to neighborhood programs to try to hear what staff know about needed supports for students. I know deans trying ways of pairing students with various mentors for Life Talk. I know administrators systematically starting to lead dialogues about who is disciplined or assigned to which programs and why. I know teachers asking colleagues to rethink a specific label they use for students or specific ways they discuss students' progress. I know program staff trying out specific motivational statements to use when talking to youth, curriculum writers adding more accurate history to units, and university faculty hosting conversations about creating new local opportunities to learn. I know parents figuring out particular ways schools can tap parents' ideas, teachers trying new ways of talking with parents, and youth trying new ways to investigate and dialogue about improving opportunity in their own schools.

And I've also launched various design efforts that didn't successfully catch on. I just had to pick myself up and try again.

So keep asking questions about designing equity in education—and share what you've learned. Remember that people need to hear all of the warts and flaws—your humble efforts to pursue equity and your own struggles to learn. Rather than just tell people the amazing endpoint, engage them in conversation about the process—the shared struggle of designing actions like schooltalk for equity, and the things that didn't work as well as those that did.

So share your redesigned conversations—and your questions.

Design equity!

#schooltalking

Appendix

A Guide to Talking Effectively with Colleagues

This entire book is about designing schooltalk that supports young people. In education, we talk about students in all sorts of ways—face-to-face, on paper, online. Some of our dialogues are small, some huge. Some are forced, some voluntary. Some are scheduled conversations, some just happen. Any such conversation can pursue equity if it gets colleagues inquiring about supporting young people better.

So, this guide offers initial Strategies for talking to colleagues effectively. (By "colleagues," I mean anyone we might include in efforts to support young people. By "effective" schooltalk, I mean talk that keeps folks partnering in equity effort—effort to support the full human talent development of every young person and all groups of them.)

STRATEGY　Use the Equity Line to matter-of-factly invite inquiry into the consequences for young people of specific actions and situations.

The Equity Line is this book's key dialogue tool. At any time, you can draw a two-sided arrow (below) and ask colleagues to join you in evaluating whether specific actions and situations support young people sufficiently. For this book's purposes, we evaluate the pros and cons of everything people say about young people:

Does **this communication** help support **equity** (the full human talent development of *every* student, and *all groups* of students)? Or not?

NOT supporting each/all
students' talent development

SUPPORTING each/all students'
talent development

No need to fear disagreement: it's core to good work. Anthropologist Norma González once noted how Spanish distinguishes an ongoing *problemática* or issue from a quickly resolvable "problem" or *problema*. Equity design efforts pose many ongoing *problemáticas*. How and when should we label students in schools? How might educators reorganize communications about students' progress, lives, and opportunities? Many actions have both pros and cons. The Equity Line helps us welcome multiple perspectives on supporting students, so we design better supports.

STRATEGY   Focus discussion on evaluating specific things that people can do to support young people better (not on debating people's presumed intentions or character).

If you've worked in education, you know that conversations about students often drift to what's wrong with students,[1] what can't be done to assist them, or what other people should do to assist them. So focusing discussion repeatedly on what people in the room would do to support young people better is often critical. And as you evaluate student support efforts (particularly actions by folks in the room), keep the focus on actions' consequences for students. I'd avoid unwinnable debates over folks' intentions or character. Investigating discrimination complaints at the U.S. Department of Education's Office for Civil Rights, I saw endless dead-end debates over people's intentions and character waste months of people's time.[2] We didn't need to debate who was a good person. We needed to debate the effects of actions and situations for young people.

So to head off unwinnable debates over people's character or intentions, I often say something like this: "I think everyone here is a good person who came here to figure out how best to support young people. Let's keep the focus on supporting them." I've also seen that when folks reflect first on actions' effects for young people, they can actually talk through and even question the beliefs undergirding their actions.

When discussion turns to harmful actions, including harmful schooltalk, I've also found it productive to frame people as shaped by a shared society, rather than as "bad" people who hold individually "bad" ideas. As we'll see throughout this book, many harmful actions happen in school after school and need repeated attention. Most schooltalk too is patterned, with many predictable "scripts" that are in the air waiting to be used, not invented by any individual.[3]

So, here's a related Strategy for reacting to a distressing comment a colleague makes in the middle of a conversation:

> **STRATEGY**   Position someone's comment as a common thing said by many people.

> **STRATEGY**   Attack the script, not the speaker. (Go after the thing said, not the person who said it.)

When you position a comment as a common thing many people say, rather than as some "bad" idea held only by an individual, people can more easily discuss and rethink a thing they just said. I often frame even very damaging ideas about students or families as rampant "in the world" or "in the air we breathe," not just in someone's (bad) head individually. I say explicitly that research shows we hold lots of damaging ideas about young people despite ourselves,[4] and that common ideas are "programmed" into our heads even if we don't want them to be there. Then I address the common idea's *effects* for young people—and I return to discussing supports for them. (I used this Strategy when quoted for this article: http://www.huffingtonpost.com/2015/01/06/black-white-discipline -gap_n_6425096.html.)

To position a comment as a common thing people say, I try responses like, "You know, I've heard lots of people say that. But (cite alternative here). . ."

As Michelle Alexander, author of *The New Jim Crow*[5]—a book that has sparked many a fraught dialogue about bias in criminal justice—put it to me via email,

> "What's important isn't pointing fingers at each other (or ourselves) for our biases, but acknowledging our biases, blind spots, or areas of ignorance so that we can better educate ourselves and express greater care and compassion for others."

Go after the thing said, not the person who said it.

Equity talk is full of common "scripts."

"Attack" the script, not the speaker.

When someone challenges something *you* just said, here's a suggestion:

STRATEGY   Act like a learner.

The goal of dialogue toward equity is not only to inform others, but to learn to support young people better in real places. Even if you feel equipped with sufficient information about any issue discussed, you probably always have more to learn about discussing that information. If you end up in conflict about something you just said, then, great—more info for you about where conversations can lead. Every conflict over divergent perspectives teaches me how to address the issue more effectively next time.

I've also learned over time that I actually feel more secure when admitting to others that I'm always learning—and in retrospect, I try to frame even people who truly shook my confidence as people who taught me something useful. Carol Dweck suggests that in all domains of life, taking a stance as a constant learner—a *growth mindset*—actually helps you succeed. A growth mindset is a powerful orientation to learning through trial and error. In Dweck's words, for people with a "growth mindset,"

> It's not about looking smart or grooming their image. It's about a commitment to learning—taking informed risks and learning from the results, surrounding yourself with people who will challenge you to grow, looking frankly at your deficiencies and seeking to remedy them. Most great business leaders have had this mindset, because building and maintaining excellent organizations in the face of constant change requires it.[6]

Researchers argue that the most successful educators keep questioning how to improve their work along all dimensions.[7] Equity work is no different: with colleagues, we keep asking how to support students better, hypothetically and in the real organizations we know.

But acting like a learner isn't always easy. I've had others quit collaborations with me because I didn't grapple with conflicting ideas; I just barreled through with restating my own perspective and didn't truly listen. Audrey Thompson describes a different form of conversational dominance—the person who positions herself as the "holier than thou" instructor of everyone else. This behavior tends to turn off even potential allies.[8] So, acting like a learner probably will serve you better overall than acting like a person with little to learn.

STRATEGY   Plan to stay engaged even if there is some conflict.

One time in graduate school I was trying to express how my own experiences as a white person diverged from the article we were reading, and several fellow students heard my comments as a predictable and infuriating effort to deny being treated as "white" by the world. (They were also frustrated that I was taking so much class time talking about myself.) I could've quit at that moment because the interaction was so upsetting and embarrassing. Instead, I talked more one on one to the colleagues in the class and then wrote a paper about the scripts I'd repeated without meaning to. That got me started on twenty years of effort to improve race talk. And since I showed up every day in class after that to continue the dialogue, this was also an experience where I learned to stay engaged so *I* could learn. Later, in *Colormute*, I suggested that "to disarm fears of error, we can state directly [to colleagues] that the task at hand is to work together through inevitable errors."[9]

Glenn Singleton notes that people often want to escape conversations when ideas get contentious. Instead, he asks people to pledge in advance to stay in the game even if disagreement arises, by committing to these Four Agreements of Courageous Conversation:

✳ Stay engaged (don't "let your heart and mind 'check out' of the conversation"; "resist the natural inclination to move away")

✳ Experience discomfort (stay "personally responsible for pushing [yourself] into a real dialogue" that can get "uncomfortable but also will lead to real growth")

✳ Speak your truth (be "absolutely honest about your thoughts, feelings, and opinions . . . not just saying what you perceive others want to hear")

✳ Expect and accept non-closure ("commit to an ongoing dialogue"; "the more we talk, the more we learn").[10]

Sometimes, colleagues' learning *to* "disagree" is key to working together successfully.[11] And sometimes the most valuable thing to experience in a discussion is a perspective or piece of evidence that makes you think differently about something.

This quote really resonated with me at the end of a meal, so I kept it:

> "The purpose of argument should not be victory, but progress."
> —*fortune cookie, 2009*

STRATEGY   Don't ignore your feelings; try to notice them and dialogue through them with young people in mind.

Believe me, I like to debate things intellectually, but interpersonally, I'm pretty conflict averse. While seeing conflicts and debates as predictable and patterned is my ultimate savior, I find these suggestions from Teaching Tolerance (designed for students) useful to help adults talk, too, as we experience strong emotions:

Reiterate. Contemplate. Respire. Communicate.

Step 1: Reiterate. *Restate what you heard.* . . . Repeating what [you] have heard limits miscommunication and misinformation.

Step 2: Contemplate. *Count to ten before responding.*

Step 3: Respire. *Take a breath to check-in with self.*

Step 4: Communicate. *Speak with compassion and thoughtfulness* . . . assuming good intentions and seeking understanding (http://www.tolerance. org/publication/teaching-new-jim-crow).

We also shouldn't dismiss anyone who shares strong emotions while schooltalking.[12] Of course we get emotional when we speak about real lives and serious consequences. Emotion is part of what gets us up in the morning to support young people.

Here's another classic schooltalk issue: Have you ever said something and then immediately wanted to explain all the stuff you didn't say? In conversations about equity particularly, everything we say is just the tip of the iceberg of all the stuff we are thinking. What's above the surface is what you said; what's below is everything you might have said!

Source: Uwe Kils

I've found it productive to literally say out loud before a dialogue that people might say just a fraction of what they actually think or know. ("So what you are about to share is just the tip of the iceberg of what you know and are thinking"; "Everyone here is just scratching the surface of what they could say about the subject at hand.") That way, everyone hears each other's words as partial rather than comprehensive.

Since so many comments just scratch the surface of things, here's another dialogue skill we'll hone in this book: asking people to consider or share additional evidence and information.

STRATEGY Ask people to consider (or offer) additional evidence related to their claims.

Pure opinion about how others live or what others should do ("those parents really need to . . .") isn't very convincing in discussion, especially if folks are talking about people who have had life experiences different from their own. So we can ask for evidence about the claims people make. Evidence can come from one's own lived experience, from one's informal investigation of the world, or from research. It's very important to acknowledge people's lived experience as evidence of that experience, but it might not be evidence of others' experiences.[13] And we can't ever ask people to "represent" for a larger community when they speak.[14]

What we can do is invite people into deeper inquiry about supporting young people better—in general and in specific places. Questions like these can get students discussing the evidence and reasoning behind their claims (http://inquiryproject.terc.edu/shared/pd/TalkScience_Primer.pdf, p. 11). It's good advice for adults, as well:

"Say More" questions:

"Can you say more about that?" "What do you mean by that?" "Can you give an example?"

"So, Are You Saying?" questions:

"So, let me see if I've got what you're saying. Are you saying . . . ?" (always leaving space for the original [speaker] to agree or disagree and say more)

"Asking for Evidence or Reasoning" questions:

"Why do you think that?" "What's your evidence?" "How did you arrive at that conclusion?"

Singleton and Hays suggest these follow-up questions to help pump more evidence into a discussion:[15]

✳ *"Can you tell me what you mean when you say . . . ?*

✳ *"Is it possible for you to say more about . . . ?*

✳ *"Have the thoughts you shared been shaped by others, or is this your personal perspective?"*

✳ *"Why do you think others might want to challenge your perspective?"*

When someone challenges me, I've also learned to say things like, "Well, I hear what you're saying. What I'm trying to say is . . ."

Shari Saunders and Diana Kardia offer a similar method for dialogue in "inclusive college classrooms": Listen, Affirm, Respond, Add Information.[16]

You might be thinking: *do we need to do all this work just to talk to colleagues?* Can't I just dismiss or ignore comments I disagree with?

Well, people might retreat when smacked down—but often with their ideas intact. (One time in a collaboration I was part of, one partner started screaming at me a lot to get me to hear him. Instead, I became even more unable to hear him and learn from him. And as I stated earlier, I've been guilty of shutting other people down problematically by just replacing their ideas with my own until they stopped talking. They, too, stopped listening to me.)

Smacking or shutting people down (rather than engaging them in inquiry) might not lead to progress, but ignoring comments doesn't either: because statements about young people are actions with consequences in the world, troubling statements require response.

As Alice McIntyre notes, for the first years of her university teaching career she just ignored comments in class that felt underinformed, because engaging speakers (especially in front of others) just felt too adversarial. (One such comment was, "Inner-city kids, and most of them are kids of color, and this is not racism, this is a fact, most inner-city kids don't want to learn. They just don't care.") Then she realized that it was her responsibility to young people to press toward more informed analysis. So, she learned to respond to comments with questions like, "Well, how do you know that?"[17]

We might worry about offending colleagues by engaging their words, but to improve supports for young people, "We need to mix compassion for our conversation partners with compassion for those harmed explicitly by the orders being described."[18] Ali Michael also urges us to ask "untouchable questions"—questions that we fear might make us sound ignorant, but would leave inequality untouched if *not* asked.[19] As an undergrad put it to me after reading Glenn Singleton's advice above to "speak your truth,"[20] "if you don't say what you need to say, people won't learn from your experience or ideas. And, you too will miss out on chances to learn."

If in speaking your truth you still seem to shut a colleague down in a way you think inhibited learning necessary for progress, you can always apologize for aspects of the interaction the person found hurtful (not for your equity commitments), explain the urgency behind your "truth," and state a commitment to learning and joint effort with young people in mind. Even if you are certain you're right, acknowledging harm experienced by others can be key interpersonally if you plan to keep working together.[21] Investigating discrimination complaints at OCR, I saw educators and parents battle for far longer than needed because educators simply failed to acknowledge the harm that parents experienced in interactions.

Just remember the bigger point that relationships are key to equity work too. If people are going to keep showing up for the work, they need to feel like the others in a partnership care about them and about their growth as contributors to a joint effort to support young people.

As a black friend noted on Facebook at one of our tough national moments,

"There is no need to unfriend the folks that disagree with you about Ferguson & Mike Brown. It's better for them to see/hear your perspective and you theirs. We don't win by turning away. We win by engaging in the work."

So, here's a final comprehensive Strategy for engaging effectively with colleagues. We'll use it throughout this book:

STRATEGY Seek clarifying takeaways for equity effort while you talk.

Discussion that raises difficult issues but never names clarifying takeaways for real work can drive people crazy. For example, teachers approach professional development on equity issues with a relentless and necessary question: "But what can I *do*?"[22]

I constantly seek useful, clear, and concise ideas about equity effort that people can take directly into their work and lives. In *Everyday Antiracism*, I called such valuable takeaways "gold nuggets."

Here are three forms of clarifying takeaway I suggest you collect as you read or talk.

✳   Great Quotes

✳   Principles/Strategies/Try Tomorrows

✳   Core Tensions

I suggest you keep a journal where you gather these takeaways and that you literally restate them out loud when you hear them in conversation. Trust me, this really helps to make dialogues productive.

Name Great Quotes that clarify equity efforts

Whenever you hear a quote that you find really useful and clarifying for equity work, say so!

* (in a conversation): "I love what Jessica just said: 'any label describes just a fraction of a person's experience.'"
* (when reading): "I found this quote from Chapter 1 really clarifying. . . ." (quote it, and discuss why).

Name Principles, Strategies, and Try Tomorrows for equity effort

At any given time in a conversation about education, someone is likely considering a foundational idea about what should be done to support young people (a Principle), a concrete plan for action anywhere (a Strategy), or a very specific thing to do "tomorrow" in a very specific situation (a Try Tomorrow). So, I ask people to name clear ideas for equity effort at all three "levels."

A **Principle** is a lofty statement in your own words about what should be done to support young people.

Every time you hear a big, clear idea about necessary equity effort, name it as a useful Principle! For example, in one class I taught for aspiring teachers, we were reading an essay by Dorinda Carter about how teachers (or peers) can problematically "spotlight" students by forcing them to represent a whole group in front of the class (essentially asking, "Can you speak for 'your' group on this issue?"). Generations of students have found this moment harmful, but teachers still do it all the time.[23] As we discussed Dorinda's piece, one teacher spoke up. "I think she's saying that people can speak as ethnic or racial group members if they want to in class, but no one should be asked to speak *for* a 'group,'" she said. We stopped and restated this advice as a memorably clear "Principle" from Dorinda's piece:

PRINCIPLE   People can speak as ethnic/racial group members if they want, but no one should be asked to speak for a "group."

To help people name such Principles as we discuss readings or real-life situations, I often literally ask, *"OK, is there a Principle under what you're saying?"*

A **Strategy** offers a concrete plan for action that someone could take in many places to pursue equity. (I'll offer a lot of Strategies in this book.) For example, the readers of Dorinda's piece suggested a Strategy to activate the Principle above:

STRATEGY   Teachers can take the spotlight off of students by explicitly inviting input from anyone in the room who'd like to share their take on the topic.

A **Try Tomorrow** is a really specific equity action to take with particular people in a specific setting. For example, a teacher considered this Try Tomorrow for her classroom out loud:

TRY TOMORROW   In my own class's discussion of Muslim experiences in America, if people start asking Mohammad to weigh in, I might say, "Mohammad doesn't speak for all Muslims, of course, and he shouldn't be asked to!"

Sometimes, I invite people to role-play a proposed Try Tomorrow to see if it really could work. ("OK, so how about you be the teacher. Try actually saying that.")[24]

As seen in this book's **THINK/DISCUSS** questions, I will often ask people to name equity Principles, Strategies, or Try Tomorrows as they are talking or writing about a topic, or to finish a dialogue. ("So at the level of Principle, are you saying that people should always strive to . . . ?" "What's a Strategy an administrator might try to live out that Principle across a school?" "OK, so at the Try Tomorrow level, what would you actually say to the parent?")

You and your colleagues may not come to consensus on Try Tomorrows, Strategies, or Principles. At times, you might agree on a Principle (e.g., "teachers should talk to students about their lives as well as academics") but not on a Strategy (to support students emotionally, should teachers text students?) or a more specific Try Tomorrow (should a teacher answer a student's text about a personal crisis sent after 11 p.m.?). Also, don't force yourself to name all three every time.

Here's the last kind of equity takeaway worth naming.

Name Core Tensions of equity effort

A **Core Tension** articulates an unsolvable dilemma of equity effort—a way people are "trapped between a rock and a hard place" when they try to take action for equity.

I find naming Core Tensions of equity effort extremely productive for people trying to make change in real places, and I do it a lot. Here are some examples:

> **CORE TENSION**   Adding tech to school communications helps broaden access to information, but it also widens disparities of access. (Chapter 7)

> **CORE TENSION**   People are individuals too complex for labels. But we also have to label shared experiences and needs in order to address them. (Chapter 1)

> **CORE TENSION**   When we don't have data, we don't know how students are doing. But just "more" talk about "more" data isn't always good. (For example, is it always helpful if a data display shows a young person's suspensions next to his face?) (Chapter 5)

> **CORE TENSION**   "OK, folks, some people seem to want us to [do something] and other people seem to want us to [do just the opposite]" (typical comment from me in a staff meeting at the Center I direct).

Every time you sense a Core Tension of equity effort—a seemingly unresolvable dilemma—I suggest you name it explicitly: "So I hear a Core Tension here! On the one hand, X; on the other hand, Y." I think you'll be surprised at how much it frees people up to talk.

Core Tensions of pursuing equity are there under the surface even if we don't name them. So, explicitly naming them helps people consider opposing perspectives rather than have a dead-end debate where nobody hears the other side. As Martin Luther King Jr. put it about nonviolent activism in the civil rights movement, "there is a type of constructive, nonviolent tension which is necessary for growth":

> We who engage in nonviolent direct action are not the creators of tension. We merely bring to the surface the hidden tension that is already alive. We bring it out in the open, where it can be seen and dealt with.[25]

So, here's an overall model for productive discussion with colleagues. I suggest you use this model as you discuss or write about the **THINK/ DISCUSS** questions in this book, or as you debate any action or situation in a real setting you know.

Discussion model

A. **Discuss** a real-world issue affecting young people.

B. **Evaluate** an existing situation or possible actions using the Equity Line, considering the pros and cons for young people. Ask for perspectives:

Does **this action/situation (for this book's purposes, this communication)** help support **equity** (the full human talent development of *every* student, and *all groups* of students)? Or not?

NOT supporting each/all students' talent development   SUPPORTING each/all students' talent development

C. As you go and definitely before ending the conversation, **restate some clarifying takeaways** regarding equity effort.

* Do any **Great Quotes** from colleagues or other sources help you think about equity effort?

* Can you name a **Principle, Strategy,** or **Try Tomorrow** for equity effort that came up in this discussion?

* Can you name one or more **Core Tensions** (unresolvable dilemmas) of equity effort that came up in this discussion?

Discuss
Evaluate
Pinpoint

→

- **Great Quote**
- **Principle / Strategy / Try Tomorrow**
- **Core Tension**

ACTION ASSIGNMENTS

1. Choose one Strategy from this guide that resonates with you and read or explain it to a friend, family member, or colleague.

   Then, ask him or her: has he or she faced this schooltalking issue in her own conversations with others? Does he or she feel the Strategy presented would help? Why or why not? Use our Equity Line to evaluate the pros and cons of the Strategy.

   Does this communication **(with colleagues)** help support **equity** (the full human talent development of *every* student and *all groups* of students)? Or not?

   NOT supporting each/all students' talent development — SUPPORTING each/all students' talent development

   Now consider a Strategy from this guide that does *not* resonate with you, based on prior experience. What alternative schooltalking Strategy would you suggest?

2. If you are dialoguing with others as you read this book, consider together:

   > Did you see any Strategies in this guide that you'd particularly like to adopt in your small group?

   > What additional norms would you appreciate from one another in your conversations?

   > Each person in your group should share at least one additional norm that you'd like to apply as you talk in your small group. Agree on a short list of Group Norms. Post your list somewhere where you can refer to it.

3. Discuss the following scenario with someone. Imagine that a colleague just said something that you consider underinformed about a racial/ethnic group, language group, gender group, or other group. You're feeling really frustrated. What's the first thing you could say next?

Role-play your response at the Try Tomorrow level. Use our Equity Line to evaluate the pros and cons of specific things you could say. End by pinpointing a Principle/Strategy and Core Tension behind your thinking.

For example, undergraduate students and I have debated the pros and cons of responding to a colleague who makes an uninformed comment about a group by saying, "You're stupid!" Students have suggested that while the response might feel good, if it shut down the other person he'd carry away his underinformed idea intact. Or you might not learn some piece of knowledge he actually has. We ended our discussion by pinpointing the following general Strategy and overall Principle to go with our final Try Tomorrow, and a Core Tension of communicating for equity that came up:

PRINCIPLE   If you disagree with someone, shutting them down altogether isn't as productive as getting them to think differently.

STRATEGY   Try saying something that states your own counter-perspective and asks the other person to offer more evidence for their claim.

TRY TOMORROW   (the specific thing you might literally say in this case): "That's a common thing to say, George. Is that really what you think? I'd say that the reality is [something else], but why don't you tell me where you learned any evidence behind what you said."

CORE TENSION   To learn more about a topic, people need to talk more with others. But talking more can also just give more airtime to an underinformed perspective.

Acknowledgments

This book benefited from thousands of people's ideas and efforts, and from some extremely generous readers' eyes. Tara Grove, at the New Press, gave me the first vote of confidence to pursue the project; Marc Favreau and Emily Albarillo helped with final finishes. Katie Sciurba was my first (and last!) draft reader and gave me confidence to keep writing (and stop). Students at UC San Diego read congealing chapters hours after I wrote them each week in winter 2014–15 and spring 2015, and completed chapters in spring 2016. John Bartholomew, Tiveeda Stovall, Milton Reynolds, Bob Jarvis, Terece Moret, Lisa Thomas, Barbara Edwards, Sherry Deckman, Rachel Garver, Sonia Nieto, and Paul Gorski each made it through the whole manuscript at different points; their enthusiasm for the project and advice on improving it buoyed me forward. Ali Michael, Carol Mukhopadhyay, Anita Wadhwa, Rich Milner, Makeba Jones, Rosemary Henze, Nicole Mirra, Amanda Datnow, Frances Contreras, Nan Renner, Bud Mehan, Jeff Elman, Rolf Straubhaar, Ana Maria Nieto, Connie Chung, Alice Mello, Jedd Cohen, Katrine Czajkowski, Marit Dewhurst, Rich Reddick, John Diamond, Fred Erickson, Andrea Dyrness, Glenn Singleton, Leisy Wyman, Bryan Brayboy, Dorinda Carter Andrews, Debbie Costa-Hernandez, Sumie Okazaki, Erica Frankenberg, Prudence Carter, Vajra Watson, Robert Sternberg, Ted Hamann, and Vivian Louie offered advice on targeted chapters. Others enthusiastically reviewed or offered targeted examples, including Kevin Foster, Christine Sleeter, Norma González, Karolyn Tyson, Thandeka Chapman, Kevin Welner, Gretchen Brion-Meisels, Gary Orfield, John Rogers, Liliana Garces, Yolanda Moses, Alan Goodman, Lee Baker, Susan Yonezawa, and Marlene Pollock. Muhammad Qassimyar tended the extensive list of works cited. I thank my parents, Estera and Sheldon, my sister, Nira (plus Rick and my nieces), the Castigliones, and the CREATE colleagues who tolerated my ongoing attention to this project over holidays, weekends, and workdays. Most of all, I thank my dearest Elea, Jonah, and Joe, for supporting me every day of my life. It takes a network to finish a book, and I'm deeply grateful for mine.

Notes

Introduction

1. For a first use, see Mica Pollock, ed., *Everyday Antiracism: Getting Real About Race in School* (New York: The New Press, 2008).
2. John Dewey, "My Pedagogic Creed," *School Journal* 54 (1897): 77–80. See http://dewey.pragmatism.org/creed.htm.
3. Vincent Harding, *There Is a River: The Black Struggle for Freedom in America* (Harcourt Brace and Company, 1981), 325–326.
4. Linda Darling-Hammond, *The Flat World and Education: How America's Commitment to Equity Will Determine Our Future* (New York: Teachers College Press, 2010), 12. This bilingual handout offers six well-worded sub-goals of equity effort as food for thought: http://www.idra.org/images/stories/Six_Goals_of_Education_Equity_Bilingual_2011.pdf.
5. Hugh Mehan, *In the Front Door: Creating a College-Going Culture of Learning* (Boulder, CO: Paradigm Publishers, 2012).
6. Alan M. Blankstein and Pedro Noguera, *Excellence Through Equity: Five Principles of Courageous Leadership to Guide Achievement for Every Student* (Thousand Oaks, CA: Corwin, 2015), 3, emphasis added.
7. Karolyn Tyson, "Providing Equal Access to 'Gifted' Education," in *Everyday Antiracism: Getting Real About Race in School*, ed. Mica Pollock (New York: The New Press, 2008), 129.
8. Blankstein and Noguera, *Excellence Through Equity*.
9. Martin Luther King Jr., "Letter from a Birmingham Jail," archived at African Studies Center, University of Pennsylvania, last modified July 1, 2015, http://www.africa.upenn.edu/Articles_Gen/Letter_Birmingham.html.
10. Mica Pollock, "From Denial to Creation," *Anthropology News* 55, no. 6 (June 2014).
11. Sarah Michaels and Catherine O'Connor, "Talk Science Primer," *The Inquiry Project: Seeing the World Through a Scientist's Eyes*, last modified 2012, http://inquiryproject.terc.edu/shared/pd/TalkScience_Primer.pdf, 4.
12. On U.S. multilingualism, see, e.g., Patricia Baquedano-López and Sera Hernandez, "Language Socialization Across Educational Settings," in *A Comparison to the Anthropology of Education*, ed. Bradley A.U. Levinson and Mica Pollock (West Sussex, UK: Wiley-Blackwell, 2011), 197–211; Teresa L. McCarty and Tiffany S. Lee, "Critical Culturally Sustaining/Revitalizing Pedagogy and Indigenous Education Sovereignty," *Harvard Educational Review* 84, no. 1 (Spring 2014).
13. Mica Pollock, *Colormute: Race Talk Dilemmas in an American School* (Princeton, NJ: Princeton University Press, 2004).
14. Mica Pollock, *Because of Race: How Americans Debate Harm and Opportunity in Our Schools* (Princeton, NJ: Princeton University Press, 2008).
15. Pollock, *Everyday Antiracism*.
16. Mica Pollock, "It Takes a Network to Raise a Child: Improving the Communication Infrastructure of Public Education to Enable Community Cooperation in Young People's Success," *Teachers College Record* 155, no. 7 (2013): 1–28.

17. Mica Pollock, "Smart Tech Use for Equity," *Teaching Tolerance* 52, (Spring 2016): 39–41 (http://www.tolerance.org/sites/default/files/general/TT52_Smart%20Tech%20Use%20for%20 Equity.pdf).

18. Long ago, I particularly learned to think about the power of language from Ray McDermott, Fred Erickson, and Bud Mehan, who also introduced me to the work of many others. Their work is cited elsewhere in the book; Erickson's *Talk and Social Theory* offers an overview. See Frederick Erickson, *Talk and Social Theory: Ecologies of Speaking and Listening in Everyday Life*, First Edition (Malden, MA: Polity Press, 2004). For a useful review of other school-related studies of language as action, see Stanton Wortham and Angela Reyes, "Linguistic Anthropology of Education," in *A Companion to the Anthropology of Education*, ed. Bradley A.U. Levinson and Mica Pollock (West Sussex, UK: Wiley-Blackwell, 2011), 137–153. Late in the process of copyediting this book, I read in full Richard R. Valencia's book *Dismantling Contemporary Deficit Thinking: Educational Thought and Practice* (New York: Taylor and Francis, 2010) and found it a kindred spirit resource calling similarly for adding more "facts" to claims about young people in education. For another kindred spirit resource that focuses with similar urgency on the use of language by school leaders particularly, see Felecia M. Briscoe, Gilberto Arriaza, and Rosemary C. Henze, *The Power of Talk: How Words Change Our Lives* (Thousand Oaks, CA: Corwin Press, 2009).

19. Daniel G. Solórzano and Tara J. Yosso, "Critical Race and LatCrit Theory and Method: Counter-storytelling," *International Journal of Qualitative Studies in Education* 14, no. 4 (2001): 471–495, p. 481.

Chapter 1: Group Talk

1. Wendy Luttrell, "Responding to the 'N-Word,'" in *Everyday Antiracism: Getting Real About Race in School*, ed. Mica Pollock (New York: The New Press, 2008).

2. See https://www.splcenter.org/20160413/trump-effect-impact-presidential-campaign-our-nat ions-schools.

3. Joseph G. Kosciw, Emily A. Greytak, Mark J. Bartkiewicz, Madelyn J. Boesen, and Neal A. Palmer, *The 2011 National School Climate Survey: The Experiences of Lesbian, Gay, Bisexual and Transgender Youth in Our Nation's Schools* (Gay, Lesbian and Straight Education Network [GLSEN], 2012), http://files.eric.ed.gov/fulltext/ED535177.pdf, xiv; Emily S. Fisher and Karen Komosa-Hawkins, ed., *Creating Safe and Supportive Learning Environments: A Guide for Working with Lesbian, Gay, Bisexual, Transgender and Questioning Youth and Families*, ed. (New York: Routledge, 2013).

4. Mica Pollock, *Colormute: Race Talk Dilemmas in an American School* (Princeton, NJ: Princeton University Press, 2004).

5. Carol C. Mukhopadhyay, Rosemary C. Henze, and Yolanda T. Moses, *How Real Is Race? A Sourcebook on Race, Culture, and Biology*, Second Edition (Lanham, MD: Rowman & Littlefield, 2014).

6. In 2011, almost two-thirds of LGBT students surveyed nationally heard frequent negative remarks from both educators and peers about "not acting 'masculine enough' or 'feminine enough.'" Kosciw et al., *The 2011 National School Climate Survey*, xiv.

7. Some key anthropological texts that first helped me understand labels as things people make were Fredrik Barth, *Ethnic Groups and Boundaries: Social Organization of Culture Differences* (Boston: Little, Brown and Company, 1969); Claude Levi-Strauss, *The Savage Mind* (Chicago: University of Chicago Press, 1966); Michael Moerman, "Being Lue: Uses and Abuses of Ethnic Identification," in *Essays on the Problem of Tribe*, ed. Jane Helm (Seattle: University of Washington Press, 1968); and Charles Frake, *Language and Cultural Description* (Stanford: Stanford University Press, 1980 [1975]).

8. Felecia M. Briscoe, Gilberto Arriaza, and Rosemary C. Henze, *The Power of Talk: How Words Change Our Lives* (Thousand Oaks, CA: Corwin Press, 2009), 113, 120.

9. Mica Pollock, *Because of Race: How Americans Debate Harm and Opportunity in Our Schools* (Princeton, NJ: Princeton University Press, 2008).

10. Russell J. Skiba, Robert S. Michael, Abra Carroll Nardo, and Reece L. Peterson, "The Color of Discipline: Sources of Racial and Gender Disproportionality in School Punishment," *Urban Review* 34, no. 4 (2002): 317–342; Daniel J. Losen, *Closing the School Discipline Gap: Equitable Remedies for Excessive Exclusion* (New York: Teachers College Press, 2014); www.colorincolorado

.org/article/reasons-misidentification-special-needs-among-ells, and http://www.colorincolorado.org /article/40715.

11. See http://www2.ed.gov/about/offices/list/ocr/ell/lau.html.

12. Laurie Olsen, "School Restructuring and the Needs of Immigrant Students," in *Immigrant Children: Theory, Research, and Implications for Educational Policy*, ed. Ruben Rumbaut and Wayne A. Cornelius (San Diego, CA: Center for U.S.-Mexican Studies, 1995.

13. Ted Hamann, "Standards vs. 'Standard' Knowledge," in Pollock, *Everyday Antiracism*.

14. Laurie Olsen, "Reparable Harm: Fulfilling the Unkept Promise of Educational Opportunity for California's Long Term English Learners," *A Californians Together Research & Policy Publication*, 2010, http://edsource.org/wp-content/uploads/ReparableHarm1.pdf, 17.

15. Teresa L. McCarty and Tiffany S. Lee, "Critical Culturally Sustaining/Revitalizing Pedagogy and Indigenous Education Sovereignty," *Harvard Educational Review* 84, no. 1 (Spring 2014): 106.

16. Erik Stegman and Victoria F. Phillips, *Missing the Point: The Real Impact of Native Mascots and Team Names on American Indian and Alaska Native Youth* (Center for American Progress: July 2014).

17. Lesley Bartlett and Ofelia Garcia, *Additive Schooling in Subtractive Times: Bilingual Education and Dominican Immigrant Youth in the Heights* (Nashville, TN: Vanderbilt University Press, 2011); Marjorie Faulstich Orellana, Presidential Address, Council on Anthropology and Education, American Anthropological Association Annual Meetings, November 19, 2015.

18. Patricia Gándara, "Strengthening Student Identity in School Programs," in Pollock, *Everyday Antiracism*.

19. Claude M. Steele, "Thin Ice: Stereotype Threat and Black College Students," *The Atlantic*, August 1999, http://www.theatlantic.com/magazine/archive/1999/08/thin-ice-stereotype-threat-and -black-college-students/304663; Paul Tough, "Who Gets to Graduate?" *New York Times Magazine*, May 18, 2014, http://www.nytimes.com/2014/05/18/magazine/who-gets-to-graduate.html.

20. Ward H. Goodenough, "Multiculturalism as the Normal Human Experience," *Anthropology and Education Quarterly* 7, no. 4 (1976): 4–7.

21. Kimberlé Crenshaw, "Demarginalizing the Intersection of Race and Sex: A Black Feminist Critique of Antidiscrimination Doctrine, Feminist Theory and Antiracist Politics," *University of Chicago Legal Forum* 1989, no. 1 (1989): 139–167.

22. Shaun R. Harper, Cameron C. Wardell, and Keon M. McGuire, "Man of Multiple Identities: Complex Individuality and Identity Intersectionality Among College Men," in *Masculinities in Higher Education*, ed. Jason A. Laker and Tracy Davis (New York: Routledge, 2011), 81–96; 92–93.

23. Mica Pollock, "Race Bending: 'Mixed' Youth Practicing Strategic Racialization in California," *Anthropology and Education Quarterly* 35, no. 1 (March 2004): 30–52.

24. Na'ilah Nasir, *Racialized Identities: Race and Achievement Among African American Youth* (Stanford, CA: Stanford University Press, 2011).

25. Django Paris and H. Samy Alim, "What Are We Seeking to Sustain Through Culturally Sustaining Pedagogy?" *Harvard Educational Review* 84, no. 1 (Spring 2014).

26. Laurie Olsen, *Made in America: Immigrant Students in Our Public Schools*, Tenth Edition (New York: The New Press, 2008).

27. Lory Jannelle Dance, *Tough Fronts: The Impact of Street Culture on Schooling* (New York: Routledge, 2002).

28. Tiffany S. Lee and Patricia D. Quijada Cerecer, "(Re) Claiming Native Youth Knowledge: Engaging in Socio-culturally Responsive Teaching and Relationships," *Multicultural Perspectives* 12, no. 4 (2010): 199–205; Gándara, "Strengthening Student Identity."

29. Kimberly Chang and Rachel Conrad, "Following Children's Leads in Conversations about Race," in Pollock, *Everyday Antiracism*.

30. Ashley Montagu, *Man's Most Dangerous Myth: The Fallacy of Race*, Sixth Edition (Walnut Creek, CA: AltaMira Press, 1997).

31. Max S. Torres, Maria Elena Martinez, and David Nirenberg, *Race and Blood in the Iberian World* (London, UK: LIT Verlag, 2012), 16.

32. Audrey Smedley, *Race in North America: Origin and Evolution of a Worldview* (Boulder: Westview Press, 1999).

33. Roger Sanjek, "The Enduring Inequalities of Race," in *Race*, ed. Steven Gregory and Roger Sanjek (New Brunswick, NJ: Rutgers University Press, 1994), 1–17.

34. Smedley, *Race in North America*, 53–62; James H. Sweet, "The Iberian Roots of American Racist Thought," *The William and Mary Quarterly* 54, no. 1 (1997): 143–166.

35. Michael Omi and Howard Winant, *Racial Formation in the United States: From the 1960s to the 1990s*, Second Edition (New York: Routledge, 1994), 62; Smedley, *Race in North America*, 23.

36. Carol C. Mukhopadhyay, "Getting Rid of the Word 'Caucasian,'" in Pollock, *Everyday Antiracism*, 12. See also Smedley, *Race in North America*, chapter 5.

37. David R. Roediger, *The Wages of Whiteness: Race and the Making of the American Working Class* (Brooklyn, NY: Verso Books, 2007), 21 and chapter 2.

38. Winthrop Jordan, *White over Black* (Baltimore: Penguin Books, 1969), cited in Tomás Almaguer, *Racial Fault Lines: The Historical Origins of White Supremacy in California* (Berkeley: University of California Press, 1994), 21.

39. Smedley, *Race in North America*, chapter 5.

40. For a quick history of U.S. citizenship policies, see http://flowofhistory.org/c_toolkit/essays/citizenship.html.

41. Ian Haney López, *White by Law: The Legal Construction of Race* (New York: New York University Press, 2006), 1. See also http://www.pbs.org/race/000_About/002_03_d-godeeper.htm.

42. See https://history.state.gov/milestones/1937-1945/chinese-exclusion-act-repeal.

43. Tomás Almaguer, *Racial Fault Lines: The Historical Origins of White Supremacy in California* (Berkeley: University of California Press, 1994), 56.

44. Almaguer, *Racial Fault Lines*. 57.

45. Haney López, *White by Law*, 38; Gilbert G. González, "The Ideology and Practice of Empire: The U.S., Mexico, and the Education of Mexican Immigrants," in *Latinos and Education: A Critical Reader*, Second Edition, ed. Antonia Darder, Rodolfo D. Torres, and Henry Gutierrez (New York: Routledge, 1997).

46. See Haney López, *White by Law*, particularly appendix A, 203–208.

47. Noel Ignatiev, *How the Irish Became White*, First Edition (New York: Routledge, 1995); Karen Brodkin, *How Jews Became White Folks and What That Says About Race in America* (New Brunswick, NJ: Rutgers University Press, 1998). See also https://history.state.gov/milestones/1921-1936/immigration-act.

48. Mukhopadhyay et al., *How Real Is Race?* See also http://www.pbs.org/race/000_About/002_03_d-godeeper.htm for a timeline of racialized policies.

49. Smedley, *Race in North America*, 161.

50. For a film treatment of this history, see http://newsreel.org/transcripts/race2.htm.

51. Stephen Jay Gould, *The Mismeasure of Man* (New York: W.W. Norton & Company, 1981). See also Faye V. Harrison, "The Persistent Power of 'Race' in Cultural and Political Economy of Racism," *Annual Review of Anthropology* 24, (1995): 47–74.

52. González, "The Ideology and Practice of Empire," 34.

53. Paraphrased from Smedley, *Race in North America*, 165.

54. Jennifer L. Eberhardt, "Imaging Race," *American Psychologist* 60, no. 2 (Feb–Mar 2005): 181–190.

55. Mahzarin R. Banaji and Anthony Greenwald, *Blindspot: Hidden Biases of Good People* (New York: Delacorte Press, 2013).

56. See Alan H. Goodman, Yolanda T. Moses, and Joseph L. Jones, *Race: Are We So Different?* (Malden, MA: Wiley-Blackwell, 2012), the companion book to the American Anthropological Association's museum exhibit; see also http://www.understandingrace.org/home.html.

57. Mukhopadhyay et al., *How Real Is Race?*

58. Nina G. Jablonski, *Skin: A Natural History* (Berkeley and Los Angeles, CA: University of California Press, 2006). See also https://www.hhmi.org/biointeractive/biology-skin-color.

59. Mukhopadhyay et al., *How Real Is Race?*, 16.

60. See also http://www.pbs.org/race/004_HumanDiversity/004_01-explore.htm and http://www.genomenewsnetwork.org/resources/whats_a_genome/Chp4_1.shtml.

61. Mukhopadhyay et al., *How Real Is Race?*, 54–55.

62. Agustin Fuentes, http://www.psychologytoday.com/blog/busting-myths-about-human-nature/201204/race-is-real-not-in-the-way-many-people-think.

63. See http://www.pbs.org/race/000_General/000_00-Home.htm.

64. See http://www.understandingrace.org/humvar/index.html and Mukhopadhyay et al., *How Real Is Race?*

65. Henry Louis Gates, http://www.theroot.com/views/exactly-how-black-black-america.

66. See, e.g., http://www.pbs.org/race/004_HumanDiversity/004_01-explore.htm.

67. Mukhopadhyay et al., *How Real Is Race?*, 10.

68. Alan H. Goodman, "Exposing Race as an Obsolete Biological Concept," in Pollock, *Everyday Antiracism*.

69. See http://www.understandingrace.org/humvar/index.html and Mukhopadhyay et al., *How Real Is Race?*

70. See the traveling exhibit's notes, http://www.understandingrace.org/humvar/sickle_01.html, on sickle cell, and Goodman et al., *Race: Are We So Different?*, the companion book.

71. See the *Race: Are We So Different?* traveling exhibit's notes; http://www.understandingrace.org /humvar/looks_hyper01.html on the lived precursors to diseases; and Goodman et al., *Race: Are We So Different?*, the companion book. See also http://www.unnaturalcauses.org.

72. Agustin Fuentes, "Anthropology and the Assault on Common Sense," 2012, at http://www.huff ingtonpost.com/american-anthropological-association/anthropology-and-the-assa_b_1834358.html.

73. See Goodman, "Exposing Race as an Obsolete Biological Concept," 2008.

74. Mukhopadhyay et al., *How Real Is Race?*, 6.

75. See http://www.pbs.org/race/000_About/002_04-background-02-05.htm.

76. For the Bike Thief, see https://www.youtube.com/watch?v=S0kV_b3IK9M. Milton Reynolds, a trainer with Facing History, likes to show another film called "The Lunch Date": https://www.you tube.com/watch?v=epuTZigxUY8.

77. See http://www.ncbi.nlm.nih.gov/pmc/articles/PMC3603687/ and http://www.ncsc.org/~/ media/Files/PDF /Topics/Gender%20and%20Racial%20Fairness/IB_Strategies_033012.ashx.

78. Nasir, *Racialized Identities*, 66.

79. Pollock, *Colormute*, 218.

80. Pollock, *Everyday Antiracism*, xviii–xix.

81. Stuart Hall, "New Ethnicities," in *Race, Culture and Difference,* First Edition, ed. James Donald and Ali Rattansi (Newbury Park, CA: Sage Publications in association with The Open University, 1992); Pollock, "Race Bending"; Sanjay Sharma, "Noisy Asians or 'Asian Noise'?," in *Dis-Orienting Rhythms: The Politics of the New Asian Dance Music*, ed. Sanjay Sharma, John Hutnyk, and Ashwani Sharma (London: Zed Books, 1996), 32–57.

82. Ta-Nehisi Coates, *Between the World and Me* (New York: Spiegel and Grau, Random House, 2015), 149.

83. Carlos Munoz Jr., "The Militant Challenge: the Chicano Generation," in *Youth, Identity, Power: The Chicano Movement*, ed. Carlos Munoz Jr. (London: Verso, 1989), 47–74.

84. See, e.g., Angel R. Oquendo, "Re-imagining the Latino/a Race," and Alex M. Saragoza, Concepcion Juarez, Abel Valenzuela Jr., and Oscar Gonzalez, "Who Counts? Title VII and the Hispanic Classification," both in *The Latino/a Condition: A Critical Reader*, ed. Richard Delgado and Jean Stefancic (New York: New York University Press, 1998).

85. Paul Ongtooguk and Claudia S. Dybdahl, "Teaching Facts, Not Myths, About Native Americans," in Pollock, *Everyday Antiracism*. Angelina E. Castagno and Bryan McKinley Jones Brayboy, "Culturally Responsive Schooling for Indigenous Youth: A Review of the Literature," *Review of Educational Research* 78, no. 4 (December 2008): 941–993. See also http://www.ncai.org/about-tribes/indians_101.pdf.

86. Yen Le Espiritu, "Coming Together: The Asian-American Movement," in *Asian-American Panethnicity: Bridging Institutions and Identities* (Philadelphia: Temple University Press, 1992), 20.

87. See, e.g., Theresa Perry, Claude Steele, and Asa Hilliard III, *Young, Gifted, and Black: Promoting High Achievement Among African-American Students* (Boston, MA: Beacon Press, 2003).

88. Briscoe et al., *The Power of Talk*, 9.

89. See http://www.census.gov/census2000/raceqandas.html.

90. See http://www.census.gov/prod/cen2010/briefs/c2010br-11.pdf, 14.

91. Geneva Gay, *Culturally Responsive Teaching: Theory, Research, and Practice*, Second Edition (New York: Teachers College Press, 2010).

92. The Op Ed Project, https://theopedproject.wordpress.com/2015/01/29/how-to-make-an-idea -go-viral.

93. Ali Michael and Eleonora Bartoli, "What White Children Need to Know About Race," *Independent School Magazine* (Summer 2014), at http://www.nais.org/Magazines-Newsletters/ISMag azine/Pages/What-White-Children-Need-to-Know-About-Race.aspx#sthash.Dw334ZYj.dpuf; Beverly Daniel Tatum, *Why Are All the Black Kids Sitting Together in the Cafeteria? And Other Conversations About Race* (Basic Books, Revised Edition, 2003).

94. For more resources on this, see http://www.tolerance.org/blog/fear-and-rewriting-trayvon-edu cator-thoughts. See also Mica Pollock and Tanya Coke, "Race and Overreaction: On the Streets and in Schools," *The Atlantic*, February 2015, http://www.theatlantic.com/education/archive/2015/02 /race-and-overreaction-on-the-streets-and-in-schools/385076. See also Prudence Carter, Russell Skiba, Mariella Arredondo, and Mica Pollock, "You Can't Fix What You Don't Look At: Acknowl-edging Race in Addressing Racial Discipline Disparities," *Atlantic Philanthropies Discipline Dis-parities Series*, December 2014, http://www.atlanticphilanthropies.org/sites/default/files/uploads /Acknowledging-Race_121514.pdf.
95. The RPI lost: 64% said no and 36% said yes. See https://ballotpedia.org/California_Proposition _54,_the_%22Racial_Privacy_Initiative%22_(October_2003).

Chapter 2: Inequality Talk

1. Linda Darling-Hammond, *The Flat World and Education: How America's Commitment to Equity Will Determine Our Future* (New York: Teachers College Press, 2010) 22–23.
2. "Report of The Sentencing Project to the United Nations Human Rights Committee: Regarding Racial Disparities in the United States Criminal Justice System," *The Sentencing Project: Research and Advocacy for Reform*, August 2013, http://sentencingproject.org/doc/publications/rd_ICCPR%20 Race%20and%20Justice%20Shadow%20Report.pdf, 1.
3. David J. Knight, "Don't Tell Young Black Males That They Are 'Endangered,'" *Washington Post*, Oct. 10, 2014, http://www.washingtonpost.com/opinions/young-black-males-trapped-by-rhetoric /2014/10/10/dcf95688-31e2-11e4-9e92-0899b306bbea_story.html.
4. See http://www.indiana.edu/~atlantic/briefing-papers.
5. Mahzarin R. Banaji and Anthony Greenwald, *Blindspot: Hidden Biases of Good Peo-ple* (New York: Delacorte Press, 2013); Ann Arnett Ferguson, *Bad Boys: Public Schools in the Making of Black Masculinity* (Ann Arbor, MI: University of Michigan Press, 2000). See also Mica Pollock and Tanya Coke, "Race and Overreaction: On the Streets and in Schools," *The Atlantic*, February 2, 2015, http://www.theatlantic.com/education/archive/2015/02 /race-and-overreaction-on-the-streets-and-in-schools/385076.
6. On middle-class schools, see Amanda E. Lewis and John B. Diamond, *Despite the Best Intentions: How Racial Inequality Thrives in Good Schools* (New York: Oxford University Press, 2015), described at http://www.c-span.org/video/?400024-2/book-discussion-despite-best-intentions.
7. Anne Gregory, James Bell, and Mica Pollock, "How Educators Can Eradicate Disparities in School Discipline: A Briefing Paper on School-Based Interventions," *Atlantic Philanthropies Discipline Disparities Series*, December 2014, http://www.indiana.edu/~atlantic/wp-content /uploads/2014/03/Disparity_Interventions_Full_031214.pdf.
8. Prudence Carter, Russell Skiba, Mariella Arredondo, and Mica Pollock, "You Can't Fix What You Don't Look At: Acknowledging Race in Addressing Racial Discipline Disparities," *Atlantic Philanthropies Discipline Disparities Series*, December 2014, http://www.atlanticphilanthropies.org /sites/default/files/uploads/Acknowledging-Race_121514.pdf.
9. Michelle Alexander, *The New Jim Crow: Mass Incarceration in the Age of Colorblindness* (New York: The New Press, 2012), and http://rethinkingschoolsblog.wordpress.com/2011/12/20/michelle -alexander.
10. Carter et al., "You Can't Fix What You Don't Look At." See also Anne Gregory, James Bell, and Mica Pollock. "How Educators Can Eradicate Disparities in School Discipline," in *Disparate Opportunity: Understanding and Addressing Inequality in School Discipline*, ed. Russ Skiba, Kavitha Mediratta, and Karega Rausch (forthcoming, Palgrave Macmillan).
11. See also Eduardo Bonilla-Silva, *Racism Without Racists: Color-Blind Racism and the Persistence of Racial Inequality in America*, Third Edition (Lanham, MD: Rowman & Littlefield Publishers, 2006).
12. Richard R. Valencia, *Dismantling Contemporary Deficit Thinking: Educational Thought and Practice* (New York: Taylor and Francis, 2010).
13. See http://www.niusileadscape.org/bl/?p=72; see also Mica Pollock, "Some Myths About Race That Every Educator Needs to Unlearn," in *Race: Are We So Different?*, ed. Alan H. Goodman, Yolanda T. Moses, and Joseph L. Jones (Malden, MA: Wiley-Blackwell, 2012).
14. Rebecca M. Blank, "Tracing the Economic Impact of Cumulative Discrimination," *American Economic Review* 95, no. 2 (2005): 99–103.

15. E.g., Gloria Ladson-Billings, "From the Achievement Gap to the Educational Debt: Understanding Achievement in U.S. Schools," *Educational Researcher* 5, no. 7 (October 2006): 9; Prudence L. Carter and Kevin G. Welner, *Closing the Opportunity Gap: What America Must Do to Give Every Child an Even Chance* (New York: Oxford University Press, 2013); Edward M. Telles, Vilma Ortiz, and Joan W. Moore, *Generations of Exclusion: Mexican-Americans, Assimilation, and Race* (New York: Russell Sage Foundation, 2008).

16. Children's Defense Fund, *Child Poverty in America 2010*, September 2011, http://www.childrens defense.org/library/data/child-poverty-in-america-2010.pdf., 3; David C. Berliner, "Effects of Inequality and Poverty vs. Teachers and Schooling on America's Youth," *Teachers College Record* 115, no. 12 (2013): 1–26.

17. Children's Defense Fund, *Child Poverty in America 2010*, 3.

18. See "A New Majority Research Bulletin: Low Income Students Now a Majority in the Nation's Public Schools," *Southern Education Foundation*, 2015, http://www.southerneducation .org/Our-Strategies/Research-and-Publications/New-Majority-Diverse-Majority-Report-Series/A -New-Majority-2015-Update-Low-Income-Students-Now.

19. David R. Roediger, *The Wages of Whiteness: Race and the Making of the American Working Class* (Brooklyn, NY: Verso Books, 2007); Carol C. Mukhopadhyay, Rosemary C. Henze, and Yolanda T. Moses, *How Real Is Race? A Sourcebook on Race, Culture, and Biology*, Second Edition (Lanham, MD: Rowman & Littlefield, 2014), chapters 6–7.

20. See Ian Haney López, *White by Law: The Legal Construction of Race* (New York: New York University Press, 2006). See also http://flowofhistory.org/c_toolkit/essays/citizenship.html.

21. Mukhopadhyay et al., *How Real Is Race?*, chapters 6–7. On this story in California, for example, see Tomas Almaguer, *Racial Fault Lines: The Historical Origins of White Supremacy in California* (Berkeley: University of California Press, 1994). See also http://www.civilrights.org/publications/reports /fairhousing/historical.html.

22. Paul C. Gorski, *Reaching and Teaching Students in Poverty: Strategies for Erasing the Opportunity Gap* (New York: Teachers College Press, 2013).

23. David Tyack, *The One Best System: A History of American Urban Education* (Cambridge, MA: Harvard University Press, 1974). See also David B. Tyack, "Constructing Difference: Historical Reflections on Schooling and Social Diversity," *Teachers College Record* 95, no. 1 (Fall 1993): 8–34; Charles Wollenberg, *All Deliberate Speed: Segregation and Exclusion in California Schools, 1855– 1975* (Berkeley: University of California Press, 1976). See also http://www.npr.org/templates/story /story.php?storyId=16516865.

24. James D. Anderson, *The Education of Blacks in the South, 1860–1935* (Chapel Hill: University of North Carolina Press, 1988); James D. Anderson, "A Long Shadow: The American Pursuit of Political Justice and Education Equality," *Educational Researcher* 44, no. 6 (August/September 2015): 319–335.

25. Rubén Donato, *The Other Struggle for Equal Schools: Mexican Americans During the Civil Rights Era* (Albany, NY: State University of New York Press, 1997), 13, 12–17; Gilbert G. González, "The Ideology and Practice of Empire: The U.S., Mexico, and the Education of Mexican Immigrants," in *Latinos and Education: A Critical Reader*, Second Edition, ed. Antonia Darder, Rodolfo D. Torres, and Henry Gutierrez (New York: Routledge, 1997).

26. Melvin L. Oliver and Thomas M. Shapiro, *Black Wealth/White Wealth: A New Perspective on Racial Inequality* (New York: Routledge, 2006), 22–23.

27. Manning Marable, "Staying on the Path to Racial Equality," in *The Affirmative Action Debate*, ed. George E. Curry (Reading, MA: Addison-Wesley, 1996), 3–15.

28. Ta-Nehisi Coates, "The Past Ain't Even the Past," *The Atlantic*, October 2012, http://www .theatlantic.com/national/archive/2012/10/the-past-aint-even-the-past/263853.

29. Christine Sleeter, "Multicultural Curriculum and Critical Family History," *Multicultural Education Review* 7, no. 1–2 (2015): 1–11.

30. Mara Tieken, "Making Race Relevant in All-White Classrooms: Using Local History," in *Everyday Antiracism: Getting Real About Race in School*, ed. Mica Pollock (New York: The New Press, 2008).

31. Karen Brodkin, *How Jews Became White Folks and What That Says About Race in America* (New Brunswick, NJ: Rutgers University Press, 1998).

32. Ira Katznelson, *When Affirmative Action Was White: An Untold History of Racial Inequality in Twentieth-Century America* (New York: W.W. Norton & Company, 2005), 163.

33. Karen Brodkin Sacks, "How Did Jews Become White Folks?" in *Race*, ed. Steven Gregory and Roger Sanjek (New Brunswick: Rutgers University Press, 1994), 89–92; Stokeley Carmichael and Charles V. Hamilton, *Black Power: The Politics of Liberation* (New York: Vintage, 1992), 22.

34. Melissa Murray, "When War Is Work: The G.I. Bill, Citizenship, and the Civic Generation," *California Law Review* 96, no. 4 (August 2008): 967–998.

35. Katznelson, *When Affirmative Action Was White*, 2005; Sacks, "How Did Jews Become White Folks?," 88, 92–97.

36. Oliver and Shapiro, *Black Wealth/White Wealth*, 18. See also http://www.nytimes.com/2016/01/03/opinion/debt-and-the-racial-wealth-gap.html.

37. Helen F. Ladd, Rosemary A. Chalk, and Janet S. Hensen, *Equity and Adequacy in Education Finance: Issues and Perspectives* (Washington, D.C.: National Academy Press); John Rogers, Melanie Bertrand, Rhoda Freelon, Sophie Fanelli, *Free Fall: Educational Opportunities in 2011* (Los Angeles: UCLA IDEA, UC/ACCORD, 2011).

38. See the Encyclopedia of Cleveland History, http://ech.case.edu/cgi/article.pl?id=SH3 and http://ech.case.edu/cgi/article.pl?id=AA.

39. See, e.g. Barbara Ehrenreich, "Dead, White, and Blue," *Huffington Post*, December 1, 2015, http://www.huffingtonpost.com/barbara-ehrenreich/middle-class-life-expectancy_b_8687694.html.

40. NCCP, "Poverty by the Numbers," http://nccp.org/media/releases/release_34.html.

41. NCCP, "Basic Facts About Low-Income Children," http://www.nccp.org/publications/pub_1145.html.

42. Rakesh Kochhar and Richard Fry, "Wealth Inequality Has Widened Along Racial, Ethnic Lines Since End of Great Recession," *Pew Research Center Report* (December 12, 2014), http://www.pewresearch.org/fact-tank/2014/12/12/racial-wealth-gaps-great-recession.

43. Oliver and Shapiro, *Black Wealth/White Wealth*, 23.

44. Peggy McIntosh, "White Privilege: Unpacking the Invisible Knapsack," *Peace and Freedom Magazine* (July–August 1989): 10–12, http://www.nymbp.org/reference/WhitePrivilege.pdf.

45. Brian Lowery and Daryl A. Wout, "When Inequality Matters: The Effect of Inequality Frames On Academic Engagement," *Journal of Personality and Social Psychology* 98, no. 6 (June 2010): 956–966.

46. Vivian Louie, "Moving Beyond Quick 'Cultural' Explanations," in *Everyday Antiracism: Getting Real About Race in School*, ed. Mica Pollock (New York: The New Press, 2008).

47. See http://christinesleeter.org/hidden-four-ps.

48. Children's Defense Fund, *Child Poverty in America 2010*, 3.

49. Prudence L. Carter and Kevin G. Welner, *Closing the Opportunity Gap: What America Must Do to Give Every Child an Even Chance* (New York: Oxford University Press, 2013).

50. Darling-Hammond, *The Flat World and Education*, 22.

51. Anurima Bhargava, Erica Frankenberg, and Chinh Q. Le, "Still Looking to the Future: Voluntary K–12 School Integration (A Manual for Parents, Educators, and Advocates)," NAACP Legal Defense and Educational Fund/The Civil Rights Project, 2008, 11. See also https://civilrightsproject.ucla.edu/research/k-12-education/integration-and-diversity/brown-at-60-great-progress-a-long-retreat-and-an-uncertain-future/Brown-at-60-051814.pdf, 12.

52. Gary Orfield, Genevieve Siegel-Hawley, and John Kucsera, "Divided We Fail: Segregated and Unequal Schools in the Southland," *Civil Rights Project/Proyecto Derechos Civiles*, March 18, 2011, http://civilrightsproject.ucla.edu/research/metro-and-regional-inequalities/lasanti-project-los-angeles-san-diego-tijuana/divided-we-fail-segregated-and-unequal-schools-in-the-southfield, 8.

53. John Kucsera and Greg Flaxman, "The Western States: Profound Diversity but Severe Segregation for Latino Students," *Civil Rights Project / Proyecto Derechos Civiles*, September 2012, http://civilrightsproject.ucla.edu/research/k-12-education/integration-and-diversity/mlk-national/the-western-states-profound-diversity-but-severe-segregation-for-latino-students, 4.

54. Kucsera and Flaxman, "The Western States," 4.

55. Gary Orfield, Jongyeon Ee, Erica Frankenberg, and Genevieve Siegel-Hawley, "Brown at 62: School Segregation by Race, Poverty and State." Civil Rights Project/Proyecto Derechos Civiles, May 16, 2016.

56. Orfield et al., "Brown at 62," 7.

57. Bhargava et al., "Still Looking to the Future," 14.

58. Orfield et al., "Divided We Fail," 5, 34.

59. Sharon Noguchi, "Report: California Among Worst in the Nation in School Segregation," *San Jose Mercury News*, May 14, 2014, http://www.mercurynews.com/education/ci_25762891 /report-california-among-worst-nation-school-segregation.

60. Orfield et al., "Brown at 62."

61. Richard Rothstein, *Class and Schools: Using Social, Economic, and Educational Reform to Close the Black-White Achievement Gap* (New York: Teachers College Press, 2004).

62. See also Sue Books, "What Teachers Need to Know About Poverty," in *City Kids, City Schools: More Reports from the Front Row*, ed. William Ayers, Gloria Ladson-Billings, Gregory Miche, and Pedro A. Noguera (New York: The New Press, 2008), 184–194; H. Richard Milner IV, "Analyzing Poverty, Learning, and Teaching Through a Critical Race Theory Lens," *Review of Research in Education* 37, (March 2013): 1–53; and Paul C. Gorski, *Reaching and Teaching Students in Poverty*.

63. Darling-Hammond, *The Flat World and Education*, 12; Jennifer L. Hochschild, "Social Class in Public Schools," *Journal of Social Issues* 59, no. 4 (2003): 821–840, http://scholar.harvard.edu /jlhochschild/publications/social-class-public-schools.

64. John Rogers, "Without Dollars and Sense: The Budget Crisis and California's School Funding," (presentation, Institute for Democracy, Education, and Access at the University of California, Los Angeles, October 22, 2012), http://idea.gseis.ucla.edu/newsroom/presentations/Rogers-Without _Dollars_and_Sense.pdf/view?searchterm=without%20dollars%20or%20sense, 16; Rogers et al., *Free Fall*.

65. Orfield et al., "Divided We Fail," 9.

66. See http://www.cde.ca.gov/eo/ce/wc/wmslawsuit.asp.

67. Public Advocates, "Williams v. California," http://www.publicadvocates.org/our-work/education /williams-v-california.

68. Rogers et al., *Free Fall*; Rogers, "Without Dollars and Sense."

69. See, e.g. Linda Darling-Hammond, http://www.forumforeducation.org/news/recruiting-and -retaining-teachers-what-matters-most-and-what-can-government-do, and *Flat World*, 22.

70. Emma Brown, "Five Eye-Opening Figures from the U.S. Education Department's Latest Civil Rights Data Dump," *Washington Post*, June 7, 2016. See also Patricia Gándara, "Meeting the Needs of Language Minorities," in Carter and Welner, *Closing the Opportunity Gap*, 156–168; Frances Contreras, *Achieving Equity for Latino Students: Expanding the Pathway to Higher Education Through Public Policy* (New York: Teachers College Press, 2011).

71. As described in Marjorie Faulstich Orellana, Presidential Address, Council on Anthropology and Education, American Anthropological Association Annual Meetings, November 19, 2015.

72. Darling-Hammond, *The Flat World and Education*, 18–24.

73. Berliner, "Effects of Inequality and Poverty vs. Teachers and Schooling on America's Youth," 1–26.

74. David L. Kirp, *The Sandbox Investment: The Preschool Movement and Kids-First Politics* (Cambridge, MA: Harvard University Press, 2009).

75. Oliver and Shapiro, *Black Wealth/White Wealth*, 19–22.

76. Sean F. Reardon, Lindsay Fox, and Joseph Townsend, "Neighborhood Income Composition by Household Race and Income, 1990–2009," in *The ANNALS of the American Academy of Political and Social Science* (July 2015, 660): 78–97, discussed in https://www.washingtonpost.com/news/wonk /wp/2015/06/24/poor-whites-live-in-richer-neighborhoods-than-middle-class-blacks-and-latinos.

77. See john a. powell, "A New Theory of Integrated Education: True Integration," in *School Resegregation: Must the South Turn Back?*, ed. John Charles Boger and Gary Orfield (University of North Carolina Press, 2005); Gary Orfield and Susan E. Eaton, *Dismantling Desegregation: The Quiet Reversal of Brown vs. Board of Education* (New York: The New Press, 1996); Gary Orfield, "Housing Segregation Produces Unequal Schools: Causes and Solutions," in Carter and Welner, *Closing the Opportunity Gap*, 40–60; and Camille Zubrinsky Charles, "Who Will Live Near Whom?" *Poverty & Race Research Action Council*, September/October 2008, http://civilrightsdocs.info/pdf/reports /Resource-Equity-Report-WEB.pdf.

78. Orfield et al., "Brown at 62," 6.

79. David C. Berliner, Gene V. Glass, and Associates, *50 Myths and Lies That Threaten America's Public Schools: The Real Crisis in Education* (New York: Teachers College Press, 2014).

80. Darling-Hammond, *The Flat World and Education*; Kirp, *The Sandbox Investment*.

81. Orfield et al., "Brown at 62"; United States Department of Education, "Dear Colleague Letter: Resource Comparability," October 1, 2014, http://www2.ed.gov/about/offices/list/ocr/letters/ colleague-resourcecomp-201410.pdf.

82. See research cited at https://m.whitehouse.gov/administration/eop/aapi/data/critical-issues.

83. Vivian Louie, "Complicating the Story of Immigrant Integration," in *Writing Immigration: Scholars and Journalists in Dialogue*, ed. Marcelo Suarez-Orozco, Vivian Louie, and Roberto Suro (Berkeley and Los Angeles, CA: University of California Press, 2011), 218–235; https:// civilrightsproject.ucla.edu/research/k-12-education/integration-and-diversity/historic-reversals -accelerating-resegregation-and-the-need-for-new-integration-strategies-1/orfield-historic-reversals -accelerating.pdf; Orfield et al., "Brown at 62."

84. Martha E. Gimenez, "Latino/'Hispanic'—Who Needs a Name?: The Case Against a Standard-ized Terminology," in *Latinos and Education: A Critical Reader*, Second Edition, ed. Antonia Darder, Rodolfo D. Torres, and Henry Gutierrez (New York: Routledge, 1997), 93–104, 101–2.

85. Jennifer C. Ng, Sharon S. Lee, and Yoon K. Pak, "Contesting the Model Minority and Per-petual Foreigner Stereotypes: A Critical Review of Literature on Asian Americans in Education," *Review of Research in Education* 31 (March 2007): 111–112.

86. Laurie Olsen, "Reparable Harm: Fulfilling the Unkept Promise of Educational Opportunity for California's Long Term English Learners," *A Californians Together Research & Policy Publication*, 2010, http://edsource.org/wp-content/uploads/ReparableHarm1.pdf. Contreras, *Achieving Equity for Latino Students.*

87. Milner, "Analyzing Poverty."

88. Alan M. Blankstein and Pedro Noguera, *Excellence Through Equity: Five Principles of Courageous Leadership to Guide Achievement for Every Student* (Thousand Oaks, CA: Corwin, 2015), 21.

89. Mica Pollock, "An Intervention in Progress: Pursuing Precision in School Race Talk," in *Toward Positive Youth Development: Transforming Schools and Community Programs*, First Edition, ed. Mary-beth Shinn and Hirokazu Yoshikawa (New York: Oxford University Press, 2008), 102–114; Mica Pollock, "Talking Precisely About Equal Opportunity," in Pollock, *Everyday Antiracism*, 26.

90. Charles Payne, *Getting What We Asked For: The Ambiguity of Success and Failure in Urban Edu-cation* (Westport, CT: Greenwood, 1984).

91. Darling-Hammond, *The Flat World and Education*, 8.

92. NEPC, "Lifting All Children Up," March 21, 2016, http://nepc.colorado.edu/publication/lift ing-all-children.

93. Mica Pollock, "From Denial to Creation," *Anthropology News* 55, no. 6 (June 2014).

94. http://www.teenempowerment.org/pdfs/VCLB.pdf.

95. Jeannie Oakes, *Keeping Track: How Schools Structure Inequality* (New Haven, CT: Yale Univer-sity Press, 1985); Jeannie Oakes, Tor Ormseth, Robert Bell, and Patricia Camp, *Multiplying Inequal-ities: The Effects of Race, Social Class, and Tracking on Opportunities to Learn Mathematics and Science* (Santa Monica, CA: Rand Corporation, 1990).

96. George Spindler and Louise Spindler, *Fifty Years of Anthropology and Education, 1950–2000: A Spindler Anthology* (Mahwah, NY: Lawrence Erlbaum Associates, Inc., Publishers, 2000).

97. In an analogous strategy, researcher Jennifer Eberhardt is slowing down video analysis of police body-camera recordings to help police see which of their interactions with suspects snowball into conflict, which don't, and why. Sam Scott, "A Hard Look at How We See Race," *Stanford Magazine* 44, no. 5 (September/October 2015): 46–51.

98. Anita Wadhwa, *Restorative Justice in Urban Schools: Disrupting the School-to-Prison Pipeline* (New York: Routledge, 2016).

99. Berliner, "Effects of Inequality and Poverty vs. Teachers and Schooling on America's Youth," 1–26.

100. Paul C. Gorski, *Reaching and Teaching Students in Poverty: Strategies for Erasing the Opportunity Gap* (New York: Teachers College Press, 2013), 2. For evidence of this, see Rogers et al., *Free Fall.*

101. Pedro Noguera, http://www.inmotionmagazine.com/er10/pn_crights.html.

102. Jaqueline Jordan Irvine, "Foreword," in *Culture, Curriculum, and Identity in Education*, ed. H. Richard Milner IV (New York: Palgrave Macmillan, 2010), xii.

103. Berliner, "Effects of Inequality and Poverty vs. Teachers and Schooling on America's Youth."

104. Mica Pollock, Sherry Deckman, Meredith Mira, and Carla Shalaby, "'But What Can I Do?' Three Necessary Tensions in Teaching Teachers About Race," *Journal of Teacher Education* 61 (May/June 2010): 211–224; Mica Pollock, Candice Bocala, Sherry L. Deckman, and Shari Dickstein-Staub, "Caricature and Hyperbole in Preservice Teacher Professional Development for Diversity," *Urban Education* (May 1, 2015): 1–30.

105. John B. Diamond, "Focusing on Student Learning," in Pollock, *Everyday Antiracism: Getting Real About Race in School.*

106. Milner, "Analyzing Poverty," 23.

107. Diamond, "Focusing on Student Learning"; Felecia M. Briscoe, Gilberto Arriaza, and Rosemary C. Henze, *The Power of Talk: How Words Change Our Lives* (Thousand Oaks, CA: Corwin Press, 2009).

108. See the work of the Carnegie Foundation, described in Anthony S. Bryk, Louis M. Gomez, Alicia Grunow, and Paul G. LeMahieu, *Learning to Improve: How America's Schools Can Get Better at Getting Better* (Cambridge, MA: Harvard Education Press, 2015). For related protocols as honed by educators, see High Tech High, *High Tech High Graduate School of Education Improvement Tools*, http://gse.hightechhigh.org/centerForResearchOnEquityAndInnovation.php.

109. Susan Szachowicz, "Brockton High School, Brockton, Massachusetts," in *Excellence Through Equity: Five Principles of Courageous Leadership to Guide Achievement for Every Student*, ed. Alan M. Blankstein and Pedro Noguera (Thousand Oaks, CA: Corwin Press, 2015).

110. See also Kysa Nygreen, *These Kids: Identity, Agency, and Social Justice at a Last Chance High School* (Chicago, IL: University of Chicago Press, 2013).

111. Jeffrey M.R. Duncan-Andrade, "Note to Educators: Hope Required When Growing Roses in Concrete," *Harvard Educational Review* 79 no. 2 (Summer 2009).

112. W. Steven Barnett and Cynthia E. Lamy, "Achievement Gaps Start Early: Preschool Can Help," in Carter and Welner, *Closing the Opportunity Gap*.

113. John Dewey, *Experience and Education* (New York: Touchstone, 1938), 39.

114. See Benjamin Herold, "Is 'Grit' Racist?" *Education Week*, January 24, 2015, http://blogs.edweek.org/edweek/DigitalEducation/2015/01/is_grit_racist.html.

115. Alfie Kohn, "The Downside of 'Grit': What Really Happens When Kids Are Pushed to Be More Persistent?" *Washington Post*, April 6, 2014.

116. Carla O'Connor, "Dispositions Toward (Collective) Struggle and Educational Resilience in the Inner City: A Case Analysis of Six African-American High School Students," *American Educational Research Journal* 34, no. 4 (1997): 593–629; Jeffrey Duncan-Andrade, "Teaching Critical Analysis of Racial Oppression," in Pollock, *Everyday Antiracism*. See particularly Paulo Freire, *Pedagogy of the Oppressed*, Third Edition (New York: Bloomsbury Publishing, 2000; first published 1968).

117. Julio Cammarota, "A Social Justice Approach to Achievement: Guiding Latino/a Students Toward Educational Attainment with a Challenging, Socially Relevant Curriculum," in *Latinos and Education: A Critical Reader*, Second Edition, ed. Antonia Darder and Rodolfo D. Torres (New York: Routledge, 2014), 270–71. See also Julio Cammarota, "The Gendered and Racialized Pathways of Latina and Latino Youth: Different Struggles, Different Resistances in the Urban Context," *Anthropology and Education* 35, no. 1, (2004): 53–74.

118. Julio Cammarota and Michelle Fine, eds., *Revolutionizing Education: Youth Participatory Action Research in Motion*, First Edition (New York: Routledge, 2008).

119. Maria Elena Torre and Michelle Fine, "Engaging Youth in Participatory Inquiry for Social Justice," in Pollock, *Everyday Antiracism*. See also http://whatkidscando.org/featurestories/previous_years/color_of_learning/index.html.

120. Gloria Ladson-Billings, "But That's Just Good Teaching! The Case for Culturally Relevant Pedagogy," *Theory into Practice* 34, no. 3 (Summer 1995): 159–165.

121. Ana Maria Villegas and Tamara Lucas, "Preparing Culturally Responsive Teachers," *Journal of Teacher Education* 53, no. 1 (January 2002): 20–32.

122. Paul C. Gorski and Katy Swalwell, "Equity Literacy for All," *Educational Leadership* 72, no. 6 (March 2015): 34–40.

123. See, e.g., Theresa Perry, Claude Steele, and Asa Hilliard III, *Young, Gifted, and Black: Promoting High Achievement Among African-American Students* (Boston, MA: Beacon Press, 2003) and Duncan-Andrade, "Teaching Critical Analysis of Racial Oppression."

124. Jeffrey M. Duncan-Andrade and Ernest Morrell, "Pan-ethnic Studies," in *The Art of Critical Pedagogy: Possibilities for Moving from Theory to Practice in Urban Schools* (New York: Peter Lang Publishing, 2008), 133–156.

125. Sonia Nieto, "Nice Is Not Enough: Defining Caring for Students of Color," in Pollock, *Everyday Antiracism*.

126. H. Richard Milner IV, *Rac(e)ing to Class: Confronting Poverty and Race in Schools and Classrooms* (Cambridge, MA: Harvard Education Press, 2015), 150–151.

127. See http://www.buzzfeed.com/alisonvingiano/21-black-harvard-students-share-their-experiences-through-a#.um1x8b82q0.

128. Tara J. Yosso, William A. Smith, Miguel Ceja, and Daniel G. Solorzano, "Critical Race Theory, Racial Microaggressions, and Campus Racial Climate for Latina/o Undergraduates," *Harvard Educational Review* 79, no. 4 (Winter 2009): 659–690.

129. Liliana M. Garces noted at a briefing to the American Educational Research Association that in admissions policies like UT's, "we are just talking about consideration of race as [a] factor of a factor of a factor. . . it's just about considering the student fully, all students fully." See http://thinkprogress.org/education/2015/12/09/3729321/affirmative-action-arguments-research. See also http://www.propublica.org/article/a-colorblind-constitution-what-abigail-fishers-affirmative-action-case-is-r, which explores the details of the Fisher admissions decision.

130. Scalia's remarks, and Richard Reddick's public responses, can be found here: http://diverse education.com/article/79419.

131. See https://www.law.cornell.edu/supct/html/02-241.ZO.html; see also note 129.

132. Sigal Alon, *Race, Class, and Affirmative Action* (New York: Russell Sage, 2015).

133. For example, http://admissions.ucsd.edu/freshmen/requirements.html.

134. Rogers et al., *Free Fall*, 13.

135. Orfield et al., "Divided We Fail," 9. See also http://www.ppic.org/content/pubs/report/R_200 JBR.pdf.

136. See http://ucsdnews.ucsd.edu/pressrelease/uc_san_diego_offers_admission_to_24552_fresh men_for_fall_2014_quarter.

137. William B. Armstrong, Heidi M. Carty, Greg Martin, and Jason R. Thornton, "UC San Diego Student Digest, 2010–2011," University of California San Diego, 2011, http://studentresearch.ucsd .edu/_files/publications/digest/Digest2010.pdf, 29.

138. See http://admission.universityofcalifornia.edu/campuses/files/freshman-profiles/freshman _profile_san_diego.pdf.

139. See http://www.ppic.org/content/pubs/report/R_200JBR.pdf.

140. Orfield et al., "Divided We Fail."

141. See http://ucsdnews.ucsd.edu/pressrelease/uc_san_diego_offers_admission_to_24552_fresh-men_for_fall_2014_quarter.

142. See, e.g., http://economix.blogs.nytimes.com/2009/08/27/sat-scores-and-family-income.

143. Rogers et al., *Free Fall*, 16.

144. Rogers et al., *Free Fall*, 15.

145. See Benjamin L. Castleman and Lindsay C. Page, *Summer Melt: Supporting Low-Income Students Through the Transition to College* (Cambridge: Harvard Education Press, 2014). See also Patricia M. McDonough, *Choosing Colleges: How Social Class and Schools Structure Opportunity* (Albany: State University of New York Press, 1997).

146. Rogers, "Without Dollars and Sense," 7.

147. Caroline M. Hoxby and Sarah Turner, "Informing Students About Their College Options: A Proposal for Broadening the Expanding College Opportunities Project," *Brookings Institution*, June 26, 2013, http://www.brookings.edu/research/papers/2013/06/26-expanding-college-opport unities-hoxby-turner.

148. Robert Teranishi and Tara L. Parker, "Social Reproduction of Inequality: The Racial Composition of Feeder Schools to the University of California," *Teachers College Record*, 112 no. 6 (2010): 1575–1601.

149. For more information on UC students' family income and first-generation demographics, see http://universityofcalifornia.edu/infocenter/ucs-commitment-social-mobility.

150. Liliana Garces, Counsel of Record, "Brief of American Social Science Researchers as *Amici Curiae* In Support of Respondents," in *Abigail Noel Fisher* vs. *University of Texas at Austin*, et al., (No. 11-345), 19. On implications for faculty and staff, see also Liliana M. Garces and Courtney D. Cogburn, "Beyond Declines in Student Body Diversity: How Campus-Level Administrators Understand a Prohibition on Race-Conscious Postsecondary Admissions Policies," *American Educational Research Journal* (2015), http://aer.sagepub.com/content/early/2015/07/29/00028312155 94878.full.pdf+html.

151. Pollock, "Talking Precisely About Equal Opportunity"; Pollock, "An Intervention in Progress."

152. Carter and Welner, *Closing the Opportunity Gap*.

153. Gloria Ladson-Billings, "From the Achievement Gap to the Educational Debt: Understanding Achievement in U.S. Schools," *Educational Researcher* 5, no. 7 (October 2006).

154. See also Hugh Mehan, *In the Front Door: Creating a College-Going Culture of Learning* (Boulder, CO: Paradigm Publishers, 2012); see http://preuss.ucsd.edu.

Chapter 3: Smarts Talk

1. See, e.g., http://www.thecrimson.com/article/2005/1/14/summers-comments-on-women-and-science.

2. Ray C. Rist, "Student Social Class and Teacher Expectations: The Self-Fulfilling Prophecy in Ghetto Education," *Harvard Educational Review* 40, no. 3 (August 1970): 411–451.

3. Karolyn Tyson, "Providing Equal Access to 'Gifted' Education," in *Everyday Antiracism: Getting Real About Race in School*, ed. Mica Pollock (New York: The New Press, 2008), 127.

4. Ulric Neisser, Gwyneth Boodoo, Thomas J. Bouchard Jr., A. Wade Boykin, Nathan Brody, Stephan J. Ceci, Diane F. Halpern, John C. Loehlin, Robert Perloff, Robert J. Sternberg, and Susana Urbina, "Intelligence: Knowns and Unknowns," *American Psychologist* 51, no. 2 (February 1996): 77–101.

5. Howard Gardner, "Cracking Open the IQ Box," in *The Bell Curve Wars: Race, Intelligence, and the Future of America*, ed. Steven Fraser (New York: Basic Books, 1995).

6. Edmund T. Hamann, "Standards vs. 'Standard' Knowledge," in Pollock, *Everyday Antiracism*.

7. Guadalupe Valdés, *Expanding Definitions of Giftedness: The Case of Young Interpreters from Immigrant Communities* (Mahwah, NJ: Lawrence Erlbaum Associates, 2003).

8. Neisser et al., "Intelligence: Knowns and Unknowns."

9. Robert J. Sternberg et al., "The Rainbow Project: Enhancing the SAT Through Assessments of Analytical, Practical, and Creative Skills," *Intelligence* 34 (2006): 321–350, 324, 325; Robert J. Sternberg and Elena L. Grigorenko, *Teaching for Successful Intelligence to Increase Student Learning and Achievement*, Second Edition (Thousand Oaks, CA: Corwin Press, 2007).

10. See http://multipleintelligencesoasis.org/about/the-components-of-mi/#box-7.

11. Barbara Rogoff, *The Cultural Nature of Human Development* (New York: Oxford University, 2003).

12. Michael Cole and John Gay, *The Cultural Context of Learning and Thinking: An Exploration in Experimental Anthropology* (New York: Basic Books, 1971); Robert J. Sternberg, Elena L. Grigorenko, and Kenneth K. Kidd, "Intelligence, Race, and Genetics," *American Psychologist* 60, no. 1 (January 2005): 46–59, 47.

13. Kris D. Gutierrez and Barbara Rogoff, "Cultural Ways of Learning: Individual Traits or Repertoires of Practice," *Educational Researcher* 32, no. 5 (June–July 2003): 19–25.

14. Peter Murrell, "Making Uncommon Sense: Critically Revisioning Professional Knowledge about Diverse Cultural Perspectives in Teacher Education," in *Proceedings of the Fourth National Forum of the Association of Independent Liberal Arts Colleges for Teacher Education*, ed. Mary Diez (Milwaukee, WI: Alverno College, 1990), 50.

15. Carol Dweck, *Mindset: The New Psychology of Success* (New York: Ballantine Books, 2007).

16. Na'ilah Nasir, *Racialized Identities: Race and Achievement among African American Youth* (Stanford, CA: Stanford University Press, 2011).

17. Jo Boaler, "The Myth of Being 'Bad' at Math: How Neuroscience Is Changing Our Mathematical Future," *A Medium Corporation*, Aug. 25, 2015, https://medium.com/aspen-ideas/the-myth-of-being-bad-at-math-b8c823ac7f75.

18. With third graders: http://studentvideos.hightechhigh.org/video/444/Growth+Mindset.

19. Amanda E. Lewis and John B. Diamond, *Despite the Best Intentions: How Racial Inequality Thrives in Good Schools* (New York: Oxford University Press, 2015).

20. Erica N. Walker, *Beyond Banneker: Black Mathematicians and the Paths to Excellence* (Albany: State University of New York Press, 2014).

21. Luis C. Moll and Stephen Diaz, "Change as the Goal of Educational Research," in *Minority Education: Anthropological Perspectives*, ed. Evelyn Jacob and Cathie Jordan (Westport, CT: Ablex Publishing, 1993), 67–79.

22. Herve Varenne and Ray McDermott, *Successful Failure: The School America Builds* (Boulder, CO: Westview Press, 1999).

23. Frederick Erickson, "Learning and Teaching About Race, Privilege, and Disprivilege," in *Interrogating Whiteness and Relinquishing Power: White Faculty's Commitment to Racial Consciousness in STEM Classrooms*, ed. Nicole M. Joseph, Chayla Haynes, and Floyd Cobb (New York: Peter Lang, 2016), 74.

24. Nasir, *Racialized Identities*; Carol D. Lee, *Culture, Literacy, and Learning: Taking Bloom in the Midst of the Whirlwind* (New York: Teachers College Press, 2007).

25. Douglas Edwin Sperry, Peggy J. Miller, and Linda Sperry, "Is There Really a Word Gap?" (presentation, American Anthropological Association 114th AAA Annual Meeting, Denver, CO, November 18–22, 2015). See also Netta Avineri, Eric Johnson, Shirley Brice Heath, Teresa McCarty, Elinor Ochs, Tamar Kremer-Sadlik, Susan Blum, Ana Celia Zentella, Jonathan Rosa, Nelson Flores, H. Samy Alim, and Django Paris, "Invited Forum: Bridging the 'Language Gap,'" *Journal of Linguistic Anthropology* 25, no. 1 (May 2015): 66–86.

26. Hugh Mehan, "Beneath the Skin and Between the Ears: A Case Study in the Politics of Representation," in *Understanding Practice: Perspectives on Activity and Context*, ed. Seth Chaiklin and Jean Lave (New York: Cambridge University Press, 1993).

27. Ibid., 260.

28. See http://qz.com/334926/your-college-major-is-a-pretty-good-indication-of-how-smart-you -are/?utm_source=SFFB.

29. See, e.g., Nick Anderson, "George Washington University Applicants No Longer Need to Take Admissions Tests," *Washington Post*, July 27, 2015. See also Lani Guinier, *The Tyranny of the Meritocracy: Democratizing Higher Education in America* (Boston: Beacon Press, 2015), and Sternberg, "The Rainbow Project."

30. Claude M. Steele, "Thin Ice: Stereotype Threat and Black College Students," *The Atlantic*, August 1999, http://www.theatlantic.com/magazine/archive/1999/08/thin-ice-stereotype-threat-and-black -college-students/304663.

31. Linda Darling-Hammond, *The Flat World and Education: How America's Commitment to Equity Will Determine Our Future* (New York: Teachers College Press, 2010).

32. Linda McNeil and Angela Valenzuela, "The Harmful Impact of the TAAS System of Testing in Texas: Beneath the Accountability Rhetoric," in *Raising Standards or Raising Barriers? Inequality and High Stakes Testing in Public Education*, ed. Gary Orfield and Mindy Kornhaber (New York: Century Foundation, 2001); Lois Weis, Kristin Cipollone, and Heather Jenkins, *Class Warfare: Class, Race, and College Admissions in Top-tier Secondary Schools* (Chicago: University of Chicago Press, 2014).

33. Nicholas Lemann, *The Big Test: The Secret History of the American Meritocracy* (New York: Farrar, Straus and Giroux, 2000).

34. E.g., as interviewed in http://www.pbs.org/wgbh/pages/frontline/shows/sats/interviews/guinier .html.

35. See http://hackeducation.com/2015/03/19/sra.

36. Neisser et al., "Intelligence: Knowns and Unknowns," 88; Robert J. Sternberg, "Culture and Intelligence," *American Psychologist* 59, no. 5 (July–August 2004): 325–338, 330.

37. Hugh Mehan, "Why I Like to Look: On the Use of Videotape as an Instrument in Educational Research," in *Qualitative Voices in Educational Research*, ed. Michael Schratz (New York: Falmer Press, 1992), 93–105.

38. Boaler, "The Myth of Being 'Bad' at Math"; Shonkoff et al., *From Neurons to Neighborhoods: The Science of Early Childhood Development* (Washington, D.C.: The National Academies Press, 2000), 53.

39. Cited in Annie Murphy Paul, "It's Not Me, It's You," *New York Times*, October 6, 2012.

40. Ray McDermott, "Achieving School Failure: 1972–1997," in *Education and Cultural Process: Anthropological Approaches*, Third Edition, ed. George D. Spindler (Prospect Heights, IL: Waveland, 1997), 110–135; Jules Henry, *Culture Against Man* (New York: Vintage Books, 1963).

41. Boaler, "The Myth of Being 'Bad' at Math."

42. Steele, "Thin Ice."

43. Winthrop D. Jordan, *White over Black: American Attitudes Toward the Negro, 1550–1812*, Second Edition (Chapel Hill, NC: University of North Carolina Press, 1968). See also http://newsreel.org /transcripts/race2.htm.

44. Stephen Jay Gould, *The Mismeasure of Man* (New York: W.W. Norton & Company, 1981), 23, 40.

45. Mica Pollock, "No Brain Is Racial," in *Everyday Antiracism*. See also Carol C. Mukhopadhyay, Rosemary C. Henze, and Yolanda T. Moses, *How Real Is Race? A Sourcebook on Race, Culture, and Biology*, Second Edition (Lanham, MD: Rowman & Littlefield, 2014).

46. David B. Tyack, "Constructing Difference: Historical Reflections on Schooling and Social Diversity," *Teachers College Record* 95, no. 1 (Fall 1993): 8–34, 14.

47. Gould, *The Mismeasure of Man*, 196.

48. Rubén Donato, *The Other Struggle for Equal Schools: Mexican Americans During the Civil Rights Era* (Albany, NY: State University of New York Press, 1997), 26, 23–29.

49. John Baugh, "Valuing Nonstandard English," in Pollock, *Everyday Antiracism*.

50. See, e.g., Steven Fraser, ed, *The Bell Curve Wars: Race, Intelligence, and the Future of America* (New York: Basic Books, 1995).

51. Arthur Allen, "Charging into the Minefield of Genes and Racial Difference: Nicholas Wade's 'A Troublesome Inheritance,'" *New York Times*, May 15, 2014. For more on the long history of such arguments, see Richard R. Valencia, *Dismantling Contemporary Deficit Thinking: Educational Thought and Practice* (New York: Taylor and Francis, 2010), chapter 2.

52. Maria Ong, "Challenging Cultural Stereotypes of 'Scientific Ability,'" in Pollock, *Everyday Antiracism*.

53. See, e.g., Adam Liptak, "Supreme Court Justices' Comments Don't Bode Well for Affirmative Action," *New York Times*, December 9, 2015.

54. Mahzarin R. Banaji and Anthony Greenwald, *Blindspot: Hidden Biases of Good People* (New York: Delacorte Press, 2013).

55. Steele, "Thin Ice."

56. Dorothy M. Steele and Esther Rebecca Cohn-Vargas, *Identity Safe Classrooms: Places to Belong and Learn* (Thousand Oaks, CA: Corwin, 2013).

57. Jennifer C. Ng, Sharon S. Lee, and Yoon K. Pak, "Contesting the Model Minority and Perpetual Foreigner Stereotypes: A Critical Review of Literature on Asian Americans in Education," *Review of Research in Education* 31 (March 2007): 95–130.

58. Vivian Louie, "Moving Beyond Quick 'Cultural' Explanations," in Pollock, *Everyday Antiracism*, 258.

59. Julio Cammarota, "The Gendered and Racialized Pathways of Latina and Latino Youth: Different Struggles, Different Resistances in the Urban Context," *Anthropology and Education* 35, no. 1 (2004): 67.

60. See Lewis and Diamond, *Despite the Best Intentions*, discussed at http://www.c-span.org/video /?400024-2/book-discussion-despite-best-intentions.

61. See Tyson, "Providing Equal Access to 'Gifted' Education." See also Karolyn Tyson, *Integration Interrupted: Tracking, Black Students, and Acting White After Brown* (New York: Oxford University Press, 2011).

62. See ACORN.org, *Secret Apartheid I: A Report on Racial Discrimination Against Black and Latino Parents and Children in the New York City Public Schools* (particularly see "Executive Summary" and "Findings"), https://web.archive.org/web/20070714173837/http://www.acorn.org/index.php?id=549.

63. Darling-Hammond, *The Flat World and Education*.

64. See   http://www.nytimes.com/2013/01/13/education/in-one-school-students-are-divided-by -gifted-label-and-race.html." On intelligence testing, see Sternberg et al., 2005, 47.

65. Tyson, "Providing Equal Access to 'Gifted' Education."

66. Roslyn Arlin Mickelson and Linwood H. Cousins, "Informing Parents About Available Opportunities," in Pollock, *Everyday Antiracism*.

67. Ong, "Challenging Cultural Stereotypes of 'Scientific Ability'"; College Board's *2012 8th Annual AP Report to the Nation*.

68. Tyson, "Providing Equal Access to 'Gifted' Education," 129.

69. Amanda Datnow and Vicki Park, "Data Use for Equity," *Educational Leadership* 72, no. 5 (2015): 50.

70. Annette Lareau, "Social Class Differences in Family-School Relationships: The Importance of Cultural Capital," *Sociology of Education* 60, no. 2 (1987): 73–85; Annette Lareau, *Unequal Childhoods: Class, Race, and Family Life* (Berkeley and Los Angeles, CA: University of California Press, 2011).

71. Beth C. Rubin, "Grouping in Detracked Classrooms," in Pollock, *Everyday Antiracism*.

72. Tyson, "Providing Equal Access to 'Gifted' Education," 127.

73. Prudence L. Carter, *Keepin' It Real: School Success Beyond Black and White*, First Edition (New York: Oxford University Press, 2005).

74. Hugh Mehan, *In the Front Door: Creating a College-Going Culture of Learning* (Boulder, CO: Paradigm Publishers, 2012).

75. See, e.g., Darling-Hammond, *The Flat World and Education*.

76. Samuel R. Lucas, "Constructing Colorblind Classrooms," in Pollock, *Everyday Antiracism*.

77. Joshua Aronson, "Knowing Students as Individuals," in Pollock, *Everyday Antiracism.*
78. Meira Levinson, "Finding Role Models in the Community," in Pollock, *Everyday Antiracism.*
79. Theresa Perry, Claude Steele, and Asa Hilliard III, *Young, Gifted, and Black: Promoting High Achievement Among African-American Students* (Boston, MA: Beacon Press, 2003).
80. Ibid., 96, 98.
81. Ibid., 99.
82. Carter Godwin Woodson, *The Mis-Education of the Negro* (New York: AMS Press, 1972).
83. See http://www.livescience.com/27853-who-invented-zero.html and Kim Plofker, *Mathematics in India* (Princeton, NJ: Princeton University Press, 2009).
84. *Alaska Standards for Culturally-Responsive Schools* (Anchorage: Alaska Native Knowledge Network, 1998), http://www.ankn.uaf.edu/publications/culturalstandards.pdf.
85. http://www.zalafilms.com/navajo/synopsis.html, 16.
86. See http://www.pbs.org/independentlens/precious-knowledge, http://www.huffingtonpost.com /2013/03/11/arizona-mcxican-amcrican-studies-curriculum-constitutional_n_2851034.html, and http://www.huffingtonpost.com/2015/01/13/in-laketch_n_6464604.html.
87. Lisa Delpit, "Lessons from Teachers," in *City Kids, City Schools: More Reports from the Front Row,* ed. Willian Ayers, Gloria Ladson-Billings, Gregory Miche, and Pedro A. Noguera (New York: The New Press, 2008), 113–135.
88. Nasir, *Racialized Identities,* 165.
89. Julio Cammarota, "A Social Justice Approach to Achievement: Guiding Latino/a Students Toward Educational Attainment with a Challenging, Socially Relevant Curriculum," in *Latinos and Education: A Critical Reader,* Second Edition, ed. Antonia Darder and Rodolfo D. Torres (New York: Routledge, 2014), 268.
90. Patricia Gándara, "Strengthening Student Identity in School Programs," in Pollock, *Everyday Antiracism,* 46.
91. Bryan McKinley Jones Brayboy and Emma Maughan, "Indigenous Knowledges and the Story of the Bean," *Harvard Educational Review* 79, no. 1 (Spring 2009).
92. Janie Victoria Ward, "Helping Parents Fight Stereotypes About Their Children," in Pollock, *Everyday Antiracism.*
93. Geoffrey L. Cohen, "Providing Supportive Feedback," in Pollock, *Everyday Antiracism.*
94. Ronald F. Ferguson, "Helping Students of Color Meet High Standards," in Pollock, *Everyday Antiracism.*
95. Perry et al., *Young, Gifted and Black,* 103.
96. Carol D. Lee, *Culture, Literacy, and Learning,* 124.
97. Amanda Taylor, "Teaching and Transcending Basic Skills," in Pollock, *Everyday Antiracism.*
98. Carol Corbett Burris, "Building a School of Opportunity Begins with Detracking," in *Excellence Through Equity: Five Principles of Courageous Leadership to Guide Achievement for Every Student,* ed. Alan M. Blankstein and Pedro Noguera (Thousand Oaks, CA: Corwin Press, 2015).
99. Jeannie Oakes, *Keeping Track: How Schools Structure Inequality* (New Haven, CT: Yale University Press, 1985).
100. John Baugh, "Valuing Nonstandard English." Bambi R. Schiefflin, Kathryn A. Woolard, and Paul V. Kroskrity, *Language Ideologies: Practice and Theory* (New York: Oxford University Press, 1998).
101. Ivette Sanchez, "Everyday Equity for Latin@ Students: Practices that Teachers and Students Identify as Supporting Secondary Mathematics Learning," Unpublished doctoral dissertation, University of California San Diego, 2015.
102. Cohen, "Providing Supportive Feedback," 83.

Chapter 4: Culture Talk

1. Norma González, Leisy Wyman, and Brendan H. O'Connor, "The Past, Present and Future of 'Funds of Knowledge,'" in *A Companion to the Anthropology of Education,* First Edition, ed. Bradley A. Levinson and Mica Pollock (West Sussex, UK: Wiley-Blackwell, 2011).
2. Mica Pollock, "From Shallow to Deep: Toward a Thorough Cultural Analysis of School Achievement Patterns," *Anthropology and Education Quarterly* 39, no. 4 (2008): 369–380. Some of the material in this chapter appeared first in that article.

3. Gloria Ladson-Billings, "It's Not the Culture of Poverty, It's the Poverty of Culture: The Problem of Teacher Education," *Anthropology and Education Quarterly* 37, no. 2 (2006): 104–109.

4. Evelyn Jacob and Cathie Jordan, "Understanding Educational Anthropology: Concepts and Methods," in *Minority Education: Anthropological Perspectives*, ed. Evelyn Jacob and Cathie Jordan (Westport, CT: Praeger Publishing, 1993).

5. Kris D. Gutierrez and Barbara Rogoff, "Cultural Ways of Learning: Individual Traits or Repertoires of Practice," *Educational Researcher* 32, no. 5 (June–July 2003): 19–25. See also Ward H. Goodenough, "Multiculturalism as the Normal Human Experience," *Anthropology and Education Quarterly* 7, no. 4 (1976): 4–7.

6. See Frederick D. Erickson, "Culture and Education," in *Encyclopedia of Diversity in Education*, ed. James A. Banks (Sage, 2012).

7. Kimberlé Crenshaw, "Demarginalizing the Intersection of Race and Sex: A Black Feminist Critique of Antidiscrimination Doctrine, Feminist Theory and Antiracist Politics," *University of Chicago Legal Forum* 1989, no. 1 (1989): 139–167.

8. Chimamanda Ngozi Adichie, "The Danger of a Single Story," http://www.ted.com/talks/chimamanda_adichie_the_danger_of_a_single_story.

9. Gloria Ladson-Billings, "It's Not the Culture of Poverty," 107.

10. Donna Deyhle, "What Is on Your Classroom Wall? Problematic Posters," in *Everyday Antiracism: Getting Real About Race in School*, ed. Mica Pollock (New York: The New Press, 2008), 191.

11. Ladson-Billings, "It's Not the Culture of Poverty," 106.

12. Adapted from Thea Abu El-Haj, "Arab Visibility and Invisibility," in Pollock, *Everyday Antiracism*.

13. Doug Foley, "Questioning 'Cultural' Explanations of Classroom Behaviors," in Pollock, *Everyday Antiracism*.

14. Angelina E. Castagno and Bryan McKinley Jones Brayboy, "Culturally Responsive Schooling for Indigenous Youth: A Review of the Literature," *Review of Educational Research* 78, no. 4 (2008): 941–993. See also Alaska Native Knowledge Network, *Alaska Standards for Culturally-Responsive Schools*, http://www.ankn.uaf.edu/publications/culturalstandards.pdf, 5–9. See also Dorothy M. Steele and Esther Rebecca Cohn-Vargas, *Identity Safe Classrooms: Places to Belong and Learn* (Thousand Oaks, CA: Corwin, 2013).

15. Christine E. Sleeter, "Preparing White Teachers for Diverse Students," in *Handbook of Research in Teacher Education: Enduring Issues in Changing Contexts*, Third Edition, ed. Marilyn Cochran-Smith, Sharon Feiman-Nemser, D. John McIntyre, and Kelly E. Demers (New York: Routledge, 2008), 559–582.

16. Paul C. Gorski, *Reaching and Teaching Students in Poverty: Strategies for Erasing the Opportunity Gap* (New York: Teachers College Press, 2013), 7.

17. Richard R. Valencia, *Dismantling Contemporary Deficit Thinking: Educational Thought and Practice* (New York: Taylor and Francis, 2010), 79, 81.

18. Akhil Gupta and James Ferguson, *Anthropological Locations: Boundaries and Grounds of a Field Science* (Berkeley, CA: University of California Press, 1997).

19. Bradley A. Levinson and Mica Pollock, *A Companion to the Anthropology of Education*, First Edition (West Sussex, UK: Wiley-Blackwell, 2011).

20. Ladson-Billings, "It's Not the Culture of Poverty," 104–109.

21. Frederick Erickson, "Learning and Teaching about Race, Privilege, and Disprivilege," in *Interrogating Whiteness and Relinquishing Power: White Faculty's Commitment to Racial Consciousness in STEM Classrooms*, ed. Nicole M. Joseph, Chayla Haynes, and Floyd Cobb (New York: Peter Lang, 2016), 74.

22. See http://studentresearch.ucsd.edu/_files/stats-data/profile/Profile2015.pdf.

23. "Vivian Louie, "Complicating the Story of Immigrant Integration," in *Writing Immigration: Scholars and Journalists in Dialogue*, ed. Marcelo Suarez-Orozco, Vivian Louie, and Roberto Suro (Berkeley and Los Angeles, CA: University of California Press, 2011), 218–235. Vivian's article itself leans on Vivian's two books: *Compelled to Excel* (on various Chinese American experiences) and *Keeping the Immigrant Bargain* (on the various U.S. experiences of Dominicans and Colombians). See Vivian Louie, *Compelled to Excel: Immigration, Education, and Opportunity Among Chinese Americans*, First Edition (Stanford, CA: Stanford University Press, 2004) and Vivian Louie, *Keeping the Immigrant Bargain: The Costs and Rewards of Success in America* (New York: Russell Sage Foundation, 2012).

24. See http://studentresearch.ucsd.edu/_files/stats-data/enroll/ugethnic.pdf.

25. "The State of Higher Education in California (Latinos)," *The Campaign for College Opportunity*, April 2015, http://collegecampaign.org/wp-content/uploads/2015/04/2015-State-of-Higher-Education_Latinos.pdf, 6–7.

26. Julianne Hing, "Asian Americans to Pew Study: We're Not Your 'Model Minority,'" *Hartford Guardian* (Hartford, CT), June 22, 2012.

27. Jie Zong and Jeanne Batlova, "Asian Immigrants in the United States," Migration Policy Institute (January 6, 2016), http://www.migrationpolicy.org/article/asian-immigrants-united-states. See also the *Community of Contrasts* reports put out by Asian Americans Advancing Justice, e.g., Asian Pacific American Legal Center and Asian American Justice Center, *A Community of Contrasts: Asian Americans in the United States, 2011* (Asian American Center for Advancing Justice), http://www.scribd.com/doc/94071413/APALC-Community-of-Contrast, or more regional reports like http://advancingjustice-la.org/media-and-publications/publications/community-contrasts-asian-americans-native-hawaiians-and-pacif-2 and http://www.upacsd.com/wp-content/uploads/2015/05/Community-of-Contrasts-Report-6-1-15.pdf.

28. Jennifer C. Ng, Sharon S. Lee, and Yoon K. Pak, "Contesting the Model Minority and Perpetual Foreigner Stereotypes: A Critical Review of Literature on Asian Americans in Education," *Review of Research in Education* 31 (March 2007): 95–130.

29. Vivian Louie, "Ethnicity Everywhere and Nowhere: A Critical ApproachTowards Parsing Ethnic and Non-ethnic Processes," *Ethnic and Racial Studies* 37, no. 5 (2014): 820–828.

30. Stacey J. Lee, *Up Against Whiteness: Race, School, and Immigrant Youth* (New York: Teachers College Press, 2005).

31. Gilberto Q. Conchas, "Structuring Failure and Success: Understanding the Variability in Latino School Engagement," *Harvard Educational Review* 71, no. 3 (2001): 475–504.

32. Frances Contreras and Gilbert J. Contreras, "Raising the Bar for Hispanic Serving Institutions: An Analysis of College Completion and Success Rates," *Journal of Hispanic Higher Education* 14, no. 2 (2015): 151–170.

33. Prudence L. Carter, *Keepin' It Real: School Success Beyond Black and White*, First Edition (New York: Oxford University Press, 2005); Pamela Perry, *Shades of White: White Kids and Racial Identities in High School* (Durham: Duke University Press, 2002).

34. Annette Lareau, *Unequal Childhoods: Class, Race, and Family Life* (Berkeley and Los Angeles, CA: University of California Press, 2011).

35. Guadalupe Valdés, *Con Respeto: Bridging the Distances Between Culturally Diverse Families and Schools: An Ethnographic Portrait* (New York: Teachers College Press, 1996).

36. Castagno and Brayboy, "Culturally Responsive Schooling," 960.

37. Kris D. Gutiérrez and Barbara Rogoff, "Cultural Ways of Learning: Individual Traits or Repertoires of Practice," *Educational Researcher* 32, no. 5 (June–July 2003): 23.

38. Amanda E. Lewis and John B. Diamond, *Despite the Best Intentions: How Racial Inequality Thrives in Good Schools* (New York: Oxford University Press, 2015), discussed at http://www.c-span.org/video/?400024-2/book-discussion-despite-best-intentions.

39. Frederick Erickson, "Going For the Zone: The Social and Cognitive Ecology of Teacher-Student Interaction in Classroom Conversations," in *Discourse, Learning, and Schooling*, First Edition, ed. Deborah Hicks (Cambridge, MA: Cambridge University Press, 1996).

40. On how teachers reward familiar speech patterns, see, e.g., Shirley Brice Heath, *Ways with Words: Language, Life and Work in Communities and Classrooms* (New York: Cambridge University Press, 1983).

41. Frederick Erickson, "The Gatekeeping Encounter as a Social Form and as a Site for Face Work," in *Handbook of Communication in Organisations and Professions*, ed. Christopher N. Candlin and Srikant Sarangi (De Gruyter Mouton, 2011), 433–454.

42. John Diamond, at http://www.c-span.org/video/?400024-2/book-discussion-despite-best-intentions.

43. Lisa Delpit, "The Silenced Dialogue: Power and Pedagogy in Educating Other People's Children," *Harvard Educational Review* 58 (1988): 280–298.

44. Ray P. McDermott, "Achieving School Failure 1972–1997," in *Education and Cultural Process: Anthropological Approaches, 3rd Edition*, ed. George D. Spindler (Prospect Heights: Waveland, 1997), 129.

45. Pollock, "From Shallow to Deep," 376.

46. David L. Kirp, *The Sandbox Investment: The Preschool Movement and Kids-First Politics* (Cambridge, MA: Harvard University Press, 2009).

47. Roslyn Arlin Mickelson and Linwood H. Cousins, "Informing Parents About Available Opportunities," in Pollock, *Everyday Antiracism*.

48. Prudence Carter, "Teaching Students Fluency in Multiple Cultural Codes," in Pollock, *Everyday Antiracism*, 110.

49. Django Paris and H. Samy Alim, "What Are We Seeking to Sustain Through Culturally Sustaining Pedagogy?," *Harvard Educational Review* 84, no. 1 (Spring 2014).

50. Angela Valenzuela, *Subtractive Schooling: U.S.-Mexican Youth and the Politics of Caring* (Albany: State University of New York Press, 1999).

51. Castagno and Brayboy, "Culturally Responsive Schooling."

52. Eugene E. García, "Valuing Students' Home Worlds," in Pollock, *Everyday Antiracism*, 110.

53. McDermott, "Achieving School Failure 1972–1997," 129.

54. Erickson, "Learning and Teaching About Race, Privilege, and Disprivilege," 83. Erickson also asks educators to interview each other about a typical dinner in their childhood homes ("who shopped for the food, who prepared it, how was it served, what kinds of conversation took place during the meal"), to begin to see how each home is itself a community of practice.

55. Steele and Cohn-Vargas, *Identity Safe Classrooms: Places to Belong and Learn*, with activities at http://www.corwin.com/identitysafe/materials/Teaching_for_Understanding.pdf.

56. Tyrone C. Howard, *Why Race and Culture Matter in Schools: Closing the Achievement Gap in America's Classrooms* (New York: Teachers College Press, 2010), 64.

57. Rosemary C. Henze, "Metaphors of Diversity, Intergroup Relations, and Equity in the Discourse of Educational Leaders," *Journal of Language, Identity, and Education* 4, no. 4 (2005): 247.

58. Henze, "Metaphors of Diversity," 254.

59. Interviewed at http://www.isthmus.com/news/cover-story/the-next-civil-rights-fight-scholar-gloria-ladson-billings-believes-african-american-students-deserve-better.

60. Ng et al., "Contesting the Model Minority," 109.

61. Ng et al., "Contesting the Model Minority."

62. See https://en.wikipedia.org/wiki/Asian_Americans, accessed 2014.

63. Louie, "Complicating the Story of Immigrant Integration," 222.

64. Ibid., 225.

65. Ibid. (citing Kasinitz et al., 2008, 363), 226.

66. Ibid., 225.

67. Ibid., 223.

68. Lee, *Up Against Whiteness*.

69. Ng et al., "Contesting the Model Minority," 98.

70. Wesley Yang, "Paper Tigers: What Happens to All the Asian-American Overachievers When the Test-Taking Ends," *New York Magazine*, May 16, 2011, http://nymag.com/news/features/asian-americans-2011-5/index6.html; Margaret M. Chin, "Asian Americans, Bamboo Ceilings, and Affirmative Action," *Contexts* (Winter 2016): 70–73.

71. Mia Tuan, *Forever Foreigners or Honorary Whites?: The Asian Ethnic Experience Today* (New Brunswick, NJ: Rutgers University Press, 1999).

72. Leisy Wyman and Grant Kashatok, "Getting to Know Students' Communities," in Pollock, *Everyday Antiracism*.

73. Dorinda J. Carter Andrews, "Black Achievers' Experiences with Racial Spotlighting and Ignoring in a Predominantly White High School," *Teachers College Record* 114, no. 10 (2012): 1–46.

74. Teresa L. McCarty, "Evaluating Images of Groups in Your Curriculum," in Pollock, *Everyday Antiracism*, 183, citing Joseph Bruchac, *Our Stories Remember: American Indian History, Culture, and Values Through Storytelling* (Golden, CO: Fulcrum Publishing, 2003), 8–9.

75. Adichie, "The Danger of a Single Story."

76. Sleeter, "Preparing White Teachers for Diverse Students," 2008.

77. Jacqueline Jordan Irvine, *Educating Teachers for Diversity: Seeing with a Cultural Eye* (New York: Teachers College Press, 2003), 74, emphasis added.

78. Sleeter, "Preparing White Teachers for Diverse Students," 2008.

79. Erickson, "Learning and Teaching about Race, Privilege, and Disprivilege," 85–86.

80. Wyman and Kashatok, "Getting to Know Students' Communities."

81. Deyhle, "What Is on Your Classroom Wall? Problematic Posters," 192.

82. García, "Valuing Students' Home Worlds."

83. Abu El-Haj, "Arab Visibility and Invisibility."

84. McCarty, "Evaluating Images of Groups in Your Curriculum," 182–3.

85. Christine E. Sleeter, "Involving Students in Selecting Reading Materials," in Pollock, *Everyday Antiracism: Getting Real About Race in School*, ed. Mica Pollock (New York: The New Press, 2008), 150.

86. Sanjay Sharma, "Teaching Representations of Cultural Difference Through Film," in Pollock, *Everyday Antiracism*.

87. Geneva Gay, "Preparing for Culturally Responsive Teaching," *Journal of Teacher Education* 53, no. 2 (March–April 2002): 109.

88. Katherine Schultz, "Interrogating Students' Silences," in Pollock, *Everyday Antiracism*; Doug Foley, "Questioning 'Cultural' Explanations of Classroom Behaviors," in Pollock, *Everyday Antiracism*.

89. See http://www.theweek.co.uk/world-news/61314/who-wants-to-be-a-volunteer-video-parodies-voluntourism.

90. Adichie, "The Danger of a Single Story."

Chapter 5: Data Talk

1. Barbara Taveras, Caissa Douwes, Karen Johnson, with Diana Lee and Margaret Caspe, "New Visions for Public Schools: Using Data to Engage Families" (2010), http://www.hfrp.org/family-involvement/publications-resources/new-visions-for-public-schools-using-data-to-engage-families.

2. Amanda Datnow and Vicki Park, "Data Use for Equity," *Educational Leadership* 72, no. 5 (2015): 49–54; Amanda Datnow, Vicki Park, and Priscilla Wohlstetter, *Achieving with Data: How High-Performing School Systems Use Data to Improve Instruction for Elementary Students* (Los Angeles: Center on Education Governance Univ. of Southern California, 2007); Kathryn Parker Boudett, Elizabeth A. City, and Richard J. Murnane, *Data Wise: A Step-by-Step Guide to Using Assessment Results to Improve Teaching and Learning*, Fifth Edition (Cambridge, MA: Harvard Education Press, 2005).

3. Amanda Datnow, "How Do We Ensure That All Students Have Access to High Quality Mathematics Teaching?," American Educational Research Association annual meetings, Washington, D.C. (April 9, 2016).

4. Na'ilah Nasir, *Racialized Identities: Race and Achievement Among African American Youth* (Stanford, CA: Stanford University Press, 2011), 45. See also Geoffrey L. Cohen, "Providing Supportive Feedback," in *Everyday Antiracism: Getting Real About Race in School*, ed. Mica Pollock (New York: The New Press, 2008); John Hattie and Helen Timperley, "The Power of Feedback," *Review of Educational Research* 77, no. 1 (March 2007): 81–112. See also http://www.ascd.org/publications/books/108019/chapters/Feedback@-An-Overview.aspx. Ronald F. Ferguson, "Helping Students of Color Meet High Standards," in Pollock, *Everyday Antiracism*.

5. Boudett et al., *Data Wise*, 17.

6. Teresa L. McCarty and Tiffany S. Lee, "Critical Culturally Sustaining/Revitalizing Pedagogy and Indigenous Education Sovereignty," *Harvard Educational Review* 84, no. 1 (Spring 2014).

7. Ethan Mintz, Sarah E. Fiarman, and Tom Buffett, "Digging into Data," in Boudett et al., *Data Wise*.

8. Datnow et al., *Achieving with Data*.

9. Larry Cuban, "Data-Driven Teaching Practices: Rhetoric and Reality," *Larry Cuban on School Reform and Classroom Practice*, October 6, 2015, https://larrycuban.wordpress.com/2015/10/06/another-look-at-data-driven-teaching-practices.

10. Linda Darling-Hammond, "Designing the 'New Accountability': How Public Scholars Can Contribute to a Productive Policy Framework for Education," American Educational Research Association annual meetings, Washington, D.C. (April 8, 2016).

11. On the "deficit" thinking packed into the longstanding term "at risk," see Richard R. Valencia, *Dismantling Contemporary Deficit Thinking: Educational Thought and Practice* (New York: Taylor and Francis, 2010), chapter 4.

12. Datnow and Park, "Data Use for Equity," 49.

13. See, e.g., http://www.everyday-democracy.org/resources/education.

14. See the work of the Carnegie Foundation, described in Anthony S. Bryk, Louis M. Gomez, Alicia Grunow, and Paul G. LeMahieu, *Learning to Improve: How America's Schools Can Get Better at Getting Better* (Cambridge, MA: Harvard Education Press, 2015). For related protocols as honed by educators, see High Tech High, *High Tech High Graduate School of Education Improvement Tools*, http://gse.hightechhigh.org/centerForResearchOnEquityAndInnovation.php.

15. Prudence Carter, Russell Skiba, Mariella Arredondo, and Mica Pollock, "You Can't Fix What You Don't Look At: Acknowledging Race in Addressing Racial Discipline Disparities," *Atlantic Philanthropies Discipline Disparities Series*, December 2014, http://www.atlanticphilanthropies.org/sites/default/files/uploads/Acknowledging-Race_121514.pdf.

16. Amanda Datnow and Vicki Park, "Compilation of Data-Driven Tools," *NewSchools Venture Fund*, October 31, 2008, http://www.newschools.org/files/Compilationofdatadriventools.pdf.

17. Ilana Seidel Horn, 2015; https://teachingmathculture.wordpress.com/2015/06/09/facilitating-conversations-about-student-data.

18. Carter et al., "You Can't Fix What You Don't Look At."

19. Datnow and Park, "Data Use for Equity," 50.

20. See wiki.oneville.org for the many contributors to this collective project. See also Mica Pollock, "It Takes a Network to Raise a Child: Improving the Communication Infrastructure of Public Education to Enable Community Cooperation in Young People's Success," *Teachers College Record* 155, no. 7 (2013): 1–28.

21. Adriene Hill, "Using Data to Head Off High School Dropouts," *Marketplace*, November 12, 2014, http://www.marketplace.org/topics/education/learningcurve/using-data-head-high-school-dropouts.

22. "Being Black Is Not a Risk Factor: A Strength-Based Look at the State of the Black Child," *National Black Child Development Institute*, http://www.nbcdi.org/resource. See also Richard R. Valencia, *Dismantling Contemporary Deficit Thinking*.

23. Dalia Topelson, Christopher Bavitz, Ritu Gupta, and Irina Oberman, "Privacy and Children's Data: An Overview of the Children's Online Privacy Protection Act and the Family Educational Rights and Privacy Act," *The Berkman Center for Internet & Society at Harvard University*, November 14, 2013, http://papers.ssrn.com/sol3/papers.cfm?abstract_id=2354339.

24. Joseph G. Kosciw, Emily A. Greytak, Mark J. Bartkiewicz, Madelyn J. Boesen, and Neal A. Pa25mer, *The 2011 National School Climate Survey: The Experiences of Lesbian, Gay, Bisexual and Transgender Youth in Our Nation's Schools* (Gay, Lesbian and Straight Education Network [GLSEN], 2012).

25. Mariella Arredondo, Chrystal Gray, Stephen Russell, Russell Skiba, and Shannon Snapp, "Documenting Disparities for LGBT Students: Expanding the Collection and Reporting of Data on Sexual Orientation and Gender Identity," *Atlantic Philanthropies Discipline Disparities Series* (March 2016).

26. Barbara Taveras, Caissa Douwes, Karen Johnson, with Diana Lee and Margaret Caspe, "New Visions for Public Schools: Using Data to Engage Families," 2010, http://www.hfrp.org/family-involvement/publications-resources/new-visions-for-public-schools-using-data-to-engage-families.

27. National Association of Elementary School Principals, *Leading Pre-K-3 Learning Communities: Competencies for Effective Principal Practice* (Alexandria, VA, 2014).

28. R.J. Marzano, *Transforming Classroom Grading* (Alexandria, VA: Association for Supervision & Curriculum Development, 2000), 1. (For many provocative thoughts on letter grades as descriptions of student performance, see http://www.gfps.k12.mt.us/sites/default/files/Ken%20O'Connor%20GFPS%20Aug%2013,%202012.pdf.)

29. Ilana Seidel Horn, "Fast Kids, Slow Kids, Lazy Kids: Framing the Mismatch Problem in Mathematics Teachers' Conversations," *Journal of the Learning Sciences* 16, no. 1 (2007): 37–79.

30. Susan Szachowicz, "Brockton High School, Brockton, Massachusetts," in *Excellence Through Equity: Five Principles of Courageous Leadership to Guide Achievement for Every Student*, ed. Alan M. Blankstein and Pedro Noguera (Thousand Oaks, CA: Corwin Press, 2015).

31. Kris D. Gutiérrez and Barbara Rogoff, "Cultural Ways of Learning: Individual Traits or Repertoires of Practice," *Educational Researcher* 32, no. 5 (June–July 2003): 23.

32. See http://www.ascd.org/publications/books/108019/chapters/Feedback@-An-Overview.aspx.

33. Hattie and Timperley, "The Power of Feedback," 87.

34. Amanda Datnow, "How Do We Ensure That All Students Have Access to High Quality Mathematics Teaching?" American Educational Research Association annual meetings, Washington, D.C. (April 9, 2016).

35. See http://mrssarahlewis.wordpress.com/category/march.

36. Datnow and Park, "Data Use for Equity," 52; see also Hattie and Timperley, "The Power of Feedback."

37. The educators adapted their "learning target" assessment approach from Ron Berger, Leah Rugen, and Libby Woodfin, *Leaders of Their Own Learning: Transforming Schools Through Student-Engaged Assessment* (Jossey-Bass, 2014), described at http://eleducation.org/resources/leaders-of-their-own-learning.

38. Hattie and Timperley, "The Power of Feedback," 101–2.

39. Mintz et al., "Digging into Data," in Boudett et al., *Data Wise*; Makeba Jones and Susan Yonezawa, "Inviting Students to Analyze Their Learning Experience," in Pollock, *Everyday Antiracism*.

40. Mintz et al., "Digging into Data," in Boudett et al., *Data Wise*, 93.

41. On shaping conversations via technology design, see Beth Simone Noveck, *Wiki Government: How Technology Can Make Government Better, Democracy Stronger, and Citizens More Powerful* (Washington, D.C.: Brookings Institution Press, 2009).

42. Linda McNeil and Angela Valenzuela, "The Harmful Impact of the TAAS System of Testing in Texas: Beneath the Accountability Rhetoric," in *Raising Standards or Raising Barriers? Inequality and High Stakes Testing in Public Education*, ed. Gary Orfield and Mindy Kornhaber (New York: Century Foundation, 2001).

43. Kavitha Mediratta, Seema Shah, and Sara McAlister, *Building Partnerships to Reinvent School Culture: Austin Interfaith* (Providence, RI: Annenberg Institute for School Reform at Brown University, 2009), 17.

44. Linda Darling-Hammond and Ray Pecheone with Ann Jacquith, Susan Schultz, Leah Walker, and Ruth Chung Wei, *Developing an Internationally Comparable Balanced Assessment System That Supports High-Quality Learning* (Washington, D.C.: Educational Testing Service, 2010). See also Boudett et al., *Data Wise*.

45. McCarty and Lee, "Critical Culturally Sustaining/Revitalizing Pedagogy," 111.

46. John Dewey, "My Pedagogic Creed," *School Journal* 54, (1897): 77–80.

47. Vincent Harding, *There Is a River: The Black Struggle for Freedom in America* (Houghton Mifflin Harcourt, 1981), 325–6.

48. Sonia Nieto, "Nice Is Not Enough: Defining Caring for Students of Color," in Pollock, *Everyday Antiracism*.

49. Norma González, Luis C. Moll, and Cathy Amanti, *Funds of Knowledge: Theorizing Practices in Households, Communities, and Classrooms*, First Edition (New York: Routledge, 2005).

50. Leisy Wyman and Grant Kashatok, "Getting to Know Students' Communities," in Pollock, *Everyday Antiracism*.

51. H. Richard Milner IV, "Five Easy Ways to Connect with Students," *Harvard Education Letter* 27, no. 1 (January/February 2011), http://hepg.org/hel-home/issues/27_1/helarticle/five-easy-ways-to-connect-with-students_492.

52. Nasir, *Racialized Identities*, 35.

53. Susan Klimczak, Michelle Li, Chris Clynn, and Joe Beckmann, "ePossibilities: The Power of a Grassroots Approach to Student-Curated ePortfolios in an Urban High School," *Student-Centered Interactive E-Portfolios in the Cloud*, last modified June 5, 2012. See also http://wiki.oneville.org/main/Eportfolio.

54. Felecia M. Briscoe, Gilberto Arriaza, and Rosemary C. Henze, *The Power of Talk: How Words Change Our Lives* (Thousand Oaks, CA: Corwin Press, 2009), 85–86.

55. See, e.g., https://www.hightechhigh.org/schools/HTH/?show=dp.

56. See https://sites.google.com/site/shsportfolio and then, e.g., https://sitesgoogle.com/site/shseportfolio/documents/verified-resume; https:/sites.google.com/site/shseportfolio/home/learning-goals.

57. Mica Pollock, "It Takes a Network"; http://wiki.oneville.org/main/Eportfolio.

58. The full video is also available at https://www.youtube.com/watch?v=9dUuCxV5D7c.

59. Klimczak et al., "ePossibilities."

60. Carol D. Lee, *Culture, Literacy, and Learning: Taking Bloom in the Midst of the Whirlwind* (New York: Teachers College Press, 2007).

61. Cohen, "Providing Supportive Feedback" and Amanda Taylor, "Teaching and Transcending Basic Skills," both in Pollock, *Everyday Antiracism*.

62. Marcia Theresa Caton, "Black Male Perspectives on Their Educational Experiences in High School," *Urban Education* 47, no. 6 (November 2012): 1067.

63. As Reverend Jamaal Bryant put it in a eulogy for Freddie Gray in Baltimore in April 2015, "One of the greatest tragedies in life is to think that you are free, but to still be confined to a box, living in a box of stereotypes, other people's opinion[s], sweeping generalizations and racial profiling." http://www.npr.org/2015/04/27/402632411/thousands-say-goodbye-to-freddie-gray-in-baltimore.

64. Nasir, *Racialized Identities*, 160–161.

65. Theresa Perry, *Young, Gifted, and Black: Promoting High Achievement Among African-American Students* (Boston, MA: Beacon Press, 2003).

66. M. Casey, Roger K. Warren, Fred L. Cheesman II, and Jennifer K. Elek, "Helping Courts Address Implicit Bias: Resources for Education," *National Center for State Courts*, 2012, http://www.ncsc.org/~/media/Files/PDF/Topics/Gender%20and%20Racial%20Fairness/IB_Strategies_033012.ashx.

67. Citing James P. Comer, "Educating Poor Minority Children," *Scientific American* 259, no. 5 (November 1, 1988): 42–48, in Kenneth M. Zeichner, "Educating Teachers for Cultural Diversity," National Center for Research on Teacher Learning Special Report, September 1992, 7.

68. Markus J. Newsom, "A Journey Toward Equity and Excellence for All Students in Chesterfield," in *Excellence Through Equity*, ed. Alan M. Blankstein and Pedro Noguera (Thousand Oaks, CA: Corwin, 2015), 242.

69. Django Paris and H. Samy Alim, "What Are We Seeking to Sustain Through Culturally Sustaining Pedagogy?," *Harvard Educational Review* 84, no. 1 (Spring 2014).

70. Edmund T. Hamann, "Standards vs. 'Standard' Knowledge," in *Everyday Antiracism: Getting Real About Race in School*, ed. Mica Pollock (New York: The New Press, 2008).

71. See https://sites.google.com/site/shseportfolio/documents/verified-resume.

72. See http://www.nytimes.com/2014/09/28/education/college-admissions-goucher-video.html.

Chapter 6: Life Talk

1. Alan M. Blankstein and Pedro Noguera, *Excellence Through Equity: Five Principles of Courageous Leadership to Guide Achievement for Every Student* (Thousand Oaks, CA: Corwin, 2015), 21.

2. Susan Yonezawa, Larry McClure, and Makeba Jones, "Personalization in Schools," The Students at the Center Series (Teaching and Learning in the Era of the Common Core), A Jobs for the Future Project, April 2012, http://www.studentsatthecenter.org/sites/scl.dl-dev.com/files/Personalization%20in%20Schools.pdf.

3. Jacqueline Jordan Irvine, *Educating Teachers for Diversity: Seeing with a Cultural Eye* (New York: Teachers College Press, 2003), 74.

4. Kenneth M. Zeichner, "Educating Teachers for Cultural Diversity," National Center for Research on Teacher Learning Special Report, September 1992, 6.

5. Geneva Gay, *Culturally Responsive Teaching: Theory, Research, and Practice*, Second Edition (New York: Teachers College Press, 2010).

6. Jeffrey M.R. Duncan-Andrade, "Note to Educators: Hope Required When Growing Roses in Concrete," *Harvard Educational Review* 79 no. 2 (Summer 2009). See, e.g., Bryan McKinley Jones Brayboy and Emma Maughan, "Indigenous Knowledges and the Story of the Bean," *Harvard Educational Review* 79, no. 1 (Spring 2009).

7. Christine Sleeter, "Standards and Multicultural Education," *Christine Sleeter* (blog), June 18, 2015, http://christinesleeter.org/standards-and-multicultural.

8. Carol D. Lee, "Intervention Research Based on Current Views of Cognition and Learning," in *Black Education: A Transformative Research and Action Agenda for the New Century*, First Edition, ed. Joyce E. King (Mahwah, NJ: Lawrence Erlbaum Associates, 2005).

9. See also Bryan McKinley Jones Brayboy, Amy J. Fann, Angelina E. Castagno, and Jessica A. Solyom, *Postsecondary Education for American Indian and Alaska Natives: Higher Education for Nation Building and Self-Determination*, ASHE Higher Education Report 37, no. 5 (2012).

10. Tiffany S. Lee and Patricia D. Quijada Cerecer, "(Re)Claiming Native Youth Knowledge: Engaging in Socio-culturally Responsive Teaching and Relationships," *Multicultural Perspectives* 12, no. 4 (2010), 201; Angela Valenzuela, *Subtractive Schooling: U.S.-Mexican Youth and the Politics of Caring* (Albany: State University of New York Press, 1999), 263.

11. Na'ilah Nasir, *Racialized Identities: Race and Achievement Among African American Youth* (Stanford, CA: Stanford University Press, 2011), 163–164.

12. Yonezawa et al., "Personalization in Schools," 1, citing the work of Ethan Yazzie-Mintz, e.g., "Charting the Path from Engagement to Achievement: A Report on the 2009 High School Survey of Student Engagement," *HSSSE High School Survey of Student Engagement*, 2010, http://ceep.indiana .edu/hssse/images/HSSSE_2010_Report.pdf.

13. Katherine Newman, *Rampage: The Social Roots of School Shootings* (Boulder, CO: Perseus Books, 2004).

14. Niobe Way, *Deep Secrets: Boys' Friendships and the Crisis of Connection* (Cambridge, MA: Harvard University Press, 2011).

15. Emily S. Fisher, "Supporting Lesbian, Gay, Bisexual, Transgender, and Questioning Students and Families," in *Creating Safe and Supportive Learning Environments: A Guide for Working with Lesbian, Gay, Bisexual, Transgender and Questioning Youth and Families*, ed. Emily S. Fisher and Karen Komosa-Hawkins (New York: Routledge, 2013), 5, citing C.S. Chan.

16. On engaging stressors, see Duncan-Andrade, "Note to Educators." On college supports, see Benjamin L. Castleman and Lindsay C. Page, *Summer Melt: Supporting Low-Income Students Through the Transition to College* (Cambridge: Harvard Education Press, 2014).

17. Yonezawa et al., "Personalization in Schools," 7, citing Marcia Gentry, Saiying Steeenbergen-Hu, and Byung-yeon Choi, "Student-Identified Exemplary Teachers," *Gifted Child Quarterly* 55, no. 2 (2011): 111–125.

18. Susan Yonezawa and Makeba Jones, "Student Voices: Generating Reform from the Inside Out," *Theory into Practice* 48, no. 3 (Summer 2009): 205–212; Antero Garcia, Nicole Mirra, and Ernest Morrell, *Doing Youth Participatory Action Research: Transforming Inquiry with Researchers, Educators, and Students* (New York: Routledge, 2015); Anita Wadhwa, *Restorative Justice in Urban Schools: Disrupting the School-to-Prison Pipeline* (New York: Routledge, 2016).

19. See http://www.exeter.edu/about_us/171.aspx.

20. American School Counselor Association, *Position Statement: The School Counselor and Comprehensive School Counseling Programs*, https://www.schoolcounselor.org/asca/media/asca/Position Statements/PS_ComprehensivePrograms.pdf.

21. John Rogers, "Without Dollars and Sense: The Budget Crisis and California's School Funding" (presentation, Institute for Democracy, Education, and Access at the University of California, Los Angeles, October 22, 2012), 7.

22. See also John Rogers, Melanie Bertrand, Rhoda Freelon, Sophie Fanelli, *Free Fall: Educational Opportunities in 2011* (Los Angeles: UCLA IDEA, UC/ACCORD, 2011).

23. Carol D. Lee, *Culture, Literacy, and Learning: Taking Bloom In the Midst of the Whirlwind* (New York: Teachers College Press, 2007), 5.

24. H. Richard Milner IV, "Five Easy Ways to Connect with Students," *Harvard Education Letter* 27, no. 1 (January/February 2011), http://hepg.org/hel-home/issues/27_1/helarticle/five-easy-ways -to-connect-with-students_492.

25. See http://preuss.ucsd.edu/current-students/university-prep.html. See also Hugh Mehan, *In the Front Door: Creating a College-Going Culture of Learning* (Boulder, CO: Paradigm Publishers, 2012).

26. Mica Pollock and Uche Amaechi, "Texting as a Channel for Personalized Youth Support: Participatory Design Research by City Youth and Teachers," *Learning, Media, and Technology* 38, no. 2 (2013): 128–144. On one-on-one interviews, see Sonia Nieto, *Affirming Diversity: The Sociopolitical Context of Multicultural Education*, Fourth Edition (Allyn & Bacon, 2004).

27. Patricia Gándara, "Strengthening Student Identity in School Programs," in *Everyday Antiracism: Getting Real About Race in School*, ed. Mica Pollock (New York: The New Press, 2008).

28. Ibid.

29. Nieto, *Affirming Diversity*, 20, 17.

30. Ibid., 171–172.

31. Ibid., 17.

32. Thea Abu El-Haj, "Practicing for Equity from the Standpoint of the Particular: Exploring the Work of One Urban Teacher Network," *Teachers College Record* 105, no. 5 (2003): 817–845.

33. Milner, "Five Easy Ways to Connect with Students," 2011.

34. Gloria Ladson-Billings, "It's Not the Culture of Poverty, It's the Poverty of Culture: The Problem of Teacher Education," *Anthropology and Education Quarterly* 37, no. 2 (2006): 108.

35. Gloria Ladson-Billings, "But That's Just Good Teaching! The Case for Culturally Relevant Pedagogy," *Theory into Practice* 34, no. 3 (Summer 1995): 159–165.

36. Mica Pollock, Candice Bocala, Sherry L. Deckman, and Shari Dickstein-Staub, "Caricature

and Hyperbole in Preservice Teacher Professional Development for Diversity," *Urban Education* (May 1, 2015): 1–30. See also Rosemary C. Henze, "Curricular Approaches to Developing Positive Interethnic Relations," *The Journal of Negro Education* 68, no. 4 (Autumn 1999): 529–549.

37. Geneva Gay, "Preparing for Culturally Responsive Teaching," *Journal of Teacher Education* 53, no. 2 (March–April 2002): 106–116; Duncan-Andrade, "Note to Educators."

38. Ben Rampton, "Observing Students Sharing Language," in Pollock, *Everyday Antiracism*.

39. Lee, *Culture, Literacy, and Learning*, 129.

40. See, e.g., Lissa Soep and Vivian Chavez, *Drop That Knowledge: Youth Radio Stories* (Berkeley: University of California Press, 2010). See also 3rdeyeunlimited.wordpress.com.

41. See, e.g., Mizuko Ito, ed., *Hanging Out, Messing Around, and Geeking Out: Kids Living and Learning with New Media* (Cambridge, MA: MIT Press, 2009), http://mitpress.mit.edu/books /hanging-out-messing-around-and-geeking-out; youthmedia.org; Cathy N. Davidson and David Theo Goldberg, *The Future of Thinking: Learning Institutions in a Digital Age* (Cambridge, MA: MIT Press, 2010).

42. Ito et al., *Hanging Out*, 16, 91. danah boyd argues in the book that "while social media have the potential to radically alter friendshipmaking processes, most teens use these tools to maintain pre-existing connections, turn acquaintances into friendships, and develop connections through people they already know" (91).

43. Michele L. Ybarra, Kimberly J. Mitchell, Neal A. Palmer, and Sari L. Reisner, "Online Social Support as a Buffer Against Online and Offline Peer and Sexual Victimization Among U.S. LGBT and Non-LGBT Youth," *Child Abuse and Neglect* (September 2014); Joseph G. Kosciw, Emily A. Greytak, Mark J. Bartkiewicz, Madelyn J. Boesen, and Neal A. Palmer, *The 2011 National School Climate Survey: The Experiences of Lesbian, Gay, Bisexual and Transgender Youth in Our Nation's Schools* (Gay, Lesbian and Straight Education Network [GLSEN], 2012), xiv (http://files.eric.ed .gov/fulltext/ED535177.pdf). See also glsen.org.

44. See Castleman and Page, *Summer Melt*; as one example, see http://beyond12.org.

45. Ito et al., *Hanging Out*, 27.

46. See, e.g., Julio Cammarota and Michelle Fine, eds., *Revolutionizing Education: Youth Participatory Action Research in Motion*, First Edition (New York: Routledge, 2008). See also Maria Elena Torre and Michelle Fine, "Engaging Youth in Participatory Inquiry for Social Justice," in Pollock, *Everyday Antiracism*.

47. Denise Pope, Maureen Brown, and Sarah Miles, *Overloaded and Underprepared: Strategies for Stronger Schools and Healthy, Successful Kids* (San Francisco, CA: Jossey-Bass, 2015), 10.

48. Milner, "Five Easy Ways to Connect with Students."

49. Anita Wadhwa, *Restorative Justice in Urban Schools: Disrupting the School-to-Prison Pipeline* (New York: Routledge, 2016).

50. Ilana Seidel Horn, "Learning on the Job: A Situated Account of Teacher Learning in High School Mathematics Departments," *Cognition and Instruction* 23, no. 2 (2005): 216.

51. See John Hattie and Helen Timperley, "The Power of Feedback," *Review of Educational Research* 77, no. 1 (March 2007): 81–112. See also http://www.ascd.org/publications/books/108019/chapters /Feedback@-An-Overview.aspx.

52. Angelina E. Castagno and Bryan McKinley Jones Brayboy, "Culturally Responsive Schooling for Indigenous Youth: A Review of the Literature," *Review of Educational Research* 78, no. 4 (December 2008): 970.

53. Yonezawa et al., "Personalization in Schools," 17.

54. H. Richard Milner IV, *Start Where You Are, but Don't Stay There: Understanding Diversity, Opportunity Gaps, and Teaching in Today's Classrooms* (Cambridge, MA: Harvard Education Press, 2010); Duncan-Andrade, "Note to Educators."

55. Makeba Jones and Susan Yonezawa, "Inviting Students to Analyze Their Learning Experience," in Pollock, *Everyday Antiracism*.

56. Yonezawa and Jones, "Student Voices: Generating Reform from the Inside Out," 205–212. See also Makeba Jones and Susan Yonezawa, "Student Voice, Cultural Change: Using Inquiry in School Reform," *Journal of Equity and Excellence in Education* 35, no. 3 (September 2002): 245–254.

57. See Garcia, Mirra, and Morrell, *Doing Youth Participatory Action Research*.

58. Yonezawa et al., "Personalization in Schools," 2. See also Rachel A. Poliner and Carol Miller Lieber, *The Advisory Guide: Designing and Implementing Effective Advisory Programs in Secondary Schools* (Cambridge, MA: Educators for Social Responsibility, 2004) and Patricia Gándara,

"Strengthening Student Identity in School Programs," in *Everyday Antiracism.*

59. Mark R. Warren, "Communities and Schools: A New View of Urban Education Reform," *Harvard Education Review* 75, no. 2 (2005): 133–173, 10.

60. Anne Gregory, James Bell, and Mica Pollock, "How Educators Can Eradicate Disparities in School Discipline: A Briefing Paper on School-Based Interventions," *Atlantic Philanthropies Discipline Disparities Series*, December 2014, http://www.indiana.edu/~atlantic/wp-content/uploads/2014/03/Disparity_Interventions_Full_031214.pdf.

61. Felecia M. Briscoe, Gilberto Arriaza, and Rosemary C. Henze, *The Power of Talk: How Words Change Our Lives* (Thousand Oaks, CA: Corwin Press, 2009), 149–50.

62. Gretchen Brion-Meisels, *Supporting Teens Their Way: An Exploration of Urban High School Students' Interpretations of Support in the Context of School* (unpublished doctoral dissertation, Harvard Graduate School of Education, Cambridge, MA, 2013).

63. See Castleman and Page, *Summer Melt.*

64. Nasir, *Racialized Identities*, 52.

65. Ibid., 57.

66. Ibid., 51–52.

67. Leisy Wyman, *Youth Culture, Language Endangerment and Linguistic Survivance* (Bristol, UK: Multilingual Matters, 2012), 207–208.

68. Milner, *Start Where You Are*, 133–134.

69. Lee, "The Home-School-Community Interface in Language Revitalization."

70. Hattie and Timperley, "The Power of Feedback," 86.

71. Jeffrey M. Duncan-Andrade and Ernest Morrell, "What a Coach Can Teach a Teacher," in *The Art of Critical Pedagogy: Possibilities for Moving from Theory to Practice in Urban Schools* (New York: Peter Lang Publishing, 2008), 69–88.

72. Amanda Lenhart, Rich Ling, Scott Campbell, and Kristen Purcell, "Teens and Mobile Phones," *Pew Research Center*, April 20, 2010, http://pewinternet.org/Reports/2010/Teens-and-Mobile-Phones.aspx.

73. For a full account, see Mica Pollock and Uche Amaechi, "Texting as a Channel for Personalized Youth Support: Participatory Design Research by City Youth and Teachers," *Learning, Media, and Technology* 38, no. 2 (2013): 128–144. Some of the material in this chapter also appeared in that article. See also http://wiki.oneville.org/main/Summary:_Texting_for_Rapid_Youth_Support.

74. See http://www.inquisitr.com/1180386/terrence-roberts-inspires-young-people-to-stand-against-discrimination.

75. Angela Valenzuela, *Subtractive Schooling: U.S.-Mexican Youth and the Politics of Caring* (Albany: State University of New York Press, 1999), 263.

76. Gretchen Brion-Meisels, "It Starts Out with Little Things: An Exploration of Urban Adolescents' Support-Seeking Strategies in the Context of School," *Teachers College Record* 118, no. 1 (2016): 1–38.

77. Hirokazu Yoshikawa, *Immigrants Raising Citizens: Undocumented Parents and Their Young Children* (New York: Russell Sage Foundation, 2012).

78. Jennifer A. Mott-Smith, "Exploring Racial Identity Through Writing," in Pollock, *Everyday Antiracism.*

79. *Alaska Standards for Culturally-Responsive Schools* (Anchorage: Alaska Native Knowledge Network, 1998), http://www.ankn.uaf.edu/publications/culturalstandards.pdf.

80. Kimberly Chang and Rachel Conrad, "Following Children's Leads in Conversations About Race," in Pollock, *Everyday Antiracism.*

81. Torre and Fine, "Engaging Youth in Participatory Inquiry for Social Justice," and Alexandra Lightfoot, "Using Photography to Explore Racial Identity," both in Pollock, *Everyday Antiracism*; Marit Dewhurst, *Social Justice Art: A Framework for Activist Art Pedagogy* (Cambridge, MA: Harvard Education Press, 2014).

82. Amanda Datnow and Vicki Park, "Data Use for Equity," *Educational Leadership* 72, no. 5 (2015): 49–54.

83. Thandeka K. Chapman, "Interrogating Classroom Relationships and Events: Using Portraiture and Critical Race Theory in Education Research," *Educational Researcher* 36, no. 3, (April 2007): 160.

84. Dorinda Carter Andrews, manuscript in preparation.

85. Leisy Wyman and Grant Kashatok, "Getting to Know Students' Communities," in Pollock, *Everyday Antiracism.*

86. Lee and Cerecer, "(Re)Claiming Native Youth Knowledge," 203. On two-way sharing, see bell hooks, *Teaching to Transgress: Education as the Practice of Freedom* (Routledge, 1994), 21.

87. Julio Cammarota and Augustine Romero, "A Critically Compassionate Intellectualism for Latina/o Students: Raising Voices Above the Silencing in Our Schools," *Multicultural Education* (Winter 2006): 19.

88. Heather M. Pleasants, "Showing Students Who You Are," in Pollock, *Everyday Antiracism*, 71.

89. Christine Sleeter, "Multicultural Curriculum and Critical Family History," *Multicultural Education Review* 7, no. 1–2 (2015): 1–11. See also Gary R. Howard, *We Can't Teach What We Don't Know*, Second Edition (New York: Teachers College Press, 2006) and Nasir, *Racialized Identities*, 160–164.

90. Gretchen Brion-Meisels, "The Challenge of Holistic Student Support: Investigating Urban Adolescents' Constructions of Support in the Context of School," *Harvard Educational Review* 84, no. 3 (2014): 314–340.

91. Dorothy M. Steele and Esther Rebecca Cohn-Vargas, *Identity Safe Classrooms: Places to Belong and Learn* (Thousand Oaks, CA: Corwin, 2013). For these supplemental activities, see http://www.corwin.com/identitysafe/materials/Positive_Student_Relationships.pdf and http://www.corwin.com/identitysafe/materials/Teacher_Warmth_and_Availability.pdf.

92. Linda Harper, "The Voices and Hearts of Youth: Transformative Power of Equity in Action," in *Excellence Through Equity: Five Principles of Courageous Leadership to Guide Achievement for Every Student*, ed. Alan M. Blankstein and Pedro Noguera (Thousand Oaks, California: Corwin Press, 2015), 89.

93. Rosemary C. Henze, "Metaphors of Diversity, Intergroup Relations, and Equity in the Discourse of Educational Leaders," *Journal of Language, Identity, and Education* 4, no. 4 (2005): 259.

94. See http://www.humansofnewyork.com/post/110254545971/you-dont-do-things-alone-nobody-does-things.

Chapter 7: Opportunity Talk

1. Angelina E. Castagno and Bryan McKinley Jones Brayboy, "Culturally Responsive Schooling for Indigenous Youth: A Review of the Literature," *Review of Educational Research* 78, no. 4 (December 2008): 946.

2. Alan J. Daly, ed., *Social Network Theory and Educational Change* (Cambridge, MA: Harvard Education Press, 2010).

3. Robert D. Putnam, "Community-Based Social Capital and Educational Performance," in *Making Good Citizens: Education and Civil Society*, ed. Diane Ravitch and Joseph P. Viteritti (New Haven: Yale University Press, 2001), 58–95.

4. Amanda E. Lewis and John B. Diamond, *Despite the Best Intentions: How Racial Inequality Thrives in Good Schools* (New York: Oxford University Press, 2015), discussed at http://www.c-span.org/video/?400024-2/book-discussion-despite-best-intentions.

5. Django Paris and H. Samy Alim, "What Are We Seeking to Sustain Through Culturally Sustaining Pedagogy?," *Harvard Educational Review* 84, no. 1 (Spring 2014): 87–88.

6. See the work of Susan Yonezawa and Makeba Jones in Daniel Solorzano, Amanda Datnow, Vicki Park, and Tara Watford, "Pathways to Postsecondary Success: Maximizing Opportunities for Youth in Poverty," *University of California All Campus Collaborative on Outreach, Research, and Dissemination*, 2013, http://pathways.gseis.ucla.edu/publications/PathwaysReport.pdf. See also Benjamin L. Castleman and Lindsay C. Page, *Summer Melt: Supporting Low-Income Students Through the Transition to College* (Cambridge: Harvard Education Press, 2014).

7. Mica Pollock, Susan Yonezawa, and Barbara Edwards, "Can We Solve San Diego's Math Problem Together?," *San Diego Union Tribune*, May 23, 2014, http://www.sandiegouniontribune.com/news/2014/may/23/tp-can-we-solve-san-diegos-math-problem-together.

8. Roslyn Arlin Mickelson and Linwood H. Cousins, "Informing Parents About Available Opportunities," in *Everyday Antiracism: Getting Real About Race in School*, ed. Mica Pollock (New York: The New Press, 2008), 318–324; Lewis and Diamond, *Despite the Best Intentions*; Annette Lareau, *Unequal Childhoods: Class, Race, and Family Life* (Berkeley and Los Angeles, CA: University of California Press, 2011).

9. Lewis and Diamond, *Despite the Best Intentions*.

10. John Rogers, Melanie Bertrand, Rhoda Freelon, and Sophie Fanelli, *Free Fall: Educational*

Opportunities in 2011 (Los Angeles: UCLA IDEA, UC/ACCORD, 2011).

11. Karolyn Tyson, "Providing Equal Access to 'Gifted' Education," in Pollock, *Everyday Anti-racism*; Richard Rothstein, *Class and Schools: Using Social, Economic, and Educational Reform to Close the Black-White Achievement Gap* (New York: Teachers College Press, 2004); John B. Diamond and Kimberley Gomez, "African American Parents' Educational Orientations: The Importance of Social Class and Parents' Perceptions of Schools," *Education and Urban Society* 36, no. 4 (2004): 383–427.

12. Lewis and Diamond, *Despite the Best Intentions*.

13. Mica Pollock, "From Denial to Creation." *Anthropology News* 55, no. 6 (June 2014).

14. See, e.g., "What's Up: Turning Local News into Information Empowerment," MIT Center for Civic Media, 2013, https://incouragecf.org/wp-content/uploads/2013/03/whatsupwhitepagesweb.pdf.

15. See, e.g., Soo Hong, *A Cord of Three Strands: A New Approach to Parent Engagement in Schools* (Cambridge, MA: Harvard Education Press, 2011); Kavitha Mediratta, Seema Shah, and Sara McAlister, *Building Partnerships to Reinvent School Culture: Austin Interfaith* (Providence, RI: Annenberg Institute for School Reform at Brown University, 2009); Mark R. Warren, "Communities and Schools: A New View of Urban Education Reform," *Harvard Education Review* 75, no. 2 (2005): 133–173.

16. Anne T. Henderson, Vivian Johnson, Karen L. Mapp, and Don Davies, *Beyond the Bake Sale: The Essential Guide to Family/School Partnerships* (New York: The New Press, 2007), 15.

17. Andrea Dyrness. "How Can Well-Intentioned School Practices Limit Parental Participation/Leadership? How Can Educators Address this Challenge When Working with Parents of English Language Learners/Emergent Bilinguals?," in *Common Core, Bilingual and English Language Learners: A Resource for Educators*, ed. Guadalupe Valdés, Kate Menken, and Mariana Castro (Philadelphia: Caslon, 2015), 94–95.

18. Tyson, "Providing Equal Access to 'Gifted' Education."

19. Castagno and Brayboy, "Culturally Responsive Schooling for Indigenous Youth," 960, 975–6, also citing *Alaska Standards for Culturally-Responsive Schools* (Anchorage: Alaska Native Knowledge Network, 1998), http://www.ankn.uaf.edu/publications/culturalstandards.pdf, 20.

20. Mediratta et al., *Building Partnerships*, 11.

21. Ann M. Ishimaru, "Rewriting the Rules of Engagement: Elaborating a Model of District-Community Collaboration," *Harvard Educational Review* 84, no. 2 (Summer 2014): 199, 201.

22. See Mediratta et al., *Building Partnerships*, 7.

23. Warren, "Communities and Schools."

24. Mediratta et al., *Building Partnerships*; Susan Yonezawa and Makeba Jones, "Student Voices: Generating Reform from the Inside Out," *Theory into Practice* 48, no. 3 (Summer 2009): 205–212; Julio Cammarota and Michelle Fine, eds., *Revolutionizing Education: Youth Participatory Action Research in Motion*, First Edition (New York: Routledge, 2008). See also "Lessons in Racial Justice and Movement Building: Dismantling the School-to-Prison Pipeline in Colorado and Nationally," *Padres & Jovenes Unidos*, November 18, 2014, http://padresunidos.org/reports/lessons-racial-justice-and-movement-building.

25. Jeannie Oakes, John Rogers, and Martin Lipton, *Learning Power: Organizing for Education and Justice* (New York: Teachers College Press, 2006).

26. Elaine Simon, Marcine Pickron-Davis, and Chris Brown, "Case Study: New York ACORN. Strong Neighborhoods, Strong Schools. The Indicators Project on Education Organizing," *Research for Action with Cross City Campaign for Urban School Reform*, March 2002, https://www.researchforaction.org/wp-content/uploads/2016/02/Simon_E_Strong_Neighborhoods_Strong_Schools_Case_Study_NY_Acorn.pdf, 7. For many more examples, see Mark R. Warren, Karen L. Mapp, and the Community Organizing and School Reform Project, *A Match on Dry Grass: Community Organizing as a Catalyst for School Reform* (New York: Oxford University Press, 2011) and Oakes et al., *Learning Power*.

27. Emma H. Fuentes, "Practicing Citizenship: Latino Parents Broadening Notions of Citizenship through Participatory Research," in *Latinos and Education: A Critical Reader*, Second Edition, ed, Antonia Darder and Rodolfo D. Torres (New York: Routledge, 2014).

28. Mediratta et al., "Building Partnerships," 11.

29. Barbara Taveras, Caissa Douwes, Karen Johnson with Diana Lee and Margaret Caspe, "New Visions for Public Schools: Using Data to Engage Families" (2010), http://www.hfrp.org/family-involvement/publications-resources/new-visions-for-public-schools-using-data-to-engage-families.

30. Norma González, James Greenberg, and Carlos Velez, "Funds of Knowledge: A Look at Luis Moll's Research into Hidden Family Resources," *USC Department of Education,* http://www.usc.edu /dept/education/CMMR/FullText/Luis_Moll_Hidden_Family_Resources.pdf, 4–5; Norma González, Luis C. Moll, and Cathy Amanti, *Funds of Knowledge: Theorizing Practices in Households, Communities, and Classrooms,* First Edition (New York: Routledge, 2005).

31. Gloria Ladson-Billings, "It's Not the Culture of Poverty, It's the Poverty of Culture: The Problem of Teacher Education," *Anthropology and Education Quarterly* 37, no. 2 (2006): 108. See also Beverly Daniel Tatum, "Cultivating the Trust of Black Parents," in Pollock, *Everyday Antiracism.*

32. Keith R. Krueger, "Digital Equity Strategies for Bridging Home/School Connection" (presentation, Consortium for School Networking, presented at the Digital Divide Roundtable, San Diego, CA, November 4, 2015), http://www.cosn.org/sites/default/files/pdf/Digital%20Equity%20-%20 Krueger.pdf.

33. John Hansen and Justin Reich, "Socioeconomic Status and MOOC Enrollment: Enriching Demographic Information with External Datasets," *HarvardX Leading Through Learning,* http:// harvardx.harvard.edu/files/harvardx/files/ses_and_mooc_enrollment_lak_colloquium_hx_work ing_paper_submission3.pdf; Justin Reich, Richard Murnane, and John Willett, "The State of Wiki Usage in U.S. K–12 Schools: Leveraging Web 2.0 Data Warehouses to Assess Quality and Equity in Online Learning Environments," *Education Researcher* 41, no. 1 (2012): 7–15; Susan P. Crawford, "The New Digital Divide," *New York Times,* December 3, 2011.

34. For just a few of many examples, see http://computers2sdkids.org (on computer refurbishing); see the historic efforts of the South End Technology Center @ Tent City, tech-center-enlightentcity. tv (on computer skill) and http://code.org. On use of phones (specifically texting) for sharing college information specifically, see also Castleman and Page, *Summer Melt.*

35. Mary Ann Zehr, "Civil Rights Deal Signals Federal Push for Translation Services," *Education Week* 30, no. 3 (March 2011): 8–9.

36. Also see some Parent Connectors explaining the work on YouTube, at https://www.youtube.com /watch?v=1mFxerWXo3c.

37. Mica Pollock, "It Takes a Network to Raise a Child: Improving the Communication Infrastructure of Public Education to Enable Community Cooperation in Young People's Success," *Teachers College Record* 155, no. 7 (2013): 1–28.

38. Henderson et al., *Beyond the Bake Sale,* 75.

39. Frances Contreras, *Achieving Equity for Latino Students: Expanding the Pathway to Higher Education Through Public Policy* (New York: Teachers College Press, 2011); Marjorie Faulstich Orellana, *Translating Childhoods: Immigrant Youth, Language, and Culture* (New Brunswick, NJ: Rutgers University Press, 2009); Lesley Bartlett and Ofelia Garcia, *Additive Schooling in Subtractive Times: Bilingual Education and Dominican Immigrant Youth in the Heights* (Nashville, TN: Vanderbilt University Press, 2011); Teresa L. McCarty, Mary Eunice Romero, and Ofelia Zepeda, "Reclaiming the Gift: Indigenous Youth Counter-Narratives on Native Language Loss and Revitalization," *American Indian Quarterly* 30, no. 1–2 (Winter–Spring 2006): 28–48; Leisy Thornton Wyman, *Youth Culture, Language Endangerment and Linguistic Survivance* (Tonawanda, NY: Multilingual Matters, 2012); Django Paris and H. Samy Alim, "What Are We Seeking to Sustain Through Culturally Sustaining Pedagogy?" On training youth to interpret at public events, see the Welcome Project, http:// www.welcomeproject.org/content/liaison-interpreters-program-somerville-lips.

40. Warren, "Communities and Schools," 15.

41. Mediratta et al., "Building Partnerships," 19.

42. Warren, "Communities and Schools"; Daly, *Social Network Theory and Educational Change.*

43. Mica Pollock, *Because of Race: How Americans Debate Harm and Opportunity in Our Schools* (Princeton, NJ: Princeton University Press, 2008).

44. Anthony S. Bryk and Barbara Schneider, *Trust in Schools: A Core Resource for Improvement* (New York: Russell Sage Foundation, 2002).

45. Warren, "Communities and Schools," 4–5.

46. Daly, *Social Network Theory and Educational Change.*

47. Tiffany S. Lee, "The Home-School-Community Interface in Language Revitalization in the USA and Canada," in *Indigenous Language Revitalization in the Americas* (forthcoming).

48. Paul C. Gorski, *Reaching and Teaching Students in Poverty: Strategies for Erasing the Opportunity Gap* (New York: Teachers College Press, 2013), 13. See also the work of James Comer,   discussed   in   https://creativesystemsthinking.wordpress.com/2015/10/30/this-yale

-psychiatrist-knows-how-to-shut-down-the-school-to-prison-pipeline-so-why-is-he-ignored.

49. *Alaska Standards for Culturally-Responsive Schools*, 3, 11.

50. Tatum, "Cultivating the Trust of Black Parents."

51. Warren, "Communities and Schools," 4.

52. Mediratta et al., "Building Partnerships."

53. Andrea Dyrness, "Research for Change Versus Research as Change: Lessons from a Mujerista Participatory Research Team," *Anthropology & Education Quarterly* 39, no. 1 (2008): 30, citing bell hooks, *Yearning: Race, Gender and Cultural Politics* (Boston: South End, 1990), 152.

54. Dyrness, "Research for Change," 30.

55. Ibid., 34.

56. Andrea Dyrness, *Mothers United: An Immigrant Struggle for Socially Just Education* (Minneapolis, MN: University of Minnesota Press, 2011), 223–224.

57. Dyrness, "Research for Change," 38, 41.

58. Elizabeth Schlessman, "'When Are You Coming to Visit?' Home Visits and Seeing Our Students," *Rethinking Schools* 27, no. 2 (Winter 2012–2013): 19–23.

59. Tatum, "Cultivating the Trust of Black Parents," 312; Sara Lawrence-Lightfoot, *The Essential Conversation: What Parents and Teachers Can Learn from Each Other* (New York: Random House, 2003).

60. Lewis and Diamond, *Despite the Best Intentions*, 2015.

61. Pollock, "It Takes a Network."

Conclusion

1. For some examples of these documents, see https://sites.google.com/site/smarttech4equity/, discussed in Mica Pollock, "Smart Tech Use for Equity," *Teaching Tolerance* (Spring 2016): 39–41.

2. See http://preuss.ucsd.edu/current-students/university-prep.html.

3. On teacher action research, see Margaret Riel, "Understanding Action Research," *Center for Collaborative Action Research*, http://cadres.pepperdine.edu/ccar/define.html. See also http://ccar .wikispaces.com. On "improvement science" by educators, see Anthony S. Bryk, Louis M. Gomez, Alicia Grunow, and Paul G. LeMahieu, *Learning to Improve: How America's Schools Can Get Better at Getting Better* (Cambridge, MA: Harvard Education Press, 2015). See also Marilyn Cochran-Smith and Susan L. Lytle, *Inquiry as Stance: Practitioner Research in the Next Generation* (New York: Teachers College Press, 2009).

4. Cynthia E. Coburn, Amy K. Catterson, Jenni Higgs, Katie Mertz, and Richard Morel, "Spread and Scale in the Digital Age: A Memo to the John D. and Catherine T. MacArthur Foundation," *Informal Science*, December 31, 2013, http://informalscience.org/research/ic-000-000-010-860 /Spread_and_Scale_in_the_Digital_Age; Louis Gomez, "Connecting Practices" (keynote address, MacArthur Foundation Digital Media and Learning Conference, Boston, MA, March 6, 2014); Bryk et al., *Learning to Improve*.

5. See, e.g., William R. Penuel, Barry J. Fishman, Britte Haugan Cheng, and Nora Sabelli, "Organizing Research and Development at the Intersection of Learning, Implementation, and Design," *Educational Research* 40, no. 7 (October 2011): 331–337; Sasha Barab, "Design-Based Research: A Methodological Toolkit for the Learning Scientist," in *The Cambridge Handbook of the Learning Sciences* (New York: Cambridge University Press, 2006), 153–170; Allan Collins, Diana Joseph, and Katerine Bielaczyc, "Design Research: Theoretical and Methodological Issues," *Journal of the Learning Sciences* 13 (2004), 15–42.

Appendix

1. See Richard R. Valencia, *Dismantling Contemporary Deficit Thinking: Educational Thought and Practice* (New York: Taylor and Francis, 2010).

2. Mica Pollock, *Because of Race: How Americans Debate Harm and Opportunity in Our Schools* (Princeton, NJ: Princeton University Press, 2008).

3. For other "scripts" found by researchers, see, e.g., Richard R. Valencia, *Dismantling Contemporary Deficit Thinking*; Michele Lamont, *The Dignity of Working Men: Morality and the Boundaries of*

Race, Class, and Immigration (Cambridge, MA: Harvard University Press, 2000); Eduardo Bonilla-Silva, *Racism Without Racists: Color-Blind Racism and the Persistence of Racial Inequality in America*, Third Edition (Lanham, MD: Rowman & Littlefield Publishers, 2006); and M.M. Bakhtin, *The Dialogic Imagination: Four Essays* (Austin, TX: University of Texas Press, 1982).

4. Mahzarin R. Banaji and Anthony Greenwald, *Blindspot: Hidden Biases of Good People* (New York: Delacorte Press, 2013).

5. Michelle Alexander, *The New Jim Crow: Mass Incarceration in the Age of Colorblindness* (New York: The New Press, 2012).

6. Carol Dweck, *Mindset: The New Psychology of Success* (New York: Ballantine Books, 2007).

7. See, e.g., Etta Hollins and Maria Torres Guzman, "Research on Preparing Teachers for Diverse Populations," in *Studying Teacher Education: The Report of the AERA Panel on Research and Teacher Education*, ed. Marilyn Cochran-Smith and Kenneth M. Zeichner (Mahwah, NJ: Lawrence Erlbaum Associates, 2005), 477–548; Ilana Seidel Horn, "Learning on the Job: A Situated Account of Teacher Learning in High School Mathematics Departments," *Cognition and Instruction* 23, no. 2 (2005): 207–236; Marilyn Cochran-Smith and Susan L. Lytle, "Relationships of Knowledge and Practice: Teacher Learning in Communities," *Review of Research in Education* 24 (January 1999): 137–163.

8. Audrey Thompson, "Resisting the 'Lone Hero' Stance," in *Everyday Antiracism: Getting Real About Race in School*, ed. Mica Pollock (New York: The New Press, 2008).

9. Mica Pollock, *Colormute: Race Talk Dilemmas in an American School* (Princeton, NJ: Princeton University Press, 2004), 219.

10. Glenn E. Singleton, *Courageous Conversations About Race: A Field Guide to Achieving Equity in Schools*, Second Edition (Thousand Oaks, CA: Corwin Press, 2015), 27, 70–76. See also Glenn E. Singleton and Cyndie Hays, "Beginning Courageous Conversations About Race," in Pollock, *Everyday Antiracism*, 20.

11. Alice McIntyre, "Engaging Diverse Groups of Colleagues in Conversation," in Pollock, *Everyday Antiracism*.

12. Daniel G. Solórzano and Tara J. Yosso, "Critical Race and LatCrit Theory and Method: Counter-storytelling," *International Journal of Qualitative Studies in Education* 14, no. 4 (2001): 482.

13. Pollock, *Because of Race*.

14. Dorinda J. Carter, "On Spotlighting and Ignoring Racial Group Members in the Classroom," in Pollock, *Everyday Antiracism*.

15. Singleton and Hays, "Beginning Courageous Conversations About Race," 21.

16. See, e.g., http:///www.crlt.umich.edu/gsis/p3_1.

17. Alice McIntyre, "Engaging Diverse Groups of Colleagues in Conversation," in Pollock, *Everyday Antiracism*, 279.

18. Pollock, *Colormute*, 218.

19. Ali Michael, *Raising Race Questions: Whiteness and Inquiry in Education* (New York: Teachers College Press, 2014).

20. Singleton and Hays, "Beginning Courageous Conversations About Race," 21.

21. Anita Wadhwa, *Restorative Justice in Urban Schools: Disrupting the School-to-Prison Pipeline* (New York: Routledge, 2016).

22. Mica Pollock, Sherry Deckman, Meredith Mira, and Carla Shalaby, "'But What Can I Do?' Three Necessary Tensions in Teaching Teachers about Race," *Journal of Teacher Education* 61 (May/June 2010): 211–224.

23. Carter, "On Spotlighting and Ignoring Racial Group Members in the Classroom."

24. If you are drawn to role-plays, check out the "Forum Theatre" process, developed by Brazilian Augusto Boal. In Forum Theatre, participants role-play extended efforts to resolve conflicts and solve problems. See http://en.wikipedia.org/wiki/Forum_theatre.

25. Martin Luther King Jr., "Letter from a Birmingham Jail," archived at *African Studies Center, University of Pennsylvania*, http://www.africa.upenn.edu/Articles_Gen/Letter_Birmingham.html.

Index

Boldface page numbers represent images and graphics.